Kill the
Messenger

The War on Standardized Testing

Kill the Messenger

With a foreword by
Herbert J. Walberg

and a preface by
J. E. Stone

Richard P. Phelps

Transaction Publishers
New Brunswick (U.S.A.) and London (U.K.)

Figures 1.1a and 1.1b have been reproduced with the permission of Yale University Press from: Max Eckstein and Harold Noah, *Secondary School Examinations: International Perspectives on Policies and Practice* (1993), figures 2 on p. 149 and 7 on p. 167.

Tables 7.4a and 7.4b have been reproduced with permission of the American Psychological Association from: Schmidt, Frank L. and John E. Hunter. 1998. "The Validity and Utility of Selection Methods in Personnel Psychology: Practical and Theoretical Implication of 85 Years of Research Findings," *Personnel Psychology*, v.51, tables 1 and 2 on pages 265 and 266.

Figures 7.1 and 7.2 have been reproduced with permission of Sage Publications from: Phelps, Richard P. "Benchmarking to the World's Best in Mathematics: Quality Control in Curriculum and Instruction Among the Top Performers in the TIMSS." *Evaluation Review*, v.25, n.4, pages 419 and 420, figures 1 and 2.

Library of Congress Catalog Number: 2002042999
ISBN: 0-7658-0178-7
Printed in the United States of America

Library of Congress Cataloging-in-Publication Data

Phelps, Richard P.
    Kill the messenger : the war on standardized testing / Richard P. Phelps.
        p. cm
    Includes bibliographical references and index.
        ISBN 0-7658-0178-7 (cloth : alk. paper)
    1. Educational tests and measurements—United States. 2. Education—Standards—United States. 3. Educational accountability—United States. I. Title.

LB3051.P54 2003
371.26|2—dc21   2002042999

"Once upon a time there was a King who received a messenger from a far off land. The messenger brought news that the King's favorite daughter was about to marry the son of one of his most hated old enemies. The King was so angry that he killed the messenger on the spot. As the King's guards came to remove the body he discovered to his horror that the messenger was his daughter in disguise. Too late he realized that she had disguised herself hoping to prepare him and dampen his angry reaction so that she could eventually reconcile him to her marriage and receive his blessings—for they loved each other deeply."—Anonymous

"Kill the umpire!"—Anonymous

"If you don't like the temperature, break the thermometer."—Anonymous

"If something exists, it exists in some amount. If it exists in some amount, then it is capable of being measured."—Rene Descartes, *Principles of Philosophy*, 1644

Contents

List of Tables viii

List of Figures xi

Foreword xiii

Preface xv

Acknowledgments xix

Reveille—Prelude to Battle (Introduction) 1

1. The Battlefield (Testing Systems and Testing Interests) 9

2. Attack Strategies and Tactics 35

3. Campaigns: The Big, Bad SAT 87

4. Campaigns: Texas, the Early Years 105

5. Campaigns: Texas, the Presidential Election Year 2000 121

6. War Correspondence (Media Coverage of Testing) 147

7. The Fruits of Victory (Benefits of Testing) 215

8. The Spoils of War (Valid Concerns about Testing) 265

9. The Agony of Defeat (The Consequences of Losing the War: The Alternatives to Standardized Testing) 277

Appendix—An Anti-Testing Vocabulary 287

Glossary 297

References 301

Index 321

Tables

1.1a. Countries with Nationally Standardized High-
Stakes Exit Exams, by Level of Education   13

1.1b. Countries with High-Stakes Entrance Requirements,
by Level of Education   14

1.2. The Battlefield of the War on Testing, According to
Anti-Testing Advocates   23

1.3. The Battlefield of the War on Testing, as It Really is   24

1.4. The Battleground of the Testing "Experts"—
Some of the "Expert Groups"   27

2.1. Typology of Testing Opponent Fallacies,
Organized by "Attacks"   78

3.1. Percentage of Admissions Counselors Citing Factor as
Influential in Admission Decisions, by Level: 1997   94

4.1. Costs and Benefit of the Texas Teacher Test
According to CRESST   107

4.2. CRESST's *The Texas Teacher Test* as a Benefit-Cost Analysis—
A Summary of the Cost Mis-Allocations   108

4.3. Social Net Benefits of the Texas Teacher Test According
to CRESST—Corrected for Mistakes   112

4.4. Private Net Benefits of the Texas Teacher Test Using
CRESST Base Numbers, but Recalculated to Reflect
Texas Teachers' Perspective, with Salary Increase Included   114

4.5. Texans' "Willingness-to-Pay" for Assurance of a
Minimal Level of Teacher Literacy   114

5.1. Percentages of IEP and LEP Students Excluded from   129
      NAEP State Math Assessments, Texas and Nation

5.2. Percentages of IEP and LEP Students Excluded from   130
      NAEP State Math Assessments, Texas and State Averages

5.3. Grade 9 Retention and High School Completion   138
      in the States

5.4. High School Completion Rates of 18- through   141
      24-Year-Olds, Not Currently Enrolled in High School
      or Below, by State: October 1990-92, 1993-95 and
      1996-98

6.1. Dow Jones Interactive Search Results   152

6.2. Who Ya Gonna Call?—*Education Week*'s Preferred   184
      Expertise on Testing

6.3. Testing Experts in *Education Week*, by Type of Expert and 185
      Type of Mention: 1981-2001

6.4. Your Tax Dollars at Work—Resources cited in *The Progress* 195
      of Education Reform 1999-2001: Assessment,
      Education Commission of the States,
      Vol.1, No.6, March-April 2000.

7.1. Summary of Decision Point Information   221

7.2. Some of the Studies Finding Benefits to Testing   231

7.3. Bishop's Estimates of the Impact of Curricular-Based   243
      External Examination Systems on Student Outcomes,
      by Type of Outcome and Study

7.4a. Predictive Validity for Overall Job Performance of General 246
      Mental Ability Scores Combined with a Second
      Predictor Using (Standardized) Multiple Regression

7.4b. Predictive Validity for Overall Performance in Job Training 247
      Programs of General Mental Ability Scores Combined
      with a Second Predictor Using (Standardized) Multiple
      Regression

7.5. Average All-Inclusive, Stand-Alone per-Student Costs   254
      of Two Test Types in States Having Both

7.6. Average Marginal Cost per Student of Systemwide   254
      Testing in the United States with Adjustments,
      by Type of Test

7.7. Average 8th-Grade Student Report of Hours per Day   259
      Spent on Various Activities, by Activity and
      World Region, 1994

Figures

1.1a. Eckstein and Noah's Scale Comparing the   15
Burden of Examinations Across Countries

1.1b. Eckstein and Noah's Scale Comparing the Overall   15
Difficulty of Examinations Across Countries

1.2. Cumulative Net Change in Number of Tests in   16
31 Countries and Provinces: 1974-1999

5.1. New Rand Report Says Texas No Better than Average: 125
Net Cumulative Scale Score Gains on State NAEP
in the 1990s, by State

5.2. Average SAT-Verbal Scores, Texas and   142
National: 1972-1999

6.1. Number of Articles about Testing in 550   154
Newspapers in Which Opponents or Defenders
of Testing Were Mentioned, 1998-2000

6.2. Number of "Hits" for Names of Certain Testing   169
Experts at Web Sites Pertaining to the Issue of
Standardized Testing

6.3. Number of "Hits" for Names of Certain Testing   170
Experts at Web Sites Pertaining to the Issue of
Standardized Testing (with some high outliers excluded)

6.4. Whom Do *Education Week* Reporters Call for Testing   183
Expertise Among Former NCME Presidents?

6.5. Number of "Mentions" for Names of Certain Testing   186
Experts in *Education Week* Stories about Testing: 1981-2001

7.1. Average TIMSS Score and Number of Quality Control   222
      Measures Used, by Country

7.2. Average TIMSS Score and Number of Quality   223
      Control Measures Used (each adjusted by GDP/capita),
      by Country

Foreword

Richard Phelps has written a scholarly book that legislators, citizens, parents, scholars, and educators should read. The book is not only scholarly but is entertainingly written. It informs us about the one-sided "testing wars" that have gone on for two decades.

In the 1983, *A Nation at Risk* report to the U.S. Secretary of Education, the National Commission on Excellence in Education first pointed out how poorly American schools compare in achievement in mathematics, science, language, and other fundamental subjects. The distinguished citizens on the Commission argued that the nation's welfare and students' futures were jeopardized by insufficient knowledge and skills learned in school.

Subsequent research showed that the Commission underestimated the seriousness of the problem. Despite the third highest levels of per-student spending among economically advanced countries, American students fall further behind the longer they are in school.

Many educators and even testing experts resisted the obvious implication that our K-12 schools should improve substantially and that educators should be held accountable for progress. They have argued long and loudly that knowledge and skills measurable on tests are only a small part of schooling, that achievement tests cannot capture the "higher-level" learning they are imparting, and that tests are expensive and take too much time. The implications are that accountability should be left to professional educators. In telling the other side of the story, Richard Phelps shows why they are largely wrong.

Though a self-serving resistance and view has prevailed for many years in education circles, federal and state legislators and the public are increasingly demanding objective accountability and better performance from our schools. To varying degrees, state legislatures have begun requiring the development of achievement tests and standards for K-12 schools. The new federal act "No Child Left Behind" requires an even more ambitious and uniform testing system for the nation.

For reasons Richard Phelps makes clear in this book, this movement is all to the good. Taxpayers who pay the school bills have a right to know the quality of results their hard-earned money buys. Legislators and school boards cannot be stewards of children's academic progress without objective information on what students learn.

Educators, above all, should welcome achievement tests. They provide information on what students have and have not learned which should guide their daily lessons and help them to revise curricula and methods of instruction.

Students also benefit from frequent testing since it encourages them to be prepared for class and to find out what they have and have not learned. Parents, too, can be helpful in their children's learning when they are well informed about their progress, strengths, and weaknesses.

Because achievement has not generally improved since the *A Nation at Risk* report, achievement tests are playing an increasingly larger role in "high-stakes" policy. States are considering and, in some cases, passing legislation that provides for the closing of schools that continue to fail. In these cases, students may be allowed to attend other public and private schools. Students who fail, moreover, may not be promoted or graduate.

As Richard Phelps shows, tests make for better decisions on these hugely important issues. Our obligation as citizens, parents, educators, and scholars is to inform ourselves of the side of the story he makes clear.

Herbert J. Walberg
University Scholar and Emeritus Research
Professor of Education and Psychology, University
of Illinois at Chicago; and Distinguished Visiting
Fellow, Hoover Institution, Stanford University

Preface

Why a War?

Public education's providers and consumers view education differently. Both want quality schooling and quality outcomes but they differ with respect to priorities. To parents, taxpayers, and their policymaking representatives, student achievement is indispensable—especially basic knowledge and skills. Schooling that fails to produce acceptable levels of knowledge and skills is considered defective no matter what else it produces.

To educators, knowledge and skills are important but not indispensable. So-called thinking skills, attitudes, and developmental outcomes are of equal importance. For example, many educators would consider students who have merely acquired positive self-esteem and an ability to work well with others to be educational successes. Whatever their view with respect to knowledge and skills, few educators believe that schooling should be judged primarily on the basis of standardized test results.

The war on standardized testing arises from this difference. Parents and policymakers favor testing as a way of knowing how much students are learning. By contrast, educators and their intellectual allies would prefer to replace tests with assessments such as portfolios of student work. *Kill the Messenger: The War on Standardized Testing* shows what is being done to achieve this goal and how it is being reported to the public.

Most of what is written about standardized testing in today's education journals is critical and disapproving. The absence of sympathetic scholarship creates the impression that standardized tests have few advantages and many shortcomings. Naïve journalists convey this sense of the situation to the public even though the opposite is closer to the truth.

Forgotten is the fact that for most of the twentieth century, teachers and schools routinely used standardized achievement tests to document student, teacher, and school performance. It was only when policymakers began holding schools accountable for test results that familiar limitations came to be regarded as fatal flaws. So long as test results could be publicized or ignored in accordance with local preferences, standardized tests were considered a perfectly legitimate educational tool.

Once mandated, however, they became a threat to educator control of schools. Test-based accountability made it possible for the lay public and their elected representatives to form an accurate opinion of teacher, school, and district performance and to intervene if dissatisfied.

The Real Issue: Accountability

The public schools are a regulated monopoly and, as such, they must be concerned with public satisfaction. Until the publication of *A Nation at Risk*[1] and similar reports, the effectiveness of the public schools went largely unquestioned. Their academic deficiencies were mostly unnoticed and tended to be blamed on the student, not the school.

Strict accountability applied more to budgetary matters, not learning outcomes. *A Nation at Risk* and subsequent research and reports, however, validated recurrent criticisms of achievement outcomes, and test-based accountability became an accepted element of the education landscape.

Policymakers generally came to recognize that schools need external accountability for the same reasons that banks and corporations need it. Organizations have an inherent conflict of interest in reporting on themselves. They seek to convey a positive image of their performance not the accurate one sought by consumers.

The recent spate of corporate accounting scandals well illustrates the phenomenon and the consequences of over-reliance on self-reports. Given the nature of organizational self-interest, rational consumers must trust, but verify.

The war on testing is characterized by technical analysis and high-flown rhetoric, but the underlying issue is far simpler: Whose interests will be served? From the standpoint of education's consumers, standardized tests may be imperfect but they increase the likelihood that the consumer's aims will be served and reduce the likelihood that reports of student, teacher, and school performance reports will be colored by educator self-interest. From the standpoint of education's providers, standardized tests are undesirable because they restrict the ability of schools to set their own goals and priorities, and interpret outcomes accordingly.

Standardized tests assess student performance in light of announced objectives, and they do so in a uniform and objective manner. The portfolio assessments preferred by educators assess student work products selected ad hoc and evaluated in a relatively subjective manner.

The Larger Conflict

The issue of testing is only one facet of a larger conflict over the public's ability to control its schools. For decades, educators worked to convince Americans that scientifically trained educators could provide the highest quality schooling only if they were generously funded and free from social, political, and parental interference. Thus, independence for public schools became a cause advanced by teacher organizations, PTAs, school boards, and state education agencies. All became parts of an institutional arrangement that supports and defends the independence of public schools as enlightened public policy.

Today an increasingly dissatisfied public is trying to reassert control but the buffers that were created to ensure independence are preventing reform. The complaints about schooling today are not from people who are anti-education but from parents, policymakers, and taxpayers who are dissatisfied with the quality resulting from the education community's stewardship.

There is growing public doubt as to whether schools are capable of or willing to carry out that which parents and the public expect of them. Many believe that schools have violated the public trust by putting their own needs and their own agenda ahead of the public's.

The War over Standardized Testing

The battle rages. As anyone who has been publicly critical of education can confirm, the schools are vigorously defended. Education-friendly voices are recognized and validated. Those that disagree are marginalized and attacked. The war on testing can be understood as an attempt to disarm the critics and quell the insurrection. Richard Phelps describes the defenders, the critics, and the conflict.

First, he sketches the battlefield—both the establishment forces and the emerging consumer groups. The consumer groups tend to be unfamiliar because educators disparage them and the media tend to ignore them.

Second, he provides the most comprehensive listing and description of anti-testing attacks and strategies available today.

Third, he gives detailed accounts of three separate anti-testing "campaigns"—against the Scholastic Assessment Test (SAT), against a 1980s teacher literacy test used in Texas, and the attacks on the now-famous Texas Assessment of Academic Skills (TAAS) during the 2000 presidential campaign. Studies of these three campaigns demonstrate how the attacks and strategies described previously are employed in practice.

Fourth, Phelps analyzes media coverage of standardized testing as an issue—in print, on television, in the education "trade press," and even on the Worldwide Web. Using computer searches, he presents extensive evidence that the prevailing coverage poorly serves the public's ability to understand both sides of the issue. Almost all of the published sources draw from education's providers—the same sources relied on by school boards and other officials.

Fifth, he provides a compilation of the substantial body of research on standardized testing's benefits—a literature that is mostly ignored by education's providers.

Sixth, Phelps describes the limitations of standardized testing that should be widely known and accurately understood, but are so often the subjects of distortion and propaganda.

Finally, Phelps reminds us of the real-world need for external standardized testing. Schools are taking 12 years and spending $100,000 per student to produce substantial numbers of illiterate teenagers. The public schooling establishment may argue that standardized tests are imperfect, but the consuming public and their children cannot wait. The economic and human costs of ineffective schooling are already horrendous. Standardized tests have limitations, but from the consumer standpoint they are superior to the known alternatives.

J. E. Stone
Education Consumers ClearingHouse &
Consultants Network

Note

1.   In the early 1980s, then U.S. Secretary of Education, T. H. Bell, formed the National Commission on Excellence in Education, which later produced the famous report *A Nation at Risk: The Imperative for Educational Reform*. Some excerpts from the report's first paragraph:

> Our once unchallenged preeminence in commerce, industry, science, and technological innovation is being overtaken by competitors throughout the world. ...the educational foundations of our society are presently being eroded by a rising tide of mediocrity that threatens our very future as a Nation and a people. What was unimaginable a generation ago has begun to occur—others are matching and surpassing our educational attainments.
>
>   If an unfriendly foreign power had attempted to impose on America the mediocre educational performance that exists today, we might well have viewed it as an act of war." (National Commission on Excellence in Education 1983: 5)

Acknowledgments

Important help from the following individuals deserves to be acknowledged while, at the same time, all should be absolved of responsibility for any possible errors and all annoying opinions: Greg Cizek helped to clarify and organize the book's outline and earliest proposed structure; Don Powers and Steve Ferrara reviewed some of the more psychometrically weighty sections; Victor A. Smith, Scott Oppler, Frank Schmidt, Deb Wetzel, and Chris Sager laid some of my basic foundation in psychometric concepts and pointed me toward the gems in the scholarly measurement literature; Bruce Kaplan, David Freund, Debbie Kline and Nancy Caldwell clued me in on NAEP exclusion rate calculations; parts of the book benefited from conversations with Rob Kremer, Chris Patterson, Larry Toenjes, George Cunningham, Lisa Leppin, Wayne Bishop, David Klein, Marilyn Reed, Richard Innes, Bruce Thompson, Sue Sahardy, Donna Garner, Bas Braams, Erich Martel, Tom Reese, David Carvalho, Don Crawford, Ann Mactier, Jay Stannard, John Kinkaid, Patrick Groff and others associated with the Education Consumers ClearingHouse; early drafts of some sections appeared on Jimmy Kilpatrick's *EducationNews.org* (what would we do without it?); Eric Hawkins and Connie Shumway conducted much of the computer search analysis; and, finally, special thanks are due the collegial and tolerant Anne Schneider, the book's editor.

Reveille—Prelude to Battle

This book is as much about censorship and professional arrogance as it is about testing.

As a judge in a popular television program asserted to public school officials gathered in his courtroom for a trial concerning their behavior toward students, "We give you our children." We also give the public school system lots of our money. Given the scale and the stakes, one would think that U.S. public education professionals would be highly accountable to the public and deeply imbued with an ethic of public service. Unfortunately, the opposite seems too often the case. (See Cutler 2000; Coulson 1999; Finn 1991; Gross 1999; Hirsch 1996; Kramer 1991; or Kozloff 1998.)

Though a novice to the debate over standardized testing can easily become confused by the flurry of arguments and counter-arguments over details, some of them silly and arcane, the key, essential point of debate is *who* gets to measure school performance—the education "professionals" or those of us who are footing the bills and giving up our children. The essential point of debate is whether testing, and other methods of quality control, should be done "internally" or "externally."

I became involved in the standardized testing debate purely by chance. I did not begin as an advocate for standardized testing. And, if truth be told, I am still not motivated primarily by a fondness for standardized testing, despite the fact that I have come to deeply appreciate its benefits and strengths. I am strongly motivated, however, against censorship, dishonesty, and arrogance, traits that can be found in profusion among some opponents of standardized testing.

A decade ago, while working at the U.S. General Accounting Office, I completed a study that I thought interesting but most would probably consider to be pretty dull—estimating the extent and cost of standardized testing in the United States. We did, I think, a remarkably good job with that study. We developed surveys carefully, reviewed and pretested them, and through enormous persistence achieved very high response rates. I alone worked 60-70-hour weeks for 18 months. A Who's Who of notables in the evaluation, statistical, and psychometric worlds reviewed various aspects of the study. Nothing like it in quality or scale had ever been done before. One would think the education research community would have been interested in the results (U.S. General Accounting Office 1993b).

I left the GAO for other employment before the report was actually released, however, and, apparently, the pressure to suppress the report and its findings (essentially that standardized testing is not that burdensome and does not cost that much) descended even before it was released.[1] Over the ensuing months, I became gradually aware of more efforts to suppress the report's findings. Panels were held at conferences criticizing the report—panels to which I was not invited. Reports were written by the federally funded research center at UCLA, the Center for Research on Evaluation, Standards and Student Testing (CRESST), and elsewhere, lambasting it and suggesting that better studies were needed.[2] The characterizations of the GAO report were completely false—the critics claimed that information was left out that, in fact, was not, and that information was included that, in fact, was not. But reasonable people, allowed to hear only one version of the story, believed it, and the GAO report, along with the most thorough and detailed data base on testing practices ever developed, started fading into obscurity.

In its place, other reports were written and presented at conferences, and articles published in mainstream education journals, purporting to show that standardized tests cost an enormous amount and were overwhelming school schedules in their volume. The studies were based on tiny samples, a single field trial in a few schools, a few telephone calls, one state, or, in some cases, the facts were just fabricated. The cost studies among them that actually used some data for evidence tended to heap all sorts of non-test activities into the basket and call them costs of tests.

I wrote dozens of polite letters and made dozens of polite telephone calls to the researchers making the erroneous claims about the GAO study and to the heads of the organizations sponsoring their work.[3] In most cases, I was simply ignored. In a few cases, I received assurances that the matter would be looked into, but it never was. I submitted articles based on the GAO study to mainstream education journals and they were rejected for outlandish and picayune reasons, or because "everyone knew" that the GAO report was flawed.

Ultimately, after years of being polite to no effect, I felt forced to take the issue public and wrote an Op/Ed concerning the censorship of the GAO report in an education finance journal that had published a lead article, again, mischaracterizing and dismissing it (Phelps 1996b). Ultimately, an article based on the GAO report won a national prize and was published in the *Journal of Education Finance*.[4] I suspect, however, that if the GAO report had arrived at politically "correct" conclusions (i.e., that standardized tests are enormously expensive and otherwise bad) any article derived from it could easily have been published several years earlier in most any education journal.

Gradually, I learned of and met many others with similar experiences. In "mainstream" education circles, quality research is often discouraged and suppressed. Often, the quality of research methodology is irrelevant in the consideration of what gets published. Too often, it is only "correct" *conclusions* that matter, and it may matter little, if at all, how those conclusions are reached.

Unlike most other countries, where education schools serve primarily to provide short, practical apprenticeship programs for new teachers, after those prospective teachers have gained the subject-area knowledge they need by majoring in the appropriate subject areas at university, the United States has developed education schools that control the entire gamut of education training and evaluation. Here, college students can major in education as undergraduates, taught by education professors. Graduate students can obtain a doctorate in "education" at an education school. Education schools, then, hire these doctoral graduates of education schools as their professors.

Prospective teachers do not take history courses in history departments or math courses in math departments so often as they take courses with titles such as "History for Teachers" or "Mathematics for Teachers" in *education* schools, taught by *education* professors, along with the many required subject-area-free education courses in pedagogy and social policy. It is a huge, self-contained, vertically integrated enterprise that supports an enormous population of co-opted adherents to the status quo.

The more one looks at those education policy issues in our society that stimulate controversy (e.g., school choice, teacher certification requirements, union work rules, and "external" testing) the clearer it becomes that there are two very distinct interest groups involved, groups whose interests are often diametrically opposed. There are education providers—education professors, teachers' unions, and a proliferation of education administrator groups, all with large memberships and nationwide organization. With some notable, brave exceptions, these enormously wealthy and politically well-connected groups, oppose "external" testing. They favor only that standardized testing which they, themselves, can fully control from initial development or purchase through the scoring, analysis, reporting, and interpretation of results (see, for example, Cutler; Coulson; Kramer 1991; Hirsch 1996; Stone 1996; or Farkus, Johnson, and Duffet 1997).

As a cynic might say, "self-evaluation is an oxymoron." Nonetheless, that is the type of evaluation strongly preferred by many mainstream education professors and administrators. After all, who else understands the U.S. education system as well as they do?[5]

On the other side of education debates are education *consumers*— the general public, parents, students, and employers—who, in overwhelmingly proportion, strongly support standardized testing and, in particular, standardized testing with consequences (i.e., "stakes") (Phelps 1998b). With the exception of employers, however, this group is neither well-organized nor well-financed. Though education consumers outnumber education providers in vast numbers, they do not have the money, organization, time, or political power to compete with the provider organizations in a fair fight. Even for the one organized group with some resources to fight the fight for education consumers—employers—education is only a peripheral issue. It is important to them, but much less immediately important than international trade legislation, macroeconomic policy, OSHA or EPA regulations, tax or anti-trust policies, and so on.

Though there are two sides to the debate on external standardized testing, often only one side gets an opportunity to talk.

In elementary school we learned that research and discussion on public policy issues in a democracy works like this: people on all sides of issues do their research and they make their arguments and all sides have an opportunity to be heard; academic journals publish all points of view; and the media publish all points of view. Done this way, those who have not already made up their minds on an issue can hear all sides and all the evidence and make up their own minds based on a wide range of available information. With this sort of public debate, democracy can thrive, and the wealthy, vested interests can not dominate public decision-making to their own advantage.

But, that is not how it typically works in education. Within the education "mainstream," too often only certain points of view and only certain researchers and advocates are considered acceptable, and others are considered to be wrong or aberrant.[6] It is common for "mainstream" education researchers to tell their students, policymakers, or journalists, that "all the research" supports their point of view on an issue when, in fact, it does not. What they mean by "all the research" is that portion of it that they prefer—that done by "mainstream" education professors and education administrator associations. They simply pretend that the rest does not exist, or else they deride it as somehow aberrant or evil. "Ideologically-motivated" or "political" are terms often used when dismissing research with inconvenient results. That is how E. D. Hirsch, for example, a prominent critic of mainstream education research, but a social and cultural liberal and registered Democrat, gets labeled a "right-wing extremist" or "reactionary ideologue" (Lindsay 2001).

Indeed, some scholars and journalists have only heard one side of the debate on standardized testing. They may have first contacted researchers at CRESST or at the even more extreme National Center for Fair and Open Testing (FairTest), and the anti-testing advocates at CRESST and FairTest steered them toward the "correct" research and away from the rest. (see, for example, Jacob 2001). Entire, full-length books are concocted from compilations of the "research" on only one side of the debate (see, for example, Sacks 1996b).

Because some mainstream education journals place a higher priority on "correct" conclusions than methodological quality, some education research of awful quality gets published, and other education research of stellar quality may only be found in academic journals outside the education "mainstream," in psychology, economics, sociology, and political science journals, for example.

One can visit several dozen websites of professional organizations of education professors, research centers such as CRESST, administrator associations, and, with one exception (the American Federation of Teachers) those of teacher groups, and find gobs of "research studies" on standardized testing. A quick glance will show, however, that, with only rare exceptions, the selection of research is completely one-sided. Professional educators, those to whom we "give our children" only get to hear one side of the story, as their leaders allow only one side of the story to be told.

Many professional educators are "cause" oriented. They tend to go in the direction they think is "right" and "just," and if they can be convinced that standardized testing is "unjust," they may well join the crusade against it. If all they are allowed to hear in six years of education school indoctrination is...tests are bad...the innocent among them (which may be most of them) will believe it firmly.

A couple of years ago, I contacted the Webmasters at a couple dozen professional educator organization websites, suggesting that their listings of research reports were one-sided, and I provided links to research reports that would provide some balance and perspective to the issue of standardized testing. With only one exception out of a couple of dozen organizations, I was given the cold shoulder. Only one side is allowed to talk in most of these groups.

The totalitarian impulse towards absolute conformity endemic to many education groups extends even to Worldwide Web research directories where anti-testing advocates have taken control of some editorships and allow only anti-testing links to be listed. With that, anyone doing research at the Web on the issue of standardized testing has access to sources on only one side of the issue.

This is censorship. It is the ethical equivalent of a political candidate driving around town tearing down the campaign posters of his opponent. It is especially disturbing, moreover, that *educators*, of all people, so effortlessly, willingly, and forcefully practice censorship. And, they do it, for the most part, with the help of our tax dollars.

But, it works.

As many advertising experts assert, the key to successful sales is repetition. The most outlandish, unsupported, illogical anti-testing assertions are repeated so often by so many professional educators that many outside the testing field have come to assume they must be facts. Conversely, the counterarguments have been just as successfully quashed by the overwhelming power of the vested interests who wish to quash them. The result is a huge education research spin machine that would be the envy of any wartime propagandist.

Education graduate students and prospective teachers who hear only one side of the story may easily come to believe that it is the only side. Remarkably, and sadly, the same holds true for journalists.

Most journalists who cover the topic of standardized testing (and other education topics for that matter) have become convinced by the upside-down logic of testing opponents. Some education professors, defending their legally protected monopoly, tell journalists that they are "independent" researchers studying standardized testing systems imposed by biased, selfish "corporations," "conservatives," and "politicians." Moreover, they argue that they are motivated to oppose "external" testing only out of concern for the students whom, they claim, are unfairly affected. Amazingly, many journalists fall for this self-serving characterization.

When only one side gets to talk, of course, it can say pretty much anything it pleases. With no counterpoint allowed, "facts" can be made up out of thin air, with no evidence required. Solid research supportive of opposing viewpoints is simply ignored, as if it did not exist. It is not mentioned to reporters, it is not cited in footnotes or reference lists. It is treated as if it was never done.[7]

Ironically, groups often characterized as forming the "other side" of the debate on standardized testing, the same groups often vilified by educators and the press, as greedy, self-interested, and mean "corporations," "conservatives," and "politicians," do not practice censorship like so many testing opponents do. One can attend conferences, visit the web sites, or read the journals of the more open-minded National Council of Measurement in Education (NCME), the National Association of Testing Directors (NATD), Business Roundtable, the Association of American Publishers—School Division (i.e., the test publishers), the Educational Testing Service (ETS), among others, and one will find research and opinions on all sides of the issue, both pro- and anti-testing. Indeed, ETS regularly hands out career achievement awards to some of its most vigorous opponents.

What does that suggest about the relative merits of the arguments on the two sides of the debate? One side is willing to let all points of view be heard, and the other side aggressively suppresses the opposing point of view. If you knew only this about the behavior of the two opposing sides in the debate, and knew nothing of the arguments themselves, whom would you be more inclined to trust?

Notes

1.   One result of the pressure was a change in the cover title of the report from an accurate one—"Extent and Cost of Testing"—to an inaccurate one—"Extent and Expenditures." In fact, the GAO report used no budgetary expenditure data whatsoever, but critics for several years thereafter asserted that that was all it used (and, thus, the report would not have included opportunity costs). The change made the study seem more limited than it was and, thus, easier to attack.

2. For example, 1993 CRESST Conference: Assessment Questions: Equity Answers: *What Will Performance Assessment Cost?*, Monday, September 13; 1994 CRESST Conference: Getting Assessment Right: *Practical and Cost Issues in Implementing Performance Assessment*, Tuesday, September 13; 1995 CRESST Conference: Assessment at the Crossroads: *What are the Costs of Performance Assessment?*, Tuesday, September 12. CRESST report #441 still contains mostly erroneous claims related to the GAO report, on pages 5 and 64—66, and mostly erroneous claims about CRESST's work on the issue, in the first seventeen pages.

3. Among the researchers directly contacted were Picus and Monk. Organizations directly contacted were the U.S. Education Department, the *Journal of Education Finance*, the federally funded, taxpayer-supported CRESST and CPRE (for Center for Policy Research in Education, based at U. Wisconsin and U. Penn), and the New Standards Project. Individuals at those organizations directly contacted include: Baker, Dietel, Linn, Resnick, Anthony, Sweet, and Odden. With the exceptions of Lauren Resnick, of the New Standards Project, and the brave Patricia Anthony, then editor of the *Journal of Education Finance*, who treated the matter in a professional manner, my appeals were met with years of inaction and animosity.

4. Even then, however, the article was published probably only because a forthright reviewer from the American Federation of Teachers—the only "establishment" organization with a pro-testing position—advocated for it. If the AFT had not had a pro-testing position, I doubt that the article would ever have been published in an education journal. It finally appeared in print in March 2000, more than seven years after the release of the GAO report and only through extraordinary persistence and effort on my part (Phelps 2000).

5. In an example that one can only hope is an extreme case, the Owens Library at Northwest Missouri State University instructs its students to judge the quality of education research this way: "Authors should have education or experience related to the subject of the source.... Educational institutions, organizations, or companies providing information are credible if they have a respected reputation in the field of education." In other words, trust *only* those with a vested interest! (www.nwmissouri.edu/library/courses/evaluation/EDWWWW.html).

6. This self-contained enterprise may be larger and tighter than even some cynics think. Some of the best known education journalists are education school graduates, for example, and many other education journalists may be as well, which may explain why so much U.S. education news coverage features viewpoints popular with status quo defenders. Furthermore, because education schools tend to maintain professorates experts in education construed as widely as possible, their presence at most colleges precludes the hiring of education experts in other university departments, independent of the education school's interests. A budget-conscious university president will balk at the prospect of hiring an education policy expert for the Public Policy School faculty or Political Science or Economics Departments if the Education School already employs an education policy expert. Interested students can walk over to the Ed School for those types of courses, making them more remunerative for the university. It may be of lesser importance, or not considered at all, that the tenor and content of the courses are likely to be completely different when offered within an education school than they would be in a school or department with no conflict of interest in education policy matters.

7. When not simply ignored, solid research with inconvenient or politically "incorrect" results can be dismissed by one of at least two other methods. If a researcher

is so prominent that she cannot simply be ignored, her research, instead, may be submerged in a sea of "correct" research. One recently published collection of essays on standardized testing research, for example, includes an essay by John Bishop, the most prominent economist studying the empirical evidence of high-stakes testings' benefits, submerged in the middle of several other essays, all written by testing opponents. A naive reader might jump to the conclusion that "most of the research," if not quite all of it, finds standardized testing to be a bad thing (Orfield and Kornhaber 2000).

The other method for dismissing "incorrect" research on standardized testing, other than simply ignoring it, is through condescension. Some education professors, for example, have dismissed out-of-hand an abundance of empirical evidence accumulated by thousands of industrial/organizational (I/O) psychologists simply by ridiculing it. Luckily for these testing opponents, they found a kindred soul directing the National Research Council's Board on Testing and Assessment, who refused to invite any of the hundreds of academic psychologists expert in personnel selection research to participate in a review of that research. Instead, she invited several education professors who were well-known and outspoken opponents of high-stakes testing. The end result was a travesty and an affront to the taxpayers who funded the study. But, that study is cited widely by testing opponents as, by itself, proving that thousands of studies conducted by the world's foremost personnel psychologists are just no good. Has the NRC also done the converse by, say, inviting I/O psychologists with favorable views toward testing to sit on panels reviewing educational testing topics? No (Phelps 1999a).

1

The Battlefield
(Testing Systems and Testing Interests)

Each of us faces many tests in life. Only a small portion of those tests are given in school. Of those school tests, only a tiny portion are "standardized tests"[1] (see Phelps 1997). Of those school tests that are standardized, only a minority are "external" standardized tests with "high stakes"—predetermined consequences for the students who take them based on the results.[2]

But, oh boy, do those *external* high-stakes standardized tests cause a ruckus! What makes these tests so different from other school-based tests and so controversial? Education providers may not control the process nor the effect or the interpretation of the results.

Someone else does. That "someone else" may include elected state officials, college admissions committees, citizen committees that write academic standards, local parents, and general public opinion. For U.S. education professionals who, unlike their counterparts in most other countries, have gotten used to pretty much running all of the education enterprise as they see fit (or, as their critics charge, as best suits their own purposes)—and evaluating their own performance—this outside "interference" comes as quite a shock.[3]

Testing, American Style

Until recently, the United States had a testing system that matched the preferences of school officials. In most places, standardized tests were used only for "diagnostic" purposes. Local school officials purchased the "nationally normed" tests directly from test publishers, administered them on their own and in their own way, and then sent the completed test forms back to the test publishers for scoring. Those scores provided school officials with some rough comparison of their own students' academic progress to national averages.

Commercial test publishers liked this system well enough. They made many separate sales of essentially the same product to many separate customers. There was no extra work involved in "aligning" the tests to state standards or curriculum; the tests were sold right "off-the-shelf." Since local school officials could use the tests (and the resulting scores) any way they wanted to use them, they were generally happy with the system, too. Generally, these tests had no "stakes" and so they aroused little controversy, which could also have been considered a plus for both local school officials and the test publishers.[4]

Then, in the 1980s, a West Virginia physician named John J. Cannell investigated a statistical anomaly that he had discovered: statewide average scores for students on some widely used standardized tests were above the national average in every state in which they were given (Cannell 1987). It was dubbed the "Lake Wobegon Effect" after the fictional public radio community where "all the children are above average."[5]

The Lake Wobegon anomaly might have been caused—observed Cannell and some test researchers—by a number of factors, including: schools reusing old (i.e., identical) tests year after year and growing familiar with their specific content; test publishers waiting years before "renorming" the reference scales; and the fact that student achievement really was improving throughout the 1980s, as verified by independent testing, such as that for SAT, ACT, and NAEP exams (Phillips and Finn 1988).

The Lake Wobegon Effect controversy led to calls for more state government control over test content and administration and less local discretion. In most states, those calls were answered. Probably the single most important recent innovation to improve the quality and fairness of testing in the United States is the addition of managerial and technical expertise in state education agencies. At that level, it is possible to retain an adequate group of technically proficient testing experts, adept at screening, evaluating, administering, and interpreting tests, who are not "controlled by commercial publishers" or naive about test results. They, along with governors and legislatures, are currently calling the shots in standardized testing. Some of the most important decisions that affect the design and content of standardized tests, and the character of the testing industry and the nature of its work, are today being made by state testing directors.

State testing directors, for example, can utilize a number of relatively simple solutions to the problems of test-score inflation (and other alleged problems with standardized tests, such as curricular compression and teaching to the test), including: do not reveal the contents of tests beforehand; do not use the same test twice; include items on the test that sample very broadly from the whole domain of the curriculum tested; require that non-tested subjects get taught (or test them, too); and maintain strict controls against cheating during test administrations. Most states now either use tests that are custom built to their state standards and curricula or that are adapted for that purpose from commercial publishers' huge test item banks. Indeed, all of the apparent causes of the Lake Wobegon effect are fairly easily avoided.[6] (Phillips and Finn 1988: 10-12; Phelps 1999b: 12-13)

The Lake Wobegon Effect overwhelmingly involved the use of "no-stakes" tests purchased by local education officials, whose results and interpretation were entirely under the control of those same local educators. Some testing opponents, however, assert that, despite the overwhelming prima facie evidence to the contrary, the Lake Wobegon Effect is really more applicable to the use of high-stakes tests (see, for example, Linn 2000). This is like arguing that the police initiating new patrols in a high crime neighborhood are the *cause* of the crime that occurred in the neighborhood before they showed up.

Testing opponents attribute the Lake Wobegon Effect to *high stakes* testing despite the fact that high-stakes tests tend to have extremely high profiles, with their operations and results shone under a bright media glare and difficult to hide. High-stakes tests also are more commonly administered at the level of a state or a nation, and subject to widespread evaluation and scrutiny, unlike the Lake Wobegon tests that were sometimes administered in any old manner that local educators preferred.

This criticism is most ironic given that the Lake Wobegon Effect was a direct product of the very system to which most testing opponents advocate we return, one where local school officials maintained complete control over all information related to their own schools' performance.

Nonetheless, it is high-stakes tests that have endured virtually all the public scrutiny and entrenched opposition in the years since Cannell's study. Inevitably, the persistence of the opposition carried the accusations into state courtrooms across the United States. The primary precedent-setting case was *Debra P. v. Turlington* (1984), in which a student, Debra P., denied graduation because she failed a state graduation examination, sued Florida's superintendent of education, arguing that the test—a national "off-the-shelf," "norm-referenced" examination included content not explicitly in the Florida curriculum to which she had been exposed.

The Florida court responded sympathetically to the argument that a graduation test should cover content which students have had an opportunity to learn in the classroom. Other arguments made by the plaintiffs regarding alleged unfairness based on psychometric (i.e., technical) aspects of the test were summarily dismissed. As testing expert Greg Cizek (2002) observes:

> Although legal challenges to such high-stakes tests still occur..., they are remarkably infrequent. For the most part, those responsible for mandated testing programs responded to the *Debra P.* case with a heightened sense of the high standard that is applied to high-stakes measures. It is a fair conclusion that, in terms of legal wranglings concerning high-stakes tests, the psychometric characteristics of the test are rarely the basis of a successful challenge.

Cizek concludes that this heightened scrutiny of high-stakes tests has had the effect of dramatically improving the quality of standardized tests over the past two decades.

The high-stakes tests of today are surely the most meticulously developed, carefully constructed, and rigorously reported. Many criticisms of tests are valid, but a complainant who suggests that today's high-stakes tests are "lower-order" or "biased" or "not relevant" is almost certainly not familiar with that which they purport to critique.... high-stakes tests have evolved to a point where they are: highly reliable; free from bias; relevant and age appropriate; higher order; tightly related to important, public goals; time and cost efficient; and yielding remarkably consistent decisions.

Testing Outside the United States

Most foreign observers would likely be confused or bemused by the controversy over external, high-stakes standardized testing in the United States. Or they might even be peeved, because the overwhelming majority of media coverage and anti-testing research in the United States implicitly assumes that no other country on earth has any experience with testing or is worth talking to about it.

Surprise! The majority of other advanced industrialized nations in the world have been administering large-scale national- or state-level high-stakes tests for decades. U.S. testing opponents caution incessantly that we should not develop high-stakes tests here until we know what will happen if we do this or that. More research is called for, presumably from those researchers who can be relied upon to produce negative results. It is never suggested that all one needs to do is make a few overseas telephone calls and one can learn exactly what happens when one does this or that.

Moreover, most other countries are increasing their use of standardized testing and high stakes. Most citizens of the world could not imagine an education system—or one that made any sense—without them. The dire "sky is falling" consequences predicted by opponents here if we adopt high-stakes testing should have befallen most of the population of the globe by now, if they were accurate.

In Table 1.1a, I list those countries with high-stakes exit examinations and those with high-stakes entrance requirements, by level of education—primary, lower secondary (i.e., junior high), and upper secondary (i.e., senior high). I do not include here the testing systems of all the countries of the world; rather, just those "like us." Specifically, I looked at the testing systems of the 29 member countries of the Organisation for Economic Co-operation and Development (OECD), essentially the wealthier countries of the world, plus China, Russia, and Singapore[7] (Phelps 1996a; Phelps 2000g).

A casual observation of Tables 1.1a and 1.1b demonstrates that, if anything, the United States, in its relative paucity of high stakes testing, exit, and entrance requirements, is the odd country out. While a few of the tests indicated for other countries are "medium stakes," in that they are used only in combination with other criteria in diploma decisions, most are fully high

Table 1.1a
Countries with Nationally Standardized High-Stakes
Exit Exams, by Level of Education

Primary school	Lower secondary school	Upper secondary school
Belgium (French)	Belgium (French)	Belgium: (Flemish)
Italy	Canada: Quebec	& (French)
Netherlands	China	Canada: Alberta,
Russia	Czech Republic	British Columbia,
Singapore	Denmark	Manitoba, New
Switzerland (some	France	Brunswick,
cantons)	Hungary	Newfoundland,
	Iceland	Quebec
	Ireland	China
	Italy	Denmark
	Japan	Finland
	Korea	France
	Netherlands	Germany
	New Zealand	Hungary
	Norway	Iceland
	Portugal	Italy
	Russia	Japan
	Singapore	Netherlands
	Sweden	Norway
	Switzerland	Portugal
	United Kingdom: England	Russia
	& Wales, Scotland	Singapore
		Sweden
		Switzerland
		United Kingdom:
		England & Wales,
		Scotland

stakes—students who do not pass the examinations are denied a diploma, entry to the next level of education, or entry to the school or university of their choice. Moreover, they are generally timed tests, given only once a year, with few chances to retake, and cover a wide range of subjects. Finally, they can be grueling, lasting days, or even weeks. The average student in a dozen European countries surveyed in 1991 endured well over forty hours total in high-stakes nationally standardized examinations during her elementary-secondary school career, and over 60 hours in all kinds of standardized testing. A Danish student could expect 170 hours of high-stakes testing, some of it in oral examinations before a jury spread out over several days (Phelps 1996a: 19-27).

Table 1.1b
Countries with High-Stakes Entrance Requirements, by Level of Education

Upper secondary school	University
Belgium (French)	Belgium (French)
Czech Republic	Czech Republic
Denmark	Denmark
France	Finland
Iceland	France
Japan	Germany
Korea	Greece
Netherlands	Iceland
Singapore	Italy
Switzerland	Japan
	Korea
	Netherlands
	Russia
	Singapore
	Sweden
	Switzerland

In their landmark collection of case studies of testing systems in eight large countries, Education professors Max Eckstein and Harold Noah (1993: chap. 7) rated the "Burden of Examination Requirements" and the "Overall Difficulty of Examinations" in the countries on a comparative scale. "Burden" was a measure combining tests' number of required subjects, average duration in hours, and total duration across all required tests. "Difficulty" had more to do with the level of the subject matter. Their comparisons are in Figure 1.1.

Mind you, Eckstein and Noah conducted their study in the early 1990s, a period when most U.S. states administered high-stakes minimum competency examinations. Even then, however, many testing opponents cried that U.S. testing was too difficult and too burdensome. Yet, the difficulty and burden paled in comparison to other large, advanced countries (and still does today).

In the section of their book titled "Lessons for the United States," Eckstein and Noah (1993: 238, 239) wrote:

The United States is unique among the countries we have studied in having no coordinated, public, national system for assessing student achievement at the end of secondary school. It lacks any systematic and general way of certifying completion of a specified course of secondary school study and, unlike other countries, has no consistent national criteria or means for selection beyond that stage, whether for employment or for particular types of postsecondary education or training. In addition to certification and selection, other countries use their end-of-secondary-school

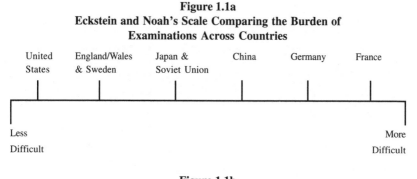

Figure 1.1a
Eckstein and Noah's Scale Comparing the Burden of
Examinations Across Countries

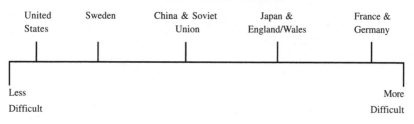

Figure 1.1b
Eckstein and Noah's Scale Comparing the Overall Difficulty of
Examinations Across Countries

examinations for a variety of other functions.... Although none of these functions is fulfilled by a national examination system alone, it does serve to support them.

Moreover, as previously mentioned, the popularity of standardized testing in other countries is increasing (see Figure 1.2). Indeed, more and more, as other countries learn the technology, they are adopting machine-scoreable multiple-choice formats for their new tests (Phelps 2000g: 11–21)

The American Public Wants More Standardized Testing, with Consequences

The U.S. public has often been asked how it feels about testing. Over several decades and in a variety of contexts, the American people have consistently advocated greater use of standardized student testing, preferably with consequences for failure (i.e., "stakes"). The margins in favor have typically been huge, on the order of 70-point spreads between the percentage in favor of more testing and the percentage against. Testing's strong popularity extends across most stakeholder groups, including parents, students, employers, and teachers[8] (Phelps 1998b).

People like standardized testing, particularly when it has high stakes, for a number of reasons, including:

Figure 1.2
Cumulative Net Change in Number of Tests in 31 Countries and Provinces:
1974-1999

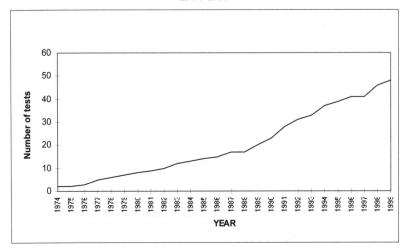

- standardized tests provide information from a unique (i.e., outside-of-the-school-building) perspective;
- standardized tests provide valuable *comparable* (i.e., standardized) information that cannot be reliably acquired by any other means;
- when they have high-stakes, tests motivate students to learn more than they otherwise do;
- standardized test scores provide affirmation to students who work hard toward academic pursuits, just as other types of affirmation, so pervasive in our public schools and our society at large, reward those who work hard toward athletic or dramatic pursuits;
- by imposing an "external" standard on students' behavior, high-stakes tests allow teachers to become partners or coaches aiding the students' quest for achievement, rather than the ones imposing the standards and a judge or antagonist;
- standardized tests help provide clarity, focus, direction, and coherence to curriculum and instruction systems;
- standardized tests are usually superior in quality, often far superior than teacher-designed measures; few teachers have had any training in testing and measurement;
- test scores can save employers and higher education institutions considerable time and expense by adding useful, complementary information to an applicant's portfolio;
- as teachers more and more are encouraged in their education school training to evaluate their students subjectively, standardized tests more and more become the *only objective measure* of student achievement;

- it has gotten to the point in the United States where standardized tests are the only pure measure of subject-matter mastery, because teachers, with the encouragement of their teachers, grade students according to a variety of criteria, of which subject-matter mastery is only one, and far from the most important one;
- local public school officials have strong disincentives against enforcing high standards because they will do relative harm to their own graduates in the larger world if they judge them rigorously while other school districts judge their graduates liberally;
- parents and the general public, by an overwhelming proportion, want more standardized testing, with high stakes, and the public schools are supposed to belong to the public;
- it is far more difficult to cheat on a standardized test than in regular classroom work; it is also easier to prevent cheating with standardized tests (e.g., using different forms with different question orderings) and to detect cheating (e.g., with computer matching);
- the process of standard-setting, and writing tests aligned to those standards, involves many parents, teachers, and other citizens personally in the large-scale management of the school system; and
- for these, and other reasons as well, standardized tests induce improvements in student academic achievement.

Testing's popularity remains steadfast today, despite an onslaught of extraordinarily one-sided media coverage of testing, and despite the efforts of testing opponents (and naive or sympathetic journalists) to drum up a "backlash"(Public Agenda 2000, 2001, 2002; Dreisler 2001; Business Roundtable 2001; Phelps 2000e). Testing opponents certainly want you to think there's a public backlash against testing; they know it will not work to reveal their self-interest in opposing testing (or, in the case of some, their ideology). Their opposition has usually been couched in propositions of defending the defenseless, whom they claim are harmed by tests. As such, it has always been inconvenient to them that the vast majority of Americans strongly support high-stakes testing. Nor does it work to claim that the public is ignorant about tests as virtually every adult has completed at least ten years of education and has encountered many tests, for better or for worse.

Reacting to testing's popularity, some opposition groups have generated their own opinion polls, with crudely worded, transparently biased questions and atrociously low response rates.[9] One national association of school administrators, for example, hired a political polling firm—one of those that conducts quickly-written, untested, low-cost, quick-and-dirty polls conducted over only a few days time (Phelps, 2000b).

After the poll was completed, the association's president wrote: "Any farmer knows that you do not fatten cattle simply by weighing them every day"(Houston 2000). Moreover, he added, "Standardized tests cannot reliably measure...honesty and perseverance." On that point, he is right. They cannot. Nor are they supposed to. Nor should regular classroom teachers try to measure them; that's not their job. Standardized tests, however, do a terrific job of measuring academic knowledge and skills, which is their purpose.

Even with that, however, the association president disagrees. He proclaims tests to be: "unreliable, unrealistic, and unfair;" "imprecise;" and "invalid for...high-stakes decisions such as promotion or graduation." They "measure factoids," "distort" and "narrow" curriculum and "cannot reliably measure problem solving." Their effect on instruction is to "narrow" it; turn teachers into "drill sergeants;" "taint the atmosphere;" and promote "memorization and repetition." All these terrible things happen to our cattle-children, *just by weighing them*!

This is rhetoric, of course. This advocate of honesty and perseverance shouts a plethora of bad-sounding words at standardized tests in hopes of overwhelming the reader's disposition to consider another side of the story.

School administrators enjoy job situations most would envy. They receive high salaries, only rarely are fired or laid-off, and half the year they are either on leave or working with schools out of session. Moreover, for decades, they have largely maintained control over the evaluation of their own organizations' performance. Unfortunately, some of them succumbed to the inertia toward low standards, social promotion, inflated grades, and fluffy, low-content courses. Some of them presented a Lake Wobegon story to their students' parents. Ironically, some used commercial, off-the-shelf standardized tests in uncontrolled conditions in a manner that helped them to fabricate the "good news" for parents. They did not complain about the "tyranny of test scores" or "narrow, multiple choice" standardized tests then (Cannell 1987).

Now, some school administrators are being held accountable for improving student achievement; they regard the accountability measures to be imperfect and unfair, and they're understandably feeling some pressure. Welcome, school administrators, to the world in which the rest of us live.

Surely, there are circumstances where the pressure on school administrators might be unfair or test administration could be handled better. Unlike in most of the rest of the world's education systems, high-stakes standardized tests are fairly new in the United States. New programs are bound to have kinks.

Most testing opponents do not direct our attention to such legitimate concerns, however. They want us to return to the Wobegon days when all students were above average and there was little accountability for learning. As Lawrence J. Peter (1993), that most famous of education administrators and education professors, wrote:

> "Bureaucracy defends the *status quo*, long past the time when the *quo* has lost its status."

Research...Lots and Lots of "Research"

But, the school administrators' poll is still "research" after all and, like much research conducted by testing's opponents, whatever its quality, it still serves two purposes:

- it gives testing opponents "evidence" they can cite to support their position (while they ignore or deny the existence of higher quality, contradictory evidence); and
- it helps to obfuscate the issue, which is particularly helpful in dealing with journalists.

Richard Rothstein, of the union-sponsored Economic Policy Institute, who now writes weekly from a soapbox at the *New York Times*, mixes up the genuine with the bogus and biased in order to declare that opinion poll results are all over the map and just cannot be relied on to make public policy. In one of his many *Times* columns belittling standards and testing entitled, "Polls Only Confuse Education Policy" (Rothstein 2000), he urges us to ignore the polls:

> Citizens cannot be expected to balance complex educational alternatives in response to multiple-choice questions posed by pollsters.... If we paid less heed to polling, we'd have more, not less, democratic decision making about education.

So, American taxpayers and parents are too stupid to make education policy decisions, which should be left to the "professionals." Rothstein uses a turn of phrase very common among defenders of the status quo in education. By "democratic decision making about education" he means public school officials control all the information and tell the public what they want the public to hear, free of outside scrutiny.[10]

Up until recently, the providers of education services in our country have maintained close to full control of all the information the consumers of those services have been allowed to hear. No *Consumers' Reports*. No Underwriters' Laboratories. No Securities and Exchange Commission. No Food and Drug Administration. No independent auditors. No government health or safety inspectors. Public school officials have controlled all evaluations of their own work. That is called "democratic decision making about education." Under that system, the evaluations are almost always good.[11]

Rothstein bristles most pointedly toward the work of Public Agenda, an organization that conducts professionally responsible public opinion polls (with high response rates, pretested, valid, and reliable questions, in polls conducted over several weeks' time), that usually collect results that Rothstein does not like. At a conference held just before the 2000 presidential election, Deborah Wadsworth (2000) of Public Agenda asserted:

...public opinion endorses higher academic standards. "Support for raising standards is rock-solid in every part of the country and among people of every background.... Members of the press insist on finding a backlash to standards that we do
not find.'

Organizations like Public Agenda, that remain steadfastly true to the ethics of their profession and continue to produce high-quality, objective surveys, may have become the most important "education institutions" in the
country, worthy of bodyguards and barricades. That is because so few education groups any more remain above the fray; much, if not most, education
research has become politicized. The few groups that do remain reliably
objective and trustworthy should be considered precious national resources.

Nor do some education provider groups stop with bogus public opinion
polls in their efforts to tell the public how to think about testing. One charac-
teristic of public education professionals that sets them apart from most other
producer groups or "quasi-industries" interested in protecting their turf is the
vast size of their store of in-house research expertise. This storehouse of
expertise is largely funded by us—the taxpayers—at a charge of about a
billion dollars a year. These tax dollars pay the salaries of education school
faculty and for the work of dozens of federally funded education research
centers, staffed largely by education school professors and graduates.

Given their occupational position and their self-selection to that occupation within the current industry structure, one should not be too surprised that
many education professors might feel an inherent dislike of objective, external testing. The commonly accepted notion that all university professors are
objective or that, at least in the aggregate, the mechanisms for open debate in
academia work to achieve objectivity and truth, should be put into some
context. The public probably can feel a high degree of confidence in the
objectivity of the collective opinion of, say, astronomy professors in regard
to their current views of the cosmos. In terms of the cosmos, there is no
collective self-interest in shaping the debate.

But, what of astronomy professors' opinions regarding government funding for astronomy research or requirements that university students take astronomy courses? These issues affect astronomers personally and, depending
on how these issues are resolved, some astronomers' careers and means of
livelihood could be ruined. Would we expect astronomy professors to express completely neutral, objective positions on these issues? Would they
even know how, given their rather narrow perspective on the world from
inside their discipline, inside academia? Moreover, even if we found brave
astronomy professors willing to risk their livelihoods in the interest of being
honest and forthright, given that they chose astronomy for a living, how
likely is it that they could genuinely feel opposed to more funding for astronomy? Finally, even if there were an astronomer who genuinely felt that
too many taxpayer dollars were being spent on astronomy research, how

willing would he be to speak up publicly against the wishes of his colleagues, upon whom he depends for his own career advancement?

Ownership of the Means of Instruction

For education school professors, much, if not most, of the research they conduct has implications for the structure of the education enterprise in our country and, in turn, for their own livelihoods and those of their colleagues. Allow parents to choose schools or free up certification requirements for educators, for example, and thousands of education faculty positions could disappear forthwith. Education administrators could then be recruited who have management degrees from business or public administration schools or management experience in non-profits or the private sector. Teachers could be recruited who have degrees or work experience in the fields in which they plan to teach, rather than education degrees. Without their traditional guaranteed supply of captive students, many education professors could find themselves out of work.[12] So, how many education professors are willing to conduct research that might support school choice or a relaxation of certification requirements? There are some very brave education professors who are, but they are not many, and they pay a steep price in reduced prospects for career advancement within their profession (see Hirsch 1996, chap. 3).

How is high-stakes standardized testing a threat to the profession? It is capable of exposing flaws in the current system, thereby opening the system to criticism and inducing calls for change. Moreover, testing can publicly expose a pervasive practice of which most citizens remain blissfully unaware, but that could potentially outrage many of them: for many education professors and the education professionals they train, academic achievement is only one of many, and far from the most important goals they have in educating *our* children (see, for example, Kramer 1991; Hirsch 1996; Farkus, Johnson, and Duffet 1997). From that perspective, standardized testing that focuses "only" on academic achievement can seem quite narrow, unfair, and distracting (Farkus, Johnson, Duffet, 1997; Johnson, Immerwahr 1994).

In some situations, tests themselves represent direct marketplace competition for teachers. This occurs whenever a potential student is offered a choice between completing a classroom course and passing a test, as a demonstration of the subject matter mastery required to attain a credential or gain admission to a position. The more applicants who can pass the test on their own and, thus, avoid the time and expense of the classroom coursework, the less need there is for teachers and school administrators.

Probably largely for these reasons of self-interest, much research conducted by education professors on the topic arrives at emphatically anti-testing conclusions, with "external" and "high stakes" testing, in particular, attracting a cornucopia of invective. Much, if not most, of this research is then passed on to the public by journalists as if it were neutral, objective, unbiased research, like that which we might expect from astronomy professors on the topic of the origins of the cosmos.

Between early 2000 and early 2001, the American public was informed, with virtually no counter-evidence ever offered, of the following testing "research" results:

- time spent preparing for or studying for exams is not "real learning";
- students also learn absolutely nothing *while* they are taking tests;
- what happens inside the classroom when there are no high-stakes tests "corrupting" "natural" instructional practice is necessarily superior to what happens under the pressure of high-stakes tests;
- drills, practice, worksheets, and teacher-centered, highly structured lessons are bad instructional practice;
- only the individual classroom teacher can determine what is best for her students to learn;
- standardized tests cannot cover all the curriculum;
- multiple choice tests only elicit factual recall;
- "teaching to the test" and "narrowing the curriculum" are always bad practice;
- a single test can only validly be used for a single purpose;
- states are making high-stakes decisions about students based on a single test performance rather than using multiple measures in graduation decisions;
- we test more than other countries do;
- other countries are reducing their amount of testing;
- there is little evidence for testing's benefits;
- standardized tests are expensive; and
- politicians and businesspersons are the prime movers behind high-stakes tests, whereas most teachers, parents, and students oppose them.

Anyone whose only source of information on the subject of testing was the U.S. news media should believe all of this. Unfortunately for education consumers, most journalists seem to accept all anti-testing research at face value and only rarely is any counter to it sought or offered. Ergo, the public "debate" over standardized testing ends up replete with misinformation, as well as being extremely one-sided.

> The quality of education research in this country is sporadic at best," says Eugene Hickok, the undersecretary of education at the U.S. Department of Education and former education secretary in Pennsylvania. "It's a system that is totally designed to protect itself forever." (Meyers 2001)

Indeed, much anti-testing advocacy presented as "technical" research from "independent" sources is neither technical nor independent. One often detects a sense of ownership from mainstream education researchers (of our schools, children, tax dollars...), and genuine resentment toward *public* efforts to exert some control over the *public* schools. Some testing opponents sincerely believe that the public and their elected representatives have no business in determining testing policy. Indeed, many of them have developed the knee-jerk habit of labeling *anyone* who disagrees with them for any reason as "political." They are the testing "experts" after all, so they believe that they alone should determine testing policy.[13]

It is remarkable, and reassuring for our democracy that despite the inundation of one-sided "coverage" from hundreds of news stories soaking the airwaves and newsprint the past few years, the vast majority of the public still does not believe the anti-testing litany above.

The Battlefields of the War on Testing

In most wars, it is fairly clear who is on which side. It should be clear in the War on Testing, too, and if it were, perhaps our country could conduct the War in a relatively orderly manner. The source of confusion is the anti-testing advocates who present their own version of the battlefield and the identity of the combatants. Their version is shown in Table 1.2.

This characterization of the opposing sides in the War on Testing is remarkable for several reasons:

- a crude one-dimensional simplicity;
- a gross misrepresentation of reality;
- a rather obvious bias; and
- many journalists who cover the testing issue seem to accept it as valid.

Briefly, we know that the characterization of the general public, students, parents, and teachers as opponents of testing is wrong unless:

Table 1.2
The Battlefield of the War on Testing, According to Anti-Testing Advocates

Those in favor of high-stakes standardized testing are:	Those opposed to high-stakes standardized testing are:
right-wing ideologues	"educators"
Republicans	"testing experts"
Texans	"progressive thinkers"
politicians (who hope to gain from "school bashing")	students
corporate interests	parents
racists and bigots	teachers
narrow-minded authoritarians	the general public
mean ogres who hate kids	"all the research"
	good and tolerant people

- we are willing to accept as truth the fairly obviously biased interpreta-
  tions, of fairly obviously biased polls, conducted by fairly obviously
  biased groups, that achieved response rates to not even a third of the
  minimally accepted level of the legitimate scientific survey community;
  and
- we are willing to ignore forty years of results from reputable survey firms
  in polls that achieved response rates between 50 and 95 percent.

A large majority of "educators" are opposed to testing, if one defines "educator" exclusively as someone working inside the public schools or graduate
schools of education. If one defines "educator" more broadly, say, to include
those who do not happen to work as public school administrators or education school professors, then this classification—with all educators lined up
against testing—is wrong, too.

Similarly, for "testing experts" and "all the research"—they are against
testing only if you define them very narrowly as, say, all the testing experts
who agree with the "mainstream" "educator" view, or who publish in "mainstream" education journals, or who teach on education school faculty (outside the testing and measurement departments, of course).

As for the other side, the pro-testing side, we know from poll data that
testing proponents are hardly limited to the Republican Party, Texas, or the
"right wing." Indeed, many true "right wingers" oppose standardized testing
as a "big government" intervention into local affairs. Some oppose it because
they desire to have their children schooled at home, or at charter or private
schools, and they want the government to have nothing to do with determining the content of that schooling.

Table 1.3
The Battlefield of the War on Testing, as It Really is

Those in favor of high-stakes standardized testing are: *education consumers*	Those opposed to high-stakes standardized testing are: *education providers:*
the vast majority of the public	most of those vested in the current
most students	public education system and
most parents	structure (primarily public school
most employers	administrators and education
most teachers[8]	school professors); and
most testing researchers outside the	those with ideological orientations:
"mainstream" of education faculty	libertarians, proponents of small
(e.g., testing & measure-ment	government (opposing intrusion
professors, psychologists,	into local affairs)
economists)	radical egalitarians
political moderates (i.e., centrists)	radical constructivists

Despite anti-testing advocates efforts to demonize the opposition, or their wish to be seen as "liberals" (even while they support, or are the vested interests) opposing "conservatives," the War on Testing is actually being fought by centrists, who favor testing, against a combination of vested interests and those of far left *and* far right ideological persuasions.

For some readers, the terms "radical egalitarian" and "radical constructivist," listed on the right-hand side of Table 1.3, might require explanation. Most of us are "egalitarians" to some degree. That is, we believe that people should be treated equally in certain circumstances. The most popular and celebrated form of equality in the United States is "equality of opportunity," which spawns such aphorisms as the "level playing field" and an "equal chance." *Radical* egalitarians want there to be an equality of *outcomes* as well as opportunity—the score at the end of the game played on the level playing field should always be a tie[14] (Wildavsky 1991; Rauch 2002).

"Constructivists" are those who believe that learners "construct" knowledge in their own way from their own set of "found materials" in their memory. Most educators believe that there is something to the notion of constructivism, and any teacher using what used to be called the Socratic Method (a question-and-answer technique) is practicing it to some degree. "Radical constructivists" believe that it is the *only* proper, legitimate, durable, or acceptable form of instruction. They believe in "student centered" learning, construction as a complete replacement for instruction. They express outrage at any use of such traditional instructional methods as teacher lectures, memorization, review, drills, and most structured forms of instruction (see, for example, Kozloff 1998: Stone 1996; Hirsch 1996).

Radical constructivists tend to oppose school practices that they think "fix" behavior. They see standardizing curricula and instructional practice as restricting teacher behavior and multiple-choice standardized tests as shackling student responses to problems.

Despite all the trustworthy evidence from decades of controlled experiments on instructional styles that radical constructivist techniques do not work as well as traditional methods or do not work at all on the least prepared children, supporters remain undaunted. They counter, for example, that these experimental studies have used as their measurement tool standardized test scores, a "flawed" measurement device. They would prefer that more "rich, creative" (i.e., arbitrary, subjective) means were used to measure student achievement.

Ultimately, a cynic might argue, it all comes down to this: Those who really want to know if and how students are learning want usable, objective, reliable, accurate measures. Those who do not really want to know (or, want others to know) want vague, fungible, subjective measures that they can control...or no measures at all.

Battleground of the "Testing Experts"

Inside the War on Testing is another, smaller, but still important battle-ground where the "testing experts" fight. Anyone reading U.S. journalists' "coverage" of the War on Testing these past few years might be surprised to learn this. Most of their accounts would lead one to believe that *all* testing experts in America oppose testing. It often seems that they are the only ex-perts that journalists are able to find (or are interested in talking to).

Most journalists' stories about testing start with some criticism of it. The journalist interviews some anti-testing expert, usually a mainstream educa-tion professor or anti-testing advocacy group spokesperson. Often, these ex-perts work at institutions with prestigious names. Who to call to add some "balance" at the end of the news story? A testing expert on the other side of the issue? Another university professor or advocacy group spokesperson with a favorable attitude toward testing? Almost never.

Typically, a telephone call goes out to either: a more "moderate" expert who also opposes standardized testing, but maybe just a little less, a "caught in the middle" state testing official (who may, personally, not like a testing program, either), or the education spokesperson at an employer group. The end result is a news story in which it appears that all those who are most knowledgeable about testing—the "testing experts"—hate it, and only unin-formed corporate blue suits support it.

There are hundreds, perhaps thousands, of pro-testing experts at universi-ties, in think tanks, and working in test development. Unfortunately, most education journalists do not seem to have their telephone numbers.

A schema for the "expert" battlefield is displayed in Table 1.4.

Expert Defenders. Yes, there is objective research conducted on testing. Indeed, there's plenty. The objective research on testing tends to be con-ducted by academics outside of education schools (such as in psychology, sociology, or economics departments), by testing and measurement profes-sors in education schools who may be shunned or ignored by their profession's leadership, and by thousands who work inside test development firms.

Many of these researchers believe that the benefits of tests vastly out-weigh their drawbacks and so should be used. Often, they are not that picky about the type of test used (e.g., multiple-choice or performance format), provided that they are valid, reliable, and fair. Pro-testing experts tend not to be very well organized, unfortunately (or, at least, not organized into *advo-cacy* groups). The American Federation of Teachers has dedicated just a few of its research staff to the effort. More recently, a very small organization named Achieve, financed by employers and sponsored by state governors, has started and, gratefully, some journalists do seem to have become aware of it. But, it is tiny; an infinitesimally small representation of the population of expert test-ing defenders, and massively outgunned by its billion-dollar opposition.

Table 1.4

The Battleground of the Testing "Experts"—Some of the "Expert Groups"

Defenders of testing / Consumers' Groups	Those "caught in the middle"	Opponents of testing / Provider Groups

employer groups:
Achieve
 	
higher education interests:
The College Board
Standards for Success
National Assn. of College
  Admissions Counselors
  (NACAC)
 	
advocates:
The Education Consumers
  ClearingHouse (ECC)
The Education Trust
 	
researchers:
ECC Consultants Network
Thomas P. Fordham
  Foundation
Center for Advanced
  Human Resource
  Studies (CAHRS),
  Cornell University
most testing and
  measurement faculty
  not in education
  schools (i.e., in
  psychology,
  economics, sociology,
  or public policy
  departments)
	test publishers:
	Assn. of American
	  Publishers (AAP) -
	  School Division
	
	practitioners:
	National Association of
	  Testing Directors
	  (NATD)
	Council of Chief State
	  School Officers
	  (CCSSO)
	Education Leaders' Council
	  (ELC)
	
	researchers:
	National Council on
	  Measurement in
	  Education (NCME)
	Society of Industrial-
	  Organizational
	  Psychologists (SIOP)
	
	politicians' groups:
	Southern Regional
	  Education Board (SREB)
	Education Commission of
	  the States (ECS)
	National Governors' Assn.
	  (NGA)
	National Conference of
	  State Legislators (NCSL)
		advocates:
		National Center for Fair
		  and Open Testing
		  (FairTest)
		Independents (e.g.,
		  Kohn, Bracey, Kozol,
		  Sacks, Meier)
		
		researchers:
		American Educational
		  Research Association
		  (AERA)
		Center for Research on
		  Evaluation,
		  Standards and
		  Student Testing
		  (CRESST), UCLA
		Center for Education,
		  National Research
		  Council (NRC)
		Center for the Study of
		  Testing, Evaluation,
		  and Educational
		  Policy (CSTEEP),
		  Boston College
		Libertarian groups (e.g.,
		  CATO, Maple River,
		  Reason Public Policy
		  Institute)
		most non-testing &
		  measurement
		  education school
		  faculty

Experts "in the Middle." There also exists a "middle group" of testing experts who are, by the circumstance of fate, "caught in the middle." They include:

- *State Testing Directors,* not all of whom are big fans of high-stakes testing. After all, they pay the highest price when a state implements a high-stakes program—they can become besieged, criticized and pilloried by the vast power and resources of the vested interests (who likes being the messenger who bears bad news?). Moreover, they may well have mixed feelings about high-stakes testing to begin with. After all, most of them are education school Ph.D.s, likely exposed to quite a bit of anti-testing philosophy in their course work. Finally, as public servants and state officials, they are restricted in what they can say, anyway, and thus are not good candidates for being "advocates" of any stripe.

- *Test Publishers.* The pure self interest of test publishers is to sell many tests at high profit. Generally, high-stakes tests are very costly, in part because they are controversial and buffeted by political storms and changes of mind and political party. Standardized tests from the Lake Wobegon days—no-stakes tests—were not costly, either to produce or to administer, and more reliably profitable. Test publishers actually lobbied against President Clinton's Voluntary National Tests even though almost all of them were involved in the contract to develop them. They feared that a single, big, nationwide test would harm their more profitable business of making many sales of the same test to many local districts.
- *State Executives and Legislators.* Many testing opponents make the ludicrous claim that politicians benefit by "school bashing" and deliberately try to make schools look bad to win votes. Everything is wrong with that story. First, the vast majority of voters like their public schools and do not want to hear bad news about them. Second, all the relevant powerful, vested interests, their checkbooks, and their lobbyists in the capitol rotunda oppose high-stakes testing; it is the vast majority of the unorganized public that favors it. It takes quite a bit of political courage for a politician to support high-stakes testing in the face of virtually unanimous interest group opposition.

Expert Opponents. That leaves testing opponents on the "expert battlefield." There are really two groups here, and they do disagree on some issues and use different tactics.

Because there are differences, as minor as they are, some journalists run stories in which they use one group of testing opponents to "balance" the other group of testing opponents. They then publish the story, having interviewed only testing opponents, as a "balanced" piece of journalism. Testing opponents help to reinforce this practice by obfuscating their positions. Some testing opponents present themselves as testing supporters and, thus, available to provide balance to anti-testing news stories. Only problem is that these "testing supporters" support testing only in theory and oppose all current or feasible tests.

The first group is *the radicals*—those who will say virtually anything in their opposition to standardized tests. The radicals are very popular in certain circles. Some of them make a comfortable living on the "rubber chicken" circuit, in paid appearances at conferences of school administrator or teacher groups or at "professional development" workshops sponsored by school districts (and, unwittingly, funded by taxpayers). The rhetoric and factual claims of the radicals is unrestrained and often quite outlandish. They are, however, quoted often in the press and relied on by journalists as "testing experts" and sources of factual information. As we shall see later, just several of these most radical testing opponents account for *the majority* of the expert commentary in stories on testing in all U.S. print media.

The second group consists of *the mainstream, "legitimate," or "established" experts.* They can be found on most education school faculty and in two institutions particularly popular with journalists: the federally funded Center for Research on Evaluation, Standards, and Student Testing (CRESST) and the Center for Education at the federally funded National Research Council (NRC). These latter two groups share membership to such a degree that they might as well be considered one group.

The *shtik* of the "mainstream" testing opponents is to appear reasonable and open-minded about testing even when they are not. Most of them will say, for example, that they do not oppose testing outright, but want testing to be done "right." In practice, however, "done right" can mean suffocating standardized testing's use to such a degree that only a tiny fraction of its potential power is exploited (e.g., allowing only no-stakes administrations and, even then, only of samples of students, so no individual information could ever be used, even for diagnostic purposes).

Or, these "false supporters" might say that they favor testing, but more "research" needs to be done (presumably by them) on the effects of testing before it can be reliably used. Then, after we have worked out the "problems" with standardized testing, perhaps in the far distant future, we might safely use them...maybe...we'll have to wait and see.... Thus, they may present themselves to journalists as "supporters" of high-stakes standardized tests, but there just happen to be no high-stakes tests currently available anywhere in the world that they support.

The taxpayer-supported work at UCLA's Center for Research on Evaluation, Standards and Student Testing (CRESST) fits this bill nicely. CRESST retains a staff of experts who represent a range of points of view on testing. At the extremes are those who favor the use of standardized portfolios, the least reliable of all forms of standardized assessment, for high-stakes use. At the other extreme are those who criticize the use of portfolios for high-stakes use because they are unreliable and favor the use of highly reliable multiple-choice tests...but, only under conditions of no-stakes. What all the CRESST researchers share in common is an opposition to highly reliable, high-stakes, external tests—the most effective and informative form of testing and exactly the type favored by the overwhelming majority of education consumers.

The existence of the radical testing opponents, who will say virtually anything, no matter how outrageous, serves the interests of the "legitimate mainstream" testing opponent experts who couch their rhetoric in more reasonable-sounding language. The latter group seems moderate in contrast. The end result of trusting either group, however, would be exactly the same— the elimination of the use of reliable high-stakes standardized tests in our country.

Journalistic "Balance"

Those familiar with journalists' coverage of testing will notice that the groups on the right side of Table 1.4 tend to get many telephone calls from reporters. The groups in the center get some. The groups on the left side get few to none. For many news stories, only testing opponents are contacted and, oftentimes, as mentioned above, one "expert" radically opposed to testing is "balanced" by one somewhat less radically opposed to testing.

Some more reasonable journalistic efforts at balance have pitted testing opponents against middle-of-the-roaders, like state testing directors or politicians who are always, it seems, presumed by journalists to be testing proponents, even though they may not be. Indeed, a quick trip through the website of the National Association of Testing Directors (NATD) will clearly demonstrate that state and local testing directors are not necessarily proponents of high-stakes standardized testing. Some are. Some are outright opponents. Others are various shades in between.

Indeed, in terms of their basic self-interest, state and local testing directors have far more in common with external high-stakes testing's opponents than with its defenders. Most are education school graduates and so have been exposed to the standard indoctrination in the mores and philosophies preferred there (decidedly anti-accountability). Moreover, they work in state education agencies or local school districts and, thus, have a strong professional incentive to make their organizations look good, even when the real news may be bad. It is easier to make their organizations look good when all testing is done "internally" and all aspects of the testing, including the interpretation of the results, is controlled by insiders. Releasing the data that show the school system to be not performing very well may gain the testing director all the popularity of a whistle-blower inside a secretive corporation or government agency. One should remember, testing directors are, first and foremost, *education* professionals. Their prospects for career advancement are determined by their reputation within the field of education professionals and not by that among politicians or education consumers.

Finally, as public servants, state and local testing directors are greatly constrained in what they can tell reporters, anyway. One slip of the tongue could attract a lawsuit. All things considered, they tend to be good representatives for defending the administrative aspects of their particular testing program, but poor advocates for testing in general.

It might also legitimately be asked why journalists only "balance" a state or local testing director with a testing opponent. If that can be considered balance, why not a story in which a testing director is "balanced" against a pro-testing advocate who thinks the test in question is too easy, or that there should be more testing than there is?

To put journalists' unbalanced coverage of educational testing, as well as many other education issues in some perspective, imagine the following scenarios:

- Environmental journalists produce stories in which they dependably interview chemical industry representatives who have slightly varying opinions on the issues and, sometimes, government industry and environment officials, but never any environmental group spokespersons.
- Consumer product safety journalists produce stories in which they dependably interview manufacturers who have slightly varying opinions on the issues and, sometimes, government industry and safety officials, but never any consumer group spokespersons.
- Health journalists produce stories in which they dependably interview officials of health maintenance organizations who have slightly varying opinions on the issues and, sometimes, government insurance and health officials, but never any patient or consumer groups representatives.
- War correspondents produce stories in which they dependably interview military spokespersons who have slightly varying opinions on the issues and, sometimes, civilian defense department officials, but never any soldiers, families of soldiers, or civilians caught up in the events of the war.
- Crime reporters produce stories in which they dependably interview police department officers who have slightly varying opinions on events and, sometimes, civilian government officials such as mayors and governors, but never any victims, criminals, their family members or friends, or eyewitnesses.

By letting the opponents of standardized testing and members of the vested interests monopolize the stage, U.S. journalists have let them control the debate to their advantage. A foundational principle in healthy democratic republics is the availability of well-reasoned positions capturing perspectives on all sides of the issues necessary for informed decision making. In regard to the debate over standardized testing, it would seem that only one side is allowed expression.

Why Test?

Tests provide information. Usually, they do it more reliably, more accurately, more objectively, and for less expense than the alternatives. Why be opposed to information? The reason usually is: because one does not want the results known. Students who work hard want the evidence of their work to be known. Some students who do not, do not. Those who want to improve the schools want information that will guide them toward improvement. Those who do not want to improve the schools, do not.

The British journalist Adrian Wooldridge (1998) emphasizes the information function of standardized tests and asserts that the information tests provide at the personal and classroom level is extremely important, but no more important than the information they provide to society as a whole:

The great merit of tests is that they provide us with relatively objective information about both individuals and institutions—and the great disgrace at the heart of the anti-testing movement is that it is trying to conceal information that it regards as unpalatable. What makes this even sadder is that tests are getting ever better at spotting and diagnosing learning difficulties as they unfold.

For the individual student, teacher, and school, Wooldridge argues that tests:

...provide vital information about how both schools and pupils are doing. This allows students to take corrective action and make informed choices.

Wooldridge accepts, however, that most anyone concedes the former principles. It is at the societal level in the United States where he sees the greatest effort to suppress useful information:

[Standardized testing] also allows society to judge the performance of its educational institutions—and to put pressure on them if they seem to be failing in their basic tasks. For all their imperfections, standardized tests are probably the most powerful instruments of accountability in education that America has.

What we need is more testing rather than less—and more willingness to act on the results of those tests so that the poor of whatever race are no longer given such a rotten deal by America's schools.

Opposing the use of standardized testing is like opposing weather research. Weather reports sometimes predict bad weather and then, sometimes, we get bad weather. So, one could suppose, we can fix the problem of bad weather by banning reports that predict bad weather. Moreover, weather reports are not completely reliable. In fact, they are sometimes wrong! So, perhaps we should ban weather reports because they sometimes give us information we do not like to hear and because they are not perfect.

As we shall see in the ensuing chapters, most of the arguments used against standardized testing could be used just as validly against weather reporting, or any one of thousands of other ordinary, familiar systems of measurement in common use. While watching the War on Testing, the healthy skeptic should always keep in mind two questions—if we were to do this, who would benefit?...and, are the alternatives better? Who would benefit if we were to ban weather reporting, and are the alternatives better?[15]

Who benefits if we ban standardized testing?...and, are the alternatives better?[16]

Notes

1.   I use the term "standardized" in its most general meaning. Any test that is consistent in any respect (e.g., format, time of administration, scoring) is standardized (see Glossary). Some may use the term "standardized test" in a more restrictive sense

(e.g., some people use the term to mean only multiple-choice tests, some use the term to mean only norm-referenced tests).

2. I use the term "external test" to mean one over which local school and district administrators do not have discretion. The rules of administration, the content, and the scoring are controlled by those outside, at a higher level of government or by an independent agency or firm. I use the term "high stakes" to apply to tests with serious consequences tied to the results (e.g., promotion/retention, entry/exit). See Glossary for longer definitions.

3. Generally, absent the use of external standardized tests, district and school-level administrators control all the information pertaining to student achievement. That is true even if standardized tests are used. Districts and schools can purchase commercially available standardized tests and administer (and even score) them themselves. In that way, it is possible for them to influence performance and outcomes measures.

4. State "minimum competency" examinations, which surfaced in many states starting in the 1970s, and whose passage was required for graduation from high school, did arouse some controversy. But, the exams were generally set at a very low level of difficulty (even as low as 6th grade), students were given many chances to pass in untimed conditions and, so, few failed.

5. See a discussion of the phenomenon that includes the physician, John Jacob Cannell, and many others in full-issue coverage, in *Educational Measurement: Issues and Practice*, summer 1988.

6. It should be noted that few of the tests were used in high-stakes situations, however, and, where they were, the bias would have been toward passing unqualified students rather than failing qualified ones.

7. For a variety of reasons, such as changing circumstances, and poor or conflicting sources of information, I felt unable to precisely determine the testing system structure in a number of countries. None of those countries, therefore, have been considered in this exercise (e.g., Austria, Finland, Luxembourg, Mexico, Poland, Spain, Turkey).

8. Though teachers do equivocate when they, themselves, are judged based on their students' academic achievement, over which they do not have total control, most teachers, and the unions, favor testing with consequences for students, but prefer that teachers be judged "up front," with stiff literacy requirements for entry to education schools, and rigorous tests on subject-matter specialties and pedagogy that must be passed after education school, perhaps, but before entry to the profession.

9. Chapter 7 provides more detail and description of the benefits of testing and the research and evidence on the topic

10. Opinion surveys with response rates far below minimally acceptable levels include the annual *Phi Delta Kappan* teacher poll and a survey conducted by the American Association of School Administrators (AASA). All surveys of the public, parents, teachers, or students with response rates over 40 percent show favorable attitudes toward testing. The only surveys finding unfavorable attitudes have response rates below 25 percent and other problems as well.

11. Some education status quo defenders are masters of what George Orwell called "NewSpeak." "Democracy" in education essentially means leaving them to decide everything. Giving education consumers (i.e., students, parents, taxpayers) objective information and letting them make their own choices is "not democratic." Rather, it is given some pejorative name, such as "marketization," a word that, among many educators, has a very bad sound to it.

12. For a more extended discussion of these issues, visit www.education-consumers.com.

13. Note that relaxing certification requirements for entry into the teaching profession threatens education professors' jobs, but does not threaten teacher union membership, as teachers join their local union once they are employed, usually under union shop clauses; one of the many ways that teacher unions' self-interests differ from education faculty's.

14. While there are some education professors and testing experts who would like to speak out against the established order, many could be afraid, as E. D. Hirsch suggests.

15. Some radical egalitarians believe that basing selection decisions on test scores rewards students who work harder, and that is not "fair" to the other students. Others argue that work has nothing to do with it, as student achievement is determined exclusively by parents' income and level of education, and predestined before the first day of kindergarten. So, test scores merely reinforce the social class structure.

16. This is not a completely facetious question. The publisher of the *Farmers' Almanac* would profit from the ban, as would astrologers, probably. Property insurance companies likely would have increased business, too, as would funeral directors, ministers, and priests.

2

Attack Strategies and Tactics

As in any war, the War on Standardized Testing is fought with both tactics—specific, pointed accusations—and strategies—the deeper and more persistent arguments and practices with which a war over public policy is waged.

This chapter begins with the tactics—the negative insinuations of standardized testing's alleged shortcomings that many of you have heard mentioned so many times that, by now, you may have accepted them as principles with as solid a scientific base as the laws of physics. Indeed, some journalists now roll the terms off their tongues like they were citing the periodic table: "teaching to the test," "narrowing the curriculum," and, well...you know. Many of these accusations consist of more nonsense than sense, yet remain as steadfast in public thought as barnacles on a shipwreck. Some of the more persistent of these "tactical" maneuvers will be introduced, explained, and countered.

This chapter then turns to the strategies employed in the War on Testing. Strategies are less immediate and less obvious than tactics, usually only becoming clear when one goes behind the scenes, or watches how testing opponents operate over some period of time. They are more systemic and long term.

At first glance, the strategies employed in the War on Testing may appear unique to the topic of testing. Enough time observing testing opponents' in action, however, and some reveal themselves to be of a similar pedigree of disingenuousness as we knew in our hometowns as gossip and that journalists nowadays call "spin." Examples of anti-testing strategies include:

- *Conceal Self-Interest* (the vast majority of testing opponents are vested in the current public education system and structure, and have a clear self-interest in preventing external evaluations of their performance, but, typically, claim to be selfless protectors of our children);
- *Guilt by Association* (racists and other hateful people used standardized tests in ignorant ways back in the 1920s and 1930s, therefore all standardized testing is forever racist or classist);

- *Compare to Unavailable Alternatives, like Perfection* (standardized tests are imperfect, therefore we should not use them);
- *Ignore the Available Alternatives* (the alternatives to standardized tests, such as grade point averages, have most of the same imperfections, and worse, but testing opponents rarely talk about that);
- *Create a Diversion* (claim that we do not need standardized tests to tell us what the problems in education are; we already know what the problems in education are, and they can be fixed by this year's new, innovative, creative solution for fixing them that requires no change in the way the public school system is managed...but probably requires more taxpayer funding);
- *Only One Side Gets to Talk* (members in organizations are only allowed by their leadership to hear one side of the argument);
- *Demonize the Opposition* (characterize testing advocates as ignorant, selfish, vile—"right wingers," "corporate interests," "authoritarians," "politicians out to get votes by bashing the schools");
- *Wrap Oneself in Academic Robes* (just keep mentioning the prestigious names of the universities where some testing opponents work, even if the work they produce there is of wretchedly low quality);
- *Doctor Data, Fudge Numbers, Alter Definitions* (if journalists will believe whatever "facts" you give them, you can give them whatever "facts" you want);
- *When in Doubt, Just Make it Up* (if what you want to claim is so far beyond the reach of truth that you cannot get to it even by doctoring data, fudging numbers, or redefining terms, just declare it to be so);

The Attacks—Tactics (Overview)

This section is organized by individual "attacks" on standardized testing. I will introduce some of the arguments of the "anti-testing canon" (e.g., they tap only "lower-order thinking," encourage "teaching to the test," "narrow the curriculum," and so on) and offer a rebuttal to each. Because there are *so many* attacks on standardized testing, I impose some order on them by way of a classification scheme. The attacks are organized into four generic groups, each of which has a basic theme. They are:

- Standardized tests are not *natural*.
- Standardized tests do not work.
- Standardized tests are not fair.
- Multiple-choice standardized tests, in particular, are problematic.

Of course, these are not rigid categories; there is quite a bit of overlap across them. Some specific attacks could reasonably be classified into more than one category. However, I need here to counteract one of the strategies in the War on Testing that might be called "proliferation." So many attacks are launched that the "evidence" and "expert opinion" can seem overwhelming.

I would not be doing my job well if I did not at least provide an organized and coherent military atlas, so to speak.

Standardized tests are not natural, they:

- distort instruction;
- induce "teaching to the test" which:
    ...leads to test-score inflation (the "Lake Wobegon" Effect)
    ...and narrows the curriculum to a small domain of topics;
- induce "test preparation," which replaces "real learning;"
- "standardize minds," imposing a "one-size-fits-all" approach to thinking and learning;
- ignore each student's individuality—"reducing" each "to a number;"
- standardize instruction, penalizing the use of innovative curricula and teaching strategies; and
- employ unnatural, "extrinsic" incentives to learn.

Standardized tests do not work, they:

- produce "unintended consequences," such as:
    stress (among students, teachers, and administrators),
    cheating (among students, teachers, and administrators), and
    increased numbers of dropouts;
- produce results that are readily and often misused by politicians and misunderstood by the public;
- are overly costly in terms of both money and time;
- are overused in the United States in comparison with other countries; and
- actually reduce educational achievement (as demonstrated by research studies that employ the technique of "reverse chronological causation").

Standardized tests are not fair, they:

- are being used for multiple purposes, contrary to the wisdom that a single test can only validly be used for a single purpose;
- are being used to make high-stakes decisions about students based on a single test performance, replacing the use of multiple measures in making graduation decisions;
- are unfair to women and minorities; and, besides,
- "selecting" and "rejecting" human beings is wrong.

Multiple-choice standardized tests, in particular:

- can be "coached;" so that students learn "tricks" for doing well on them that have nothing to do with "real knowledge;"
- encourage teaching by "rote memorization" and "drills," which stunt creativity;

- tap only "lower-order thinking;" and
- are not "authentic."

The Attacks—Tactics:

Standardized tests are not *natural*, they:

...Distort instruction. Most test critics' research is derived from the simple assumption that it is good if teachers are allowed to do whatever they please in the classroom. Testing opponents wax eloquent on the alleged benefit of allowing teachers to be "creative" and "innovative" in tailoring instruction to the unique needs of their unique classes. Then, when they evaluate the implementation of "external" testing programs they, not surprisingly, find some teachers who declare that what they taught before was better than what they are now being *coerced* to teach.

Some teachers probably do believe having their own way is better; others simply may not like to make changes. In the language of the test critics' evaluations, the teachers' objections to change get translated into something like "teachers felt that the tests force them to teach contrary to what they, as trained professionals, feel is best instructional practice." In the calculations of the critics, *any* instructional change represents a net cost by comparison to the pure, organic, natural order.

What happens in the classroom then, absent standardized testing, is just assumed to be wonderful. Since it is wonderful and, since enforced standards and high-stakes standardized tests stimulate changes in classroom behavior, testing opponents classify test-induced changes as bad, as deviations from wonderfulness. These deviations are labeled "corruptions" of the natural order and standardized test scores as "pollution" of the natural evaluations of students, which can only be made by individual teachers.

It is not entertained as possible that what teachers teach in the absence of common standards could be less than wonderful. The high school athletic coach who spends as much time talking about the team's progress as the subject matter he is supposed to teach, with the complicity of many of the students...that's wonderful. Teachers who teach subject matter that they happen to like personally because, absent common standards they can teach anything they please, whether or not it serves the students' needs...that's wonderful.[1]

While not denying that some teachers might produce high-quality instruction in a laissez-faire curricular environment, there also exist other teachers who, in the absence of any controls or standards, may relax demands on themselves and their students. They may spend time with students in non-instructional ways or have students work on their own during class time. In U.S. school systems without curricular accountability, the content of courses even in the same subject area and grade level can vary widely in content and quality.

Critics who consider the imposition of "external" standards and testing to be bad things, perversions of the natural order in which teachers get to do whatever they want, deny legal reality and the will of those who pay teachers' salaries. In fact, the public has a legal right to impose curricular order on its schools. In setting common standards, the public is expressing its opinion that there is nothing sacrosanct about what happens in the classroom independent of external quality control. One method by which the public can monitor the implementation of its curricular standards is a standardized testing program. Please indulge me while I employ a sports analogy to illustrate the point.

There are, generally, three ways that basketball can be played: (1) pick-up games in the neighborhood park; (2) intra-squad games at the local high school supervised by the coach; and (3) inter-squad games in an organized league with paid referees, rules, signed liability disclaimers, standings, and maybe even journalists from the local newspaper in attendance.

Is one of these forms of basketball superior to the others? I can imagine that some folks might argue that type one is the most "natural" and "creative" form of basketball, and they may have a point. It certainly is the most natural in the sense that it is the most casual, requires the least commitment and planning, allows anyone to play (maybe), and probably most closely simulates the conditions under which basketball was originally played hundreds of years ago. Others might argue, however, that type two is the superior form for training because play can be stopped at any time by the coach (if the coach is attentive and diligent) and mistakes can be corrected right then— feedback is immediate. It is still somewhat intimate and casual, but there is adult guidance and supervision. Still others would argue, however, that type three is the superior form of basketball. It is more formal and serious, the structure of the game is known beforehand, the rules are set and enforced (though by fallible humans), and the players have an opportunity to prepare. Moreover, one is probably most likely to see the best basketball performance here.

I would argue, however, and I suspect that most people would agree with me, that none of the three forms of basketball is ubiquitously superior to the others. The three types are simply different from one another. Is basketball type three a "distortion" of basketball types one or two? After all, type one may be more "natural" and type two may be more intimate. I believe that if you polled the general public and forced them to choose one of the three types of basketball as the "superior" form, however, most would choose type three, the most formal, and standardized, of the three.

Most of the attacks on standardized testing, however, derive from the assumption that high-stakes standardized testing—basketball type three—is or causes a "distortion" of the good, organic, natural type of learning—basketball types one or two.

Here's another example of measurement-induced distortion—the use of bathroom scales. They distort body size. After all, one is more likely to be conscious of one's weight if one weighs oneself. Comparing one's weight to desired targets may induce behavioral changes that result in a "distortion" of one's body size.

...Induce "teaching to the test." "Teaching to the test" is the silliest and, probably, the most effective of all anti-testing tactics.

Most of us would argue that it is not fair to make high-stakes judgments of students based on the mastery of material to which they have not been exposed. Most testing opponents concur. They criticize vociferously when high-stakes tests cover subject matter that students have not had an opportunity to learn. Then, sometimes in the same argument or speech, testing opponents will criticize just as vociferously the process of teaching material that is covered on a test—that is wrong, too, that is "teaching to the test." Teaching *only* that material that may be covered on a test allegedly leads to other maladies, such as "narrowing the curriculum," test-score inflation, and test coaching.

"Teaching to the test" is the perfect "damned if you do, damned if you don't" argument. Do not teach material that will be covered in a test, and you will be excoriated. Teach material that will be covered in a test, and you will be excoriated. The only way out, of course, is the solution preferred by testing opponents—stop all testing (and let them run the schools the way they like).

Any more, however, the phrase "teach to the test" is employed commonly and reflexively in education research journals and conferences and even among some education journalists, as if it were just as valid a concept as one of the laws of thermodynamics. This leads to miscommunication when those conversant with the education research dialect attempt to discuss these issues with those who are not. For example, when a politician opposed to a certain test proposal several years ago argued that teachers would "teach to the test," a parent wrote a letter to the editor of the newspaper that had interviewed him:

> Ignoring the inherent illogic of the statement, I would like to know what's wrong with 'teaching to the test'?...the fundamental principle of establishing a curriculum, teaching it and then testing what has been learned, is basic to education. (Maroon 1997)

Indeed. Testing opponents are fond of research studies in which students are given two different tests over a period of time, one test that has stakes and is based on the curriculum they are taught in their classrooms, and another, unrelated test that counts for nothing. Over time, of course, scores on the test that counts and that covers material they are taught tend to improve more than the scores on the unrelated test that does not count. Anyone giving the situation a moment's thought would expect such an outcome.

Testing opponents, however, offer the test score discrepancy as "proof" that teachers are "teaching to" a particular test and "narrowing the curriculum." It is suggested that it is a bad thing that the teachers teach from the same domain of knowledge as that from which the test is derived rather than from a domain of knowledge that is different from the test's. So, they should instead teach material that the test will not cover? They should "teach away from the test?"

There is no possible way that our schools can teach our students everything there is to know. The amount of information potentially available for instruction is gargantuan, millions of times larger than can possibly be taught in twelve years of schooling. Given a limited amount of time, the schools must be selective in what they teach. This is inevitable. This is unavoidable. Testing opponents, however, exploit this truism regarding the mismatch between the enormous size of humankind's accumulated pool of knowledge and the obvious inability of any one human to master all of it, or any one school to teach all of it, as an argument to eliminate the use of external standardized tests.

The schools are no more able to teach students the entirety of humankind's accumulated pool of knowledge in an anti-testing environment than in a testing environment, of course, but testing opponents do not tell you that. All teachers "teach to" something, always have, and always will. If they are not "teaching to" the publicly mandated curriculum standards, then what are they "teaching to?" Most likely to their own personal interests and, again, why should the public pay for that? All the trustworthy evidence shows that students tend to learn more in educational environments with common standards, testing, and other forms of logical structure and quality control, than they do in the "anything goes" classrooms advocated by many testing opponents (for an extended discussion defending teaching to the test, see Cohen and Hyman 1991).

Affiliated symptoms of the teaching-to-the-test-illogic pattern are included among the following.

...Induce test-score inflation (The "Lake Wobegon" Effect). In the early 1980s, a West Virginia physician John J. Cannell investigated a statistical anomaly that he had discovered: statewide average scores for elementary school students on some widely used test batteries were above the national average in every state in which they were given[2] (Cannell 1987). It was dubbed the "Lake Wobegon Effect" after the fictional public radio community where "all the children are above average."

The Lake Wobegon anomaly might have been caused—observed Cannell and some test experts—by a number of factors, including: schools reusing old tests year after year and growing familiar with their specific content; and test publishers waiting years before "renorming" the reference scales. Other factors could have included the "non-representativeness" of the norming samples (test publishers make economic and logistical trade-offs by using convenient samples, such as Chapter 1 [federal anti-poverty program] students they are already testing to meet Chapter 1 requirements, as norming samples); school districts could pick and choose among various versions of tests the one most aligned to their curriculum and on which students would perform best; and student achievement really was improving throughout the 1980s, as verified by independent testing, such as that for SAT, ACT, and NAEP exams. There may also have been some statistical anomalies in Dr. Cannell's calculations (Phillips and Finn 1988).

The Lake Wobegon effect controversy led to calls for more state government control over test content and administration and less local discretion. In most states, those calls were answered. Today most school systems are aware of the problem of test score inflation and do not allow local districts to use tests with the exact same questions year after year. Many jurisdictions now either use tests that are custom built to their state standards and curricula and that are adapted fresh each year from commercial publishers' huge test item banks. A simple way of preventing test score inflation is to use different tests from year to year without announcing in advance which test will be used. Indeed, most of the presumed causes of the Lake Wobegon effect are fairly easily avoided[3] (Phelps 1999b: 12-13).

...Narrow the curriculum. Test critics commonly accuse high-stakes tests of "narrowing the curriculum," but it is actually the amount of instructional time available that narrows it. In fact, all educators, including those opposed to standardized tests, narrow the curriculum. They have to. There is only so much instructional time available and choices must be made as to how that time is used. It is physically impossible to teach everything that can possibly be taught.

Critics argue that important subjects, such as music, art, and drama, are being dropped from the curriculum because they are not tested, in favor of the basics, which are. What they do not say is that curriculum content is legally the product of public decisions, not of the personal preferences of education professors. Most U.S. states conducted an arduous, years-long process of reviewing and adopting new curriculum standards in the 1990s. Citizens' committees were formed, "expert" committees were formed, public hearings were held. In the end, the curriculum standards adopted through these democratic processes may not have been what some education professors preferred. Too bad.

In those cases where the students are, indeed, woefully deficient in basic skills and need extra instructional time devoted to them, however, probably few parents would object to trimming other subject matter. Primary school students may need to establish a foundation in reading, writing, and arithmetic before they can learn anything else well later on. (Farkus, Johnson, Duffet 1997). Poll results show clearly that the public wants students to master the basics skills first, before they go on to explore the rest of the possible curriculum. If that means they must spend more time on the basics, so be it (Johnson and Immerwahr 1994).

If the critics intend to continue asserting that non-tested subjects are being dropped from the curriculum, however, they should show some evidence that *student requirements* for taking music, art, language, or other non-tested subjects are being dropped.[4] If they cannot, then they have no grounds for their assertions. In principle, of course, any school system can implement high-stakes tests in art, music, language, and civics, too, or in any other "non basic" subject they consider important. Indeed, some do.

...Induce "test preparation" which replaces "real learning." According to CRESST:

> High-stakes testing misdirects instruction even for the basic skills. Under pressure, classroom instruction is increasingly dominated by tasks that resemble tests.... Even in the early grades, students practice finding mistakes rather than do real writing, and they learn to guess by eliminating wrong answers. (Shepard 1991)

Critics like CRESST claim that intensive instruction in basic skills denies slower students instruction in the "the neat stuff" in favor of "lower-order thinking" (see, for example, Shepard 1991a; Smith 1991a, 1991b, 1991c). They argue that time for preparing students for high-stakes tests reduces "ordinary instruction" and "real" learning. They cannot abide the notion that preparing students for a standardized test could be considered instruction, because it is not the kind of instruction that they favor (Shepard 1991).

Instruction to which teachers tend to resort to help students improve their scores on standardized tests tends not to be the kind CRESST researchers like (i.e., it is not constructivist—because constructivist learning is too slow and hit-and-miss). It is the type of instruction, however, that teachers feel works best and most dependably for knowledge and skill acquisition. Most teachers in high-stakes testing situations do not deliberately use instructional practices that impede learning; they use those that they find to be most dependable and successful and, yes, those tend not to be the types that constructivists promote. The fact that when student learning must be accounted for teachers tend to abandon constructivist techniques is, in reality, evidence that constructivist techniques are neither reliable nor effective. Constructivists blame the tests when, really, they should question their own beliefs.

There have been thousands of education research studies on instructional practices but, every so often, some truly rigorous ones are conducted (e.g., program evaluations using random assignment). With a couple dozen or so random assignment evaluations of thematic education programs having been performed, the evidence strongly supports the use of highly structured, highly scripted instructional methods. These are programs employing workbooks and lots of repetition, methods that look like "test preparation," methods that look like "drill and kill." Constructivist programs show less evidence of success (see, for example, Carnine 2000; Traub 1999; Ravitch 2000; Hirsch 1996; Stone 1996; Kozloff 1998).

Some "test-preparation" accusations are tautological. For example, a Center for the Study of Testing, Evaluation, and Educational Policy (CSTEEP) at Boston College did a study of several commercially available math and science tests funded by the National Science Foundation and concluded that the tests promoted "test preparation" practices. Eighty-one percent of math teachers and 53 percent of science teachers engaged in some form of "test preparation," according to CSTEEP. However, the researchers "coded 'test preparation' as 'present' when the teacher or administrator made an explicit link between a particular activity and test scores, or gave such evidence in spite of denying test preparation." Thus, if a teacher taught an ordinary math or science lesson and hoped that it would improve students' performance on a test later on, that was counted as "test preparation" in the study, even if the teacher pointedly denied that it was (West and Viator 1992).

...Standardized minds (demanding a "one-size-fits-all" approach to thinking and learning). Standardized tests measure attained knowledge and skills, they do not determine *how* one attains either. Different people may acquire the same knowledge in different ways, and often do. A student can arrive at an answer to a test question any way she wishes to. It is the subject matter itself that imposes "one size" on the material. Unless, of course, one wants to argue that every student has a right to create his or her own rules of mathematics and English grammar, and should only be judged by his or her own, unique, individualized subject matter.

...Ignore each student's individuality–"reducing" each "to a number." According to education journalist, and testing opponent, John Merrow (2001, 2002):

> Standardized tests do not allow for children to be different—as all humans are. To measure children against a national standard is inappropriate. We are saying that they all need to be good at the same things, and the worst part is that the tests do not measure the real knowledge a child may have and how they can apply their knowledge to real life experiences.... We hurt kids when we reduce them to a number.

Standardized tests are inanimate objects and standardized test scores are numerical measures representing an amount of knowledge. Standardized tests are not imbued with the power to form human beings, mold them, or change them. Humans beings can make whatever they wish of standardized tests or the scores they receive on them. Humans may ignore tests completely. Humans can read too much into tests. Or, as is probably true in most cases, humans can accept tests for what they are–limited collections of information that may, or may not, be informative.

Human children are different from each other before they take standardized tests, and they are just as different from each other after they take standardized tests. Standardized tests do not have the power to make children any more or less different. Standardized tests measure knowledge—yes, real knowledge (is there such as thing as fake knowledge?) and, yes, they measure a certain subset of that knowledge. But, in most cases, that subset of knowledge is exactly what the children are supposed to be taught in school. That subset is a legally prescribed body of knowledge, agreed upon through a democratic process with citizen involvement. High-stakes tests, in most cases in which they are used, embody the knowledge that society has determined is most useful or necessary for an adolescent to know.

Kids are not "reduced to a number" by a test score. The test score does not even attempt to describe them as individuals. A test score describes only what they know. And, the vast majority of the American public wishes to employ objective, comparable measures of what and how much their children know.

...Standardize instruction (penalizing the use of innovative curricula and teaching strategies). "Innovation" has limits as a beneficial force. Yes, indeed, teachers need flexibility in addressing the learning needs of their students. But, despite the utopian rhetoric of the radical constructivists, no teachers other than home schoolers can feasibly adapt every lesson to each individual student. The evidence shows that very few even try (see, for example, the revealing reports of Celebuski, Farris, and Burns 1998; and Nolin, Rowand, Farris, and Carpenter 1994). Besides, standardized tests do not dictate instructional technique; they require the mastery of certain knowledge. Teachers and students are free to master that knowledge in any manner that works best for them.

Some testing critics idealize the concept of teachers as individual crafts persons, responding to the unique needs of unique classes in unique ways with "creative and innovative" curriculum and instruction (Farkus, Johnson, Duffet 1997). But the most difficult jobs in the world are those that must be created anew everyday without any consistent structure, and performed in isolation, without collaboration or advice. In Public Agenda's research, "teachers routinely complained that teaching is an isolated and isolating experience" (Farkus, Johnson, and Duffet 1997: 12).

By contrast, teachers in other countries are commonly held to more narrowly prescribed curricula and teaching methods. Furthermore, because their curricula and instructional methods are standardized, they can work together and learn from each other. They seem not to suffer from this reduction in "creativity and innovation"; indeed, when adjusted for a country's wealth, teachers in other countries are paid more, and usually have greater prestige.[5]

The critics cannot accept that some teachers may *want* to conform to systemwide standards for curriculum, instruction, and testing. Standardization brings the security, convenience, camaraderie, and common professional development that accompany shared work experience.[6]

Students in education systems with more stringent curriculum and instruction quality control measures tend to learn more of the material that is required for them to learn (Phelps 2001e). Students in systems where teachers have more "flexibility" may well learn more of what each individual teacher personally prefers to teach. But, again, why should the public want to pay for and subject their children to the personal preferences of each teacher?

...Employ unnatural, "extrinsic" incentives to learn. Some opponents of external standards and quality control want to abolish more than just high-stakes standardized tests. Alfie Kohn, perhaps the country's most prolific anti-testing writer and speaker, also opposes teacher grades and ability grouping. Nothing should be done to discourage students from learning, he argues. If not discouraged (by being judged and made to conform) each student's natural, "intrinsic" desire to learn will blossom. Kohn cites much research to support his viewpoint, but much of it amounts to little more than the expression of others' similar opinions. Moreover, he conveniently ignores loads of well-done research that does not support his point of view (see Cameron and Pierce 1994, 1996; Freeman 1994, www.alfiekohn.com).

Kohn is certainly correct in asserting that all of us have an intrinsic incentive to learn. Furthermore, he is right to argue that schools should exploit that natural tendency as much as possible. Personal experience and common sense tell most of us, however, that "intrinsic" motivation has its limits. All children, at some time or another, get bored with learning. Moreover, intrinsic motivation does not operate in the same way, or at the same pace all the time, with all children.

Besides, though it may sound politically incorrect to say so, children do not always know what is best for them. Let them be in charge of their own education, to learn whatever interests each of them the most at any given moment. Would they learn what is most important for them to learn? Moreover, how could such a school possibly be organized in any kind of rational way? Finally, most parents and taxpayers would probably say, "If some 'extrinsic' incentives work, why not use them? Will not the kids be better off in the end?"

Standardized tests do not work, they:

Produce "Unintended Consequences," such as: The "unintended consequences" line of argument is just another way of saying that standardized tests do not please everybody (e.g., students who score poorly might get hurt feelings, or held back a grade, teachers who no longer get to teach their favorite subject matter). A CRESST study on the "unintended consequences of external testing," claimed "stress, frustration, burnout, fatigue, physical illness, misbehavior and fighting, and psychological distress," among the effects of testing on young students (Smith and Rottenberg 1991).

If we were to wait until everyone everywhere declared unconditional love for standardized tests before using one, we would, of course, wait forever. Everybody who has ever attended school (or lived life), however, already knows that you cannot always get what you want, and does not expect it. Testing opponents, nonetheless, take their expectation of ubiquitous happiness concept a bit further in two respects: in their idealization of the "natural" education process in which teachers and schools are left alone to do whatever they please with our tax dollars and our children; and in their insistence that standardized tests should not be allowed in use until they become perfect and have no "unintended consequences."

...Stress (among students). A favorite "unintended consequence" of testing is "stress" and many testing opponents argue that stress is ubiquitously bad. "Stress," as the belief goes, is unpleasant and because high-stakes tests cause stress, which, of course, they do, they are bad (see, for example, Kellaghan, et al. 1996, or Shepard 1991). Their belief runs contrary to the philosophy that there are many stressful events in life and we do our children no favors if we do not prepare them for them. Or, we do our children no favors if we do not make them face the normal, reasonable challenges that life has in store for them.

Nonetheless, polls and surveys show little evidence that students feel unduly stressed by tests[7] (e.g., Public Agenda 2001). About a quarter of students in one poll who claimed to be receiving a good education cited "challenging, high standards" as the reason; 11 percent of students who claimed to be receiving a bad education cited "low demands, repetition" ("good" or "poor" teachers accounted for the majority of the responses) (Erickson 1991: 42).

In *Assignment Incomplete*, the polling organization Public Agenda asked about a variety of pressures that U.S. teenagers face, "such as pressure from peers, pressure at home because of troubled families, or from crime and drugs in the neighborhood, and academic pressures come out dead last. No more than 10 percent of any group—the general public, parents, teachers, or leaders—think American youngsters are under too much academic pressure today" (Johnson et al. 1995: 27). There seems to be far more evidence that U.S. students feel bored and unchallenged than that they feel stressed or overtested.

Besides, abandoning the enforcement of high academic standards will not eliminate pressures and hurt feelings among our youth. Pressure and hurt feelings are facts of life. Abandoning academics just means the pressures will come from and the hurt feelings will be caused by non-academic aspects of their lives.

...Stress (among educators). School administrators have lived a charmed life for decades. Not accountable for reliable measures of student learning, too many of them succumbed to the inertia toward low standards, social promotion, inflated grades, and fluffy, low-content courses.

Now, some school administrators are being held accountable for doing their job, they regard the accountability measures to be imperfect, and they are feeling some pressure. Welcome to the world that the rest of us live in.

Surely, there are circumstances where the pressure on school administrators might be unfair or test administration could be handled better. Unlike in most of the rest of the world's education systems, where high-stakes standardized tests have been relied on for decades (and educators could not imagine school without them), they are fairly new in the United States. New programs are bound to have kinks. Most testing opponents do not direct our attention to such legitimate concerns, however. They want us to return to the Wobegon days when all students were above average and there was no accountability for learning.

As for teachers, there are probably no fairer systems for judging teacher performance than the "value added" testing systems like Tennessee's. It is not fair to judge teacher performance solely on students' test scores at the end of a semester or year. It could be that the students started a year well behind. Teacher performance should be evaluated on the basis of each teacher's unique performance, on the value each teacher added to the base of knowledge with which their students arrived at the beginning of the school year. Value-added testing systems do just that.

But, remember, in most states, teacher performance is not evaluated at all. All teachers get raises based on seniority, including those who, in the face of huge disincentives, work hard and succeed, as well as the irresponsible or incompetent ones who may be stifling students' educational opportunity.

...Cheating. Opponents of high-stakes standardized tests claim they induce normally good people to cheat. How standardized tests are any different in this respect than a thousand other temptations in our daily lives is confusing to me. We all have incentives to: cheat on our income taxes, run red lights if we're in a hurry, shoplift, and steal our neighbor's lawn sprinkler. Because all of us have selfish incentives to do these things does not mean that all of us do them. Some of us do. Some of us do not because we are too ethical. Some of us do not because we are afraid of the consequences.

While no one would advocate that cheating is good or that it should be allowed, many would not agree with some of the critics that the simple fact that cheating exists in high-stakes environments justifies banning the use high-stakes tests (see, for example, Toch 1992). If we were to shut down all activities in our society that provided temptations, because some weak, self-ish, and unethical people will give into those temptations, we will shut down all of society. We could then all live in fortified stone towers, like in a medieval Italian town, hoarding all we own, trusting no one.

...Cheating (among students). Yes, there are students who cheat. If youth surveys are to be believed, the overwhelming majority of students cheat in some fashion at some point in their school careers, and they do not restrict their cheating behavior to standardized test days (e.g., Durham 2000; Stricherz 2001). Students willing to cheat are likely to cheat where they can get away with it, and they can cheat on teacher-made classroom tests just as well as on standardized tests. Indeed, students can cheat far more easily on homework (or on portfolios), by having someone else do the work, or by copying text out of publications or off the Internet for a class report. Everything considered, it is far more difficult to cheat on a standardized test than in regular classroom work.

It is also easier to *prevent* cheating on standardized tests by, for example, using different forms with different question orderings and having someone who has no personal incentive monitoring the test administration. Moreover, it is easier to *detect* cheating with standardized tests, through computer matching of student responses.

...Cheating (among teachers). Some testing opponents willing to concede that the incidence of student cheating is more often than not *reduced* by the use of standardized tests, may still argue that high-stakes standardized testing increases the incidence of *teacher* cheating. If a teacher's performance is judged, in whole or in part, on the basis of their students' test results, certainly they are given an incentive to cheat.

Teachers who cheat on standardized tests do not easily get away with it, however. Teacher cheating cannot usually be done silently or singly. Someone else knows, and someone else usually tells. That produces the news headlines. The headlines provide the impression that cheating occurs, but they also provide the evidence that it was detected and the perpetrators caught.

Would the elimination of high-stakes standardized tests eliminate all incentives for teachers to cheat? No. Teachers have just as much incentive, and far better opportunity, to cheat in the absence of high-stakes tests and many, if not most, of them do. It has become a national scandal.

The two most popular types of non-test-related teacher cheating are "social promotion" and "grade inflation." Some argue that both exist in pandemic proportions in today's public schools. Grades and grade promotion decisions have become largely meaningless in many schools. They simply do not represent subject matter mastery. Social promotion and grade inflation do not often make headlines, however. It is extraordinarily difficult to prove a teacher has graded improperly and, in most cases, all the others involved—school administrators, other teachers, and students—share the same incentives.

In a 1996 survey, more than half of teachers questioned said that they had promoted unprepared students in the past year. In the same survey, 60 percent of teachers said they felt pressure from principals or other administrators to pass students, and 52 percent felt parental pressure. Without standardized testing, do we really have any idea how well our children are learning the subject matter that will determine whether they can lead happy, productive lives (Farkus, Johnson, Friedman, Bers, and Perry 1996)?

...Increased numbers of dropouts. Some opponents of high-stakes testing argue that the costs to society of denying students diplomas for any reason might be too high. One said, for example: "As a determinant of a student's life chances in American society, possessing a high school diploma is far more important than scoring well on a basic skills competency test" (Jaeger 1991). He cited statistics showing that high school dropouts are more likely to have blighted lives and argued that "the use of such tests jeopardizes the future of those young people denied a high school diploma by limiting their employ-ability, reducing their quality of life, and diminishing their opportunity to contribute to society through the productive applications of their abilities" (Jaeger 1991: 242). He implied that if states just gave poorly performing students their diplomas with no impediments, they would enjoy less crime, fewer out-of-wedlock births, and shorter welfare rolls (Jaeger: 242).

Most U.S. dropouts leave school when they reach the limit of the compulsory attendance law, however, and not when they fail an exam.[7] When students in the large-scale *Indiana Youth Poll* explained why some dropped out, either disinterest in school or non-academic-related problems (such as pregnancy or family problems) were more than four times more likely to be mentioned than any type of academic failure (Erickson 1991: 33).[8]

A careful examination of the dropout issue by Griffen and Heidorn (1996), using data from Florida from the early 1990s, examined the relationship between minimum-competency testing and dropout behavior among students in 14 Florida school districts, from 3 grade levels, who took the state test in 1990-91. They found a statistically significant likelihood of leaving school only among students who were doing well academically (as they were in a group with extremely low rates of dropout). Students with poorer academic records and minority students appeared to be unaffected by failure on the graduation exam.

More recent studies of the high-stakes test-dropout relationship have shown that it can move in either direction—the dropout rate can rise if struggling students are ignored, or decline if they are given the extra attention they need, when they need it.

Speaking about the same high-stakes exit exam in Florida, the psychologist and lawyer Barbara Lerner explained:

> On the first few tries, 80 to 90 percent of Florida's students failed the test. But they were not crushed, as the experts predicted, and they did not give up and drop out in droves without diplomas. They kept trying, and their teachers did too, working hard to help them learn from failure and, ultimately, to master the skills they needed to graduate. By the fifth try, better than 90 percent of them did just that. They left school not just with a piece of paper, but with basic skills that prepared them better for life..."
> (Gray and Kemp 1993).

We all know that slower students can catch up if they get extra help (and if they want to do the extra work). One could well argue that social justice demands they be given the opportunity. So, should we not all celebrate a system that guarantees them that extra help? Where do we find such school systems?

In states with high-stakes testing, that's where. In states *without* high-stakes testing, standards do not matter, meeting standards does not matter, and students may be promoted and graduated no matter how little they learn. There is no need for extra help, after-hours tutoring, summer school, or Saturday classes. In high-stakes testing states, students in academic trouble get the extra help they need. In states without testing, they get forgotten.

The critics who complain about the onerous effect of high-stakes tests on at-risk students usually do not recognize the lengths to which state education agencies go to make it possible for disadvantaged students to succeed. Minimum competency tests in many states are administered as "power tests," which means any student has as much time as they want to take to complete the test. Virtually all minimum competency exams, moreover, can be taken more than once—an unlimited number of times in some cases. Most states offer test administrations in several grade levels and several times a year (U.S. General Accounting Office 1993: 18-20).

In his study comparing U.S. school organization to that in four West European countries, John Bishop digresses at length on the topic of *redoublement* (repeating a grade). In European countries with curriculum-based graduation examinations, instruction emphasizes mastery of material; if students do not master the material, they will not graduate. In such an environment, it is considered detrimental to the child to pass her on to the next grade level if she has fallen behind her class in achievement. Passing her on will only make her mastery of the material worse, not better. *Redoublement* allows some students extra time to achieve very demanding learning goals. The systems emphasize achievement of a certain body of knowledge; it is not considered so important how old the student is when mastery is achieved (Bishop 1994: 26–33). If the problem with retaining students in grades in the United States is the stigma it induces, then perhaps we should do something about the stigma, as other societies have, rather than eliminating high-stakes tests.

...Produce test scores that are readily and often misused by politicians and misunderstood by the public. It is most certainly true that some politicians and parents sometimes misuse or misunderstand tests and test scores. But, so do testing opponents. Whereas politicians and parents may misinterpret because they lack sufficient understanding, testing opponents may misinterpret because it is in their interest.

The point is moot, anyway. Educators are using the public's money to care for the public's children. In a democratic society, there should be no question that full disclosure and objective evaluation as to what goes on behind school doors are in order.

...Are costly in terms of both money and time. In the early 1990s, CSTEEP, at Boston College, calculated a "high" estimate of $22.7 billion spent on standardized testing per year (Haney, Madaus, and Lyons 1993: 119). U.S. schools, the CSTEEP report claimed, suffer from "too much standardized testing" that amounts to "a complete and utter waste of resources." (Haney, Madaus, and Lyons 1993: 122). Their estimate breaks down to about $575 per student per year. A CRESST report which counted cost components in much the same way as the CSTEEP study estimated costs of a certain state test at between $848 and $1,792 per student tested ($1,320 would be mid-range) (Picus and Tralli 1998).

Testing critics exaggerate their cost estimates by counting the costs of any activities "related to" a test as costs *of* a test. In the CRESST study of Kentucky's performance-based testing program, for example, teachers were asked to count the number of hours they spent "preparing materials related to the assessment program for classroom use." In an instructional program like Kentucky's, with the intention of unifying all instruction and assessment into a "seamless" web, where the curriculum and the test mutually determine each other, *all* instruction throughout the entire school year will be "related to" the assessment and, indeed, some teachers in the CRESST survey claimed the entire school year to be "test preparation."

The CSTEEP study counted even more cost items, such as student time. The CSTEEP researchers assumed that there is no instructional value whatsoever to student time preparing for or taking a test (i.e., students learn absolutely nothing while preparing for or taking tests). Then they calculated the present discounted value of that "lost" learning time against future earnings, assuming all future earnings to be the direct outcome of school instruction. The CSTEEP researchers also counted building overhead (maintenance and capital costs) for the amount of time spent testing, even though those costs are constant (i.e., "sunk") and not affected by the existence of a test. In sum, CSTEEP counts any and all costs incurred simultaneously to tests, not just those caused by testing, that would not exist without testing.

In stark contrast to these incredible estimates are the actual prices charged for tests such as the ACT, SAT, and AP exams, ranging from $20 to $70 a student. The makers of these tests must cover all their costs, or they would go out of business.

The bipartisan U.S. General Accounting Office (GAO) (1993b) also conducted a survey of state and local testing directors and administrators to learn the costs of statewide and districtwide tests. The GAO estimate of $15 to $33 per student contrasts markedly with CRESST and CSTEEP estimates of $575 and $1,320. And, the GAO estimates counted all relevant costs, including that for teacher time used in administering tests. The GAO estimate for the total national cost of system-wide testing of about $500 million contrasts with a CSTEEP estimate *45 times higher.*

...Are far less common in other countries, where test use is declining. Scholars at the National Research Council (NRC) and CSTEEP have declared that "American students are the most heavily tested in the world" and the use of standardized testing in other developed countries is declining (Madaus 1991). They reason that other countries are dropping large-scale external tests because they no longer need them as selection devices, since places in upper secondary programs are being made available to everyone and access to higher education programs has widened. Thus, they argue, a worldwide trend toward less external testing can be found at all levels of education; "even at the postsecondary level," it is unidirectional—large-scale, external tests are being "abolished," and "standardized national examinations before the age of 16 have all but disappeared (Madaus and Kellaghan 1991).

Are U.S. students the "most heavily tested in the world?" No. U.S. students spend less time taking high-stakes standardized tests than do students in most, and perhaps all, other developed countries. A 1991 survey for the Organisation for Economic Co-operation and Development (OECD) revealed that "U.S. students face fewer hours and fewer numbers of high-stakes standardized tests than their counterparts in every one of the 13 other countries and states participating in the survey and fewer hours of state-mandated tests than their counterparts in 12 of the 13 other countries and states" (Phelps 1996).

What of a trend toward less standardized testing in other countries? As was shown in chapter 1, the primary trend appears to be toward more testing, with a variety of new test types and for a variety of purposes. The best evidence, from a study of testing programs in 31 countries and provinces from 1974 to 1999 reveals that 27 countries increased their amount of testing and only 3 decreased it; 59 new tests were added, while only 4 were dropped (Phelps 2000g).

...Actually lower student achievement (as demonstrated in research studies which employ reverse chronological causation). Objective researchers

tend to think that one thing cannot cause something in the past, unless one can travel back in time. The no-holds-barred methodologies of testing opponents are not limited by such rigid temporal ordering, however. In anti-testing research, reverse chronological causation is sometimes considered an acceptable form of logic.

For example, in its report, *High Stakes Tests Do Not Improve Student Learning*, FairTest asserted that states with high-stakes graduation exams tend to score lower on the neutral, common National Assessment of Educational Progress (NAEP). According to FairTest, this "contradicts the...common assumption of standards and tests-based school reform...that high-stakes testing...will produce improved learning outcomes"[9] (Neill 1998).

The FairTest report provides a good example of just how simplistic much anti-testing research is. FairTest argues that states with high-stakes minimum-competency test graduation requirements tend to have lower average test scores on NAEP. They make no effort, however, to control for other factors that influence test performance, and the relationship between cause and effect is just assumed to be in the direction FairTest wants[10] (Neill 1998).

More astute observers would assume the direction of cause and effect to be just the opposite—poorly performing states, mostly in the South, initiated high-stakes testing programs in an effort to improve academic performance, while high-performing states did not feel the need to. Those researchers who have handled this research issue responsibly—comparing the gains in average student achievement over time across states while controlling for state's initial starting positions and other background factors—have found states with high-stakes testing systems to have stronger student achievement gains[11] (see, for example, Grissmer, Flanagan, Kawata, and Williamson 2000; Graham and Husted 1993; Bishop 1995a-c). Chapter 7 discusses these and other studies of testing benefits at more length.

Education policies appear to have been most effective in states with comprehensive, curriculum-based, high-stakes testing programs that are well-integrated with instruction and professional development—states such as Texas and North Carolina, the states that have shown the most improvement in State NAEP results in the 1990's[12] (Grissmer and Flanagan 1998).

Standardized testing is not fair, because:

...A single test can only validly be used for a single purpose—A popular bit of folklore at the National Research Council and at CRESST. The kernel of truth behind this assertion is that when a test is used for a single purpose (e.g., individual student diagnosis; mastery of a required curriculum) it can be *optimized* for that purpose. Testing opponents say, however, that one must only use each test for one single purpose, even when it might be sub-optimal for other purposes, but still far better than any feasible alternative.

Most countries in the world use single tests for multiple purposes. Individual tests are used as high-stakes graduation requirements from one level of education; high-stakes entrance requirements to selective places in the next level of education; diagnostic tools for students, teachers, and schools; curriculum drivers; and more (see also Cizek 1994).

According to Eckstein and Noah (1993: 238-239):

> In addition to certification and selection, other countries use their end-of-secondary-school examinations for a variety of other functions: for example, to define what knowledge and skills are of most worth, to set performance expectations of students, teachers, and schools, and to provide yardsticks against which individual schools and the school system as a whole can be assessed.

If we were to only use single tests for single purposes, as testing opponents argue, we would end up with a plethora of tests. Then, some of the same testing opponents, naturally, would argue that we use too many tests.

... "Single tests" are being used to make high-stakes decisions about students (rather than "multiple measures"). No, they are not. Students are given several to many chances to pass high school exit exams in U.S. states. Moreover, these exams are typically set at a middle-school level of difficulty, or lower. Most parents do not want their children to leave high school before they have mastered the basic core subjects at a 6th- or 7th-grade level of difficulty.

Moreover, exit exam requirements are no different from any other high school completion requirement. If a state requires that students complete four levels of English to graduate, no student can graduate without passing marks in four levels of English. If a student fails a senior-level English course, she does not graduate. And, ultimately, *at the margin*, she can fail simply for not passing an end-of-semester exam in any level of English, by just one question. What is true for English is true for any other graduation requirement, from passing grades in four levels of Physical Education courses to completion of minimum amounts of community service time in some states.

...Standardized tests are unfair to women and minorities. There is a double sadness to the focus of some minority groups on the messenger instead of the message. Black and Hispanic students in the United States generally receive an education inferior to that which white students receive. It is a shame and a disgrace. By blaming standardized tests instead of the school systems that are responsible for their students' poor achievement, however, these advocacy groups waste efforts that would be more productively expended reforming bad school systems.

A Public Agenda survey of school parents on education issues pertaining to race implies that NAACP actions in Texas and other states against high-stakes standardized testing may not even reflect what most African Americans want. "Most African-American parents do not think standardized tests are culturally biased and very few want race to be a factor when choosing the best teachers for their children..." (*Education Daily* 1998). When asked why, on average, black students do not do as well as whites on standardized achievement tests, only 28 percent say it is mostly because "the tests are culturally biased against black students." Forty-four percent of black parents say "the tests measure real differences in educational achievement," and 18 percent say the reason for this difference is a failure of expectations (Farkus, Johnson, Immerwahr, and McHugh 1998).

The charge that the use of SATs in college admissions artificially depresses minority admissions may also be misguided. As the statistician David W. Murray writes:

> Nor is it even clear that relying more exclusively on grades would bump up the enrollment numbers of blacks and Hispanics, as many seem to think. While it is true that more minority students would thereby become eligible for admission, so would other students whose grade point averages (GPAs) outstripped their test scores. A state commission in California, considering the adoption of such a scheme, discovered that in order to pick students from this larger pool for the limited number of places in the state university system, the schools would have to raise their GPA cutoff point. As a result, the percentage of eligible Hispanics would have remained the same, and black eligibility actually would have dropped." (Murray 1998; see also Sandham 1998)

Testing opponents may not tell you this, but minorities tend to do relatively better on multiple-choice standardized tests than on the open-response or performance-based tests that radical constructivists favor. The reason probably refers to one of multiple-choice tests' most underappreciated advantages—when a student knows that the correct answer is among the several provided, the domain of possible answers is bounded, the *type* of answer desired is pretty clear. With open-ended formats, the domain of possible answers is, well...open ended. The respondent does not know if the question is looking for a general answer or specific answer, a long answer or a short answer, a broad answer or a deep, narrow answer. Open response formats may be culturally biased.

One of the more repulsive techniques of many testing opponents is their use of "at-risk" poor and minority students as hostages. They claim to be concerned about them and interested in protecting them. But, the future they would make for them is the same as their past—years of social promotion, a diploma "on time" if they can stand the boredom long enough, and a life of poverty and ignorance without any practical skills.

... "Selecting" and "rejecting" human beings, especially young children, is wrong. Testing's critics also complain about using test scores to make selection decisions. They say that tests are not perfect measures and, in that,

they are correct. They claim that low test scores can make students feel bad, which they well might. They assert it to be wrong to "select" and "reject" students in general, especially through an instrument as dispassionate as a standardized test.

They neglect to mention, however, that, sooner or later, the students are going to be selected or rejected, with or without the use of tests. Selection and rejection are facts of life; we cannot all get whatever we want. Without standardized tests, the selection and rejection decisions will still be made, they will just be made based on less information. The argument can be framed as a type 1/type 2 error problem:

Type 1/Type 2 Errors in Testing Policy

Type 1 Error: Tests are not perfect measurement instruments and humans are not perfectly measurable, so any one test may not accurately measure a student's achievement or ability (but, neither does the high school GPA).

Type 2 Error: Without tests, those who could benefit from an accurate evaluation of a student's achievement and abilities, such as employers in their hiring, higher education admissions personnel in their applicant selection, or students themselves, or from an accurate evaluation of a school or school system's performance, such as the taxpayers, will not be able to do so.

Two Possible Solutions for reducing Type 1 Error:

- Ban or banish all tests [*increases Type 2 error*]
- Use many tests over time and across subjects, along with other measures of student performance—multiple measures—so that no one is judged summarily on the basis of just one [*reduces both Type 1 and Type 2 error*].

Multiple-choice standardized tests, in particular, are problematic, because:

..."Test taking" can be "coached," such that students learn "tricks" for doing well on tests, that have nothing to do with "real knowledge." Testing opponents would have you believe that one can do well on a multiple-choice test without even reading the questions, just strategizing over the list of answers. One or two responses will "obviously" be wrong. How can one know that some answers are "obviously" wrong without knowing something about the topic?

Indeed, the Princeton Review, a billion-dollar company, claims that coaching is all they do in their standardized test preparation courses. They may be correct. But, if true, the objective evidence would suggest that they are sell-ing a near worthless product. The president of the for-profit Princeton Review claims, essentially, that the Scholastic Assessment Test (SAT) and other standardized tests, are fraudulent measures.

The kernel of truth inside testing opponents' claims is that it is to one's benefit to be familiar beforehand with the format of a test. The non-profit consortium of hundreds of higher education institutions that use the SAT, the College Entrance Examination Board (CollegeBoard), used to tell test-takers not to bother studying for it. This was, at the least, rather misleading.

On the one hand, the content domain covered by the SAT is so broad (e.g., tens of thousands of English words) that one cannot hope to make up for ten years of bad education in the matter of a few weeks of cramming. On the other hand, there are particular niches where some review can help, such as with about a half a dozen geometry formulae. More importantly, *familiarity with the test format and with test conditions*, as opposed to the actual study of the subject matter being tested, can help.

A couple of decades ago, then, the CollegeBoard started recommending that students take a practice SAT under simulated conditions (i.e., timed and uninterrupted) to become familiar with test taking conditions. They also provided samples of tests that they recommended students review in order to become familiar with the test format.

The advantage one gets from format familiarity, however, is raised by some testing opponents to the status of global conspiracy, though the situation is no different from that for any other activity in which standardized measures are used. All measures that compare use a structure. So, everyone should be made to know the structure and the rules and the rules should be applied the same way to everyone. It is the standard set of rules, and the uniform application of those rules, that make a measurement system fair. Any competitive athletic contest, for example, has rules and a format. Anyone who plans to participate in one of those contests would be prudent to understand those rules beforehand and become familiar with the format. It is no different with most of life's tasks, such as learning a new computer software program at work, finding the best deal on airline tickets for your next trip to see your mother, or potty training a new puppy. Every system, every organized way of doing something, has standards, rules, and formats, and much of life is about learning them.

Yes, it does take some time to learn the rules, but not that much time. Learning the structure of a standardized test is far simpler than learning successful strategies for some of the board or video games our children play routinely, and may be more fair than strategies successful in winning the favor of one's classroom teacher. Indeed, "gaming"—behavior that improves one's score or grade but is not necessarily related to mastery of the academic subject matter—is undoubtedly a larger factor in boosting grade point averages than it is in boosting standaradized test scores. Some testing and measurement experts have made their careers studying the "halo" effect behavior students adopt to make teachers like them (and garner better grades). Teachers are human, and humans cannot be perfect graders, perfect test developers, perfectly fair, or immune to manipulation. Teachers and schools are "gamed," too.

What of the "test coaching" argument, though? If courses from test-preparation companies such as Stanley Kaplan and the Princeton Review can help improve a student's college admissions test scores, does that not give wealthier students, better able to afford these expensive courses, an advantage? Only if you believe the Kaplan and Princeton review ads. The next chapter focuses on the Scholastic Assessment Test (SAT) and the discussion of test coaching will pick up again there.

...Standardized tests, particularly those in multiple-choice format, do not measure "higher order" thinking. Nonsense. Standardized tests can measure "higher" or "lower" thinking, or combinations of the two. "Higher-order" thinking is a loosely defined term, generally having to do with thinking that is indirect, like meta-analysis and lateral thinking. Despite the implication of the name, "higher order" thinking is not necessarily any more important or more essential than "lower order" thinking. Indeed, one could argue that humorist James Thurber's chronic daydreamer Walter Mitty is the penultimate higher-order thinker.

Many testing opponents certainly want us to think that "higher order" thinking is better—the font of creativity—and that traditional standardized tests do not measure it. Is "higher-order thinking" a ubiquitously superior form of thinking? Consider the type of thinking surgeons do. Surgeons are highly paid and well respected. Their study, however, consists of a considerable amount of rote memorization and their work entails a considerable amount of routine and factual recall (all "lower-order thinking"). Moreover, the medical college admissions test is largely multiple-choice, and tests administered during medical training largely elicit the recall of discrete facts.

If you were about ready to go under the knife, which kind of surgeon would you want? Perhaps one who used *only* "higher-order thinking," *only* "creative and innovative" techniques, and "constructed her own meaning" from the activity of surgery each time she performed it? Or would you prefer a surgeon who had passed her "lower-order thinking" exams and used tried-and-true methods with a history of success; ones that other surgeons had used successfully?

Certainly, there would be some situations where one could benefit from the practice of the innovator. If no aspect whatsoever of the study or practice of surgery were standardized, however, there would be nothing to teach in medical school and your regular barber or beautician would be as well qualified to "creatively and innovatively" excise your appendix as anyone else.

Ideally, most of us would want a surgeon who possessed both the "lower" and "higher" abilities; either of each type alone limits intelligent reasoning.[13]

While some education professors dreams of populating a nation entirely with Albert Einsteins and Walter Mittys, the overwhelming majority of employers and consumers would feel quite pleased if there were more precise, methodical, detail-oriented, "lower-order" thinkers available to conduct the business of everyday life.

The surgery analogy offers an illustrative counter to another of the testing critics' arguments. They say that multiple-choice tests limit students to the "one correct answer" when there may really be more than one correct answer and more than one way to get to each. Moreover, students should not get an entire exercise counted wrong if they analyze most of the problem correctly, but make one simple, careless error.[14]

Most of us would sympathize with this sentiment, but we should remember that there are countless examples in real life where there is just one right answer or the consequences of one careless error in a process can have devastating consequences—in brain surgery, for example.

...The multiple-choice format demands only rote recall, rote memorization, "lower order" thinking. Many readers would be astonished, as I still am, by the vehemence of some critics' ire toward something seemingly so dull and innocuous as test item response format. Many standard accusations leveled at multiple-choice items have little substance, however. For example, you can often find in CSTEEP and FairTest publications assertions that multiple-choice items demand only factual recall and "lower-order" thinking, while "performance-based" tests do neither. Both claims are without merit. In developing a test, for example, one could include this multiple-choice item— "What is the capital of Albania?: (a) Skopje; (b) Sofia; (c) Bamako; (d) Tirana; (e) Bratislava"—or this open-ended, performance-based item—"What is the capital of Albania? _____. The "performance-based" item demands "factual recall" just like the multiple-choice item. The point is, it is the structure of the *question*, not that of the response format, that determines the character of the cognitive processing necessary to reach a correct answer.

Test items can be banal and simplistic or intricately complex and, either way, their response format can be multiple-choice or open-ended. There is no necessary correlation between the difficulty of a problem and the type of response format. Even huge, integrative tasks that require 50 minutes to classify, assemble, organize, calculate, and analyze can, in the end, present a test-taker a multiple-choice response format. Just because the answer to the question is among those provided, it is not necessarily easy or obvious how to get from the question to the answer.

Anyone who still thinks that multiple-choice items demand only factual recall should take a trip to the bookstore and look at some SAT or ACT help books. I purchased a copy of *Cliffs SAT I Preparation Guide* and randomly picked a page. It was in the math section and 4 items are posed. Here's one: "What is the maximum number of milk cartons, each 2" wide by 3" long by 4" tall, that can fit into a cardboard box with inside dimensions of 16" wide by 9" long by 8" tall?" Five possible answers are provided, but the correct one, obviously, cannot just be "recalled," some calculations are required. Our solution was to calculate the volume, in square inches, of a carton and the box, by multiplying the 3 dimensions in each case, and then to divide the former volume into the latter. I used pen and paper for 2 of the calculations and figured the other in my head. Interestingly, the *Cliffs Notes* book solves the problem graphically, by sketching a 3-dimensional box and subdividing it along each dimension (Bobrow 1994: 63).

Indeed, much of the *Cliffs Notes* book is devoted to convincing the student that there is usually more than one way to "construct" a response to a problem. The book contains sections that each illustrate different approaches to solving similar problems. It is a very "constructivist" book; any student following its advice would make ample use in taking the SAT of pen, paper, calculator, formulas, diagrams, sketches, lateral thinking, meta-analysis, and other devices that constructivists hold dear. Students armed with multiple methods for solving problems, of course, will hit more correct answers on the SAT than students with fewer methods, other factors held equal. So, higher SAT scores should be taken as evidence of more "higher order" thinking.

All the optical scanner will read in the end, however, is a sheet of circles, some filled in with pencil and others not. Moreover, all the computer will score in the end is the number of correct filled-in circles. The calculations, sketches, and diagrams the student used to solve the problems are left behind in the test booklet, on scratch paper, or in the student's head. Just because the optical scanner and computer do not see the "process" evidence of "higher order" thinking, however, does not mean it did not take place. That is, however, what the critics assume.

The most essential point for the critics in applying the "lower-order" label to multiple-choice and the "higher-order" label to performance tests, seems to be that, with open-ended questions, a student shows her work and a scorer can see how the test-taker has approached the problem through the exposition of the answer.[15] That is a big IF, in my opinion, because a test-taker may not jot down each and every thought that comes through her head. (Besides, multiple-choice tests can also easily be set up to measure partial credit, if so desired.)

...The multiple-choice format is artificial, not "authentic." This argument is part of the "naturalist" strain common to so much anti-standardized testing sentiment. Standardized tests are not like "authentic" tests in the real world, critics argue. They are artificial. How often, after all, do we face the multiple-choice format in real life?[16]

There do exist many high-stakes tests set in "authentic" format. Most certification exams for the skilled trades are "authentic"—the student has to "show" that she knows how to wire a circuit box or edge a banister molding by doing it. Proponents of authentic assessment will often use the example of a pilot's test to press their point. After all, who would want to be a passenger in an airplane piloted by someone who had never before flown a plane, but had done very well on a paper-and-pencil exam about piloting?

Traditionally, however, we have saved "authentic" tests for last. That is, we have had students accumulate as much knowledge as quickly and as efficiently as possible in traditional classroom mode and, then, just before they "become" whatever it is they wish to become, we make them demonstrate their skill in an authentic format. There are several sound reasons for following this progression. First, one has to know something about a skill, and practice a skill, before one can adequately demonstrate a skill. Students in an airline pilot's course do not start out the very first minute of the first class flying a plane, they read the instruction manuals and some elementary physics textbooks first.

Second, "authentic" assessments can be time-consuming and expensive. We simply cannot afford, financially or practically, to give every U.S. school student an authentic test every time we wish to give them a test. For example, we would like all school students to understand how planes fly (lift and thrust and all that). But we cannot afford the time or expense of putting every U.S. school student through a pilot's course. Moreover, we really do not need to. Not every student will want to be a pilot. Those that do can put themselves into an aeronautical science program when they get to the community college level.

There are thousands of things we want our children to know. If all instruction and assessment were "authentic," it would take several lifetimes to expose them to a fraction of what we can expose them to vicariously in twelve years of traditional classroom learning.

As for the alleged ubiquitous superiority of the more general category of "performance-based" tests—a category that includes "authentic" assessments, as well as the more traditional essay and open-response formats—Walstad and Becker (1994) sum up the objective research concisely:

> The research evidence...suggests that there is little difference in the knowledge, skills, or abilities measured by multiple-choice and essay (or constructed-response) tests. A study of Advanced Placement (AP) tests in seven college subjects...concluded that "whatever is being measured by the constructed-response section is measured better by the multiple-choice section.... We have never found any test that is composed of an objectively and a subjectively scored section for which this is not true." (Wainer and Thissen 1993: 116)

Similarly, an investigation of the AP exam in computer science found "little support for the stereotype of multiple-choice and free-response formats as measuring substantially different constructs (i.e., trivial factual recognition vs. higher order processes)." (Bennett et al. 1991: 89)

A review of studies in four domains (writing, word knowledge, reading, and quantitative) was more equivocal about the value of constructed response but concluded that "if differences do exist for any domain, they are very likely to be small." (Traub 1993: 39)

Finally, a study predicting the GPA of first-year college students found that "the essay added essentially nothing" to what was predicted from high school GPA, SAT scores, and a multiple-choice test of writing skills. (Bridgeman 1991: 319)

Performance-based tests do offer some advantages over multiple-choice tests in certain situations. However, they also: cost more, take more time to administer, provide less reliable results, take longer to score (thus delaying results and their feedback to students and teachers), and minority students do relatively worse on them (see also, Feinberg 1990; Rudman 1992; Roberts 1996; Sivalingam-Nethi 1997; Lee 1997).

The Attacks—Strategies

The *strategies* employed by critics of educational testing provide interesting and colorful glimpses into how the War on Testing is waged. A list of strategies was introduced at the outset of this chapter. Here, I expand on that list and explain the strategies in further depth.

Certainly, legitimate and objective research can arrive at results that suggest problems with the use of standardized tests. Indeed, chapter 8 in this book discusses some of them. I use the term "anti-testing research" to describe anti-testing *advocacy* research, that which is conducted for the purpose of opposing testing. Anti-testing research suffers from many fallacies, some of which are clarified below.

Conceal self-interest. The vast majority of testing opponents are financially and professionally vested in the current public education system and structure, and have much to gain by preventing external evaluations of their performance. Most testing opponents are education professors, education administrators, or are otherwise connected with the current public school system structure. When they cite their "research," however, they often identify themselves as "independent," even though they are anything but. When they mention why they are so interested in opposing testing, many of them claim that their only concern is for the kids.

Wrap oneself in academic robes. Most anti-testing researchers are once or future education professors. Yes, there are some education professors who do not oppose high-stakes standardized testing (and they number among the most heroic persons in our country), but not many. Journalists, however, typically tell their readers or listeners that Professor So-and-So teaches at some prestigious university; they often do not identify them as *education* professors at that university with a profound self-interest in protecting the current public school system from outside evaluation.

Demonize the opposition. Anti-testing researchers often characterize testing advocates as ignorant, selfish, vile—"right wingers," "corporate interests," "authoritarians," and "politicians out to get votes by bashing the schools." They do not mention that most university testing experts not on education faculty tend to have much better opinions of standardized testing, along with the vast majority of parents, taxpayers, and even students.

Induce guilt by association. One way to demonize testing advocates is to continually recall what some biased people did with standardized testing over seventy years ago. Racists and bigots used standardized tests in manipulative ways back in the 1920s and 1930s, therefore all standardized testing is forever faulty. We all know of some corrupt, vile people who brush their teeth, too. So, are all of us who brush our teeth corrupt and vile?

Induce shame. I know from personal experience that if one attempts to defend the use of standardized tests, some journalists (e.g., at CBS, PBS) will ask one what one's standardized tests scores were. The implication is that one has no right to advocate for standardized testing if one "does well on standardized tests." That would be cruel, since others "do not do well on standardized tests."
Imagine if the same standards applied in, say, sports reporting. A journalist is interviewing Michael Jordan who might be speaking, as he often has, about the value of recognizing hard work and quality performance, and setting clear rules and playing by the rules. Imagine the journalist replying by telling Jordan that he has no right to be making such value judgments because, he is "good at athletics."

Kill the messenger. Perhaps the ultimate in nerve, testing opponents blame it on the tests when tests uncover problems. Some students do poorly on a standardized test and the test is blamed ("some students do not test well") rather than the schools that taught them poorly. Often, the geographic correlation between standardized test scores and household wealth is high, and so the tests are blamed, rather than the schools that are blandly similar across districts and add so little value to the achievement levels that students have already attained in their own homes.

Proliferate "validities." In the early days of the state "minimum-competency test" movement, about the late 1970s and early 1980s, many educators protested against the use of nationally normed standardized tests to make high-stakes high school graduation decisions. On the one hand, the criticism was certainly justified since the tests were developed by companies without regard to the curriculum used in any particular state. It is simply not fair to deny a student a diploma because he cannot pass a test containing subject matter to which he has either not been exposed or was never told he needed to master. On the other hand, the subject matter contained in these tests was typically set at a 6th- or 7th-grade level of difficulty and so basic and general that any responsible school district anywhere would have exposed their students to the material.

Nonetheless, the argument against using nationally normed standardized tests to make high-stakes decisions was a *validity* argument. Generally, a "valid" test measures what it is supposed to measure, or what it purports to measure. A high-stakes test, most believe, should measure a student's mastery of subject matter that he has known for some time he was supposed to master, and that he had an opportunity to master.

Tests should be valid. They should measure what they are supposed to measure. They should be used for the purposes for which they are meant to be used. It is quite obviously not appropriate to use your state's official Certified Public Accountancy Examination to measure my ability to fly an airplane. Unfortunately, "appropriateness" is not easily defined, nor easily measured. Some experts have devised measures for some types of validity, but other types of validity, like the concept of appropriateness, defy precise measurement.

Moreover, testing opponents seem to "discover" a new form of "test validity" every month. There seems to be no end to the number of different types of validities it is possible to apply to standardized testing. Indeed, some types of validity appear to be invented for the sole purpose of invalidating any and all high-stakes tests, multiple-choice tests, and so on. It is not overly cynical to suppose that, for those who oppose high-stakes testing, an effective tactic is to develop forms of or standards for validity that no standardized test can survive. Then, one can find in one's "research" that certain standardized tests are *invalid* forms of testing.

The psychometrician Robert Ebel (1961) once said: "Validity has long been one of the major deities in the pantheon of the psychometrician. It is universally praised, but the good works done in its name are remarkably few."

Compare to unavailable alternatives, like perfection. One of the primary criticisms of college-entrance examinations (the American College Test [ACT] and the Scholastic Assessment Test [SAT]) is that they are not curriculum based. So, the critics argue, we need a national, curriculum-based test which, of course, means we must impose a national curriculum. That, of course, would be politically impossible and is, thus, not an available alternative. It would likely also be unconstitutional. The U.S. Constitution says nothing about education, thus leaving it to be a state matter. Such inconvenient facts do not silence these critics, however, nor the journalists who give their suggestions serious coverage.

Standardized tests are not perfect, nor can they be perfectly administered. These are truisms. These truisms, nonetheless, represent the primary line of illogic used by anti-testing researchers: Standardized tests are not perfect, therefore we should never use them. The "problems" of standardized tests, both real and alleged, are presented as if any alternative to standardized testing would present no such problems. The alternative to schools with standardized testing is assumed to be a perfect school without flaws.

Ignore available alternatives. In reality, virtually all of the genuine imperfections of standardized tests exist with their real alternatives, too. Teacher grades, grade-point averages, and classroom tests, for example, are fraught with exactly the same problems and imperfections as are standardized tests and, in most cases, to an even greater degree. Grade-point averages, for example, are norm- not standards-based measures, normed *at the school level* and, thus, have low reliability and little validity outside a single individual school.

Moreover, few teachers have any training in testing and measurement, yet they test and measure constantly. Are their measurement efforts ubiquitously better than those of the Ph.D.s, with several years of graduate-level training in testing and measurement, who design standardized tests and administer large-scale testing programs?

Nor are our public schools the only places where standardized tests are administered. We administer standardized tests to our police, firefighters, doctors, lawyers, engineers, paramedics, accountants, nurses, and on and on. All the problems claimed for student standardized tests must exist with professional occupational tests, too. Should we not eliminate ALL standardized testing, if it is really as bad as the opponents say? Is it not even *more* important to eliminate standardized testing from use for these critical occupations, if it is really so untrustworthy?

We could then return to more subjective measures for determining who becomes a firefighter or paramedic. Opponents of student testing would have us believe that schools without standardized testing are wonderful, magical, and joyous. That some of these wonderful, magical, joyous places can occupy twelve years of our children's lives without teaching them how to read or write may not be of concern to them.

Declare contrary research nonexistent. An *Education Week* reporter is writing a story on a FairTest report which claimed proof that high-stakes standardized testing worsens student achievement. As is typical of EdWeek's style, she "balances" the FairTest testimony in her article by telephoning CRESST, one of the "legitimate mainstream" anti-testing groups. The CRESST researcher appears to express some misgiving with FairTest's methodology, but it is expressed so vaguely as to be meaningless (Viadero 1998).

On the more important point, the effect of high-stakes testing on student achievement, the CRESST researcher, a well-known, outspoken opponent of external high-stakes testing, says the right thing: the evidence for high-stakes testing's benefits is "thin." He, and other CRESST researchers, have for over a decade been pushing the results of a little research project they conducted ten years ago. One of CRESST's directors finally published a lead article on that obscure research study in mainstream education research's flagship journal *Education Researcher* (Linn 2000).

To read what was written or listen what was discussed, one would think that CRESST was the only organization to have ever conducted a study on the effect of high-stakes testing on student learning. It certainly does nothing to make its readers and listeners aware of the other research studies...that reach different conclusions. There have, after all, only been *well over a thousand* research studies, largely done by psychologists, economists and testing practitioners—not education professors—studying the benefits of high-stakes student testing on student achievement. Pretend they do not exist, and maybe they will go away.

Even better, *declare* that they do not exist, and many journalists will not bother to look for them. Even "legitimate" and reasonable-sounding research, like that done at CRESST, openly accepts and cites the findings of the most atrociously conducted anti-testing research while, at the same time, ignoring all the research with contrary findings, as if that body of research simply does not exist.

Allow only one side to talk. Why are so many education news stories so one-sided? One reason is that journalists are not even aware of those who might offer a contrary point of view. They talk to a "mainstream" education researcher, and may ask him for the name of someone who would disagree with him, but in response they will only get the name of someone who disagrees on minor points. Attend conferences or visit the websites of many of the vested interests' organizations and you will be exposed to only one point of view. To hear them tell the tale, "all the research" shows that standardized testing is a bad thing—all the research they will let their members see, that is.

Put words in their mouths. One of the advantages of having the stage to oneself, as testing opponents often do with American journalists, is that one can then define and speak for the other side. One can attribute false motives, false assertions, and false identifications. One can create "straw men" who are easy to beat up.

One prominent example of this strategy is provided by the frequently expressed claim that testing *proponents* view high-stakes standardized testing as a "silver bullet," "quick fix," or "magic potion" that will, by itself, solve all our education problems. Testing advocates are that ignorant! I have read hundreds of writings of people who have favorable attitudes toward high-stakes testing, however, and I have yet to witness one person make such a simplistic claim. At the same time, I have read or heard the claim made several dozen times by testing opponents that proponents advocate high-stakes testing as a panacea. When the other side is not allowed to talk, one can speak for them.[17]

A CRESST researcher, generously and widely cited in the education research literature, purports to explain why politicians behave the way they do in regard to standardized testing (as if he would know) (Linn 1995):

1. Tests and assessments are relatively inexpensive. Compared to changes that involve increasing instructional time, reducing class size, attracting more able people to teaching, hiring teacher aides, or enacting programmatic change involving substantial professional development for teachers, assessment is cheap.
2. Testing and assessment can be externally mandated.
3. Testing and assessment changes can be rapidly implemented. New test or assessment requirements can be implemented within the term of elected officials.
4. Results are visible. Test results can be reported to the press. Poor results in the beginning are desirable for policymakers who want to show they have had an effect.

Guess that sums it up. "Policymakers" are narrow-minded and cheap. To them, tests are merely political expedients (for another example, see NEA Today Online).

Really? It is not possible that some policymakers favor testing...because the public—whom policymakers are legally obligated to represent—overwhelmingly want testing? ...because policymakers want an objective source of information on school and student performance? ...because they do not trust school personnel (often with good reason) to provide them objective information? ...because of the demonstrated benefits of testing, in motivation, information, and organizational clarity? ...because they are legally responsible for how they spend the taxpayers' money and want to monitor the programs they pay for?

Let out the attack dogs. Most in the field know who they are—the testing opponents who practice little restraint when they throw mud. Education journalists, however, often treat these offensive folks with the utmost respect, lest, perhaps...

Use evidence selectively. Much anti-testing research is just simply one-sided—costs are tallied with no concomitant count of benefits, people affected adversely by test results are studied while those who benefit are ignored, excuses are made for the United States in international test comparisons without considering those that are equally valid for other countries—and so on.

Inconsistency, contradiction, and obfuscation. The tell-tale sign of the point where anti-testing research is really just advocacy comes when the attacks mutate freely and flexibly to counter any defense (see box at end of chapter). Standardized tests are so easy that they can be "coached," but so difficult that a generation of students will be discouraged and drop out of school. Standardized tests induce cheating, but many testing opponents advocate, instead, the use of portfolios, the equivalent of paradise for cheaters. Standardized tests allegedly impose a "one-size-fits-all" curriculum in our classrooms, but one-size-fits-all public school systems, ability groups, curricula, and teacher salary schedules are fine. Other criticisms of standardized testing have become so subtle, so picky, or so obscure that any amount of "more research is needed before..."—carried into eternity—can never lay them to rest.

Doctor data, fudge numbers, alter definitions. It has happened far too many times to be considered exceptional. Journalists claim a "fact" about testing that is not a fact. It is false. It can easily be shown to be false.

Because testing opponents know that some journalists are likely to believe whatever they tell them, some have gradually over the years learned to stretch the boundaries of what is allowable in research further and further. They have gone way beyond simply ignoring the research they do not like and accepting that with conclusions they like regardless of quality. Some of them will now say just about anything—fudging numbers, doctoring data, and, when all else fails, they may just make things up. The research on testing in the professional "mainstream" of education has become so corrupted that no one interested in accurate information should take any of it at face value.

Perhaps the most clever type of anti-testing research involves the use of "altered definitions"—sleight-of-hand changes in the meanings of words. In the early 1990s, for example, some critics of standardized testing claimed that U.S. students were "subjected to too much standardized testing" and standardized testing "devours" teaching time and "looms ominously" in students' lives. This critical study invoked the use of some rather unusual arithmetic to count standardized tests (Haney, Madaus, and Lyons 1993).

Here is one of the study's more concise passages. It refers only to college entrance exams, those administered by the College Entrance Examination Board—the Scholastic Assessment Test (SAT)—and the American College Test (ACT).

...we contacted the College Board and ACT directly and were informed that 1,980,000 SATs and 1,000,000 ACTs were given in 1986-87. We thus have relatively firm figures on the number of such college admissions tests given. But there are several ways of counting the number of separately scoreable subtests in these testing programs. The SAT has two subtests, the SAT-Verbal and the SAT-Math. Moreover, two subscores are reported for the SAT-Verbal, namely reading and vocabulary. Also, almost all students who take the SAT take the Test of Standard Written English (TSWE). Thus in calculating the number of separately scoreable tests involved in SAT testing, we have offered the alternative perspectives of 2 subtests (i.e., the SAT and TSWE) as a basis for a low estimate and 5 (Math, Verbal, Reading, Vocabulary, Verbal Total, and TSWE) as a basis for a high estimate. Similarly, the ACT assessment has four subtests, but since a composite score is also calculated we have used 4 and 5 as bases for high and low estimates. The results...indicate that between nearly 4 million and 10 million SAT subtests and 4 million to 5 million ACT subtests are administered annually.... Altogether then we estimate that in 1986-87, 13 million to 22 million college admissions "tests" were administered.

[The quote goes on to sum the total of all standardized student tests, and not just college entrance exams, but the quotation marks around the word "tests" disappear, *et voilà*, all parts of tests become whole tests.]

In sum then...we estimate that between 143 million and 395 million tests are administered annually to the nation's population of roughly 44 million elementary and secondary school students, equivalent to between 3 and 9 standardized tests for each student enrolled in elementary and secondary schools.

You are forgiven if you found this long excerpt confusing. At the beginning of the excerpt, a test is called a test. In the middle, the reader is told that tests have parts. Those separate parts are counted up and, in the next paragraph, the parts are called tests. After this semantic magic is complete, the authors feel confident in telling the public that there are from 3 to 9 times as many standardized student tests administered annually as actually are.

Using this same arithmetic, baseball games are really 9 to 10 baseball games, since each inning is a discrete part, with a separate score. Or, maybe baseball games are really 18 to 20 baseball games, since each half inning is a discrete part, with a separate score. One can imagine the semantic difficulties we would have if all parts of things became in language the things of which they are parts. What, then, would one call the wholes to distinguish them from the parts?

Another oddity of the study was the unnecessary use of "estimates"; unnecessary because two telephone calls to the SAT and ACT offices provided exact counts of the numbers of tests administered. The study contains a particularly peculiar interpretation of a "lower bound estimate." At the beginning of the excerpt above, an American College Test (ACT) is referred to in the singular, the way most people refer to it, and the total annual number of ACTs administered is declared to be 1 million. After the authors do their parts-as-wholes counting, they end up with an "estimate" for the annual number of

ACTs of from 4 to 5 million. Four million is their "lower bound estimate" for a number of tests they had just claimed for a fact to be only 1 million.[18]

This behavior is akin to a business keeping a second set of account books with fudged numbers for the IRS auditor. "Altered definitions" give testing opponents a second set of facts available to use with journalists. As disreputable as the practice of altering definitions may be, it is used often, and it works.

The Public Broadcasting System's *Merrow Report*, for example, devoted an hour-long documentary to this fictitious problem of over-testing. In all their background research, the show's producers never spoke with anyone who offered correct information, and their own research effort stopped the moment they found two separate citations to support any point, not knowing (or, perhaps, not caring) that, in most cases, both citations derived from the same original source (Phelps 1998d).

A few years later, the same author responsible for the "too much testing" ruse studied the testing program in Texas and discovered that it caused an enormous number of "dropouts." He accused the Texas testing program of increasing the number of dropouts by including in *his* definition of "dropout" any student whose graduation from high school was delayed by even a week (i.e., most of his "dropouts" never actually dropped out of school) (see Phelps 2000h). His research was covered by many journalists, however, all of whom took it at face value, all, apparently, completely unaware that altered definitions of the key terms were being used.

When in doubt, just make it up. Most journalists do not ask for evidence of factual claims, and they do not read professional journals. They take what you tell them on faith. If they also make no effort to talk to those who might have a contrary point of view, then testing "facts" can literally be simply made up.

A fairly colorful example of this method is provided in *Testing in American Schools: Asking the Right Questions*, a report from the ill-fated U.S. Office of Technology Assessment (OTA). To write its long chapter, "How Other Countries Test," the OTA might have contracted the then-current American experts on the topic, Max Eckstein and Harold Noah, for the highest quality work. In their previous work, however, Eckstein and Noah (1993) had already strongly argued that the U.S. students faced much less, and much easier, testing than their overseas counterparts.

Instead, the OTA contracted some well-known opponents of testing to write the chapter. The result has a "research-like" appearance: there are sketches of country shapes and many facts about the countries are presented. Those figures and tables presented have nothing to do with the conclusions, though, and nothing to do with testing. Rather, they are boilerplate taken from a world atlas on the population and gross national product of each country and the like.

For the chapter's conclusions, there is no evidence at all, just a single plausible rationale. It is explained that because other countries, as they have become wealthier, have made more opportunities available in high schools and universities, they no longer need to use high-stakes tests to select and exclude students from those opportunities. Sounds reasonable enough.

The chapter's conclusion, "Lessons for the United States," made the following claims:

- Other countries test less than we do.
- Other countries are dropping, not adding, large-scale, external testing.
- The trend can be found at all levels of education "even at the postsecondary level."
- External examinations are "no longer used to make decisions about students' educational paths during the period of compulsory education."
- "standardized national examinations before the age of 16 have all but disappeared."
- The trend is universal across countries and unidirectional; large-scale, external tests are being "abolished."

Did the OTA provide any evidence for any of these claims? No. Were any of these claims true? No. Indeed, all of these claims were easily proven false. In each case, just the opposite was true[19] (see, for example, Phelps 1996a, 2000g).

Made-up facts can be just as serviceable, however, as real ones (see Viadero 1994). One can find also many instances of anti-testing researchers citing as evidence another testing opponent's work when, in reality, that work included no evidence, just a declaration that something was so.

Name-calling as methodology. Many education researchers naturally drift toward the softer side of the social sciences, using methodologies somewhat akin to those anthropologists use. Cultural anthropologists, of course, have a good reason for resorting to relatively data-free, observational, non-experimental research. They have no choice. It is difficult enough simply to obtain access to a remote and completely foreign society, and can take some time before their social structure and rules are well understood. Moreover, anthropologists usually have no obvious conflict of interest in the results of their research describing another culture.

So, why do education researchers, who have access to a cornucopia of research data and who could conduct research using randomized experimental designs if they chose to, find anthropological techniques so attractive? It's a good question. Education research journals are filled to bursting with "naturalistic inquiry," observational studies, "fourth-generation evaluation," and the like. These methods have in common no control for the researcher's preferred ideology and self-interest in the results (see, for example, Phelps 2000f).

Some of the most celebrated studies in the pantheon of anti-testing research consist of "semi-structured" interviews with or "naturalistic observations" of a "purposive" sample of "stakeholders."

It should come as no surprise when the results of these studies clash with those of studies conducted with large, randomly selected, representative samples of education's consumers—students or parents—that incorporate statistical tests. It should also come as no surprise that the former studies tend to be celebrated and widely disseminated whereas the latter usually remain virtually unknown.

Commonly used to compensate for the paucity of evidence (and absence of genuine analysis) in the "naturalistic inquiries" so popular in education research is a surfeit of research-like rhetoric. Sometimes the rhetoric can be hyperbolic. After all, if one must rely on adjectives and adverbs to carry the analysis because the analysis lacks content, ultimately one must resort to using some of the more colorful ones. There are only so many times one can write "drill," "rote," "narrow," and "uncreative" about standardized tests before it becomes repetitive.

Without standardized testing, schools operate without external evaluation, and we have little choice but to accept educators' claims that they are doing the wonderful job they say they are doing. They are teaching "critical thinking," and "problem-solving." The children are "learning how to learn." Indeed, what they are learning is so profound, that it cannot be measured by anything as "crude" or "primitive" as a standardized test. We must take it on faith. They say we should get rid of standardized tests because they promote "lower-order skills," "rote recall," "memorization," "drill and kill," "low level content" and other unpleasant-sounding things. Get rid of tests and teachers can concentrate on "higher-order skills" and "real learning."

Testing opponents may employ euphemisms to describe instructional practices they favor also because they know that if they described in practical terms what they actually mean the public would be appalled.[20]

Here are some excerpts from a book about Texas testing that received quite a lot of attention during the presidential campaign of 2000.[21] The research alluded to in the book was rather free form. The author spoke with some "stakeholders" who did not much like the new high-stakes testing program in their state. It is not specified how these respondents were selected or how many there were. Apparently, they were teachers and school administrators in just a few schools in just one town that participated in one program. The interviews might have been "semi-structured" because no forms or protocols are mentioned.

scientific-sounding language:
"We present here our strong assessment..." "Our analysis draws on emerging research..." "Our investigations..." "Our investigations..." "Our research required fieldwork in schools and classrooms and frequent interactions with students, teachers,

and administrators, whose voices and experiences are vital to capture." "...empirical tracing of what happens to teaching and children when standardized testing takes control of the schools." "...gather and triangulate data from a variety of sources over a multi-year period." "...represent strong, persistent trends emerging from the data." "Our analysis reveals..."

I particularly like the cool, research-sounding "triangulate" and "empirical tracing." It does not matter that the author's research is not even remotely empirical. She claims that her research is unique to Texas and its tests but when reading her work, one may come to realize that they have read it a dozen times before, written by others. Take the word "Texas" out of what she writes and it is a generic radical constructivist's criticism of any standardized test.

standardized testing crowds out other topics:
"...crowds out other forms of learning..." "This testing system distances the content of curriculum from the knowledge base of teachers..." "...the TAAS system of testing is reducing the quality and quantity of education offered..." "... a regular education has been supplanted by activities whose sole purpose is to raise test scores on this particular test." "...fosters an artificial curriculum..." "...diverting scarce instructional dollars away from such high quality curricular resources as laboratory supplies and books toward test-prep materials and activities of limited instructional value." "...drilling students on practice exam materials." "...takes time from real teaching." "...raise test scores at the expense of substantive learning."

The crowding-out or narrowing-the-curriculum argument is one of testing opponents' favorites, of course, and most illogical. The length of the school day was not shortened when the Texas Assessment of Academic Skills (TAAS) was introduced (indeed, in some places it was lengthened); there remains as much time available for instruction as there was before. Granted, what is taught during the instructional day may be different but, after all, that's the whole point. The citizens of Texas feared that too many fluffy, low-content courses were taking time away from the primary academic subjects.

If some topics have been "crowded out," in fairness it must also be acknowledged that other topics, considered more important by the citizens of Texas, have been "added in." It may be that the selection of courses has been "narrowed" if more time is spent on reading, writing, and arithmetic and less on courses considered peripheral but, at the same time, the curricular content of those subject areas considered most important has been *broadened*, not narrowed.

standardized testing is unfair to minority students:
"...this over-reliance on test scores has caused a decline in educational quality for those students who have the greatest educational need." "The system's popularity is further bolstered by the idea that it must be improving the education of Latino and African American children, since, in many parts of the state, their test scores are also rising." "This testing system distances the content of curriculum from the knowledge base of teachers and from the cultures and intellectual capacities of the children."

"Most damaging are the effects of the TAAS system of testing on poor and minority students." "...divorced from children's experience and culture."

Just how culturally biased can mathematics be? ...or science?...or geography? Yes, reading comprehension and grammar could be if one does not insist that the test be based on Standard English but, if it is based on Standard English, how culturally biased can it be? Even history; if there are agreed-upon state standards, and teachers teach to those standards, every student has been exposed to the same material. One cannot validly argue that a test is biased because it asks a question about Hildegard von Bingen and because she was white. It is a rare white kid who knows about Hildegard without learning it in school.

As for the "intellectual capacities of the students," the nastiest part of the radical constructivist opposition to standardized tests is the way they use poor and minority children for their own purposes. First, they claim to defend them and their culture, declaring that we must teach different subject matter in every school, subject matter attuned to their culture. Conveniently, we could not then use standardized tests to measure school performance because the subject matter would not be standardized.

Second, they claim that we cannot have high academic standards because minorities will not be able to meet them. And, just why won't minorities be able to meet them? Are minorities for some reason incapable of meeting high academic standards? Who's being prejudiced?

it's low-quality instruction with standardized tests; not "real learning":
"Much of the drill time is spent learning how to bubble in answers, how to weed out obviously wrong answers, and how to become accustomed to multiple-choice, computer-scored formats." "...drilling students on practice exam materials." "...takes time from real teaching." "...raise test scores at the expense of substantive learning." "...the TAAS system of testing is reducing the quality and quantity of education offered..." "... a regular education has been supplanted by activities whose sole purpose is to raise test scores on this particular test." "...fosters an artificial curriculum..." "...not a curriculum that will educate these children for productive futures..." "...diverting scarce instructional dollars toward test-prep materials and activities of limited instructional value." "...aimed at the lowest level of skills and information..."

Some criticism of standardized testing is just silly. How long can it take to teach a student how to fill in a circle on an answer sheet?

The author makes it clear that she does not consider any learning that is measured on a standardized test to be worthwhile. She also does not consider test preparation to be "real learning." Workbooks are bad; books are good. That's her opinion. Maybe you were a more conscientious student than I was, but I "really learned" best when I was studying for exams. And, during exams, I often realized concepts for the first time or, otherwise, had some knowledge burnt into my brain by the pressure of writing the exam, information that I would have otherwise forgotten.

basing important decisions about students and schools on a single indicator is not fair:
"...a single indicator." "...the use of a single indicator to assess learning or to make decisions about tracking, promotion, and graduation violates the ethics of the testing profession." "The scores loom so large that they overshadow discussion of other, more telling indicators of quality of education."The author must know that students are not held back because of a single poor performance on the Texas test, they are given several more opportunities to pass the exam. Moreover, she also knows that the test is pretty low-level. It is not as if students are getting denied diplomas because they cannot pass a test based on 12th-grade level material, it is material at a much lower level of difficulty than that. If a student cannot pass it, and has a good grade-point average, either there is something funny about grade-point averages at his school or he has a severe case of test anxiety.

scores on a standardized test are not a valid measure of student achievement:
"Highly touted rates of improved scores (for example, that Texas was described as in the top four "most improved states") mask the fact that even after such "gains," Texas student were still at or below average, registering lower than 21 of 40 participating states." "The scores loom so large that they overshadow discussion of other, more telling indicators of quality of education, among these the degree of segregation, the level of poverty, or the number of student graduating, taking the SAT, and going to college."

You just can't win with these guys. Texas is one of the most improved states in the country on the neutral National Assessment of Educational Progress (NAEP), AFTER implementing the testing program she criticizes, but our author says it is still not among the top states. So, she means to imply that without the testing Texas would have vaulted to the top ranks? ...even though it had rested consistently near the bottom for decades before?

As for her, more "valid," outcome measures...since when did degree of segregation and level of poverty become measures of educational achievement? Most citizens of Texas are concerned that their students graduate with skills that will enable them to lead productive lives, or take the SAT with a chance of doing well and going to a good college and making good use of the opportunity. Graduating from high school without having learned how to read and write does no one any good, least of all the graduate.

Really, one must admire the people behind anti-testing semantic acrobatics, though. Their research-like prose is to real analysis what guar gum is to diet food, filler with no nutritional contribution. But, it is usually very strongly worded, uses lots of terminology that sounds "sorta scientific," is written by folks with academic credentials from education schools at (often) prestigious universities, and these folks have developed an expertise in phraseology that works (to persuade naive journalists, for example).

In an appendix to his best-seller, *The Schools We Need and Why We Don't Have Them,* E. D. Hirsch provides an enormously useful guide to the jargon and euphemisms used by the radical constructivists, "Critical Guide to Educational Terms and Phrases." As a useful public service, the Texas Education Consumers Association has abridged Hirsch's appendix and placed it on the Worldwide Web, under the title "Education Terminology Every Parent Must Understand" (http://www.math.nyu.edu/mfdd/braams/nychold/hirsch-termin.html). (See also Raimi 2000; Wolff 2002.)

Our country owes Professor Hirsch an enormous debt of gratitude for his effort and erudition in raising the linguistic facade that disguises the radical constructivist faith.

A Typology of Testing Opponent Fallacies

Some criticisms of standardized testing are valid and reasonable, and some of those will be discussed in a later chapter. In this chapter, I have focused on the invalid and unreasonable.

There are so many invalid and unreasonable attacks on standardized testing, however, that it can be confusing. For the most part, though, they seem to fit into one of just three categories of logical fallacy: (1) the assertion is a truism that ignores a more important consideration; (2) the problem described would be worse with available alternatives to standardized testing; and (3) the assertion is based on erroneous information or illogic.

Truisms, probably the most popular of anti-testing fallacies are, in most cases, just as valid for any system of measurement, such as in weather reporting, prices of goods in the marketplace, shoe sizes, body temperature, baseball statistics, and so on. If a truism is accepted as a legitimate reason for banning standardized testing, in most cases, it would be just as legitimate a reason for banning any of the other thousands of systems of measurement we use in our world.

Table 2.1 comprises a first effort to organize testing opponent attacks by type of fallacy.

How Do They Justify What They Do?

Not all, but too many anti-testing researchers conduct biased research. They stretch the truth, fudge numbers, distort data, or select only the data and sources they like in order to reach the conclusions they wish to reach. Yet, they still call themselves "Doctor So-and-So," and consider themselves to be "scientists," sworn ethically to conduct only unbiased, objective research. How do they reconcile their behavior with their persona of aloof objectivity?

One way is to constantly demonize the "enemy." The enemy, of course, consists of those evil persons whom we all know are the real forces behind the "tyranny of test scores." You know who they are—right-wing ideologues, Republicans, Texans, politicians who hope to gain from "school bashing," corporate interests, racists and bigots, narrow-minded authoritarians, and mean ogres who hate kids. Given the sinister character of those who *favor* standardized

Table 2.1

Typology of Testing Opponent Fallacies, Organized by "Attacks"

	Truism —true of any measurement of anything	Is worse with available alternatives	False fact or blatant illogic
High-stakes standardized tests... **...are not natural, they:**			
"distort" (i.e., steer) instruction	X	X	
induce "teaching to the test"...	X		
...lead to test-score inflation		X	X
...narrow the curriculum		X	X
...support change to a different curriculum	X		
induce test preparation...	X		
...and test preparation is not "real learning"			X
..."drills," worksheets, practice, and memorization are all bad instructional practice			X
standardize curriculum	X		
standardize instruction			X
employ "extrinsic" incentives to learn	X		
...do not work, they:			
produce stress	X		
induce cheating		X	
produce increased numbers of dropouts		X	X
can be misunderstood by politicians and public	X	X	
are overly costly			X
are unique to the United States			X
are being abandoned by other countries			X
reduce educational achievement			X
induce a public "backlash"			X

testing, is not *any* behavior on the part of the good and decent people who defend pure and wholesome public education justified? As for the parents and taxpayers who like standardized testing, the public is often described in anti-testing tracts as ignorant and unfair. Thus, perhaps it is OK to deceive them, too.

On one level, there is nothing wrong with those who have a self- interest in opposing testing. This is a free country, and we all have a right to lobby for our interests. On another level, it is disturbing because school administrators and education professors represent a group of public servants who should serve as models to our children. We pay them high salaries and give them very secure jobs. Then, we give them our children. Is just a little bit of external, objective evaluation of what they do with our money and our children really asking so much?

Table 2.1 (cont.)

...are not fair, they:	Truism —true of any measurement of anything	Is worse with available alternatives	False fact or blatant illogic
are being used for multiple purposes...	X		
...can only validly be used for a single purpose			X
are used to make high-stakes decisions about students based on a single test score			X
are inferior to the use of multiple measures	X		
are unfair to women and minorities		X	X
are used to make selection and rejection decisions	X	X	
...with multiple-choice formats, in particular:			
can be "coached"...	X	X	
...and students can do well on them knowing only "tricks" without understanding the subject matter		X	X
encourage teaching by "rote memorization" and "drills"...	X		
... and highly-scripted instruction and learning through practice stunt learning		X	X
tap only "lower-order thinking"...			X
...and "lower-order thinking" is bad			X
are not "authentic"	X		
can allow for only "one correct answer"			X
cannot provide partial credit			X
allow the use of "process of elimination"	X		
can be solved simply by "plugging in" answers			X

Postscript: The Impregnable Defense of Testing Opponents

Anyone who declares that they support standardized testing or high-stakes standardized testing, but opposes all the current versions and are waiting for more research to improve them, should not be believed. Most any type of standardized test one can imagine is used in a high-stakes environment somewhere in the world, and has been for decades. Given all the variety and all the experience, anyone who cannot be satisfied by any current testing program can never be satisfied with any testing program. This person is not a supporter of standardized testing, but an opponent, and should be honest about it.

Many testing opponents say that they are not against all standardized testing, they just want it "done right." Then, they may make selective attacks on particular aspects of standardized tests, implying that if only those particular features were changed, they would be satisfied. When testing officials respond by changing those particular features of tests, often with enormous difficulty and at enormous expense, however, some other feature of standardized tests usually emerges as particularly loathsome and necessary of correction before the test scores can be used to make any judgments or decisions.

The result, of course, is an endless process of tail-chasing on a massive scale, as huge state and national testing programs are continually altered to accommodate each new complaint as they go in and out of fashion among educators. For example, a state may change from a multiple-choice testing format for any of the many rationales that testing opponents use to attack the multiple choice format and adopt "constructed response" and "hands on" test formats. That state may then learn that testing opponents are still not happy. The new formats cost more money, take more time, and produce less reliable scores, for example, so the tests are still attacked.

Much anti-testing illogic is impervious to solution. Satisfy one complaint, and there will inevitably be another. That is because the arguments virtually never reflect the basic conflict over testing, which is *who* gets to evaluate educational performance. Some education provider groups want to be left alone to do as they please (with our money and our children). Most parents and taxpayers want some external, independent oversight and measurement.

When discussions of testing are manifest in those, its most essential terms, education provider groups cannot win the argument. They can only win the argument if they can divert attention toward peripheral issues. The boxed table below lists just a small number of the contradictions of testing opponents, and illustrates how impervious to logic some of their arguments can be:

A testing opponent might say:	...but, might also say:
One cannot judge students based on scores from tests not aligned to the curriculum. In fairness, students can only be judged based on material to which they have been exposed.	"Teaching to the test" (i.e., having tests based on material that is taught) and "narrowing the curriculum" (i.e., having tests based on material that is taught) are very bad practices.
A single test can only validly be used for a single purpose (one for student diagnosis, another for teacher diagnosis, another for curricular alignment, another for graduation, and so on).	If we followed this directive, we would end up with a plethora of tests. Then, some of the same testing opponents would argue that we use too many tests and they take too much time, and they would be right.
These high-stakes standardized tests are too difficult; they produce massive numbers of failures, dropouts, and demoralized students.	These standardized tests are too easy; creative, higher-order instruction has been replaced or dumbed down to the low level of these simple tests that could be passed by 5th graders.
Academic standards, course work, textbooks, instruction, and tests should all be consistent and operate from the same play book, otherwise students and teachers will be confused and the system unfair.	Teachers should be allowed to tailor instruction uniquely to each class, indeed, to each individual student. Teachers are intelligent craftpersons who should be granted creative license to choose course content and not be bound by standards and norms.

A testing opponent might say:	...but, might also say:
Tests, if used at all, should be "performance-based" and "authentic."	Performance tests and authentic testing are too expensive to use.[22]
Standardized tests do not show anything because parental income explains all the variance in student achievement.	[...therefore schooling has no effect on academic achievement] ...but we should spend more tax money on public schools, anyway.
Standardized tests inhibit creativity and critical thinking;	Arguments in favor of testing come from evil people, thus they are allowed no place in the education school curriculum. [So, prospective teachers hear only one side of the issue, inhibiting creativity and critical thinking.]
If test scores do not go up, it is proof that high-stakes external testing does not improve achievement.	When test scores rise, it is just a statistical aberration, they always go up (because of teaching to the test), and it does not really mean anything.
Standardized tests impose a "one-size-fits-all" structure on teaching, learning, and curriculum, ignoring the individuality of teachers and students.	A one-size-fits-all teacher accreditation system, a one-size-fits-all public school system without parental choice, a one-size-fits-all teacher salary schedule, one-size-fits-all teacher union work rules and grievance procedures, a one-size-fits-all (absence of) ability grouping, a one-size-fits-all list of approved textbooks...are all good practices and promote "democracy."
"Multicultural education" must teach different subject matter in every school, subject matter that is tuned to students' own cultures.	If the subject matter is different in every school, it would be unfair to use standardized tests to measure school performance because the subject matter would not be standardized.
Minimum-competency testing is bad because it teaches to a lowest-common denominator.	High standards are bad because they will discourage kids and some will fail.
Standardized tests are an affront to the professionalism of educators. They imply that we do not trust educators to do the best thing for the students and that is a shame, because U.S. educators are highly trained and professional. Their integrity should not be questioned. They should be afforded the trust and respect they deserve and that other professionals in our society receive.	With high-stakes tests, educators are motivated to cheat, and many, if not most of them do cheat; so we should eliminate high-stakes testing.

A testing opponent might say:	...but, might also say:
The Japanese secondary school grinds all creativity out of their children, numbing them with all-important multiple-choice standardized tests, which drive them to suicide, and we certainly would not want to do the same to our children [in truth, the U.S. teen suicide rate is much higher].	The Japanese elementary school is a model of Deweyist progressive education, and uses no high-stakes standardized tests [in the elementary grades], and that is the reason for Japanese educational excellence. We should consider Japanese education as a model for the U.S.
Policymakers like testing because it is a cheap "quick fix" and "real" solutions to school problems cost money.	Tests are enormously expensive, and drain scarce resources away from "regular instruction."
The testing industry has grown too huge, has too many firms, is anarchic, and needs to be regulated (by people like us). It is a "fractured marketplace" (Haney, Madaus, and Lyons 1993).	The testing industry is "tiny," has too few firms and cannot handle the increased workload required by President Bush's testing proposals (Boser 2000; Clarke, Madaus, Horn, and Ramos 2001).
High-stakes standardized tests are too difficult and millions of students will be discouraged and drop out of school because of them.	High-stakes standardized tests, particularly those with multiple-choice formats, are so easy that anyone can do well on them just by learning a few "tricks," without even knowing the material.
Standardized testing imposes an unreasonable amount of additional work on teachers and administrators, when they are already expected to do too much.	[In response to public demands for educators to focus on academic subject matter...] The problems of society are enormous and cannot be ignored in the classroom; instruction must be imbedded within the social context.
National testing would be bad because education should be a state and local issue in the United States.*	A national review board [composed of testing opponents] should be established to review the "technical quality" of high-stakes state tests.*
State tests are bad because they reduce local control and parents' influence in their children's schools.*	The public's opinions on high-stakes testing [which are overwhelmingly in favor] should be dismissed because the public is ignorant about the "technical" aspects of testing.*
High-stakes standardized tests are bad for all the reasons stated above.	Tests without stakes are bad because some students do not make an effort on tests that do not count, and the resulting test scores are meaningless.
President Clinton's Voluntary National Tests were a bad idea because they would have reduced local control (even though they were voluntary).*	With the Voluntary National Tests, "the federal government would [have been] unable to regulate how states and local districts would use the test results."*

* Found in the National Research Council's tome, *High-Stakes: Testing for Tracking, Promotion, and Graduation.*

Notes

1.   Tom Haladyna, Susan Bobbitt Nolan, and Nancy Haas are often associated with
     the term "test score pollution" (see Haladyna, Haas, and Nolan 1989; Nolan,
     Haladyna, and Haas 1992). But, they use it in a more reasonable and limited sense
     than others do. For some testing critics, if tests induce any change whatsoever in
     curriculum or instruction, they are polluting and corrupting.
         An example of what can happen in a laissez-faire curricular environment is
     provided by the fate of writing instruction in the United States, a subject that in
     many places simply has not gotten taught. An American Federation of Teachers
     (AFT)-Peter D. Hart (1994) poll of teachers nationwide found that they regard
     writing to be the subject in which students have the most need for improvement.
     Forty-eight percent of teachers rated students' abilities in writing "less than ad-
     equate" or "poor," by comparison with 29 percent who said the same for students'
     reading abilities.
         English teachers, however, are generally assigned two tasks— teaching reading
     comprehension and teaching writing. Many would probably agree that teaching
     reading comprehension can be enjoyable. A teacher picks a reading that the teacher
     likes and then discusses the various meanings of the work with the students in
     class. Such a discussion can be "creative" and expansive, can move freely from
     idea to idea as the group's minds wander among them. It can be the mental equiva-
     lent of taking a walk. It can be fun.
         Most would also agree that teaching writing, by contrast, is very difficult.
     Discussions about good writing are not expansive and "creative," they are neces-
     sarily focused and ordered. Moreover, teaching writing inevitably necessitates
     assigning and reviewing homework; giving students reading assignments does not
     necessarily. Reviewing homework for writing calls for editing and rewriting on the
     teacher's part, which can be time-consuming and tedious.
         If an English teacher is left to be "creative" and "innovative" and teach either
     reading or writing, which will they pick? The teacher who insists on teaching
     writing will likely take on work she not only does not have to do, but that the
     students do not want to do. It is not disparaging to say that most students, given the
     choice, would rather sit and discuss the big ideas in literature during class time and
     watch TV in the evenings than spend their class time and evenings struggling to
     craft meaningful and grammatically correct sentences. That's hard work.
2.   See a discussion of the phenomenon that includes the physician, John Jacob Cannell,
     and many others in full-issue coverage, in *Educational Measurement: Issues and
     Practice*, summer 1988.
3.   Few of the tests involved in Cannell's study were used in high-stakes situations,
     however, and where they were the bias would have been toward passing unquali-
     fied students rather than failing qualified ones.
4.   Some evidence from some studies shows an absence of course dropping at the
     secondary level. See John O. Anderson, Walter Muir, David J. Bateson, David
     Blackmore, and W. Todd Rogers, *The Impact of Provincial Examinations on
     Education in British Columbia: General Report*. British Columbia Ministry of
     Education, March 30, 1990; and Linda Ann Bond and Darla A. Cohen, "The Early
     Impact of Indiana Statewide Testing for Educational Progress on Local Education
     Agencies," in Rita G. O'Sullivan and Robert E. Stake, eds. *Advances in Program
     Evaluation.* Vol. 1, Part B, 1991, pp. 78-79, 86-87.
5.   See OECD, *Education at a Glance*, 1997, p. 200, for the salary figures. See also
     John H. Bishop, "Impacts of School Organization and Signaling on Incentives to

Learn in France, The Netherlands, England, Scotland, and the United States,"
Working Paper 94-30, Center for Advanced Human Resource Studies, New York
State School of Industrial and Labor Relations, Cornell University, Ithaca, New
York, December, 1994b; and "Incentives for Learning: Why American High School
Students Compare So Poorly to Their Counterparts Overseas," Working Paper
No. 89-09, Cornell University School of Industrial and Labor Relations, 1989a,
for discussions of the relationship of external tests and teacher status.
6.   See Phelps 2001e, Bond and Cohen, or George Stigler's work comparing time use
in U.S., German, and Japanese lower secondary mathematics and science classes,
in Stigler and Hiebert.
7.   See Indicator C3 in Organization for Economic Co-operation and Development,
Education at a Glance: OECD Indicators 1997, Paris: author, 1997. At age 16, the
United States has a lower percentage of students enrolled than do Austria, Belgium, Canada, the Czech Republic, Denmark, Finland, Germany, the Netherlands,
Norway, New Zealand, and Sweden, all countries with high-stakes secondary-
level exit exams. Rates in Hungary and Ireland are similar to ours. Switzerland and
the United Kingdom are the only countries, among those included, with high-
stakes exit exams and lower enrollment rates than the U.S. at age 16. Comparisons
at age 17 are similar. The implication: students drop out in the United States for
reasons other than not passing an exit exam.
8.   The Horatio Alger Association's *Mood of American Youth* survey found that not
liking exams—any type of exam—was ranked sixth (at 25 percent) behind "boring
material" (at 77 percent), "not interested in subject," and "class moves too slow"
among student complaints about school. Only 19.7 percent of students cited their
courses for moving "too fast," while 28.5 said "too slow." Only 16.3 percent said
"too much challenge," whereas 19.9 percent said "not enough challenge" (Horatio
Alger Association 1996: 23).
In the *Indiana Youth Poll*, "tests, exams" popped up as a candidate for "most
disliked aspects of going to school," but by only 5.9 percent of the school students
and 6.5 percent of the youth leaders. Eleven other candidates received more votes.
In general, the poll revealed little evidence of stress. Indeed, "stress, pressure for
grades" came in just above tests and exams at 9.3 and 7.7 percent, below "boring,
uninteresting classes," and "boring routines" (Erickson 1991: 10). When the school
students described a typical day in school in negative terms, they were six times
more likely to mention "boring" or related terms, such as "monotonous," "te-
dious," or "tiring," than they were to mention stress-related terms (Erickson 1991:
21)
9.   By contrast, FairTest advocates limiting testing to occasional no-stakes monitoring
with samples of students using the types of response formats that FairTest favors
(no multiple-choice!). Scores on "portfolios" of each student's best work would
measure individual student progress (FairTest 1998). Indeed, the only state-testing
program to garner the highest rating from FairTest in a nationwide appraisal of state
tests was Vermont, with a statewide portfolio program and no high-stakes or
multiple-choice standardized testing (FairTest 1997).
While standardized performance-based tests are thousands of years old, the
history of the large-scale, standardized use of *portfolios* is spare and brief. There
appear to be many problems with a sole reliance on portfolios to measure student
progress: they're far more susceptible to cheating, coaching, gaming, and outright
plagiarism than are standardized tests (*Education Week on the Web* 1997; and
Gearhart and Herman 1996). Moreover, they reward occasional, exceptional bril-
liance and not steady competence; and are difficult to score with consistency (Koretz

1996). These sound like the same tenor of criticisms FairTest, the most prominent advocate for the exclusive use of portfolios, makes of standardized tests.

10. Reverse chronological causation is also the primary mode of logic in the famous anti-ability grouping book, *Keeping Track*. It is assumed that students are held back *because* they are in low ability groups. It is not considered that they were put in the low ability groups in the first place because they were progressing more slowly than the other students (Oakes 1985).

11. The work of the Cornell labor economist John Bishop does not get the press attention bestowed on FairTest. Yet in a series of solid studies conducted over a decade, Bishop has shown that, when other factors that influence academic achievement are controlled for, students from states, provinces, or countries with medium or high-stakes testing programs score better on neutral, common tests and earn higher salaries after graduation than do their counterparts from states, provinces, or countries with no- or low-stakes tests (see Bishop 1989-2001).

   Bishop recently turned his attention to the very same relationship that FairTest studied, only he looked at it in some depth. He and his colleagues used individual-level data from the National Education Longitudinal Study (NELS:88), that started in 1988, and High School and Beyond (HSB), another longitudinal study that ran from 1980 to 1992. They controlled for socioeconomic status, grades, and other important factors, while comparing the earnings of graduates from "minimum-competency" testing states to those from non-testing states (Bishop 2001). "They found that test-taking students earned an average of 3 percent to 5 percent more per hour than their counterparts from schools with no minimum-competency tests. And the differences were greater for women, with as much as 6 percent higher earnings for those who had taken the tests.

12. Figure 9c in NCES's *State Indicators in Education, 1997* shows the difference in average mathematics proficiency scores of public school eighth-graders on the National Assessment of Educational Progress (NAEP) between 1990 and 1996, by state (U.S. Department of Education, National Center for Education Statistics, *State Indicators in Education, 1997*). Thirty states participated in the NAEP in both of those years. Given that each state is compared with itself, at two different time points, background factors, such as socioeconomic status, that can influence test performance, are controlled. I compared these state 1990-1996 NAEP score differences with the presence or absence of state student promotion or graduation tests and school test performance reporting in the middle of the period, the 1993-1994 school year (Roeber et al. 1994). Six of the top 10 and 8 of the top 15 states had high-stakes graduation tests, whereas only 3 of the bottom 10 and 4 of the bottom 15 states did. Moreover, 10 of the top 10 and 14 of the top 15 states publicly reported school average test performance, whereas only 5 of the bottom 10 and 8 of the bottom 15 states did. The more comprehensive the testing program, in terms of grade levels and subjects tested, the more the state's children's performance improved. Among the most improved states are Texas and North Carolina. Comparing the average NAEP score differences between states with high stakes graduation tests and those without, the difference is statistically significant. (Using a z test of two population means with known variances. The null hypothesis is rejected at p=.05, in a 1- or 2-tailed test.) Comparing the average NAEP score differences between states with public reporting of school average test scores and those without, the difference is even more decisively statistically significant. (Using a z test of two population means with known variances. The null hypothesis is rejected at p=.0001, for a 1- or 2-tailed test.) The results for reading test scores (Figure 8b) are similar.

13. E. D. Hirsch, of course, makes a more detailed and eloquent argument for the acceptance of both process and content as necessary components of intelligence. See E. D. Hirsch, Jr., *The Schools We Need and Why We Don't Have Them*, 1996.

14. Multiple-choice tests can be set up to award partial credit. Say a student may know enough to realize that the correct answer has to be b or c, and cannot be a, d, or e, but does not know which and so guesses. A student will get some of these types of answers right at a higher rate than she would just by guessing blindly. The student is raising the probability of getting a correct answer each time she does this. "Educated Guessing" can raise one's test score, but test developers can also set up the items and the test scoring such that they provide and give credit for responses that are partially correct.

15. They are made explicit, however, in the cognitive laboratory testing that some multiple-choice tests undergo when they are developed.

16. I would argue, as would others, that we actually use the multiple-choice format quite often in real life. Either we know how to get to the correct answer directly, or we use the process of elimination technique.

17. A curious form of etiquette aids this form of censorship. Some declare it to be impolite, or even rude, to identify the persons or organizations with whom one disagrees—that is an *ad hominum* attack. To me, just the opposite seems more rude. If one identifies one's opponent, the opponent is given the opportunity to defend herself. Moreover, if one identifies one's opponent, one better get the quotation right, or that opponent can accuse one of slander.

    Not identifying one's opponent may seem, superficially, more polite, but it also opens the door to dishonesty. One can put words in the mouths of one's opponents or, worse, one can create one's opponents (straw men) out of thin air, as evil, diabolical, obviously wrong and easy to beat.

18. The manner in which the study's authors count up other standardized student tests besides college entrance exams is similar, only the estimation process is even mushier. At least with college entrance tests they start their "estimation" with a known number of tests. With state and local district tests, they use another report's rough guess for how much state testing exists, and three telephone calls to three U.S. school districts form the base of their estimate for the number of district tests. Then, they do their turning-parts-into-wholes routine. Oh, and I almost forgot: they count state tests twice: once as statewide tests, and then again as districtwide tests. They used similar arithmetic to estimate the cost of tests.

19. Those responsible for the level of research quality at the OTA have, since the Congress closed the OTA down in 1994, gone to work at the National Research Council's Center on Education and, there, have done remarkably similar work.

20. Take, for instance, their opposition to facts, content, and substance in favor of and exclusive reliance on process. Most humans believe that intelligence involves both content and process. You cannot do data processing without both data and process. You cannot speak a language without both vocabulary and grammar. Most testing opponents, however, side with the radical constructivists on our education school faculty and deride content as unimportant to teach, saying you can always look it up. But, how can you even begin to know where to look up a word if you know no words? How can you know where to look up a fact on a computer if you know no facts to begin with? Testing opponents do not get into this detail.

21. McNeal, Linda M. 2000. *Contradictions of School Reform: Educational Costs of Standardized Testing*. New York: Routledge.

22. For an example where both sides of this proposition are stated flat out, see *Education Week*, 1992.

3

Campaigns: The Big, Bad SAT

The standardized test attracting the loudest and most sustained oppro-
brium from critics over the years is the Scholastic Assessment Test (SAT), used
by almost two-thirds of U.S. colleges in making admissions decisions.[1] The
SAT has been a consistently popular target for attack both from the interests
vested in the current K-12 public school system and from some journalists
who probably think of themselves as muckrakers.

Indeed, even the Nader organization has attacked it, making it a prominent exception to their usual interest in full disclosure, more information,
quality control, and the consumer's welfare. Regarding standardized testing
in general, the Naderites take an emphatically anti-consumer, pro-producer
stance, preferring to close the curtains and keep us all in the dark.[2]

The SAT is administered several times annually to about two million high
school students and costs each of them about $25. The individual student
scores are sent to higher education institutions at the request of the students.
Those institutions use SAT scores as one measure among many in their admissions decisions. Surveys of college admissions officers show that, on average,
they tend to weight SAT scores about equally with high school grade-point
averages and grades in advanced courses, and ahead of letters of recommendation, extracurricular activities, and any number of other indicators of student performance or character, with a couple of exceptions. They tend to
weigh most highly scores on certain tests that are based on a rigorous, standardized curricula, such as Advanced Placement Tests or the International
Baccalaureate, but only a small proportion of high school students take these
types of tests.

In general, college admissions officers would prefer to make admissions
decisions based on reliable information, and unstandardized indicators are
not reliable. A grade-point average, for example, can be high for several
reasons, including: the student worked very hard in tough courses; the student did not work very hard and took only easy courses; and the school has
very low standards and any student can get good grades with little effort.

High school and course standards vary widely and a college admissions officer in Lincoln, Nebraska, does not have the time to evaluate the rigor of standards, or the content of courses offered, at an unfamiliar high school in Florida. Nonetheless, she still needs to make judgments about the high school record of students from that Florida high school who apply to enter the University of Nebraska.

The SAT offers such a standard measure. It is not a perfect measure of performance, achievement, or aptitude, nor does anyone claim that it is. Used as a complement to other imperfect measures, however, college admissions officers find it to be helpful. If they did not, the SAT would not exist.

The SAT has been a source of discontent among some prominent scholars not opposed to all standardized testing (e.g., Christopher Jencks, John Bishop), because it is not based on an actual, required curriculum. They feel that a test based on the actual curriculum each student encounters in high school would be fairer and provide better incentives for students to apply themselves in school. The SAT is based on such a broad domain of knowledge, they complain, that one cannot really study for it, and what is the point of having a test for which one cannot study?[3] It is in the study for the test that one learns, after all.

Though their basic points are valid, the fact remains that there is no single national curriculum, and probably never will be. The U.S. Constitution says nothing about education and, as we should all remember from our school lessons, those areas not addressed in the federal constitution are the responsibility of this country's original, founding governmental entities, the States. Each U.S. state can set or choose not to set its own standard curriculum. If the SAT were to be curriculum-based, which curriculum would it choose? Should the SAT use Connecticut's curriculum? That might please high school students from Connecticut, but would be irresponsibly unfair to students from Alabama, where the curriculum could be quite different. Connecticut students will have been exposed to material on the SAT and the Alabama students not. Moreover, the more curricular-specific the test, the greater the advantage given to those students lucky enough to have attended better schools.

The points above, all essential to understanding why the SAT exists, how it is used, and why it is not a curriculum-based test, are seldom mentioned by the critics, or the journalists who talk to them. For example, the Public Broadcasting System's *Frontline* television documentary on the topic, "Secrets of the SAT" (see below) mentions none of them.

The extremist advocacy group, the National Center for Fair and Open Testing (FairTest), delivers monthly vituperatives to its membership attacking the validity and fairness of the SAT. Indeed, one of its primary sustaining causes is to convince colleges to quit using the SAT in their admissions decisions and to celebrate those that do. If you read only FairTest's literature, you might believe that its campaign against the SAT has been very successful (FairTest 2001).

According to them, a few hundred colleges nationwide now have optional or limited SAT requirements.[4] FairTest tends to be fairly liberal in its counting method, however. Colleges have complained to the National Association for College Admission Counseling (NACAC) about their presence on "The List" of colleges that FairTest claims waive the SAT requirement. Many colleges FairTest includes waive the requirement only for a few students under extraordinary circumstances (e.g., disabilities, remote foreign locations, etc.) (National Assn. for College Admission Counseling 1998).

Even those colleges that offer to consider applications without admissions test scores, however, may require additional proof of ability, such as a graded writing sample or an on-campus interview. Even though not required for admissions consideration at a particular college, absence of an admissions test score may still bias an application negatively in the absence of other, countervailing evidence of outstanding abilities or experience (Goldberg 1996a, 1996b).

Still, the SAT's impact is often overstated. The overwhelming majority of U.S. colleges are not selective, so a low SAT score will rarely keep a student out of college. Even at the most selective colleges, the SAT is virtually never used alone by college admissions staff to make decisions. Typically, it is one of many factors that include a student's high school grade-point average, extracurricular activities, recommendations, essays, and so on. When surveyed, however, admissions counselors rate the SAT score as a more reliable measure than these other indicators.

The criticisms of admissions tests are many, but chief among them are two: (1) that they can be gamed—with some tips, "tricks," and insights a student can score better without really studying the subject matter—so, the critics say, the test is not testing the subject matter, but the tricks; and (2) that they are inferior predictors of college performance to high school grades.

Doing Well with "Tricks"

The first criticism—that college admissions tests can be gamed—is fostered not only by test critics but by salespersons for test preparation services such as the Princeton Review and Stanley Kaplan, who stand to profit if people believe it. What the salespeople do not tell potential customers is that they can learn all the useful hints they need to know themselves directly from the ACT or SAT organizations or a $20 paperback book.

Indeed, there are ways to "game" the tests and students who spend the time to learn how may benefit. Like all systems, the tests have certain structures, forms, and procedures, and an understanding of them can help the test taker relate to the test better. Learning to game the college admissions tests will not make up for a high school career of academic abstinence, however. The gaming methods only go so far; students who did not show up for English class in high school and skipped Algebra and Geometry will not produce a stellar performance on the ACT or SAT after merely having attended a Stanley Kaplan course, no matter how many hundreds of dollars they (unwisely) spend on it.

Essentially, there are two aspects to college admissions test preparation—format familiarity and remedial instruction. Test preparation courses cannot make up for years of academic neglect (on the schools' part or of the student's own doing), and two decades of research bears this out. "Format familiarity" is something else and students who have spent years in constructivists' schools avoiding objective tests are likely to be the most shocked by the unfamiliarity of the format of something like the ACT or SAT.

Having already asserted that I do not think the test prep courses (like those of Stanley Kaplan and the Princeton Review) can make up for years of academic neglect and, thus, offer no substantial remedial help, what do I think of their ability to help students with format familiarity? Not much. Probably, these expensive test prep courses are even less able to help students with format familiarity than they are with subject matter remediation. That is because any motivated student can carefully read the free prep materials provided by SAT or ACT, or purchase a $20 test preparation book from a variety of book publishers and familiarize themselves with the format. Any student not motivated enough to do even this small amount of work will probably daydream throughout the several hundred dollar Princeton Review course, anyway.

There is nothing better than just sitting down and practicing taking a test on one's own, and preferably under timed conditions, and getting familiar with the formats and instructions. Stanley Kaplan and the Princeton Review provide illusory, artificial conditions. When the student sits down to take the SAT or ACT, there will be no Kaplan instructor there to help. He or she will be all alone. And, the best way, the most "authentic" way, to prepare for the SAT or ACT, is just like that, all alone.[5]

Granted, it is sad that some students sit down for the SAT cold, without having prepared themselves in any way. In doing so, they are not being fair to themselves. But, getting rid of the SAT, however, will not make things more fair.

The Princeton Review's advertising claims, though, go far beyond familiarizing students with the format of the ACT or SAT. The Princeton Review argues that one can do well on multiple-choice standardized tests without even understanding the subject matter being tested. They claim that they increase students' test scores merely by helping them to understand how multiple-choice items are constructed. Are they correct?

The evidence test coaching firms use to "prove" their case is in data of their own making. Some, for example, give students practice tests, score them, then put the students through a course, after which they take a real SAT. They argue that the second test scores are hugely better. Even if you could trust that their data were accurate, however, they do not subtract out the effect of test familiarity. Students generally do better after they familiarize themselves with the test format. On average, students do better on the SAT just by taking it again. Indeed, simply retaking the SAT for $25 is a far less expensive way to familiarize oneself with the test.

For decades, independent scholars have studied the effect of test preparation courses like those offered by Stanley Kaplan and the Princeton Review. Becker's (1990) meta-analysis of such studies, for example, found only marginal effects for test coaching for the SAT. Becker analyzed study outcomes in terms of some 20 study characteristics having to do with both study design and content of coaching studied. Like previous analysts, she found that coaching effects were larger for the SAT-M than for the SAT-V. She did not find that duration of coaching was a strong predictor of the effects of coaching. Instead, she found that of all the coaching content variables she investigated, "item practice," (i.e., coaching in which participants were given practice on sample test items) was the strongest influence on coaching outcomes) (Becker 1990).

Overall, Becker concluded that among 21 published comparison studies, the effects of coaching were 0.09 standard deviations of the SAT-V and 0.16 on SAT-M. That is, just 9 points for the Verbal and 16 points for the Math, on their 500 point scales. That's virtually nothing-one or two additional correct answers in the Verbal and Math sections—and far, far less than Stanley Kaplan and the Princeton Review claim.

Research completed in November 1998 by Donald Powers and Donald Rock update the earlier studies of Becker and others with new data about the minimal effects of coaching on the revised SAT, which was introduced in 1994. As described by Grade-point (2001), research director of the College Board:

> Results from the various analyses conducted in the Powers and Rock study indicate the external coaching programs have a consistent but small effect on the SAT I, ranging in average effect from 21 to 34 points on the combined SAT I verbal and math scores. That is, the average effect of coaching is about 2 to 3 percent of the SAT I score scale of 400 to 1600 (the verbal and math scales each range from 200 to 800 points). Often raw score increases may be the easiest to understand. When examining the actual increases of both coached and uncoached students we find that:
>
> • Coached students had an average increase of 29 points on SAT verbal compared with an average increase of 21 points for uncoached students. Coached students had an average increase of 40 points on SAT math compared with 22 points for uncoached students. The best esti-

mate of effect of coaching is 8 points on verbal scores and 18 points on math scores.

- Coached students were slightly more likely to experience large score increases than uncoached students. Twelve and 16 percent of coached students had increases of 100 points or more on verbal and math scores, respectively, compared with 8 percent for uncoached students (on both math and verbal scores).

- About one-third of all students actually had no gain or loss when retesting. On the verbal scale, 36 percent of coached students had a score decrease or no increase when retesting. On the math scale, 28 percent of coached students had a decrease or no increase, compared with 37 percent of uncoached students.

- Students attending the two largest coaching firms, which offer the largest and most costly programs, do fare somewhat better than students attending other external coaching programs, but again, the effects of coaching are still relatively small. The typical gains for students attending these firms were 14 and 8 points on verbal scores and 11 and 34 points on math scores (with an average increase of 10 points on verbal, 22 points on math, and 43 points on combined verbal plus math for the two major test preparation firms).

- There are no detectable differences in scores of coached students on the basis of gender and race/ethnicity, and whether initial scores were high or low.

- The revised SAT I is no more coachable than the previous SAT.

The estimated effects of coaching reported in this study (8 points on verbal and 18 points on math) are remarkably consistent with previous research published in peer reviewed scientific journals, all of which are at odds with the very large claims by several commercial coaching firms" (see also Briggs 2001; DerSimonian and Laird 1983; Kulik, Bangert-Drowns, and Kulik 1984; Messick and Jungeblut 1981; Zehr 2001; Bridgeman, McCamley-Jenkins, and Ervin 2000).

Predictive Invalidity

The second criticism of college admissions tests—that they are inferior to high school grades as predictors of college performance—deserves further attention here because it leads right into a cost-effectiveness analysis of student testing. The critics' argument starts with a kernel of truth. Neither the SAT nor the ACT is any better a predictor of performance in college than is the high school grade-point average. They are roughly equal predictors, as measured by their "predictive validity" (which, technically, is a standard Pearson product-moment correlation coefficient [typically, about .45] between one or the other factor and college [usually freshman year] grade-point average).[6]

If high school grade-point average is just as good a predictor, why bother with the ACT or SAT, say the critics? Intelligent critics, who know full well the simple answer to this question, may nonetheless withhold it from the journalists or general public they wish to convince of the evils of the tests[7] (see L. May 1995; Bracey 1989; Fiske 1989). (A cynic might respond that it seems just as appropriate to ask if it is not the high school GPA that should be tossed, if the ACT or SAT predicts college performance just as well.)

The simple answer: while high school GPA and admissions test scores might each correlate equally well with college performance, they are not perfectly correlated with each other. College admissions counselors, who require the ACT and SAT because they regard the information useful, gain more information about each student from a combination of the two pieces of information, high school GPA and admissions test score.

The critics will then retort that the additional increment of information provided by the test score is just not that much. Critics claim that the SAT adds only another 15 percent in correlation beyond what is already gained from the high school GPA.

Are the critics right? Is an increment of 15 percent too little to be worth our attention?...too little to matter?...not worth the stress and anxiety?...not worth the $25 test fee? For the critics and the journalists they have rallied to their cause, the answer to all these questions is a resounding yes.

One might keep in mind, however, that even a 15 percent correlation is higher than one obtains for other commonly used required admissions materials, such as extracurricular activities and letters of recommendation. Given the low level of their predictive power, why do we not hear calls to ban the use of recommendation letters and the consideration of extracurricular activities? Perhaps, it is because the alleged low predictive power of the SAT is not the real reason its critics wish to get rid of it.

Moreover, in cost-effectiveness terms, the incremental gain in predictive power offered by the SAT is a bargain. Again, the basic facts are that the predictive validity of the high school GPA is around 40 percent. SAT critics concede that SAT scores add an additional 15 percent. It costs society about $90,000 to educate a student up through high school graduation; a high school education alone costs about $30,000. The SAT costs about $25. For an incremental cost of 0.03 percent over the cost of education in grades 1-12, or an incremental cost of 0.08 percent over the cost of education in grades 9-12, we get a 38 percent increase in information for the college admissions counselor.[8]

The incremental benefit-cost ratio for the SAT is 1,250:1 counting the expense for grades 1-12 and 475:1 just counting the expense for high school. The "break-even" value of the SAT is over $11,000 per student.[9] If one wanted to count the Stanley Kaplan courses as "costs" in these calculations, they would have to cost at least $11,000 for each student to make the SAT cost-ineffective for society relative to regular school costs.[10]

How and Why Colleges Use Admissions Test Scores

In their admissions decisions, college admissions officers supplement high school grades and other information with SAT scores for several reasons: high schools vary quite a lot in the rigor and uniformity of their grading practices, so grade-point averages are not standard, comparable measures; students vary quite a bit in the rigor of their course selections, even within the same high school; and all aspects of curricula, even within the same high school, are not taught or learned equally well. College admissions counselors can make assumptions about the rigor of courses by course titles, but they will only be assumptions. Grades in Advanced Placement (AP) courses can tell them quite a lot, mostly because their performance standards are nationally uniform, but AP courses represent a tiny proportion of high school courses nationwide.

The annual survey by the National Association for College Admission Counseling shows that their members consider the following criteria the most important in determining admission (by percentage mentioning each criterion of considerable or moderate importance): grades in college prep courses such as the AP (90); admission test scores (82); grades in all subjects (79); class rank (71); essay or writing sample (53); counselor recommendation (66); and teacher recommendation (55). Other criteria have lower percentages (see Table 3.1) (National Association for College Admission Counseling 1996: 2, 4).

Table 3.1
Percentage of Admissions Counselors Citing Factor as Influential in Admission Decisions, by Level: 1997

Criterion	Considerable importance	Moderate importance	Limited importance	None
Grades in college preparatory courses	78	12	4	5
Admission test scores	48	34	11	7
Grades in all subjects	38	41	15	7
Class rank	36	35	19	11
Essay or writing sample	20	33	23	24
Teacher recommendation	19	46	23	12
Counselor recommendation	17	49	22	11
Interview	13	29	32	26
Work/extracurricular experience	6	39	38	18
Personal recognition program	2	12	38	48
Ability to pay	2	8	14	76

Source: National Association for College Admission Counseling, "Members Assess 1996 Recruitment Cycle in Eighth Annual NACAC Admission Trends Survey," *News from National Association for College Admission Counseling*, October 28, 1996, pp. 2, 4.

College admissions counselors are not deaf and blind; they hear and read the arguments against use of the SAT. Moreover, they are not required to use it. They can only be using it because they know, based on personal experience or based on their own readings, it is valuable—so valuable that they consider test scores to be the second most important criterion among many in making admissions decisions.

Allocative Efficiency and Restriction of Range

Allocative efficiency is predictive validity's twin. Predictive validity is the degree to which higher test scores predict higher future performance, typically in higher education or in employment. Allocative efficiency is the degree to which all graduates are well matched to those positions where they end up. The better the overall match, for both college students and colleges, for example, the greater the efficiency. It would be most efficient, for example, if students applied only to the college they most desired that is also desirous of admitting them and if each college considered only applications from students it was willing to admit and who would come if they were.[11]

Maximum allocative efficiency would benefit both students and colleges by saving them a great deal of time. Students would not waste time filling out applications for colleges they would be very unlikely to attend or to get into; colleges would spend less time considering applications from students who will not be admitted or will not come.

ACT and SAT scores produce some allocative efficiency. Students can look in any number of thick paperback college guides and see the ACT or SAT score ranges of admitted students at any college and compare their own scores to those in the published ranges. They can thus eliminate some colleges from their list of considered colleges if their scores exceed the range or fall short of the range. Likewise, colleges can eliminate some potential applicants from consideration (by not making an effort to recruit them, for example) if their test scores fall short of their normal range, given the higher probability that they will not be able to match the performance of their classmates.

It is not easy to measure allocative efficiency, however, because the benefits are so widely dispersed. One can hazard a guess as to how much time students save by applying to fewer schools, but the estimate would be pretty rough.[12]

This increase in information provided by published college average ACT and SAT scores narrows the applicant pools for colleges, as applicants with test scores beyond the end points of each college's range may decide against applying. As applicant pools become more homogeneous (i.e., their variation is reduced), predictive validity is reduced at the same time allocative efficiency is increased. [13]

The SAT and the Public Broadcasting System—
Secrets of the Journalist's Trade

The Public Broadcasting System's *Frontline* series originally produced an hour-long documentary on the SAT a few years ago, but it has been rebroadcast many times since. "Secrets of the SAT," is an award-winning, yet amateurish and irresponsible piece of journalism. Most galling, of course, is that our tax dollars and well-intended tax-deductible contributions paid for it.

Consider just a few of the narrator's statements:

- "In a few days, millions of American teenagers will take a test that will determine their future. They have spent thousands of hours and thousands of dollars, obsessed with higher scores."
- "How did the SAT become a national obsession?"
- "Nicholas Lemann has been studying the American fixation on standardized testing for the past five years."

"National obsession?" "American fixation?" What's the evidential basis for making such pejorative comments? There is none, naturally. Virtually every other industrialized country in the world tests its students more, and with greater consequences riding on the results, than we do.

Moreover, the producers seemed to regard it as perfectly fair to allow advocates on one side of the SAT controversy ten times more air time than the single SAT defender (and only interviewee with an expertise in testing research) whom they allowed to speak, and this does not even count the many minutes used by the narrator or given to test prep course teachers. The producers also let the anti-testing advocates make most of their assertions (which could easily be proven false) without any counter. In the minds of these journalists, apparently, the anti-testing advocates were revealing truth and fact, so there was no need for even an attempt at balance.

Speaker	Amount of time to speak*
SAT critics	
Nicholas Lemann, journalist	34
Bob Schaeffer, FairTest	25
John Katzman, Princeton Review	19
Claude Steele, professor	23
SAT defender	
Wayne Camara, College Board	9

*as measured by lines in transcript

The full set of background interviews, available at the web site, reveal an even stronger tilt to one side.

Speaker	Amount of time to speak*
SAT critics	
Nicholas Lemann, journalist	882
Bob Schaeffer, FairTest	368
John Katzman, Princeton Review	394
Claude Steele, professor	570
Robert Sternberg, professor	367
Christopher Jencks, professor	413
SAT defenders	
Henry Chauncey	128
Wayne Camara, College Board	33

*as measured by lines in transcript

To be complete, it must be mentioned that the interview with Henry Chauncey was mostly about his career and not the value of the SAT. Also there was another interview with Jonathan Grayer of the Stanley Kaplan test preparation firm: it was 361 lines and included statements both in defense and critical of the SAT. Jonathan Grayer gave perhaps the most interesting and insightful interview of the show, yet none of the interview was included in the broadcast. More so than anyone else interviewed, Grayer straddled the line between opposition and defense of the SAT and perhaps (just speculation, mind you) this annoyed the PBS producers. Grayer's PBS interviewer was sufficiently courteous with him so long as he criticized the SAT. When Grayer began to defend the SAT, however—asserting that it served a useful purpose and was much better than any current or foreseeable alternative—the PBS interviewer turned on him. The interviewer asked Grayer what his SAT scores were. This confrontational tactic is used by journalists opposed to standardized testing (and has been tried on me) to shame testing supporters.[14]

"Secrets of the SAT" is really a documentary on two separate topics—the SAT and affirmative action in college admissions—which the producers jumble together in a confusing and arbitrary manner.[15]

Nicholas Lemann has written a book about the SAT, and the PBS producers present him as a thoroughly reliable source of truth and fact, the font of all wisdom on the topic of standardized testing, and provide him more air time than anyone else. At one point in the show, a rare one in which the lone SAT defender is actually given an opportunity (of one sentence) to respond to a lengthy anti-SAT argument, the producers bring in Nicholas Lemann to settle the issue with the last word. One can trust what Nicholas Lemann says; after all, he's a journalist!

We know we cannot trust what Wayne Camara says. After all, he's the research director of the College Board, which profits from the SAT, according to "Secrets of the SAT." The College Board, in reality, is a nonprofit consortium of hundreds of higher education institutions in the United States that use the SAT in their admissions. It is unclear to me what incentive the College Board's members would have to use a test that is not helpful or useful to them. Further, it is absurd to think that college admissions counselors, probably some of the world's most politically liberal individuals, would favor using an admissions indicator that has the characteristics of bias, inaccuracy, or unreliability the PBS producers attribute to the SAT.

By contrast, the spokespersons for the National Center for Fair and Open Testing (FairTest), the most extreme and unrestrained anti-testing advocacy group in the country, and the Princeton Review, a private company that directly profits from the type of assertions made by the PBS documentary, are presented by the PBS producers as unbiased sources of truth and fact. The Princeton Review, incidentally, has no association whatsoever with Princeton University, but allows naive students to think that it does. "Secrets of the SAT" (and our taxes and contributions to PBS) have provided this private firm a huge amount of free advertising.

What is the value of the test-preparation services provided by this for-profit firm, at great expense to trusting students? If you believe what the "Secrets of the SAT" producers say, there is a great deal of value. If you believe, instead, the evidence provided by the little experiment set up by the producers themselves, there is none. The producers "followed" seven high school students through their senior years as they applied to the University of California (Berkeley), prepared (or not) for the SAT, received (or not) their SAT scores, and were admitted or rejected from Berkeley. The group represented a politically correct range of students—two economically very well off white students, two Hispanics, two Asians, and one African-American high school student.[16]

What was the experience of the seven students who paid the fees for expensive test-preparation programs, such as the Princeton Review? Two of the seven took such courses, one was accepted at Berkeley and one was not. Another student took a free SAT test preparation course at his high school, that was derided as inferior by the documentary, but got into Berkeley anyway. Another went through an SAT test-preparation program he purchased on a CD, and was rejected by Berkeley. Three students who endured no test preparation program were all admitted.

That, apparently, is not the "Secret" of the SAT that the PBS producers had in mind, however (i.e., that these commercial test prep programs are a waste of

SAT score	Grade-point average	Student's ethnicity	Paid for test preparation course?	Was accepted to Berkeley?
1500	4.3	White	no	yes
1390	3.9	White	no	yes*
1350	3.5	Asian-American	yes	no
1240	3.8	Hispanic	(CD course)	no
1110	4.0	Asian-American	yes	yes
920	4.0	Hispanic	no	yes
880	3.5	African-American	free course at school	yes

*Was rejected at first. He then appealed and was admitted after appeal.

money and time). PBS clearly wanted the viewer to come away with a different impression, judging from what the narrator said and from the student quotes the documentary revealed. Here is a sampling:

> [student speaking] "I had to do something about the SATs. I mean, had I not taken Kaplan, I do not even know where I'd be right now. It's just that one blemish, that one thing that could have ruined everything."
>
> [test prep teacher speaking] "You do not show up to the SAT anymore without some prep because the SAT, along with...are...most important criteria that college admissions departments look at....The bright students' scores are getting higher and higher. A 1550 used to mean everything, and a 1550 does not necessarily mean everything anymore."
>
> [another student speaking] "At first I kind of regretted going to this class, but now I just—I'll be so much prepared for the SATs that I can probably get into Stanford."
>
> [narrator] "Ninety-seven percent of all students in high school use some kind of test prep."

The latter claim is ridiculous, of course, and the producers do not reveal the source of the alleged "fact." But, I think I have found the source on my own—it is a reference to a CollegeBoard study of test-takers that reveals the proportion of students who prepare themselves in any fashion and for any amount of time for the SAT, including spending just a few seconds browsing the SAT introductory brochure. PBS lets the viewer believe, however, that they are referring to several hundred dollar Stanley Kaplan and Princeton Review type courses, and not just a few seconds of "brochure perusal."

The Princeton Review and FairTest spokespersons, predictably, claim that the SAT (and, for that matter, all multiple-choice tests) can be gamed; one can do well on it just by learning a few tricks. As one of the shadowed students explained, "the Princeton Review book...explained that the SAT is a measure of how well you take tests, rather than—rather than how smart you are or how much you know."

So, why do not all Princeton Review and Stanley Kaplan customers get perfect scores on the SAT?

The "evidence," that these test prep courses are worth the expense, of course, is that, according to the test prep course promoters, they "improve" your test scores. "Secrets of the SAT" makes this claim, too, and in exactly the same way the test prep course promoters do—they do not reveal what "improve" really means. Does it mean an improvement from one official SAT administration to another? Not necessarily. It could mean an improvement over some score calculated from any old practice exam, over a student's Preliminary Scholastic Assessment Test (PSAT) score, or pretty much anything else.[17]

Anybody can walk down to their corner bookstore, or go on line with any large-scale book seller, and purchase a test preparation booklet for $20, and simulate taking an SAT (and save the several hundred dollars one would pay to the Princeton Review or Stanley Kaplan). Anyone can get a sample test from the CollegeBoard for free. If the Public Broadcasting System had really desired to promote the public interest, it could have informed its audience of all the above, instead of suggesting to them that the quality of their future is inextricably tied to their purchase of services from these very privately inter-ested, for-profit test prep companies.

The trustworthy evidence suggests that many thousands of students are wasting their money on snake oil. What is the reaction of the PBS producers to this information? They discount the evidence because, after all, Nicholas Lemann does not trust it, and if Nicholas Lemann does not trust it...:

> You know, the studies on either side are not very good....there just isn't a good, kind of standard double-blind scientific study of this question. I sort of think, you know, 10 million freshman can't be wrong. If that many people are taking these test prep courses, they must do something.

Randomized experimental design studies are no good, we need "double blind scientific studies!" Does Nicholas Lemann understand this stuff?[18]

Not only do the fates of the seven shadowed students contradict the PBS producers' claims about the effect of expensive test preparation courses, they contradict the PBS producers' claims about the weight given to SAT scores and the effect on the admissions of minority students.

How do the documentary's producers square the admissions evidence of their seven shadowed students with their own assertions about the effect of SAT scores on diversity—the "assault on affirmative action" they assert to be a fact? They claim that Berkeley is an exception to the rule. It is not; of course, and they present no evidence that it is. They just declare it to be so. According to Nicholas Lemann, "Berkeley is still operating on the principle of merit. They're just defining merit more broadly than just that one number, the test score. And I suspect that the whole country is also going to move in that direction as this fight plays out over the years."

In point of fact, the "whole country" admits students in the same manner as Berkeley does, has for decades, and continues to do so. In point of fact, no college "defines merit" based on "just that one number." The "sky is falling" and implied bigotry rhetoric of the show is simply not justified.

Both the FairTest spokesperson and Nicholas Lemann claim that "all" the SAT does is predict "only" 15 percent of a student's first-year college grades. In truth, the actual percentage is a good deal higher than that; they are referring to the proportion of variance in first-year grades after all other predictive indicators are controlled for. They do not explain that, of course.[19] Furthermore, they do not tell the viewer that even the 15 percent unique contribution that they are willing to concede represents quite a lot of predictive power, more than letters of recommendation, extracurricular activities, and a number of other factors about which high school students may be just as "obsessed" and "fixated."

The PBS producers seem to have been successful in hiding the results of their show's experiment with the seven shadowed students and other facts inconvenient to their notions of truth and fact. At the PBS/*Frontline* web site, one can find a document listing the reactions to the show of several journalists. Their reactions reveal that most of them got the message the producers intended, and missed the evidence that was right on their television screens. Here is a summary:

Only in Pittsburgh, it seems, did other journalists see through the veneer.

Press Reaction to "Secrets of the SAT"—Excerpts

Nancy Rabinowitz (AP): Test bias -"success on SAT depends more on family income & ethnic background than on ability;" "test has strayed from original purpose of measuring merit"

Walter Goodman (*New York Times*): "no secret that advantages of privilege are still built into test system;" "Behind the criticisms of the test, as the documentary makes clear, is a larger debate over the goal of diversity in American society."

Connie Langland (*Cincinnati Enquirer*): "there are signs that the SAT may have outlived its usefulness as a predictor of success in college;" "Frontline hour comes to a surprising end"

Clarence Page (*Chicago Sun-Times*): After watching the Frontline documentary, he was "persuaded to pursue these actions" for his 10 year old child - "scrape together $700 to enroll him in one of the major preparation courses . . .; buy him one of the currently available CD-ROMS that will train him for taking the test; assure him in advance that the aptitude tests like the SAT are not really a measure of aptitude."

Additionally, he says the "program exposes how the original intent of the SAT . . . has been subverted and that there is a "high correlation with race, gender and family income and, mainly how well students are prepared in advance, technically and psychologically, to take the test"

Claims documentary is "one more nail in the coffin of standardized tests"

Jane Elizabeth Zemal (*Pittsburgh Post-Gazette*): No secrets to mastering test, "program should have been at least subtitled, 'The Fickle College Admissions Officer' or 'Dangerously Pushy Parents.' One of the only secrets of the show is which of the 6 students get into Berkeley.

Three profound contradictions must be accepted for Lemann and "Secrets of the SAT" to be credible. First, one must believe that the SAT means almost everything and that it means almost nothing (depending on which argument serves best at any given moment)—each view is promoted by the documentary several times. Second, one should believe that the SAT is given too much credence (so we should get rid of it), and that it is given very little credence (so we should get rid of it)—each view is promoted by the documentary. Finally, one should also believe that the SAT is so general (not based on any actual curriculum) that you cannot study for it, and that one can easily ace the test simply by studying some tricks—each view is promoted by the documentary.

Combine those contradictions with some vulgar language, gobs of free advertising for hucksters, and what is one left with? Not very high quality work. Perhaps the saddest aspect of this very sad piece of award-winning journalism, however, is that is does a great deal to promote the very problem it purports to try to solve—it does its very best to create a "national obsession" over the SAT.

Notes

1. The SAT is the primary admissions exam for state universities in about half the U.S. states, mostly on the East and West Coasts and in Texas. The public universities in most of the states in between the Sierras and Appalachians use the rival American College Test (ACT). Because the SAT is the admissions test of choice in more populous states, however, and in most private colleges with pretensions, it accounts for almost two-thirds of college admissions test taking.
2. Ralph Nader's organization, for example, sponsored a large tome called *The Reign of ETS*, which pulls no punches in its assault on the SAT, which is developed, analyzed, and scored by the Educational Testing Service (ETS), under contract to the College Entrance Examination Board (CollegeBoard).
3. The SAT was until several years ago, of course, named the Scholastic Aptitude Test. There was, and still is, some debate about whether one can test "aptitude," but the theory underlying the concept goes something like this. We learn largely through an accumulation of knowledge (e.g., once you have learned analytical geometry, you can learn calculus more easily and quickly). Those who have a very broad foundation of knowledge, thus, have a larger "base" from which to learn more. Put another way, they have more potential to learn more. So, one would assume that the broader one's base of knowledge is the greater potential one has for learning more and for learning it more quickly. The SAT tends to include many test items on "foundational" information—vocabulary and grammar, mathematics only through algebra and geometry, logic, and abstract analytical reasoning.

    "Achievement" tests, by contrast, focus on certain topics with strictly bounded domains. An achievement test on algebra includes only algebra test items, and so on.
4. They do not mention, however, the continual growth in the number of colleges using the SAT—102 added since 1990—bringing the total to 1,450 four-year institutions (Kiesler 1998).
5. Probably the optimal strategy for a student with genuine test anxiety would be to take and retake and retake sample ACTs or SATs right out of these test preparation

books under simulated (i.e., timed) conditions. Buy all the test prep books that exist if need be and "take the test" as many times as possible.

6. At best, a student's high school record explains only 44 percent of the variation in first year college grades. SAT scores alone explain 42 percent of the variation. To a large extent, however, high school record and SAT scores represent the same thing, mastery of academic subject matter. Thus, when both high school record and SAT scores are used together in equations to predict students' first-year college grades, the two predictive factors overlap. If SAT scores are put in the equation first, high school record adds only a comparatively smaller amount of predictive power. Likewise, if high school record is put in the equation first, SAT scores add only a comparatively smaller amount of predictive power. After subtracting the proportion of predictive power that the two predictive factors share in common, SAT scores predict an additional 15 percent of the variation in first-year college grades. This 15 percent predicted by the SAT alone represents an incremental increase in predictive power when added to the equation. See Willingham et al. 1990, *Predicting College Grades*, chapters 5 and 12; Bridgeman, McCamley-Jenkins, and Ervin 2000

7. Walter Haney of Boston College is often quoted on this issue. See, for example, L. May, D. Goldberg, or P. Sacks (1999a).

8. Recall that high school GPA predicts about 40 percent of college grades. Critics concede that the SAT predicts as much, but also that it predicts 15 percent in addition to high school GPA. That is, 15 percent of the SAT college prediction is unique to the SAT, and would not exist without the SAT. Fifteen percent is 38 percent of 40 percent. One gets a 38 percent increase in predictive power by adding the SAT to the mix. For the critics' statements, see the *Frontline* documentary transcripts at www.pbs.org, and read the comments of Bob Shaefer of FairTest, or Nicholas Lemann.

9. Recall that it cost $90,000 (in per-student public education costs) to get us to the point where we could predict 40 percent of one student's college performance (the predictive power of the high school GPA), or $30,000 if one counts just high school expenses. Meanwhile, a $25 SAT exam can predict an additional 15 percent of one student's college performance. An incremental benefit of 38 percent (15 percent added to 40 percent equals 55 percent, and 55 percent is 38 percent higher than 40 percent) requires an incremental cost of 0.03 or 0.08 percent ($25 added to an education cost of $90,000 or $30,000 is an increase of 0.03 or 0.08 percent). Thirty-eight percent divided by 0.03 equals 1,250 and, divided by 0.08 equals 475. Thirty-eight percent more additional K-12 education would cost $34,000 (using K-12 costs as a base) or $11,000 (using high school's cost as a base).

10. A Stanley Kaplan course fee should only be counted as an unnecessary and avoidable cost unless it can be shown with objective evidence that it provides some benefit over and above what a student might obtain from reading the SAT instruction materials on her own.

11. Achieving this maximum efficiency, of course, would be very difficult. One would need to have very detailed information about the characteristics and preferences of all the applicants and all the colleges in the country. It is a huge database management and optimization problem and clearly unrealistic. But, that would be required to attain maximum allocative efficiency.

12. Perhaps one could put together a survey of college applicants, asking them how much time they devote to studying candidate colleges and how much time they save by eliminating some colleges from consideration and how much they improve their probabilities of getting accepted at a college they might like by focusing their

efforts on applying to colleges that are more likely to accept them, given their ACT or SAT scores. Such a survey is certainly feasible, but far too large a project for this author alone.

13. ETS can roughly calculate the quantitative effect of the range restriction because they have information from a huge pool of SAT-takers, they know to which colleges they apply, they know at which ones they get accepted, and they know which one each accepts. Out of this pool of applicants, they can statistically create artificially diverse groups, such as might occur absent the existence of an SAT and the public dissemination of SAT score ranges, groups that are diverse because of their different grade-point averages, for example, but not because of their SAT scores.

14. The "rationale" is that one who "scores well" on standardized tests should be grateful for the "gift" that they have and not wish to punish those who just happen to not "score well on standardized tests." This rationale spins off the belief, promoted fiercely by public education's vested interests, that standardized tests are unrelated to study, learning, and knowledge. It is as if those "who do well on tests" were genetically lucky. Their superior performance has nothing whatsoever to do with them paying more attention in class, studying more, being more organized in their study habits, devoting more of their attention to academic matters and less to sports, socializing, and watching television. No, the "ability to do well on standardized tests" is completely unrelated to all those behaviors. It is, instead, a genetic trait that some lucky kids receive by accident and other, unlucky kids do not.

15. On the topic of affirmative action, there seems to have been some more effort made for balanced coverage. Three advocates in favor of Affirmative Action in admissions (not counting the documentary's narrator) were given 21 lines of commentary, according to the transcript, whereas two opponents were given 16 lines of commentary.

16. Conspicuously missing were any poor or working-class white students, who might have represented the group most directly and adversely affected by affirmative action programs.

17. Moreover, the test prep course promoters do not reveal that, on average, students who take the actual SAT a second time improve their scores slightly anyway, simply from practice and familiarity with the format and probable content, even if they have not participated in any formal preparation outside the test room. That is why some colleges discount scores from second SAT test administrations.

18. Sure, Nicholas Lemann writes well. But, writing well, of itself, does not make one...a logician, a scientist, an historian of science, a cognitive psychologist, a policy wonk, a testing expert, nor anyone Americans should necessarily trust to any degree to set policy that determines how their own children will be treated for 20,000 hours of their lives, or how $120,000 per student of tax dollars will be spent.

19. They also do not explain the effect of "restriction of range" on this "predictive validity" measure; adjust for restriction of range and the predictive power of the SAT is higher still.

4

Campaigns: Texas, the Early Years

As any Texan will tell you, Texas is unique. It is a big state with an independent inclination. Indeed, as any Texan will tell you, Texas operated as an independent nation for a while and chose, of its own volition, to join the United States. Texans are not cowed by the Northeast or the West Coast. They do not feel inferior. They do not necessarily do things the ways others would like.

So it is with the way they run the schools. Texans have the audacity to think they have a right to run their own public schools, the schools they pay for and to which they send their children. For almost two decades now, the vested interests in education have feared, hated, and focused on Texas.

A favorite bogeyman of mainstream education professors, local son and corporate leader H. Ross Perot, headed a blue ribbon commission in the early 1980s that studied the Texas school system, long considered one of the country's poorest performers. The commission made many recommendations, some of which were implemented in some form. One finding of the commission was that some Texas teachers were illiterate and there were no high-stakes requirements for new teachers. One outcome of the commission's recommendations was the development of a basic literacy test, the Texas Examination of Current Administrators and Teachers (TECAT), and a requirement that all teachers pass it. By all accounts, the test was extremely easy; nonetheless, some education researchers opposed it.

The federally funded Center for Research on Evaluation, Standards, and Student Testing (CRESST), based at UCLA's Education School, conducted a benefit-cost analysis of the test and decided the net benefits were negative, by about $70 million. Indeed, they were extremely critical of every aspect of the test. They recommended that the test not be high-stakes and that, if the test were used at all, failure should, at most, mean a teacher be required to take a literacy course.

Skirmish—The Texas Teacher Test

The TECAT was a paper-and-pencil test of basic literacy skills, was born out of a concern of the citizens of Texas that weakly regulated state teacher colleges were producing graduates unqualified to teach. Originally, the TECAT was intended to include both a basic literacy section and a content-area section, but the former section alone survived the deliberations among the legislature and the various interested groups in time for the test administration in March of 1986.

The CRESST report portrayed the acceptance of the TECAT as a quid pro quo of the teacher's union, agreed to in return for a salary increase in the midst of the state fiscal crisis caused by the collapse in oil prices in the early 1980s. The test had high stakes—a teacher was required to pass to maintain teacher certification. The test was also widely regarded to be extremely simple. The CRESST authors reported that state newspapers displayed easy questions from the TECAT alongside stories of large numbers of teachers participating in study sessions for the exam.

Among the CRESST authors' many criticisms of the test was the assertion that the costs were enormous and easily outweighed the benefits. The authors were not shy about stating their opinions, either. Points critical of the TECAT were listed along with the authors' preferred alternatives. Even in the executive summary, one finds editorial comments such as:

- An atmosphere of stress and bitterness was created by the high-stakes, of literally losing your job if you failed. *Many said the effect would have been different if not passing meant having to take a college refresher course.*
- Counting a teacher in-service day to take the test and district-sponsored workshops, the total public cost was $35.5 million. (*Alternative uses of these dollars to serve the same end might have been to create a fund to support the legal costs of districts seeking to fire incompetent teachers.*)
- Private costs in teacher time and preparation expenditures were an additional $42 million. (*Alternative uses of this resource might have been to require more advanced study by teachers.*)

The authors' clear preference was to preserve the status quo, eschew accountability requirements, and continue the citizens' sole reliance on input measures and trust in the education schools' own quality control to provide the teachers who taught their children at their expense. The authors also criticized the TECAT as simplistic, too narrow in format, and too general in content, but they did not advocate a "better" testing program. They favored eliminating teacher tests altogether.

Perhaps the most ironic of the authors' opinions coupled two conflicting assertions. The test was easy, simplistic, and beneath the dignity of professional educators, and so studying for the test should not be counted as a benefit. At the same time, the teachers, their union, and the school districts were afraid that many would fail the test, so a massive effort was undertaken to prepare the teachers for it and that should be counted as a cost. CRESST's point-of-view colored its analysis and affected its benefit-cost calculations.

Table 4.1 lists the costs and benefits as the authors calculated them. The authors decided that the TECAT produced a $53 million net cost. In their view, the development of the test itself accounted for only about $5 million, or less than 10 percent of the total cost of the test of $54 million. Three general categories of costs comprised the rest of the total: a day's worth of teachers' in-service time used for the test administration; time and materials used in test preparation workshops organized by the school districts; and time and materials spent by teachers privately.

Table 4.1
Costs and Benefits of the Texas Teacher Test According to CRESST
(figures are supposed to represent annualized values)

CRESST estimate	Cost component
-$5,065,500	Test development & administration
-26,260,000	Teacher inservice day to take test
- 4,150,000	Preparation workshops and review - done by the school districts and, thus, paid for by the taxpayer
-43,152,000	Private teacher costs in study time, paid-for workshops, and purchased study materials
+25,295,466	Salary savings from dismissed teachers
-$53,470,534	CRESST TOTAL

The authors' benefit-cost analysis of the TECAT, however, is full of mistakes. The mistakes take several forms:

• arbitrary inclusions or exclusions of benefits or costs;
• miscalculations of the value of time, specifically, the value of teachers' after-hours time and the compounded value of recurring benefits; and
• counting gross costs when net costs (that include the value of countervailing benefits) would be more appropriate and the authors are making net cost conclusions.

Correcting just the more obvious of their mistakes, pushes the TECAT program's net benefits into the black, and by a wide margin. The CRESST authors' -$53 million turns into +$300 million. A summary listing of the authors' mistakes is provided in Table 4.2. A summary of the recalculation is provided in Table 4.3, which will be discussed later.

Table 4.2
CRESST's *The Texas Teacher Test* as a Benefit-Cost Analysis—
A Summary of the Cost Mis-Allocations

- arbitrary inclusions or exclusions of benefits or costs:
    — exclusion: more than half the dismissed teachers "do not count" in the benefit calculations—those in vocational education, industrial arts, special education, business education, and kindergarten—because, the authors argue, literacy is not important in their work
    — inclusion: teacher time spent taking the test during one of their prescribed-topic in-service days is counted as a pure cost, implying that tests are not acceptable vehicles for teaching subject matter, while passive accumulation of seat time during lectures (with no accountability for listening) is an acceptable vehicle for learning
- miscalculations of the value of time:
    — they value teachers' after-hours time at their full salary rate; and
    — they ignore the future value of recurring benefits.
- counting gross costs when net costs (that include the value of countervailing benefits) would be more appropriate and the authors are making net-cost conclusions;
    — (e.g., Why would teachers take the non-required test preparation workshops on their own time if there was no benefit to be had?).

Here is how the recalculation is done. Taking their mistakes one-at-a-time, and in order:

Arbitrary Inclusions or Exclusions:

Cost of one in-service day. The authors arbitrarily include as a cost at least one item that should not be counted as a cost—$26 million for the teacher in-service day used for the test administration. By counting this as a pure cost, the authors assumed that the best alternative use for the teachers' time would have been something they considered to be fully worthwhile, like a day's teaching, or in-service workshops with topics that each teacher chose herself to meet her own most significant needs (no comment on whether teachers generally spend their in-service time productively). This implies, however, that if it had not been for the TECAT there either would not have been an in-service day or the teachers would have been able to choose their in-service topic.

Such was not the case. In Texas at the time, half of the required in-service days' topics were of the teachers' choosing, but the other half were reserved by the education authorities for subject matter of particular general import. On these latter days, the state or district education authorities required that teachers participate in in-service activities of the authorities' choosing. On

the test administration day in 1986, the teachers were scheduled to participate in an in-service activity of the authorities' choosing (Texas Education
Agency 1994). The authorities decided that teacher literacy was the most
pressing issue at the time and determined that that particular in-service day
would be devoted to that issue, as was their prerogative. The test format was
their chosen means for inducing the teachers to study to improve their literacy skills if they needed to. The "next best use" (i.e., the "opportunity
cost") of the in-service day was for some other topic *necessarily* of less importance (necessarily, because if another topic had been more important, it would
have been chosen).

The authors cannot legitimately count the teachers' time as a cost, then,
unless they wish to argue that taking a high-stakes test (and the studying and
heightened attention that it induces) is an inferior form of learning to sitting
passively in a chair while a lecturer talks at you. In order to justify counting
the in-service day a total loss (a pure cost) as they do, they must have concluded that one learns nothing from tests or the process of studying for and
taking tests and that one always learns a significant, appreciable amount by
attending someone else's lecture.

Presumably, the authors would have considered that a lecture on literacy
skills would have been an acceptable, "non-costly" use of the teachers' time
on that in-service day.

Benefit of dismissing illiterate teachers. The only benefit included in the
entire study was calculated as the sum of the salaries of the teachers who were
dismissed after failing the TECAT after multiple opportunities to pass it. If
Texans' could hire a literate teacher to replace an illiterate one, they were
presumably getting value for their investment that they previously had not.

This may seem like a crude way to count the benefits, but it's really not so
bad. Teachers were given much help to pass the TECAT—study sessions,
coaching, and multiple chances. And, by all accounts, the test was extremely
easy. It was highly likely that if a teacher could not pass the TECAT, the
teacher *was* illiterate. New teachers hired to replace the dismissed ones would
have had to pass the TECAT, and so were far more likely to be literate.

But the authors decided that only some of the dismissed teachers were
relevant to this issue, counting the salaries of 887 of the dismissed teachers,
while not counting the salaries of the other 1,063. Their rationale for this
exclusion was that the 887 counted were in "academic" jobs where their
illiteracy could adversely affect the quality of their teaching, while the 1,063
not counted were in "non-academic" jobs where their illiteracy allegedly
would not affect the quality of their work.

Superficially, the principle makes sense. A custodian, for example, may
not need basic literacy skills to perform her job effectively, whereas teachers
obviously do. So which employees did the authors' categorize as "non-academic?" The answer: kindergarten teachers; music and art teachers; ESL teach-

ers; industrial arts teachers; business education teachers; counselors; and physical education teachers. The authors asserted that, though literacy skills affect the quality of teaching in "academic" subjects, they are not important to these subjects. "Non-academic" teachers and students would likely feel shocked and insulted to hear this assertion. Parents of the affected students would likely feel outrage. The authors' assertion seems elitist and economic-class biased. It was also very presumptuous. The state of Texas decided that minimal literacy skills should be required of kindergarten, vocational education, and the other groups of teachers the authors wished to exclude. And it was, after all, Texas's decision to make, not the authors'.

Including *all* the dismissed teachers as the authors should have done, one calculates an annual benefit of $55,610,100 million rather than the $25,295,466 million of the authors. The authors arbitrarily excluded some pertinent benefits.

The authors also refused to consider another 8,000 teachers who never showed up to take the TECAT. While it is certainly fair to assume that most of these were probably teachers who had planned to leave the teaching profession, or leave Texas, anyway, probably some number of them were teachers who decided, while studying for the TECAT, that they could not pass it.

Miscalculating the value of time. Moreover, benefits from the dismissal of illiterate teachers recurred; they continued for years afterwards; they were not just one-time-only benefits.[1] A dismissed teacher was prevented from teaching for years,[2] one should presume for the average remaining duration of the average teacher's career. Applying a discount rate of 7 percent and assuming conservatively that the illiterate teachers would have held on to their teaching jobs for another five years on average (had they not been dismissed for failing the TECAT), the benefit mushrooms to $283,625,416 (the calculated net present value).[3] (Incidentally, there were no recurring costs. Each teacher needed to pass the TECAT only once.)

While the authors undervalued benefits by not considering their recurrent nature, they overvalued costs by valuing all teacher time, even their evening and weekend time, at the teachers' full-time wage rate. "Teacher study time" was the largest of the alleged costs, consisting of time teachers took away from their own personal time to study for the exam.

Studies show, however, that people do not value their personal time at their full wage rate. Economists' convention is to value personal time at a substantially lower rate—half the wage rate is typical—but some economists insist it should be less than that (see, for example, Hensher and Truong 1985; Mohring 1983). The adjustment here divides the authors' estimates by half.

In something of a mystery, the authors valued teacher time in district-sponsored test study workshops at $30 an hour. The real average hourly teacher wage at the time was about $15, not $30. Moreover, that hourly wage would be appropriate only if these workshops took place during regular business hours, but they did not. They were conducted on weekends. So the teachers' time should be valued at half their wage rate (or less)—a standard valuation for personal time. That is $7.50 an hour for Texas teachers in 1986.

Counting gross costs rather than net costs. Discussion of how to value the teachers' time begs another question. Why would the teachers have chosen to spend their free time in workshops if they had expected to get no benefit for it? The correct answer is, they would not have. If they had expected a benefit, should not that be considered, and should it not cancel out the cost of teacher time imbedded in the workshops and personal study time? The answer is, it should. There were countervailing benefits to the costs. Thus, net costs are nonexistent by comparison with gross costs.

There is some empirical evidence that the teacher study time had a payoff. On the basis of preliminary field tests, it was projected that 12 percent of teachers and administrators would fail the TECAT, yet only 3.3 percent of test-takers failed the exam on the first try. Studying, then, appears to not have been valueless. The citizens of the state of Texas had decided that minimal literacy skills were important for their teachers, and it appears that studying improved those skills.

The authors, however, asserted that the test had no value and study for the test had no value. They wrote in their executive summary, "Only 3% of teachers interviewed said they learned new skills during their test preparation." Odd statement, since one would have hoped that basic literacy skills were not new to teachers. Indeed, one would hope that the teachers did not need a refresher course on such basic skills. Nonetheless, no one forced them to go to the workshops. They went of their own volition based on their own expected values for the workshops.

Besides, the authors' statement is false and misleading on its face. The 3 percent figure is an artifact of the authors' categorization scheme for their interview responses: "Percentages were calculated based on the leading answer given by each respondent." Thus, many more than 3 percent might have claimed to have learned new skills, but the authors refused to count any responses other than a first one. Thirty-three percent of the respondents gave as their first response, "Brushed up skills and reviewed terminology." That has no value?

The authors repeatedly attacked the test for its alleged low-level nature. But, ultimately that is beside the point, because the authors would have been opposed to a "high-level" test, too. It is beside the point, too, because it is clear that the citizens of Texas wanted some accountability in their teacher certification system, and would not have been content with the minor modifications of the status quo—consisting of more input requirements—that the authors recommend. Even the authors admit that half the teachers interviewed thought that the test accomplished its purpose, "to weed out incompetent teachers and reassure the public."

Table 4.3 recalculates the authors' base numbers, correcting for mistakes in their calculations.

Table 4.3
Social Net Benefits of the Texas Teacher Test According to CRESST—
Corrected for Mistakes

Amount	Cost or benefit component/Correction
-$53,470,534	Authors' TOTAL
+30,314,634	correcting for the arbitrary exclusion of vocational education, special education and other "non-academic" teachers as not needful of basic literacy skills
-23,155,900	Sub-total
+283,625,416	accounting for the recurrent nature of the benefits
+260,469,516	Sub-total
+26,260,000	correcting for the arbitrary inclusion of the teachers' prescribed-topic in-service day that was used for the test administration as a pure cost
+286,729,516	Sub-total
+22,026,000	correcting for the overvaluation of teachers' personal time and the mystery of the $30/hour workshops
+308,755,516	Sub-total
+23,826,000	accounting for the countervailing benefits of the teacher workshop and study time
+332,581,516	CORRECTED TOTAL

Other benefits. Tests provide information. And they do so rather inexpensively. It turns out that the teachers' TECAT score, as simple a measure as it may have been, was correlated with student achievement. Ron Ferguson used TECAT scores and other data in an effort to predict student achievement in Texas (see Ferguson 1991a, 1991b). His articles have been used to argue that higher levels of education spending can, in certain circumstances, produce higher levels of student achievement, in this case because teachers with higher TECAT scores tended to get paid more.

While controlling for other, traditionally used predictors, he found that the TECAT score provides additional, significant predictive power. In the lower grades, a teacher's TECAT score was the strongest single predictor of student achievement—the same test that CRESST described as meaningless and worthless. Ferguson found that the teacher's TECAT score explained 48 percent of the variance in predicting 5th-grade student reading scores in majority black school districts, and 26 percent in predicting 9th-grade student reading scores in majority black school districts. The influence of teacher TECAT score was stronger than that of any other predictors, including parents' education, family poverty level or number of parents, or class and district size. The ethnicity of the teacher was not a significant predictor. Teacher TECAT score was the strongest predictor for 5th-grade reading scores in majority Hispanic school districts, too, and the second strongest predictor of 9th-grade reading scores in majority Hispanic school districts.

Ferguson ended his studies with quite the opposite attitude of CRESST. He noticed that disadvantaged and minority children tended to get the teachers scoring lowest on the TECAT, and he thinks it was unfair...to the students.

In another, separate article, economists Lewis Solmon and Cheryl Fagnano conducted a re-analysis of the data from the CRESST study and found the net benefits to be large, probably in excess of $1.25 billion. Among other things, they estimated the value over many students' lifetimes of the increased learning they would gain from more literate teachers (see Solmon and Fagnano 1990).

Private net benefits—Texas teachers. CRESST strongly implied that the TECAT was a failure not only for all Texans, but for the teachers and other educators, especially. The TECAT embarrassed the profession because the teachers made such a fuss over an exceptionally easy exam, and some failed. The TECAT caused unnecessary stress, and the authors view stress as a cost. The message of the authors is, do not make such a deal again.

But a brief look at the benefits and costs suggests a different story. The teachers who did not lose their jobs won big (see Table 4.4). Table 4.4 counts the salary increase that the teachers won as part of the TECAT deal, along with a promise of smaller class sizes (thus, a reduced workload) and an increase in the length of the kindergarten day from half- to full-day (thus, more work and more pay for some teachers and greater seniority for others). (Incidentally, these costs did not get counted in either the authors' social accounting or mine, for legitimate reasons. These amounts are "transfers" from the taxpayers to the teachers. From society's perspective, the cost to the taxpayers is equally balanced by the benefit to the teachers and, thus, there is no net cost or net benefit to society.)

What was a private benefit to the teachers, however, was a cost to the taxpayers. Why were they willing to pay so much? The CRESST authors made it clear that the legislative deal was a straight quid pro quo—the teachers got their salary increase, reduced workloads, and full-day kindergarten and the taxpayers got the TECAT—some assurance that their teachers met a minimal level of literacy. How much was that assurance worth to Texas taxpayers? Quite a lot. Table 4.5 summarizes Texas's willingness-to-pay for an assurance that their teachers were minimally literate. "Willingness-to-pay" is simply economists' jargon for empirical evidence of the level of demand.

Table 4.4
Private Net Benefits of the Texas Teacher Test Using
CRESST Base Numbers, but Recalculated to Reflect Texas Teachers'
Perspective, with Salary Increase Included
(all figures are net present values, single annual figures)

Amount	Cost or benefit component
-$43,766,000	Private teacher cost of workshops, materials, and supplies
+$1,732,100,000	Salary increase over five years (one year = $394.9 million — our estimate using figures from CRESST report)
(+)	Smaller class size (i.e. reduced workload)
(+)	1/2 day kindergarten required, adding more jobs
+ $1,732,100,000 + reduced workloads + more jobs	CORRECTED TOTAL (annualized, for five year period)

Table 4.5
Texans' "Willingness-to-Pay" for Assurance of a
Minimal Level of Teacher Literacy

Includes:

- *expected* nominal cost of test ($3 million)
- teachers' salary increase ($1,723 million over 5 years)
- salaries of new teachers hired
    - to reduce class sizes
    - to extend the kindergarten day

TOTAL? Well over $1.7 billion, or 4 percent of education budget annually

Texas's willingness-to-pay for an assurance of teacher literacy also demonstrates that taxpayers *are* willing to pay more for education *if they can get something in return* from the education system.

Postscript

If CRESST was right about public opinion, the TECAT controversy was a messy affair that left many people disappointed. Furthermore, according to the authors at least, the TECAT produced unanticipated costs. So, the authors concluded, do not have teacher tests.

What of the concerns of the citizens of Texas that there was no account-ability in the teacher certification system? The authors recommended putting more money into the same system, perhaps changing some input require-ments, and making no changes to the status quo.

An alternative that CRESST did not consider would have been to move the TECAT to an earlier point in the teacher training process, say at the end of graduate school, or even at the beginning of graduate school. This would have met the concerns of the citizens of Texas. It would have achieved all the same benefits. But, most of the costs that the authors enumerated would have evaporated. There would have been no loss of teacher time. The responsibil-ity for preparing the teachers for the test would have been placed on the teacher training schools or, better, on the potential education students them-selves. And, best of all, the time of unqualified would-be teachers (and their students) would not have been wasted.

A reasonable alternative to the authors' complaints about the alleged sim-plistic nature of the TECAT would have been to initiate a required "higher-level" exam for teachers, in addition to the TECAT.

As it turns out, the citizens of Texas did not follow CRESST's advice. Rather, they followed the path just drawn, making the basic literacy exam an entrance exam for education school and requiring new teachers to pass an-other, newly created exam that focused on each teacher's content area and on pedagogy and professional development. They increased the benefits and reduced the costs, even according to the authors' creative benefit-cost ac-counting criteria. And they ended up with more tests, not fewer.

"Educational Costs" of Testing and "The Contradictions of School Reform"

Another education researcher taking up the mantle against testing in Texas is a Rice University professor who has been quoted widely in the press na-tionwide in recent years.[4] Much of her work was funded by the taxpayers (through a U.S. Education Department grant) and a Mellon Fellowship. Con-veniently, her book was published in the presidential year 2000. In it, the author still invoked the decades-old legacy of the reviled H. Ross Perot who, according to another education professor, had once said, presumably in refer-ence to education groups: "'We've got to drop a bomb on them, we've got to nuke them–that's the way you change these organizations.'"

Greatly enamored of this single alleged statement of Perot's, the Rice edu-cation professor wrote:

> No policy-maker expected teachers or students to provide expertise into what schools needed…. After all, schools were the problem. Instead, a businessman was brought in to "fix" things. And to fix it, Ross Perot decided to "nuke" the system.

> When the state system was "nuked," the bombs did not fall on the...state education agency...the state bureaucracy [or]...central office administrators. The legislated reforms...fell instead on the classrooms, on the teachers and their students. Teachers and students suffered the "collateral damage" from Perot's reform "nukes." These reforms included systems for testing teachers and for evaluating their classroom performance. They included reinforcement of systems for prescribing curriculum and testing students.

So there you have it—testing and evaluating teachers, prescribing curriculum, and testing students–are bad, awful things. No, more than awful, they have an effect on children equal to that of being annihilated in the explosion of a nuclear bomb.

The Rice professor's book has been richly praised by some fairly prominent and well-funded defenders of the status quo. Some nuggets of wisdom from the book jacket:

> "...provides dramatic examples of the consequences of standardization for school reform. A seminal work! It is incisive, eloquent, and brave."
>
> "In stunning detail...new research shows for the first time what actually happens when these [standardization] policies make their way behind classroom doors.... As policymakers attempt to reform schooling with standardization and accountability, they will exacerbate the very problems they seek to solve."
>
> "...demonstrates how...impressive achievements are undermined by sometimes well-intentioned but nearly always misguided efforts at standardization of curriculum and assessment."

The lesson being, as always, that education must be left to the "professionals" to operate as they see fit. Any interference by the public, parents, or their elected representatives will only make things worse than they already are!

Postscript: CRESST Does Not Much Like Arizona, Either

In the face of overwhelming public support for high-stakes tests, the taxpayer-funded Center for Research on Evaluation, Standards, and Student Testing (CRESST) has consistently told its benefactors for twenty years, and at the cost of tens of millions of taxpayer dollars, that they should not bother with them, as the "research" shows that high-stakes tests, multiple-choice tests, and pretty much any meaningful standardized student tests can be terrible things.

CRESST has produced a substantial quantity of top-quality technical psychometric research, conducted by some of the world's foremost, scholars. The quality of CRESST's work takes a nose-dive, however, when its researchers venture into the field of testing policy.

Probably, the most important feature of CRESST research on testing policy issues is the degree to which it narrows the topic. You would think that with the many millions of dollars we taxpayers have given them over the past twenty years, CRESST reports would be expansive and wide-reaching. Just the opposite has been the case. The reports on policy issues have used very little source material, generally that to be obtained from CRESST researchers themselves and a small circle of colleagues.

This narrowness has two effects: it serves to promote the careers of CRESST researchers; and it hides the abundant research and evidence that might lead one to conclusions other than those favored by CRESST. While twenty years of CRESST reports have amply discussed a plethora of real and (mostly) imagined problems with high-stakes testing, for example, not a single one among over 500 has broached the subject of high-stakes testing's benefits. Nor have any CRESST reports broached the topic of the considerable validity, reliability, and fairness problems associated with the exclusive reliance on the traditional alternatives to standardized tests, such as student grade-point averages, that CRESST favors. Anyone who thinks they will read broadly "the state of knowledge" or the "state of the art" in testing research in CRESST reports will be disappointed. They will read only one side of a very thin slice.

One prevalent CRESST theme is that "politicians" and the general public have no business making testing policy or running testing programs. These tasks should be left to testing "experts" and "educators," who are familiar with the "research" on testing. A good example of this theme, that "noneducators" have no business involving themselves in testing issues, is provided by a series of CRESST reports that ridicule the government of the state of Arizona and vilify its then-current state superintendent, Lisa Graham Keegan. The series is comprised of, at least, CRESST reports 321, 373, 380, 381, 420, 425, 468. CRESST report number 426 bears my favorite title, "The Politics of Assessment: A Case Study of Policy and Political Spectacle."

Here are some excerpts from this series of CRESST reports on the "Political Culture" of Arizona:

> The dominant discourse was union-bating and educator-bashing, federal mandate— and court order-defying. Right-wing extremists often made the news, as did religious conservatives. Assessment policy could hardly be immune from this climate, particularly because of the relationship between political and pedagogical conservatism...
>
> ...right-wing organizations typically extol the virtues of ...phonics...and math by memorization of math facts. They repudiate the teaching of higher-order thinking, whole language and bilingual education, and other recommended approaches of progressivism and constructivism (Dewey and Vygotsky's communist leanings make these perspectives suspect)...
>
> These preferences have the characteristics of fixed ideologies, in that they seem founded in biblical interpretation, are immune to fair debate, and tend to demonize the opposition...
>
> Noneducator interests [in Arizona] dominate policy making over educators'. The primary policy value in the state is efficiency (tax savings) rather than excellence or

equity. Education was defined as an economic function long before it became so defined at the national level.... Arizona is a right-to-work state, and teachers have very little say in a climate that systematically dismisses them.

The media also play a role in [Arizona's] political culture. The two newspapers are owned by Dan Quayle's family. They express the values of efficiency and antiprofessionalism on a daily basis.... They never mention an educational issue without using the term "educational establishment." With great relish, they publish the yearly results of student assessments and use these or any indicators as the source of editorial handwringing about the failure of public schools.

In spite of Arizona being near the bottom in spending on education, health, and social programs...the legislature...passed the largest tax decrease in state history...the polluter protection bill...the "veggie hate crimes" bill...charter school legislation [and] the governor...sought to avoid the federal mandates to provide school services to immigrants and to protect endangered species and fragile ecosystems.

Against this landscape of political culture, the organization of schooling struggles.

[CRESST] is too taken aback to provide much consolation. Long since having given up on speaking truth to power, [CRESST] has the modest expectation that research should contribute to reasoned debate about the effects of state assessment policy on school practices [but] the spectacle is far from over.

In November 1994, Lisa Graham won the election as Arizona Superintendent of Public Instruction...replacing staff with backgrounds in teaching and curriculum with people experienced in the private sector.

With no advance warnings and no expert or public debate...Graham announced that the [Arizona] performance test was "suspended."...Design teams of teachers, business leaders, and parents (but no curriculum specialists) were commissioned to write standards.... Hearings would then be conducted around the state...

CRESST thought these actions should be dropped in favor of "further research."

[Governor Symington signaled] to his appointees on the Board [of Education] to follow through on his conservative agenda and not give in to the professionals....[in] the confluence of Symington's bankruptcy and criminal indictments, his plan to seek reelection anyway, Keegan's own gubernatorial ambitions, and her open criticisms of his administration and calls for his resignation. Word was, he had even tried to lure her out of town to a governors' meeting on education that coincided with the board meeting.

At this point, the reader might wonder what these biased, pompous, and catty comments, culled from four reports in the CRESST series on Arizona testing policy, have to do with the testing research we all thought we were paying for. Here's the answer:

> ...mandated assessment programs are more than marks on optical scanning sheets, assignment of rubric scores to essays.... One must examine instead the dynamics of wins and losses in the political arena.

In its defense, CRESST's public relations officer might say that individual CRESST reports are written independently by independently minded researchers, and are independent of any CRESST group point of view. Perhaps, but it is CRESST's directors who decide which researchers get our money, and the biases of the researchers who write on policy issues have in every case been clear and obvious beforehand. Moreover, the outcomes of CRESST research tack in a monotonously steady direction.

Notes

1. James Caterall noticed this, too. See p. 4 of his report.
2. Though, dismissed teachers could keep trying, as often as they wished, to pass the TECAT, which was administered a few times each year.
3. The discount rate of 7 percent assumes the government's terms of borrowing and is based on the 1986 federal funds rate (of 6.81 percent), as found in the *Economic Report of the President, 1989*, p. 390.
4. See http://www.rethinkingschools.org/Archives/1404/tex144.htm and http://www.law.harvard.edu/groups/civilrights/conferences/testing98/drafts/mcneil_valenzuela.html.

5

Campaigns: Texas, the Presidential Election Year 2000

After discussions with several testing experts, a Washington Post reporter wrote a story, in the summer of 2000, during the heat of the presidential campaign, describing the standardized testing program in the state of Texas. The Texas Assessment of Academic Skills (TAAS) had been introduced in the early 1990s to test the basic skills of elementary school students, and passage was required for graduation from high school. The Post reporter here describes Texas classrooms before the introduction of the test, a period when Texas students ranked near the bottom on most national achievement measures, this way:

"creative, productive learning environments," "[a] culture of both equity and authentic academics," "rich curricula," "creative writing, literature, and science labs," "learning a variety of forms of writing, studying mathematics aimed at problem-solving and conceptual understanding," "teaching complex biology topics," and "the joy and magic of reading," "a substantive curriculum," "authentic teaching," "changing the futures for urban children."

And, after the TAAS was introduced?

"drudgery," "going over dreary one-paragraph passages," "repetitive drills, worksheets, and practice tests," "[teachers use] aggressive test drilling" and "test coaching," "...fosters an artificial curriculum...," "...not a curriculum that will educate these children for productive futures...," "[TAAS preparation] takes time from real teaching," "artificially shift teaching away from a focus on children's learning in favor of a format that held the teacher at the center," "excessive concern with discipline, mass processing of students for credentialing, overemphasis on efficiencies to the detriment of quality instruction," "[it is] de-skilling teachers' work, trivializing and reducing the quality of the content of the curriculum"

Moreover, the Post reporter told us that the TAAS was too difficult:

"drab factories for test preparation," entire instructional budgets spent on "commercial test preparation materials," schools "handed over to 'test prep' from New Year's through April," "TAAS [test] camps," "[Friday night] lock-ins...where students do TAAS 'drills' until sunup," prizes given to students who do well, and "students cannot graduate if they fail the exams."

Or, rather, perhaps, the TAAS was too easy:

"could be passed by many fifth-graders," "'low expectations' are 'cause for concern,'" "...aimed at the lowest level of skills and information..." "Artificially simplified curricula that had been designed by bureaucrats seeking expedient curricular format."

One would certainly have cause to fault the reporter for being contradictory and unclear and for trusting, essentially, only the "expert" sources on one side of the issue. But, given whom he interviewed, he probably accurately related what they said to him.

In hindsight, the 1980s controversy over Ross Perot's teacher education reform commission and the Texas Teacher Test seems a mere skirmish in the War on Testing. The larger campaign against the TAAS in the year 2000 represented a full frontal assault. Several anti-testing books and reports just happened to be released in the year preceding the election,[1] accompanied by hundreds of newspaper and magazine articles critical of Texas's testing program. Defenses of the TAAS in the media were virtually nonexistent.

George W. Bush was Texas's governor in the year 2000, and he was running for president, using education as one of his key campaign themes. Bush declared Texas's education innovations of the 1990s a success worth emulating throughout the United States, and those innovations included high-stakes testing. Though the TAAS had been developed under the watch of the two previous Democratic governors, Bush had continued the program with little change and much support.

The "October Surprise" of the 2000 Presidential Campaign

The noisiest battle of the rather one-sided 2000 campaign against testing occurred in October, less than a month before the election.

A small group of researchers at the Rand Corporation whose two most lucrative sources of contracts were likely to be threatened if George W. Bush was elected president decided to conduct an analysis of the Texas testing program. They said it was pure coincidence that their report was released just before the presidential election. They also said it was only coincidence that they chose to study Texas, rather than any number of other states with testing programs very similar to the one in Texas. As James A. Thomson, CEO of the "scrupulously nonpartisan institution" said, "Texas was studied because the state exemplifies a national trend toward using statewide exams as a basis for high-stakes educational decisions." In an unusual move, Rand paid for the study itself. Think of it as a public service from a generous corporate benefactor.

Rand could have studied the testing system in virtually any other industrialized country at any time in the past few decades, since all but a tiny handful have had popular high-stakes testing programs in place for decades. Rand also could have studied any number of other states or Canadian provinces that have had high-stakes testing programs for years. But, it simply just occurred to them in 2000, sort of out of the blue, that it was a good time to do their study, and that Texas was a good place. Ironically, pretty much every other anti-testing group in the country seemed to have received the exact same message, sort of out of the blue, just at the same time.

It was also only coincidence, surely, that this particular group of researchers at Rand spent most of its work time on contracts with two largely overlapping organizations as outspoken in their opposition to high-stakes standardized testing as the new Rand report was—the taxpayer-funded Center for Research on Evaluation, Standards, and Student Testing (CRESST) and the National Research Council's Board on Testing and Assessment (see, for example, Phelps 1999a, 2000d, 2000i).

This new Rand study faced a number of challenges from the start. First, there was the bothersome detail of two other recent, and very thorough, studies by Rand personnel extolling the virtues and successes of the high-stakes testing programs in Texas and North Carolina. These studies were conducted by other, more independent Rand researchers, without ties to any education interest groups.[2] This new study (hereafter, "NewRand") mentions just one of them and uses the standard finesse that that report claimed "more research was needed" to discount its findings. If one picks up those two studies, by David Grissmer and others, however, one for the National Education Goals Panel and the other published under Rand's banner, one will detect little equivocation. The evidence of the success of the Texas testing program is seen in the other two, more independent Rand reports to be strong and convincing.

Second, there was the bothersome detail of the rather obvious success of the Texas program, as verified, for just one example, by the coincident and substantial improvement of Texas students on the independent National Assessment of Educational Progress (NAEP). The NAEP is a "no-stakes" test funded by the federal government that, every two years, tests 4th, 8th, and/or 12th graders in national samples of schools on their knowledge of one or more of several major academic subjects. On some occasions, the NAEP also tests representative samples within states that wish to participate. Most do, NAEP state assessments usually involve 40 or more states. NAEP scores trends can be used as an unbiased check on TAAS score trends. If the TAAS score rise was for real, they could be reflected to some degree in NAEP score trends, though one should not expect a perfect correlation as there are many differences between the two tests.

As NAEP score increases represent the least controvertible evidence that the achievement gains in Texas are real, this NewRand report chose to attack that evidence in particular. One really has to admire these Rand researchers; it is not easy to fabricate a rationale for declaring the obvious to be false, but these are clever people and, darn it, they found a way. The NewRand report supports its case on four claims:

1. While there has been an improvement in fourth-grade NAEP mathematics scores in Texas over time, there has been no improvement in eighth-grade math scores or fourth-grade reading scores.
2. What improvement there is in math and reading does not last past fourth grade. Between the fourth and eighth grades, the gain in scores over time is no greater than the average for the nation.
3. Because Texas Assessment of Academic Skills (TAAS) scores have improved by a greater proportion than Texas' NAEP scores have improved, the TAAS scores must be "inflated" and unreflective of "real" gains in achievement.
4. "Evidence" from other studies of the TAAS supports the NewRand conclusions.

Here is an illustration of what the NewRand researchers were up against. Of all the states that have participated in all the state-level NAEP assessments in math and reading in the 1990s, only one other state, North Carolina, has improved its scores more than has Texas. North Carolina, of course, tests its students even more often, and for higher stakes, than Texas does.

If one simply adds up the scale-score gains (or losses) over time from the different NAEP administrations for each state, one finds these results: North Carolina increased by 33 scale points overall, Texas by 27 points, and Connecticut by 25 points. These top three states all test their students often. In Connecticut, high stakes are not attached for the students, but the state education department uses the test information to evaluate schools and districts in a rigorous manner. Connecticut's education department is as intrusive in local affairs as many European national education departments, their quality monitoring being as thorough and intensive. After the top three states, the cumulative scale score gains drop to 19 in Kentucky (another state with plenty of testing) and on down to -10 in D.C., which had no testing in the early 1990s. Figure 5.1 presents the situation graphically.

Texas's net cumulative score gains are more than twice the national average, yet, no matter how hard the NewRand group tried to find an improvement in Texas's NAEP scores, they just could not find it. In their words, they "generally found only small increases, similar to those observed nationwide, in the Texas NAEP scores." Were they looking at the same data?

NewRand finds Texas's gains to be no different than the nation's by separating the big picture above into several smaller pictures and then relying on

Figure 5.1
New Rand Report Says Texas No Better than Average: Net Cumulative Scale
Score Gains on State NAEP in the 1990s, by State

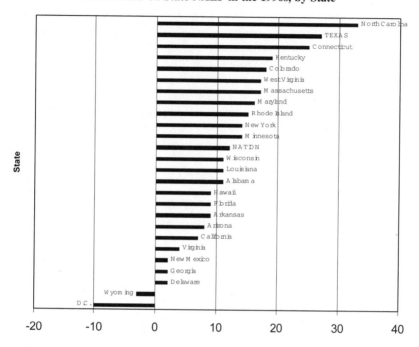

statistical-testing artifacts within each. This is invalid, of course, because the conclusion they make refers to the big picture, but they did not conduct a statistical test on the big picture. They could have, but they did not.

Instead, NewRand looked at a segment of gains in 4th-grade math, a segment of gains in 8th-grade math, and so on. With each segment they conducted a statistical test that relied on arguably standard, but still arbitrary, cutoff thresholds to determine "statistically significant" differences. For each separate case in isolation, there is nothing wrong with this. The NewRand researchers probably noticed, however, that for the segments in which the Texas gains failed to reach the cutoff points, they just barely did not make it. The Texas gains in the case of every segment were large by normal standards of "large," just not large enough in each and every segment to make the cutoff point for the statistical test NewRand chose to use in each case.

If one combines the various segments (in statistical jargon, this is called "pooling"), as in Figure 5.1, however, one can both increase the statistical power of the test (by increasing the sample size) and conduct the correct test, that for the NAEP performance of Texas as a whole, rather than for separate, discrete little bits. Combining separate tests, or subtests, at the same level of difficulty, even on different subject matter, is done all the time when identical scales are used. Witness the many studies that use SAT combined (verbal + math) scores in their analysis.[3] If the NewRand researchers want to say it is invalid to do that, even though only identical scales are used in comparison, they would also have to admit, if they were honest, that their proclamation that Texas's performance as a whole is just average is not supported by the separate little tests they used. At best, they have a "right" to make claims only about each separate little bit, not the whole. It is tempting to assume that NewRand broke the entire sample into smaller little bits deliberately, precisely so that the many separate statistical tests of the little bits would have less power. But, that would be a cynical assumption.

TAAS Gains are Disproportional to NAEP Gains, and So Cannot be "Real"

While the NewRand analysis discussed above could arguably fit into the murky category of misunderstanding or disagreements over methods, or some such, their next argument veers fairly close to gross misrepresentation.

Scores on two tests cannot be perfectly correlated without them being the exact same test. The TAAS and the NAEP are not the same test, nor are they supposed to be, so their scores cannot be perfectly correlated. The fact that the score increases in the TAAS over time were greater than Texas's students' score gains on the NAEP was to be expected. Any other result would reveal a serious problem. The TAAS contains subject matter that matches the curriculum standards of the state of Texas. The NAEP does not. Therefore, it is to be expected that Texas student scores on the TAAS will increase more than Texas student scores on the NAEP.[4]

There is nothing sacred about the content of the test used for comparison here, the NAEP. It no more represents "real" learning than the TAAS does. The NAEP tests a reasonable, but ultimately arbitrary, sample of academic subject matter. It is based on no legal curriculum, however, and NAEP content matches the curricular standards in no U.S. state. This is not to say that the NAEP is not a good test; it is. But, there is no sensible reason why performance on the TAAS should exactly match performance on the NAEP. The fact that Texas's students' score gains on the NAEP have been second best in the country provides evidence that the improved achievement of Texas's students is generalizable beyond the confines of Texas's curriculum. It can in no reasonable way be argued to be a failing.

If the NewRanders want to continue this line of reasoning, claiming that the TAAS must be deficient because its gains do not precisely mirror the NAEP's, they would also have to admit, if they were to be honest, that the situation must be worse in every other state in the country, except North Carolina. Ultimately, that is where their argument leads us if we assume that the NAEP should represent a mirror-image barometer of state test outcomes. The NewRanders would have to admit that, after North Carolina, Texas is the least worst state in the country on academic achievement gains. Relatively, even according to NewRand logic, Texas still ends up second best in the nation.

"Evidence" from Other Studies of the TAAS Supports the NewRand Conclusions

As verification of their work, the NewRanders mention the similar conclusions found by other testing-opponent researchers. Perhaps they did not read the "research" they cite, because they cite as evidence "facts" about the Texas testing program that are easily shown to be results of extraordinary research errors (accidental or otherwise) and, in some cases, complete fabrications.

For example, the NewRanders write:

> It is worth noting that even the relatively small NAEP gains we observed might be somewhat inflated by changes in who takes the test. As mentioned earlier, Haney (2000) provides evidence that exclusion of students with disabilities increased in Texas while decreasing in the nation, and Texas also showed an increase over time in the percentage of students dropping out of school and being held back. All of these factors would have the effect of producing a gain in average test scores that overestimates actual changes in student performance."

Every statement in this quotation can easily be shown to be false, and is in the section below.

Walter Haney's Texas Mirage

The most sustained, and creative, anti-testing, anti-Texas research of the year 2000 was Walter Haney's. This Boston College education professor labels the "Texas Miracle" a "mirage," and the Texas Assessment of Academic Skills (TAAS) a "sham."[5]

NAEP Scores

Haney argues that the positive correlation between TAAS score trends and National Assessment of Educational Progress (NAEP) trends for Texas are bogus because Texas manipulated NAEP participation levels, excusing an artificially high number of limited-English-proficient (LEP) students when the NAEP was administered in Texas. To arrive at this conclusion, he used the wrong numbers, otherwise miscalculated NAEP's and others' statistics, and might have just made some things up. In point of fact, NAEP score trends affirm the TAAS score gains.[6]

Haney then goes on to describe the evidence that proves, in his opinion, that "the apparent improvement" in academic achievement in Texas is not "real." His evidence consists of the following:

1. Retention rates prior to grade 4 (Haney argues that Texas holds more students back in the primary grades and, thus, its students taking the grade 4 NAEP are older than other states');
2. Rates of participation by students with disabilities (SD) and limited English proficiency (LEP) in the state NAEP (Haney argues that Texas excused more SD and LEP students from taking the NAEP, thus raising the NAEP scores for Texas, if one assumes that SD and LEP students would score low);
3. Level of effort to comply with NAEP's new criteria, as of 1996, for inclusion of SD and LEP students in the state NAEP (Haney argues that Texas did not cooperate with the national effort to include more SD and LEP students in the state NAEP and, instead, excused even more of them in 1996 than it had in 1992, thus biasing the trend of its NAEP scores upward); and
4. Relative average of state NAEP scores (Haney repeatedly points out that, regardless of what one thinks about trends in state NAEP scores, the average NAEP scores for Texas (and North Carolina) are not exemplary, they rest only near the national average.

Retention rates prior to grade 4. Haney writes:

> ...NAEP state assessments have focused on measuring the learning of students at particular grade levels, namely grades 4 and 8.... Thus, it is probably no accident that the two states identified in 1997 by the NEGP [National Education Goals Panel] as having made unusual "progress" on NAEP math assessments, Texas and North Carolina, have unusually high rates of failure and grade repetition before grade 4. (see Heubert and Hauser 1999, Table 6-1, corrected)

Haney is implying that Texas and North Carolina 4th graders do as well as they do, on average, only because so many of them are given extra time prior to 4th grade to learn. They are given the extra time—more time than students in other states get—because Texas and North Carolina hold more students back in the primary grades than other states do.

To check Haney's claims, I looked at Table 6-1 in the Heubert and Hauser book he references (pp. 138-147 in the corrected form of an errata sheet), and added up the retention rates for the primary grades (grades 1 through 3) for all the states listed in the table.

I do not get Haney's results. Out of the 19 states listed, North Carolina ranks 7th, with an 11.3 percent cumulative retention rate for grades 1-3. Texas ranks 16th out of 19, with a 5.1 percent cumulative retention rate. If one adds in kindergarten, one loses three states without data for kindergarten. After calculating the cumulative percentage retention rate for each state for grades

K-3, one finds much the same result as before. North Carolina ranks 5th out of 16 states, with a 15.5 percent cumulative retention rate, whereas Texas ranks 10th out of 16 states, with an 11 percent cumulative retention rate.

Texas and North Carolina do not have "unusually high rates of failure and grade repetition before grade 4," according to the table to which Haney refers. Indeed, Texas's rate is well below average. I encourage the reader to look at the table and check my addition. The report is *High Stakes*, by the National Research Council's Board on Testing and Assessment, Jay P. Heubert and Robert M. Hauser, editors.[7]

Exaggerating the increase in NAEP scores between 1992 and 1996—
"Illusion from Exclusion." Haney writes:

When considering average test scores, it is always helpful to pay attention to who is and is not tested.... As can be seen in this table [reproduced below as table 5.1], at the national level, between 1992 and 1996, the percentages of students excluded fell slightly.... However, in Texas, the percentages of students excluded from testing increased at both grade levels.... This means that some portion of the increased NAEP math averages for Texas in 1996 are illusory, resulting from the increased rates of exclusion of LEP and special students in Texas from NAEP testing. The gaps in rates of exclusion between Texas and the nation in 1996 also mean that comparisons of Texas with national averages in that year will be skewed in favor of Texas for the simple reason that more students in Texas were excluded from testing. In short, as with TAAS results, some portion of the apparent gains on NAEP math tests in Texas in the 1990s is an illusion arising from exclusion."

Haney argues that Texas's average NAEP test scores rose in the 1990s, in part because, over time, they excluded more and more students from the NAEP test administrations who could be expected to perform relatively poorly on the test, specifically, disabled students (those with IEPs, or "individual education plans") and limited-English proficient (LEP) students.

Table 5.1
Percentages of IEP and LEP Students
Excluded from NAEP State Math Assessments, Texas and Nation

Mathematics, Grade 4

	1990	1992	1996
Texas		8%	11%
Nation		8%	6%

Mathematics, Grade 8

	1990	1992	1996
Texas	7%	7%	8%
Nation	6%	7%	5%

Note: IEP = individual education plan (i.e., student with disability)
LEP = "Limited-English Program" (i.e., non-native speakers)
Source: Reese et al. 1997: 91, 93; Mullis et al. 1993: 324-25

Haney's argument is compelling, but his numbers are wrong. He either does not realize, or he is not telling us, that the national numbers he cites and the Texas numbers he cites come from completely different samples with completely different trends. The national numbers come from the NAEP national sample used for national trend data. It contains items that match items used in the past so that NAEP can calculate valid trends in student achievement over time. The state numbers come from state NAEP samples, and the average of the state samples is very different than the average of the national sample Haney uses.[8]

Instead of using the exclusion percentages listed for the "nation," which come from a different sample, I calculate the average of all the state percentages. You can try it yourself (note that you need to use the "S1" column from the 1996 table because the NAEP scores were calculated using those inclusion criteria). I calculate numbers that form a pattern quite different from Haney's (see Table 5.2).

Haney's disparity disappears. The trend between 1992 and 1996 for grade 4 is in the same direction for Texas as it is for the states as a whole. The trend for grade 8 is also in the same direction for Texas as it is for the states as a whole. Indeed, all exclusion percentages are trending up between 1992 and 1996. Moreover, the magnitude of the trends for Texas and for all the states are much the same, within rounding error.

The percentages in Table 5.2 make much more sense than those in Haney's table. Notice that in Haney's table (Table 5.1), Texas and the nation have exactly the same exclusion percentages in 1992 for grades 4 and 8. Anyone familiar with the situation would know that that cannot be. Texas has the second highest proportion of limited English proficient (LEP) students in the country, second only to California, and its proportion of students with dis-

Table 5.2
Percentages of IEP and LEP Students
Excluded from NAEP State Math Assessments, Texas and State Averages

Mathematics, Grade 4

	1992	1996
Texas	8%	10%
States' Average (unweighted)	5.1%	7.2%
States' Average (weighted)	6.2%	9.1%

Mathematics, Grade 8

Texas	7%	9%
States' Average (unweighted)	5.2%	6.3%
States' Average (weighted)	5.9%	7.2%

Source: Reese et al. 1997: 91, 93; Mullis et al. 1993: 324-25

abilities is not extraordinarily low. Logically, Texas must have a higher exclusion percentage than the country as a whole. Indeed, given its geographic position, it should only be surprising that Texas's exclusion percentage is not higher than it is.

Incidentally, using Haney's arithmetic, one would make any state, not just Texas, look like it was slack in its effort to decrease exclusion rates. It might also be worth noting, as it relates to motive, that Haney does not mention the continuing high rate of immigration into Texas between 1992 and 1996 in his discussion of the exclusion issue (more LEP students would justify an increase in the exclusion rate). He mentions it in other locations in his article, where it serves his purpose. Here, in this discussion, it would counter his argument.

Guidelines for excluding SD and LEP students from NAEP. Haney is correct in saying that the National Assessment Governing Board (NAGB), the body that oversees the NAEP, has encouraged states to include more SD and LEP students in their NAEP testing. Moreover, NAEP introduced new criteria in the 1990s to guide the states toward doing so. Haney cites his figures from Table 5.1 as proof that Texas was negligent in its obligation to adhere to the new criteria. Haney either does not realize, or he is not telling us, however, that the published NAEP scores for 1996 are based on the old inclusion criteria. So, his entire digression about the new criteria and his allegation that Texas was flaunting the new criteria is meaningless for explaining score trends.

Since he has leveled the rather slanderous charge, however, that Texas deliberately excludes too many SD and LEP students from NAEP testing and that it neglects to adhere to NAEP exclusion criteria, let us look into it. There is a very revealing table in the 1996 NAEP Almanac that Haney either does not know about, or is not revealing to us. Table D.4 lists the percentage of limited English proficient (LEP) students included in 1996 NAEP testing by each state with a population of LEP students large enough to provide an adequate sample for estimating summary statistics.

According to the original NAEP inclusion, Texas included (i.e., tested) 66 percent of its 4th-grade LEP students, which places it 4th out of 10 states with large LEP populations, and 55 percent of its 8th- grade LEP students, which places it 1st out of four states, ahead of Arizona, California, and New Mexico. Texas's relative position looks even better when calculated according to the newer NAEP inclusion criteria. Not only was the state of Texas not responsible for all the devious and unethical behavior of which Haney accused them in the 1990s, they were, in fact, one of the cooperative and responsible states in the country regarding their inclusion of LEP students in NAEP testing.[9]

Texas's NAEP scores are just average. As if what Haney did, described above, is not bad enough, he also chides Texas (and North Carolina) for being just average in their NAEP scores:

...review of results of NAEP from the 1990s suggests that grade 4 and grade 8 students in Texas performed much like students nationally. On some NAEP assessments, Texas students scored above the national average, and on some below.

Haney joins Linda McNeil in making this grumpy criticism. Texas (and North Carolina) used to be at the bottom of the pack. Now, they have risen to the middle. Instead of rejoicing at their progress, Haney and McNeil can only muster up resentment.

Dreams of Dropouts

Walter Haney uses dropout statistics in Texas, and makes up some of his own, in an attempt to demonstrate that the evil, devious Texas Education Agency (TEA) is cooking the stat books and that the dreaded, hated Texas Assessment of Academic Skills is, contrary to the pronouncements of the untrustworthy TEA, actually pushing more students to drop out of school.

Everybody who knows anything about dropout statistics knows that they are very complicated; come in a wide variety of forms and magnitudes, none of which are perfect; and have low reliability by comparison with other education statistics. There are a variety of reasons why dropout statistics are not very reliable. It is difficult to know when a student actually "drops out" as they fill out no form and, more often than not, only truly become dropouts after they have been truant for some time and, even then, are unlikely to give their school formal notice. For their part, schools and school districts have no incentive to report dropouts or to report them in a timely manner. They receive funding from the state based on "headcounts," the number of students they serve. If they report a dropout, they lose money.

Education statisticians, such as those at the U.S. Education Department's National Center for Education Statistics (NCES), have had many discussions over the past couple of decades about the many problems inherent in dropout data. But, in the end, they did agree on a common set of definitions as to what dropouts are in statistical terms.

Haney completely ignores these definitions and comes up with his own. Haney would have you believe that Texas's proportion of student dropouts has increased markedly since the introduction of the TAAS. It has not. He would have you believe that Texas's student dropout rate is now much higher than those in other states. Actually, it is lower. Haney would have you believe that dropout and high school completion statistics from the U.S. Education Department and the U.S. Census Bureau are all wrong, and that he has figured out what the real dropout rate is in Texas. He has not. Turns out, Texas actually has rather low rates of dropout, low by national standards, and lower than demographically similar states.

Haney's personal definition of "dropout." Take this sentence from his report's abstract:

Only 50% of minority students in Texas have been progressing from grade 9 to high school graduation since the initiation of the TAAS testing program.

...and this section from his report:

...these results lead me to conclude that since the implementation of the TAAS high school graduation test in 1991, 22-25% of White students and 35-40% of Black and Hispanic students, have not been persisting from grade 6 to regular high school graduation six years later. Overall, during the 1990s the dropout rate in Texas schools was about 30%. As appalling as this result appears...

In the first sentence from the abstract, Haney is counting any minority student from grade 9 who does not graduate three years later as a dropout without, of course, explaining that to the reader. By "not progressing to high school graduation since the initiation of the TAAS testing program," he really means not progressing to high school graduation "on time," that is, exactly three years later. Some of those students are retained in grade somewhere in between the start of grade 9 and the end of grade 12, of course. But, they become dropouts by Haney's definition. In other words, he counts many students who never actually drop out of school as dropouts.

As Haney makes plain in several parts of his report, not graduating "on time" is, in his opinion, an "appalling" scandal. He believes that no student should be restrained in any way from graduating "on time," regardless the reason.[10] His way of counting dropouts becomes more explicit in the second quote in the paragraph above where Haney uses the phrase "regular high school graduation," by which he means graduation "on time."[11]

To be complete, Haney uses more than one definition of "dropout" in his writing and it can get confusing. The "official" dropout rate, however, is apparently just one of several components of his better dropout rate, an umbrella term that includes repeating a grade, not graduating "on time," taking the G.E.D., and more. Pretty much anything Haney does not like gets defined as "dropping out."

The Texas Education Agency must be lying to us, again. Haney lambastes the TEA early and often in his report. He paints a portrait of institutionalized dishonesty and rampant incompetence. Their estimates of dropouts seem low to him, for example, so he accuses them of cooking the stat books:

It is clear that the TEA has been playing a Texas-sized shell game on the matter of counting dropouts. Every source of evidence other than the TEA (including IDRA, NCES, the Casey Foundation's KIDS Count data, Fassold's analyses and my own) shows Texas as having one of the worst dropout rates among the states. (Recall that even the Texas State Auditor's Office estimated that the 1994 dropout numbers reported by the TEA likely covered only half of the actual number of dropouts.)

Haney does not tell you that ALL states underestimate their dropout numbers. At best, dropout numbers arrive at the state level very late; at worst, schools and districts invent a variety of means of deliberately hiding those students who initially enrolled but no longer show up for class. Some states do better jobs than others at monitoring these numbers, but vigilant monitoring does not come cheap. It requires frequent state inspection of classroom attendance and cross checking names on enrollment and attendance collection forms.

Nonetheless, even though Texas's official state dropout numbers almost certainly underestimate the true magnitude of dropouts, if the data collection is consistent over the years, trends in the state averages should still be informative. The TEA shows dropout numbers trending downward during the 1990s, during the TAAS era, and asserted that the TAAS may actually have had the effect of decreasing the number of dropouts and could not have been increasing it. The TEA could be right. At least Haney's complaints to the contrary are no threat to the claim. Haney argues that since Texas's dropout numbers are underestimates, the trend must be incorrect. His reasoning is not valid. If the numbers are underestimated in a consistent way over the years, they can provide significant evidence of a trend toward fewer dropouts, even if the absolute magnitude of the numbers is off.

Evaluating Texas on reasonable and reliable dropout measures. There is a table in the NCES publication, *Dropout Rates in the United States: 1998,* that Haney does not cite, even though he cites other sections of the report. It lists all 50 states according to their "event" dropout rates, one of the accepted, standard ways of measuring dropouts. An "event" rate is the proportion of students who leave school each year without completing a high school program. Specifically, the event rate in this publication measured the number of 15 to 24 year olds who were enrolled in high school in October 1997, but were not enrolled a year later and had not completed high school. To get around the problems inherent in administrative dropout numbers, this information is captured in the U.S. Census Bureau's October *Current Population Survey.*

How does Texas compare? It has a 3.6 percent event dropout rate, lower than the U.S. average. Its Mexican border neighbors, Arizona and New Mexico, have rates of 10.0 and 7.5 (California has no rate listed). The average rate for the South is 5.1. Texas has the sixth lowest event dropout rate in the United States in 1996-97, the most recent year measured. The official statistics, calculated by some of the world's foremost statistical experts, buttress the TEA's claims about Texas's low dropout rate. Especially given Texas's demographic disadvantages (Hispanic dropout rates in the U.S. are triple the average), its school officials deserve high praise. Instead, after doing such a wonderful, commendable job, they must endure the cynical attacks of anti-testing advocates like Haney.

The same NCES publication shows a table of state-by-state high school completion rates. Texas does not look as good here compared to the national average. Haney makes a big deal out of this table in his report, even while he completely ignores the dropout table.

Remember Haney's claim: "Every source of evidence other than the TEA (including...NCES, the Casey Foundation's *KIDS Count* data, ...and my own) shows Texas as having one of the worst dropout rates among the states." Shameless. I looked. I cannot find evidence supporting Haney's claim in NCES data, nor in *KIDS Count* data.

Here is Haney on the *KIDS Count* data:

> Suffice it to say that: (1) according to both indicators of youth welfare, between 1985 and 1997, Texas had one of the poorer records among the states, consistently show-ing more than 10% of teens ages 16-19 as dropouts and more than 10% of teens not attending school and not working; and (2) if one examines the standing of Texas on these two indicators relative to those of other states, conditions in Texas seemed to have worsened in the early 1990s after implementation of TAAS.

I went to the *Kids Count* web site of the Annie B. Casey Foundation and retrieved the relevant data. I list all the states which had a statistic of 10 percent or higher.

State in 1990	Percent of 16-19 year-olds not attending school and not working	State in 1997
Hawaii	10	Alabama
Idaho		Hawaii
Indiana		Mississippi
Maryland		Nevada
Michigan		New York
New Mexico		
North Carolina		
South Carolina		
Washington		
Alaska	11	Alaska
California		Arizona
Florida		Oregon
Illinois		Rhode Island
Missouri		**Texas**
Texas		West Virginia
Georgia	12	Arkansas
Nevada		Kentucky
Oklahoma		Alabama
Arizona	13	Louisiana
Arkansas		Tennessee
Louisiana		
Mississippi		
Tennessee		
Kentucky	14	New Mexico
West Virginia	16	

Haney is using the number of 16 to 19 year-olds who are neither in school or at work (in the aboveground economy, anyway) as a proxy measure for dropouts, even though all 19-year-olds and most 18-year-olds should be out of school if they had arrived at graduation "on time." In other words, many of these young adults/old teenagers could simply be unemployed or working off the tax rolls.

Let's check out Haney's observation about Texas's relative standing on this statistic, anyway. He claims that Texas ranks very low and got lower during the 1990s TAAS era. Notice that Texas's percentage did not change at all in the 1990s. Is its rank very low? Not much by comparison to its peers—other Mexican border or Southern states (in italics). In 1990, three peers rank above, two are the same, and seven rank below. In 1997, two peer states rank above, one is the same, and four rank below. There are, of course, some peer states not included in the table because they have percentages less than ten (one in 1990 and six in 1997). There does seem to be a drift upwards in the table between 1990 and 1997 (i.e., toward lower percentages), but it is certainly neither uniform nor overwhelming.

I also retrieved from the *KIDS Count* website the dropout data for which Haney chastises Texas. Here, I list all the states which had a statistic of 12 percent or higher.

Again, Texas's percentage did not change during the TAAS era, as Haney says it did, and Texas is surrounded by peer states both years, hardly near the bottom of the rankings by itself.

State in 1990	Dropout rate	State in 1997
Georgia Kentucky Oklahoma West Virginia	12	Arkansas Florida Georgia North Carolina Rhode Island
California Florida Louisiana Tennessee Texas	13	Oregon Tennessee Texas
North Carolina	14	New Mexico
Alabama Arizona Nevada	15	Arizona
	17	Nevada

Haney brings up the topic of adjusting statistics for demographic considerations whenever it serves his goal of lambasting the TEA, and he ignores
demographic considerations when it does not serve his goal of lambasting
the TEA. Throughout his report, he criticizes Texas for being a low-ranking
state on this or that statistic. He compares Texas to all the other U.S. states—
Minnesota, Vermont, Oregon, Wyoming. On statistics that are likely to be
affected by a state's demographic profile—statistics like dropout rates and
high school completion—does it make much sense to compare Texas to Minnesota, Vermont, Oregon, and Wyoming? Of course not.

If one compares Texas to its demographic peers, the other Southern or
Mexican border states, Texas comes out above average. Probably the most
pertinent demographic factors as regards effect on dropout rate are the percentages of poor and minority student population in a state. It is, indeed,
unfortunate, that black and, particularly, Hispanic students tend to have higher
dropout rates, but they do. And, Texas has a much larger black population
than does Wyoming or Iowa. Texas has the second largest population of
Hispanic students in the country, second only to California. Moreover, Texas's
minority population tends to be poor.

Grade 9 and Its Relation to High School Completion

Haney writes about grade 9 as if it was a magic grade, much, much more
important than all the others. Haney has no tolerance for retention by any
rationale. Whether a student studies or not, whether a student learns anything
or not, whether a student shows up at school or not, all students should be
given high school diplomas "on time," regardless. To do any less is cruel, in
his opinion.

> The grade 9 retention rates in Texas are far in excess of national trends. The recent
> report of the National Research Council (NRC) also shows Texas to have among the
> highest grade 9 retention rates for 1992 to 1996 among the states for which such data
> are available (Heubert and Hauser 1999, Table 6-1).... States with the higher rates of
> grade 9 retention tend to have lower rates of high school completion.

Even at grade 9, Texas is not the retention champ, however; New York,
Mississippi, and D.C., among the states in the Table 5.3, have higher grade 9
retention rates. Pick any other grade and Texas's retention rate is relatively
low. Haney draws a scatterplot that shows an almost perfect (inverse) correlation between grade 9 retention rates and high school completion. Grade 9, he
wants us to believe, is very special, the gateway grade to high school graduation. Believe it if you like.

It just may be that Haney harps on grade 9 because it is in that grade that
Texas retains a high proportion of students (17 percent, just in front of the
required high school graduation exam they must pass in 10th grade), and he

wants to make Texas appear onerous in flunking students. In fact, looking at all grades, and not just grade 9, even using data from Haney's source, Texas has relatively low retention rates.

Comparing Texas to its peer states—other states with high minority, particularly Hispanic, and immigrant populations, Texas does not look remarkably different. Arizona, which had no high-stakes testing program in the 1990s, had a lower high school completion rate (ergo, higher dropout rate). Moreover, its grade 9 retention rate was about two-fifths the size of Texas's and it still has a lower high school completion rate, contrary to Haney's rule. Texas does not stand out as Haney wants. Accounting for its demographics, Texas seems much like the other states.

In Table 5.3, Haney attempts to show that Texas holds more students back and so more students drop out. But, I would like to compare Texas to its peer states—other states with high minority, particularly Hispanic, and immigrant populations. Unfortunately, New Mexico and California are not in Haney's table, so I settle for Arizona and other Southern states (in italics). Notice that Texas does not look remarkably different from its peers.[12]

Table 5.3
Grade 9 Retention and High School Completion in the States

State	Year	Grade 9 Retention Rate	High school completion rate 18-24 year-olds, 1996-98
Alabama	1996-97	12.6%	84.2%
Arizona	1996-97	7.0	77.1
District of Columbia	1996-97	18.7	84.9
Florida	1996-97	14.3	83.6
Georgia	1996-97	13.1	84.8
Kentucky	1995-96	10.7	85.2
Maryland	1996-97	10.3	94.5
Massachusetts	1995-96	6.3	90.6
Michigan	1995-96	4.8	91.0
Mississippi	1996-97	19.7	82.0
New York	1996-97	19.5	84.7
North Carolina	1996-97	15.8	85.2
Ohio	1996-97	11.4	89.4
Tennessee	1996-97	13.4	86.9
Texas	1995-96	17.8	80.2
Vermont	1996-97	4.8	93.6
Virginia	1995-96	13.2	85.9
Wisconsin	1996-97	8.5	90.8

Sources: Heubert and Hauser (1999) Table 6.1; Kaufman et al. (1999), Table 5.

Looking beyond grade 9, Texas looks even better. Here's my partial repro-
duction of one of Haney's favorite tables, the state-by-state retention rate
table (Table 6.1) from the Heubert and Hauser book. Starting on the book's
page 138 are several pages of state-level and grade-level retention rates. Not
all U.S. states are included in the table and, even for those that are included,
data are often missing for certain grades.

grade level state \	1	2	3	4	5	6	7	8	9	grades 1—9 sum	grades 1—9 rank
Virginia	4.3	2.4	1.9	1.6	1.1	3.6	5.3	6.0	13.2	39.4	4
Texas	5.9	2.6	1.5	1.0	0.8	1.7	2.9	2.1	17.8	36.3	7
Tennessee	5.5	2.5	1.8	1.2	1.4	2.7	7.2	5.7	13.4	41.4	3
N Carolina	5.7	3.1	2.5	1.4	1.0	2.6	3.4	2.8	15.8	38.3	5
Mississippi	11.9	6.6	5.4	6.1	6.6	7.7	15.6	12.9	19.7	92.5	1
Georgia	4.0	2.4	1.7	1.3	1.1	2.1	2.5	2.1	12.4	29.6	8
Florida	4.1	2.2	1.5	1.0	0.7	4.4	4.9	4.0	14.3	37.1	6
Arizona	2.2	1.0	0.7	0.5	0.5	1.1	2.7	2.3	7.01	8.0	9
Alabama	8.5	3.3	2.5	2.1	2.0	2.9	6.1	4.4	12.6	44.4	2
Average	5.8	2.9	2.2	1.8	1.7	3.2	5.6	4.7	14.0	41.9	N=9

Does Texas retain students at a rate much higher than other states, as Haney
claims? Absolutely not. Indeed, grade 9 is the only grade where Texas's retention rate is above average (except for grade 1's 0.1 difference). No wonder
Haney picked grade 9. At any other grade, 2 through 8, Texas looks like a
wimpy social promotion state, the kind that Haney prefers. Texas comes in
below the average sum for grades 1 through 9, ranking 7th in cumulative
retention rate out of only 9 states.[13]

"Persistence" across grades. Haney also makes a big deal out of comparing grade 9 enrollments to numbers of graduates and, for that matter, the
enrollments in other grades to the number of graduates, both his "on time
only" graduates and the kind the rest of us are familiar with. One result is the
particular type of Haney-special dropout statistic that he ends up with in his
report.

His words themselves seem breathless, as he writes:

Overall, during the 1990s the dropout rate in Texas schools was about 30%. As
appalling as this result appears.... A convergence of evidence indicates that during the
1990s, slightly less than 70% of students in Texas actually graduated from high
school."

Haney claims that this 30 percent is the "real" dropout rate for Texas. He
also strongly implies that it is unique to Texas, that uniquely evil state that

rises above all the others in ill will, dishonesty, incompetence, and bad education policy.

He gets the 30 percent by comparing enrollments in a middle-school level grade X, like grade 9 or 8 or below, to the number of graduates (12 - X) years later. To check his claims, I use his own numbers, from the spreadsheet appendix to his report. Dividing the number of graduates in Texas for the 1998-99 school year by the number of 8th graders in 1995-96, I get 0.72, almost exactly what Haney led us to expect. If I do the same for grade 9, I get 0.61, but, remember, there is that big retention bulge in grade 9 that distorts comparisons.

I was curious to see how much higher Texas is on this measure than other states. Haney writes that Texas is a lot higher in dropout rate and a lot lower in persistence to graduation than other states. But, he is comparing apples and oranges—his special measure for Texas with genuine dropout measures for other states. How do other states stack up on his measure—apples to apples?

It so happens, a lot like Texas. Texas is not unique as Haney would have us believe. I used data from the U.S. Education Department's *Digest of Education Statistics,* comparing graduates in 1997-98 to 8th graders in 1993-94 and 9th graders in 1994-95, in nine states demographically similar to Texas. The persistence rates below are calculated by dividing graduates by each grade's enrollments. These constitute measures of how many of the 8th- or 9th-grade students were still in school X years later when they were supposed to be.

	US	TX	CA	AZ	NM	LA	MS	AL	AR	TN	NC
8th gr. Enrol (000) 93-94			389	55	25	58	40	59	36	66	86
Grads (000) 97-98			269	36	17	38	24	38	26	44	59
persistence rate	0.71	**0.72**	0.69	0.65	0.68	0.66	0.60	0.64	0.72	0.67	0.69
9th gr. Enrol (000) 94-95			438	59	29	69	43	65	37	74	101
persistence rate	0.64	**0.61**	0.61	0.61	0.59	0.55	0.56	0.58	0.70	0.59	0.58

Far from standing out from the crowd with the unusually low persistence rate Haney claimed we would find, Texas has a higher-than-the-national-average persistence rate overall and a rate higher than those for all but one of the comparison states for the grade 8 comparison. For the grade 9 comparison, Texas is hobbled by the grade 9 retention bulge and, not surprising, its persistence rate of 0.61 slides under the national average this time. However, compared to its peer states, Texas is still above average, higher than six out of nine.

Looking to a more reliable data source on high school completion than Haney uses, the National Center for Education Statistics, here's what I find

Table 5.4
High School Completion Rates of 18- through 24-Year-Olds,
Not Currently Enrolled in High School or Below, by State: October 1990-92,
1993-95 and 1996-98

	1990-92	1993-95	1996-98
Total U.S.	85.5%	85.8%	85.6%
Arizona	81.7	83.8	77.1
California	77.3	78.7	81.2
New Mexico	84.1	82.3	78.6
Texas	80.0	79.5	80.2

Source: Kaufman, P., Kwon, J., Klein, S. and Chapman, C. (1999). Dropout rates in the United States: 1998. (NCES 2000-022). Washington, DC: National Center for Education Statistics, p. 20.

comparing national averages and the relevant figures for Texas's neighboring Mexican border states.

Compared to its Mexican border peers, Texas's high school completion rate seems normal and steady, just like the country's as a whole. It is not rising over the years like California's, but neither is it falling over the years like Arizona's or New Mexico's. It ends up higher than two of its peers and lower than the others.[14]

SAT Scores

Some critics, including Haney, have remarked on how low Texas's average SAT scores are relative to other states' scores (40th in math, 46th in verbal), pretty low for an "education miracle" state. The quickest rejoinder to this criticism is to say that Texas's low standing on the SAT is hardly a product of the TAAS era, but has existed for a long time. As one can see in Haney's graph of SAT average scores for Texas and the U.S. from 1970 to 1999 (see Figure 5.2), the gulf between the Texas and the U.S. SAT mean scores has been about 10 scale points for the verbal portion (and about 12 for the math portion). These TAAS-era differences are smaller than those of the mid-1980s, long before TAAS, of 13 for verbal and 16 for math. So, it would appear that TAAS is not to blame for Texas's low SAT average.

Here's a somewhat longer rejoinder. As far as the SAT is concerned, there are three groups of test-takers who influence the level of each state's average score. First, there are those students in a state who do not plan to go to college and who do not attempt the SAT. They tend to be lower achieving students who would probably bring the state average down if they did take the SAT.

Second are those students who take the SAT because their relatively low-cost and/or nearby state public higher education institutions require the SAT. This scenario plays out in less than half the U.S. states, however. That is because a slight majority of the states (or, rather, their public higher education

Figure 5.2
Average SAT-Verbal Scores, Texas and National: 1972-1999

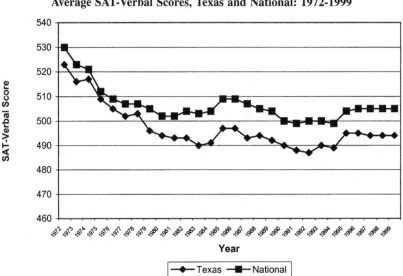

institutions) prefer or require the SAT's competitor, the American College Test (ACT). This second population of SAT test-takers does exist in Texas because its public higher education institutions require the SAT. These test-taking students tend to score higher on the SAT than the first group of non-college-bound probably would, as these college-bound are higher-achieving students.

Again, this second population of test-takers does not exist in the majority of U.S. states. A wide swath of territory from the Sierra Nevada to the Appalachians (with the exceptions of Texas and Indiana) encompasses ACT states. Students who take the SAT in these states are students who plan to attend college outside their own state, where they will pay out-of-state tuition, private school tuition, or require a scholarship or grant. These students must be high-achieving students to get into these institutions in other states which have no obligation to take them. This third population of test-takers tends to produce the highest SAT average of all. Thus, one finds the highest average SAT scores in ACT states, such as North Dakota, where the state average SAT math score is 609, more than one standard deviation above the national mean.

It simply is not fair to compare the average SAT score in an SAT state to one in an ACT state. If one compares Texas's SAT average scores only to those of other SAT states, Texas's rank does not look so awful. Twelve states have higher math and verbal scores. Seven states have one score (math or verbal) higher than Texas's, but not the other. Four states have lower math and verbal scores. Most of the other SAT states are wealthier and have a much lower population of limited-English-proficient students.

But, Haney not only chides Texas for its low relative standing on SAT means, he also observes that SAT scores for Texas are not rising in conjunction with TAAS scores, which makes him suspicious of the validity of the TAAS score rise. In response to Haney's compelling argument, I state two facts:

1. The SAT and the TAAS are different tests. The SAT, originally designed to measure "aptitude," is as wide-ranging and general as an academic test can be, whereas the TAAS is based on specific curriculum standards agreed to by the citizens of Texas. Moreover, the SAT level of difficulty is defined by the achievement level of the average college aspirant, whereas the TAAS is, by many accounts, pitched to a minimum level of achievement of something like a 6th- or 7th-grade level of difficulty.
2. More important to the point, the population of students taking each test is different, too—college aspirants for the SAT and the entire range of students for the TAAS.

A decade ago, a Ph.D. economics student at MIT, Jonathan E. Jacobson, completed a dissertation on the effect of 1980s-era minimum competency tests on academic achievement and young adult earnings. He used the National Education Longitudinal Study (NELS), which consists of a panel group questionnaire with an achievement test imbedded. He compared the most recent average NELS achievement test scores and subsequent respondent earnings between those individuals who had attended high school in minimum competency test states and those who had not.

As expected, he found that the lowest-achieving students were, indeed, made better off in the minimum-competency test states. Both their average test scores and their average level of earnings were substantially higher than those of their counterparts, the lowest-achieving students from non-test states. This was encouraging. However, he also found that the other students, particularly the middle-achieving ones in the minimum-competency testing states ended up worse off. Their average NELS achievement test scores and their subsequent average earnings were lower than those for their counterparts, the middle-achieving students from non-test states.

It is easy to speculate about what might have happened to produce these results. In test states where the only threshold to exceed was that at the minimum level of achievement, substantial effort focused on that level. Perhaps schools and teachers kept themselves so busy making sure the lowest-achieving students got over the minimum competency threshold that they neglected the higher-achieving students and the curriculum and instruction that they needed.

Given this evidence, and given the low level of the TAAS, one would expect that the average SAT scores of college-aspiring Texas high schoolers would be declining in the TAAS era. There is no logical reason why an in-

structional focus on a 6th- or 7th-grade level TAAS would help college aspirants on their SATs. The only effect that one would expect would be a negative
one, with instructional resources flowing away from the higher-achieving
students toward the lower-achieving students. The fact that Texas's SAT scores
have remained flat throughout the TAAS era (that is, the same distance in
scale points below the national average) is a credit to the Texas testing program. It apparently has not degraded instruction for its higher-achievers, as
minimum competency testing regimes can do.

Notes

1.   For example, McNeil 2000; Haney 2000; Sacks 1999b; Klein, Hamilton, McCaffrey,
     and Stecher 2000; Moore 2000; ASCD 2000; Orfield and Kornhaber 2000; Hous-
     ton 2000; Rand Corporation 2000.
2.   Why did not the anti-testing groups visit North Carolina in the year 2000? It could
     not have been because North Carolina's testing program was inaugurated and has
     been run throughout its history by Democratic administrations, could it? Despite
     the eerie similarity between the North Carolina program, inaugurated by former
     Governor (and Al Gore campaign advisor on education issues) James Hunt, and
     the Texas program, all the anti-testing groups chose to find fault with Texas instead.
3.   I refer to comparing scores on 4th-grade scales to scores on 4th-grade scales in
     later years and scores on 8th-grade scales to scores on 8th-grade scales in later
     years. It would not be the same to compare scores on 4th-grade scales to scores on
     8th-grade scales.
4.   *High Stakes* is available for order on line at [http://www.nap.edu]. Incidentally, a
     review of Heubert and Hauser's rather one-sided report appeared in the December
     2000 issue of *Educational and Psychological Measurement.*
5.   The reader is welcome to look at the table and check—Table B.4 in the *1992 NAEP
     Trial State Assessment Data Compendium,* pp. 796-797 for the 1992 exclusion
     percentages and in the *NAEP 1996 Mathematics Report Card for the Nation and
     the States,* Table D.2, p. 144. for the 1996 percentages. First, get the percentages
     for Texas (1992: 8 percent [grade 4] and 7 percent [grade 8]; 1996: 10 percent
     [grade 4] and 9 percent [grade 8]). (I have no idea where Walt Haney got his 11 and
     8 percent for Texas for 1996.) The *1996 NAEP Almanac can* be found on the Web:
     [http://nces.ed.gov/pubsearch/pubsinfo.asp?pubid=97488].
6.   The overwhelming majority of U.S. citizens, of course, disagree with Haney. They
     believe that students should graduate after they have met generally agreed-upon
     academic standards, and not before. Moreover, most citizens believe that students
     should be able to demonstrate mastery of those standards before being allowed to
     graduate.
7.   Here's another example where the ruse is even clearer (or, murkier, depending on
     your perspective): "If we adopt the common sense definition that a dropout is a
     student who leaves school without graduating from high school, analyses of data...tell
     a reasonably clear story of what has happened in Texas over the last two decades...the
     percentage of black and Hispanic students who progressed from grade 6 to gradu-
     ation *six years later* [italics ours] hovered around 65 percent. For white students,
     the corresponding percentage started at about 80 percent and gradually declined to
     about 75 percent in 1990.
         One final quote to hammer home the point: "...to be absolutely clear (and to
     avoid getting into semantic arguments about the meaning of the term 'dropout'), I

readily acknowledge that what the cohort progression analyses show is the extent of the problem in Texas of students failing to persist in school through to high school graduation-regardless whether it is caused by students having to repeat grade 9, failing to pass the exit level version of TAAS, *officially 'dropping out'* [italics mine] opting out of regular high school programs to enter GED preparation classes, or some combination of these circumstances."

8. Haney's book-length article can be found in the *Education Policy Analysis Archives* (EPAA) at: [http://olam.ed.asu.edu/epaa/v8n41]. NAEP administrators researched the large disparity between the national and the state exclusion rates. The national rate was estimated by Westat, the contractor in charge. State exclusion rates were estimated by state education department personnel. The latter estimates were systematically and substantially higher.

9. Testing opponents' cry of "teaching to the test" (in this case, to the TAAS) is obfuscation. Teaching to the test is only a problem when students are tested on material they have not been taught. When students are tested on material they have been taught, any teacher not teaching to the test is behaving irresponsibly. It may be for this reason that, despite testing opponents' (largely successful) efforts to convince journalists that teaching to the test is a horrible practice, parents continue to tell pollsters that, of course, they want their students' teachers to teach to the test.

10. As Haney, himself, describes it: "In 1997, results from the 1996 National Assessment of Educational Progress (NAEP) in mathematics were released. The 1996 NAEP results showed that among the states participating in the state-level portion of the math assessment, Texas showed the greatest gains in percentages of fourth graders scoring at the proficient or advanced levels. Between 1992 and 1996, the percentage of Texas fourth grades scoring at these levels had increased from 15 percent to 25 percent. The same NAEP results also showed North Carolina to have posted unusually large gains at the grade 8 level, with the percentages of eighth graders in North Carolina scoring at the proficient or advanced levels improving from 9 percent in 1990 to 20 percent in 1996 (Reese et al. 1997).

" ...these findings led to considerable publicity for the apparent success of education reform in these two states. The apparent gains in math, for example, led the National Education Goals Panel in 1997 to identify Texas and North Carolina as having made unusual progress in achieving the National Education Goals.

" ...the gains on TAAS...appear quite impressive. Across all three grades and all three TAAS subject areas (reading, math and writing), the magnitude of TAAS increases ranged from 0.43 to 0.72 standard deviation units. According to guidelines for interpreting effect sizes, these gains clearly fall into the range of medium to large effects. Also, the gains on TAAS clearly exceed the gains that appear possible, according to previous research, from mere test coaching. The gains on TAAS seem especially impressive when it is recalled that the gains on TAAS...represent performance of hundreds of thousand of Texas students....

"Apparent gains for Texas in NAEP math scores between 1992 and 1996 were indeed statistically significant.... Also...the NAEP math gains for Texas fourth graders between 1992 and 1996 were greater than the corresponding gains for any other state participating in these two NAEP state assessments. So any reasonable person must concede that the apparent improvement of Texas grade 4 NAEP math average from 217.9 in 1992 to 228.7 in 1996 (a gain of about one-third of a standard deviation), if real, is indeed a noteworthy and educationally significant accomplishment."

11. The dedicated, hard-working employees of the Texas Education Agency deserve better than the treatment they get from Haney. One can, perhaps, understand that

the vested interests in education attacked Texas because they felt threatened by the policies of its governor, who was running for president. But, in the manner in which they did it, they also happened to trample on the reputations of thousands of sincere and competent education professionals in Texas's education department.

12. Arizona, which had no high-stakes testing program in the 1990s has a lower high school completion rate (ergo, higher dropout rate). Moreover, its grade 9 retention rate is about two-fifths the size of Texas's and yet it still has a lower high school completion rate, contrary to Haney's rule. The other, almost-peer states have mostly lower grade 9 retention rates slightly higher high school completion rates. Texas does not stand out as Haney wants.

13. A look at the upper grades shows much the same picture. Texas ranks below average on retention for grades 10 and 12, and slightly above average for grade 11. Its cumulative retention rate for all grades 1 through 12 is well below average, ranking 6th out of only 9 states in retention.

14. The results are similar in comparing Texas to its Southern states' peers. Here, Texas does have the lowest high school graduation rates, but they are not appreciably lower than those in Louisiana and Mississippi, its neighbors, or in Florida, the only other state in the list with a sizable immigrant population.

6

War Correspondence
(Media Coverage of Testing)

Many of us in the United States believe that we are better off than those poor souls living under authoritarian governments, in part, because we benefit from freedom of the press. Journalists in the United States can say what they wish, write on any topic, talk to anyone, and get all sides of a story. Journalists enjoy a constitutionally guaranteed protection from the vested interests. They may feel free to "speak truth to power."

The operative word here is "may." In practice, they do not have to if they do not want to.

On many education issues, and especially on the issue of standardized testing, U. S. journalists in overwhelming numbers voluntarily choose to censor themselves. They talk only to advocates on one side of the story—those dedicated to maintaining the current public education system structure. Efforts at "balance" are few and far between. That journalists behave this way will be demonstrated with abundant evidence in this chapter. Why journalists behave this way will be discussed at the end of the chapter.

The net effect for the public is little different from what one would find in an authoritarian society. When only one side is allowed to speak, it can say anything it pleases. With no counters allowed, "truth" and "fact" get less and less restrained, and more and more outrageous. U.S. education journalists serve willingly, in effect, as the public relations office of the rich and powerful forces protecting the status quo.

News Sources on Standardized Testing

News stories can only be as good as their sources of information. Where do journalists get their information on testing? Or, better, where do journalists get their information on the testing research they so often cite? Forget about scientific journals; journalists rarely read journals.

Instead, they read reports—reports from advocacy groups—and the work of other journalists. Also, they speak to members of advocacy groups. It may seem ironic that members of a profession dedicated to seeking truth and fact steadfastly ignore carefully reviewed scientific journals in favor of material produced by partisan groups with obvious biases. And, while it is true that many testing research journals are simply not understandable to most journalists—many articles on research methods in particular weigh heavy with equations and technical terms—some testing research is easily accessible to the average journalist, yet still widely ignored.[1]

Why do many journalists prefer to get their facts from the sources least likely to provide them? There could be several reasons but, primary among them, several journalists have suggested to me, is convenience. Advocacy group reports arrive in the mail and appear on a journalist's desk without the journalist having to move a muscle. Moreover, the reports usually come with a one-page cover letter, a slightly longer press release, and a somewhat longer executive summary. So, a journalist can spend just a minute before deciding to invest any more time, which will just be a few minutes more, before deciding to invest any more time, which will still be less than an hour.

It's good marketing. Furthermore, the advocacy group will conveniently provide names of "research experts" who work at the group, along with their coordinates so they can be easily reached for "further, in-depth information" on the research results. Those "experts" will be coached with tested phrases readily available for the journalist to easily pop into her piece.

Journalists' news stories sometimes are written based on nothing more than an advocacy group's press release, which can differ dramatically in its "spin" from the actual research being cited. Just last year, for example, an association of school administrators opposed to testing commissioned a public opinion poll on testing from the Harris polling organization. I obtained the poll's methodology report and questionnaire and reviewed the results, which fell in line with other poll results on testing from the last forty years, with respondents strongly supportive of testing (Moore 2000).

The press release, however, selected only a tiny proportion of the results and, even with it, fudged the numbers such that the results appeared to support the association's position on testing.[2] All the news stories of that poll that followed gave the association's spin. Apparently, none of the journalists who covered the story looked at the actual poll, or talked to the actual pollsters (ASCD 2000).

Some journalists even solicit advocacy groups to write news stories for them. One can read at the Internet chat room of the anti-testing group FairTest requests from journalists to provide the information they need for a story on testing. It should be no surprise if the story ends up looking like a typical FairTest propaganda piece.

Remember the self-congratulatory claim of the journalists in the Hollywood film, *The Paper*—that no story ever knowingly gets printed with factual errors? Well, perhaps that is true in education journalism, too, but it ignores the more cogent point. Apparently, many stories get printed for which little or no effort has been expended to determine what the facts actually are.

Most advocacy groups represent the extremes of opinion. It is not clear to me that the stereotypic conservative-liberal spectrum has any meaning for the topic of student testing but, if it does, the war over testing is being fought by the center against the extremes. On this issue, journalists seem to listen mostly to the extremes that oppose testing—the organized advocacy groups—and ignore the center.

"Balance" in Journalism—Small Differences Can Mean a Lot

The standard journalistic check on bias is "balance." If the journalist is unfamiliar with an issue, or the journalist is biased on the issue, he is ethically obligated to get "both" or "all" sides of the story and, at least, let advocates for the other side represent themselves.

Unfortunately, the concept of "balance" does not work in the coverage of testing. Many do not even bother with it. Others allow only minimal token representation for the opposing point of view. Often, even when there is some reasonable attempt at balance, it is employed superficially and flippantly—any two commentators who disagree to any degree are considered to "balance" an issue. The end result is, usually, that two opponents of standardized testing, who disagree in minor ways, are allowed to represent "both" sides of the testing issue. This tendency to show "balance" over minor differences then lends credence to the assertion of testing opponents that ALL experts and testing researchers oppose the use of standardized testing, particularly for high stakes.

Do Journalists Check Their Facts?

Some do; but many do not bother. Testing is technical and it is rare that a journalist attempts to verify a "fact" delivered to them by a testing opponent. Overwhelmingly, advocates' "facts" are accepted at face value, presented to the public as such, and then repeated by other journalists as facts.

In her insightful, but frightening book about how journalists report research results, *Tainted Truth: The Manipulation of Fact in America*, Cynthia Crossen (1994: 230-231) concludes:

> It would be comforting to think the media protect us from the flood of dubious information we face every day, but they do not and they never have.... The media are willing victims of bad information, and increasingly they are producers of it. They take information from self-interested parties and add to it another layer of self-

interest—the desire to sell information.... In addition to distorting our individual facts, media self-interest also paints a world that is excessively dramatic, episodic, and ultimately confusing.

Coverage of Standardized Testing in the Print Media

I conducted a search through Dow Jones Interactive's data base of about 550 U.S. newspapers and magazines, looking for mentions of individuals who are expert in issues of educational testing policy. The time period consisted of the three calendar years 1998, 1999, and 2000. I was careful to use all different combinations of each person's name (e.g., with middle initial and without, with nickname and without) and to not double count articles. I was also careful to count only articles about testing policy and not articles on other education matters or ones that included test results as part of a different topic (e.g., test scores are used as the outcome variable for a story on research into the effects of class-size reduction).

In accumulating the list of experts, I used my own judgment to select an equal number of individuals I thought to be prominent opponents and defenders of high-stakes standardized testing (26 each for a total of 52). Generally, the opponents consist of the two groups identified in chapter 1—the radicals and the mainstream. The radicals are those willing to pull out all the stops in their opposition to testing; the mainstream opponents are the ones who try to appear more open-minded. As mentioned before, some mainstream even identify themselves as supporters of high-stakes standardized testing, except that there are no actual tests currently in existence or in history that they would support. Typically, they will say that "more research is needed" (and they are willing to do it) before they can confidently implement a high-stakes test. The difference between these two subgroups is mainly one of appearances; the end result of following either group would be the same.

Likewise, testing defenders are of two types—the "picky defenders" who only support certain types of high-stakes standardized tests (e.g., only multiple-choice, no multiple-choice; only minimum competency, no minimum competency; teacher tests, no teacher tests; aptitude tests, no aptitude tests) and the "liberal defenders" who are more flexible and willing to let the public decide on the type. Among defenders, the difference between the two subgroups has definite policy implications.

I will not pretend to have devised the perfect list, nor to have classified individual experts perfectly in all cases. The selection and the classifications are made subjectively and based only upon my knowledge of the field, which is far from exhaustive.

I have deliberately left out those experts that might fit the "stuck in the middle" category, such as politicians and state testing directors. The object is to learn how much the press pays attention to both sides of the topic, not one side against the middle.

Some readers, as well as some of those testing experts I have classified, may object that I am attempting to pigeonhole thinking beings who are too intelligent and varied in their opinions to be so narrowly described. Furthermore, some might accuse me of hypocrisy in putting labels on people, as I object, elsewhere in this book, to testing opponents' proclivity to dismiss testing defenders by calling them names, such as "ideologue," "conservative," "right winger," and so on.

To a certain extent, I sympathize with these criticisms. But, I would argue that this type of exercise, no matter how crude or distasteful, is exactly what journalists must go through every time they wish to present a "balanced perspective" on an issue.

In Table 6.1, I provide a list of all names used and the respective number of "hits" in the Dow Jones Interactive data base. The list is sorted in descending order, by the number of hits in 550 print media during the calendar years 1998, 1999, and 2000.

Journalists' seven most popular testing experts were Alfie Kohn, Nicholas Lemann, Bob Chase, Walter Haney, Peter Sacks, and the FairTest team of Monte Neill and Robert Schaeffer. They totaled 341 "hits." The 46 other experts combined had only 400. Those in the know, know, of course. This group includes the most unrelenting and unrestrained opponents of standardized testing in the United States. Add the number of hits for the just as unequivocal Deborah Meier to the top seven's and one arrives at close to an equilibrium. Just eight people, among them the country's most extreme testing opponents—Kohn, Lemann, Chase, Haney, Neill, Schaeffer, Sacks, and Meier—account for more hits (375) in the print media than all the other testing experts combined (366).

Testing Opponents vs. Testing Defenders

Generally, I classify experts into the "opponent" or "defender" camp like this: if an expert uniformly reaches conclusions opposing the implementation of external, high-stakes standardized testing programs I put them in the "opponent" camp. I include as "opponents" those I consider to be "false supporters," testing experts who claim to support high-stakes standardized testing but do not support any that could feasibly ever be used. Typically, false supporters will say "more research is needed," or they will burden any proposed test with so many restrictions and conditions that it becomes impractical to use them (which may be the intention).[3] "Defenders" are those willing to approve, at least under some realistic, practical, feasible, and current conditions, the implementation of external, high-stakes standardized testing.

Under these criteria, I found 614 articles mentioning opponents in the years 1998 through 2000, and 127 articles mentioning defenders. Six defenders received no mention at all; another six defenders received two or fewer.

Table 6.1
Dow Jones Interactive Search Results

Testing Expert	Affiliation (if any)**	Type of Opponent	Type of Defender	Number of Hits
Monty Neill	FairTest	radical		65
Nicholas Lemann		mainstream		59
Bob Chase*	NEA	mainstream		56
Bob Schaeffer	FairTest	radical		44
Alfie Kohn		radical		42
Walter Haney	CSTEEP	radical		37
Peter Sacks		radical		38
William Sanders			picky	37
Deborah Meier		radical		34
Peter Schrag		radical		25
Gerald Bracey		radical		23
Howard Gardner		radical		21
Paul Houston	AASA	mainstream		21
Stephen Klein	CRESST	mainstream		20
L. Darling-Hammond*		mainstream		17
Lorrie Shepard	CRESST	radical		17
Richard Atkinson	U. of California	mainstream		17
Linda McNeil		radical		12
Mark Musick	SREB		picky	12
Robert Hauser	NRC	mainstream		12
Brian Stecher	CRESST	mainstream		10
Eva Baker	CRESST	mainstream		10
Jay Heubert	NRC	mainstream		10
Amy Wilkins	EdTrust		picky	8
Jonathan Kozol		radical		8
Matt Gandal	Achieve/AFT		picky	8
Michael Kean	AAP		liberal	8
Chester Finn	Fordham		liberal	7
Nancy Cole			liberal	7
John Bishop	CAHRS		picky	6
Robert Linn	CRESST	mainstream		6
Robert Schwartz	Achieve		picky	6
Diane Ravitch	Fordham		liberal	5
E.D. Hirsch			picky	5
George Madaus	CSTEEP		radical	5
Michael Podgursky*	ECC		picky	4
Daniel Koretz	CRESST	mainstream		3
Susan Phillips			liberal	3
Bill Mehrens			liberal	2
Dale Ballou*			picky	2
Ronald Hambleton			liberal	2

Table 6.1 (cont.)

Testing Expert	Affiliation (if any)**	Type of Opponent	Type of Defender	Number of Hits
Susan Ohanian	FairTest		radical	2
Bella Rosenberg	AFT		picky	2
David Murray			liberal	1
Gregory Cizek			liberal	1
Herbert Walberg	ECC		picky	1
Barbara Lerner			liberal	0
Gene Bottoms	SREB		liberal	0
George Cunningham	ECC		picky	0
Katy Haycock	EdTrust		picky	0
Richard Phelps	ECC		liberal	0
Robert Costrell			liberal	0

* Most citations for this person pertain to teacher, rather than student, testing.

** Affiliations:

AASA (American Association of School Administrators);

AAP (Association of American Publishers - School Division);

AFT (American Federation of Teachers);

CAHRS (Center for Advanced Human Resources Studies - Cornell University);

CRESST (Center for Research on Evaluation, Standards and Student Testing);

CSTEEP (Center for the Study of Testing, Evaluation, and Education Policy - Boston College);

ECC (Education Consumers' Consultants Network);

EdTrust (The Education Trust);

FairTest (The National Center for Fair and Open Testing);

Fordham (the Thomas P. Fordham Foundation);

NEA (National Education Association);

NRC (National Research Council - Center for Education;

SREB (Southern Regional Education Board)

The most popular testing opponents in the print media were, in descending order, Neill, Lemann, Chase, Schaeffer, Kohn, Haney, Sacks, Meier, Schrag, Bracey, Gardner, Houston, and Klein. Each was mentioned in 20 or more articles, Neill, Lemann, and Chase in 65, 59, and 56, respectively. The only defender of testing in this stratosphere of popularity was William Sanders, the statistician who helped to develop Tennessee's value-added testing system, who was mentioned in 37 articles.

In Figure 6.1, I further subdivide experts into two groups of defenders and two groups of opponents, as described above—the "radical" and "mainstream" opponents, and the "picky" and "liberal" defenders.

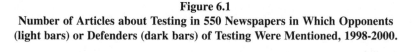

Figure 6.1
**Number of Articles about Testing in 550 Newspapers in Which Opponents
(light bars) or Defenders (dark bars) of Testing Were Mentioned, 1998-2000.**

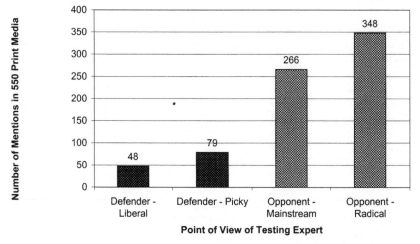

SOURCE: Dow Jones Interactive search of 550 newspapers, years 1998—2000.

Opponents:

Radicals (N=13):	Gerald Bracey; Howard Gardner; Walter Haney; Alfie Kohn; Jonathan Kozol; George Madaus; Deborah Meier; Linda McNeil; Monty Neill; Susan Ohanian; Peter Sacks; Robert Schaeffer; Lorrie Shepard
Mainstream (N=13):	Richard Atkinson; Eva Baker; Bob Chase; Linda Darling-Hammond; Robert Hauser; Jay Heubert; Paul Houston; Steven Klein; Daniel Koretz; Nicholas Lemann; Robert Linn; Peter Schrag; Brian Stecher

Defenders:

Picky Defenders (N-13):	Dale Ballou; John Bishop; Robert Costrell; George Cunningham; Matt Gandal; Katy Haycock; E.D. Hirsch; Mike Podgursky; Bella Rosenberg; William Sanders; Robert Schwartz; Herbert Walberg; Amy Wilkins
Liberal Defenders (N=13):	Gene Bottoms; Gregory Cizek; Nancy Cole; Chester Finn, Jr.; Ron Hambleton; Michael Kean; Barbara Lerner; William Mehrens; David Murray; Mark Musick; Susan Phillips; Richard Phelps; Diane Ravitch

Among those opponents mentioned in ten or more articles were Shepard, Darling-Hammond, Atkinson, Hauser, McNeil, Heubert, Baker and Stecher. The only defender of testing in this troposphere of popularity was Mark Musick, of the Southern Regional Education Board and the National Assessment Governing Board, the board overseeing the National Assessment of Educational Progress, who was mentioned in twelve articles.

All other defenders of testing—all 26 of them—lie low in the mesosphere of popularity among U.S. journalists, or on the ground. The two main FairTest spokesmen plus Alfie Kohn, all by themselves, were included in more articles than all 28 testing defenders combined. Indeed, William Sanders and Mark Musick alone represent the bulk of journalistic interest in testing defenders. But, virtually all of the articles in which they were mentioned were pure news, rather than analysis. As chairperson, Musick often served as a spokesperson for the National Assessment Governing Board (NAGB), the NAEP oversight board, for example, and got interviewed when some administrative decision was made concerning the NAEP, or when some NAEP results were released. Musick and Sanders were seldom asked to express their opinions on the value of high-stakes standardized testing (or to counter the assertions of testing opponents). Overwhelmingly, journalists sought general expertise and value judgments from testing opponents alone.

As if the numbers in the aggregate were not lopsided enough, consider this example. The now-famous Texas Assessment of Academic Skills (TAAS), that was the subject of intense media scrutiny during the 2000 presidential campaign, had a year earlier survived a legal suit (*GI Forum vs Texas Education Agency*). Each side called in testing experts. In the summer of 2000, when U.S. journalists needed Texas testing experts to call for expert news commentary, the expert witnesses from the trial represented an obvious group of potential interviewees. Indeed, dozens of telephone calls went out from journalists to those experts who had testified against the State of Texas and the TAAS. Guess how many telephone calls went out to the expert witnesses who defended the TAAS? According to the Dow Jones Interactive search, none.

Time Magazine on Standardized Testing

Some journalists' stories on standardized testing make only superficial efforts at "balance" by offering token opportunities to testing defenders to speak. These stories commonly have one testing proponent pitted against several critics. Many other stories make no attempt at balance whatsoever, not even a token one.

Time magazine has published its share of such one-sided articles. Here is a summary of one that was published during the 2000 presidential campaign. It would seem apparent that the reporters talked exclusively to testing opponents, as only testing opponents are quoted. The "facts" and language used could have come straight out of a FairTest propaganda piece.

Time: "Is This Your Final Answer" (June 19, 2000)

Subject matter:	State standardized tests
Advocates against testing	Walter Haney, Education professor
	James Popham, Education professor
	Daniel Duke, Education professor
	1 local education administrator
	2 teachers
Advocates for testing	— none —
Prejudicing the jury:	Walt Haney, one of the country's most vociferous and unrestrained opponents of standards (and unapologetic supporter of social promotion), is presented thus: "Even some backers of tough standards are taking a second look at the tests."
	"[Senator Wellstone's bill against testing] is unlikely to pass in the Republican-controlled Congress."
Preconceived bias and unsupported assertions (from reporter's statements):	"this exhaustive new breed of tests..."
	"In practice, the tests have spawned an epidemic of distressing headlines..."
	"Educators say they have had to dumb down their lessons to teach the often picayune factoids covered by the exams."
	"...questions often resemble those in Trivial Pursuit.."
	"Florida has forsaken rote multiple-choice exams..."
False or misleading "facts"	"[these tests] have spurred parents, students and teachers to rebel against the exams' harmful side effects."
	"[students protesting against a state test] are foot soldiers in a growing revolt being waged in classrooms,..."
	"protest-the-test groups have sprouted in at least 36 states"
	"...it is parents who are heeding the call to arms."
	"[parents] charge that too much is riding on a single testing session"
	"Research shows that using test scores in combination with grades results in a more valid decision."
	"People don't cheat when there's a level playing field."

	"When parents start to realize their [child's] going to take a test and may not get a high school diploma, more and more people will start raising their voices."
Tabloid sensationalism:	"Teachers are taking to the streets, with some walking out of exams or quitting the profession entirely."

Notes:

- Out of 73 sentences in the article, only one made any attempt to present a counter argument: "Advocates of greater accountability in the schools contend that teachers—not the tests—are to blame for...cheating." That's it.
- A standard anti-testing ploy is used of presenting a single test item, out of context, and asking if it is fair that students are judged by their performance on just that one test item (in this case, the item is on an event in the history of Asia). In fact, of course, students are not judged based on their performance on a single test item but, rather, on many of them. This single item may have been one of the toughest questions in an examination with hundreds of questions.
- According to these reporters, parents and students oppose tests, "Republicans" support them.
- *Time* asserts that parents who support testing will change their minds if their own children are in danger of failing. Surveys that have asked parents that question directly, however, have found just the opposite. Testing opponents choose to ignore the evidence.
- There is a backlash, it is new, with new people, and growing rapidly—spontaneous movement, grassroots, made up of parents and students, according to *Time*. This assertion, however, is the preferred view of testing opponents. The evidence shows otherwise.
- Standardized tests, it is asserted, induce cheating. It is not mentioned that it is easier to prevent, control, and detect cheating with standardized tests, and that cheating is rampant in regular classroom work—the alternative to standardized testing.
- Multiple-choice tests do not test only "rote" or "trivia." The process of getting from a question to the correct answer can be extremely complicated and time-consuming, requiring a good bit of processing, integration, and analysis.
- Contrary to *Time,* no U.S. state prevents students from graduating based on a single test performance, nor uses test scores alone to make graduation decisions.
- *Time* reporters argue that tests are too hard; and that tests are too easy.

The Washington Post Advocates State Student Testing Programs, But Not in Texas

The *Washington Post,* the paper that broke the Watergate scandal, envisions itself the country's newspaper of record on political issues, a not unrealistic aspiration given its location. The *Post* also declares itself to be a strong, uncompromising advocate of clear academic standards and the use of high-stakes student tests to enforce those standards. It has supported over the past decade and continues to encourage the efforts of the governors and their states to implement such systems.

In April 2000, in the heat of the presidential election campaign, the *Post* published a front-page story on student testing (Mintz 2000). This news story, however, was an unrestrained, wholly critical attack on one of those programs, a particular state testing program that is structured in a way typical of most of the other current state testing programs. The particular state testing program the paper did not like happened to be in Texas.

The article included 26 paragraphs attacking the program and allowed seven paragraphs of defense from state officials and organization spokespersons, stuck mostly in the middle (giving the critics the first and last words). The reporter strongly implied that all testing "experts" stood uniformly in opposition to Texas's tests. There were several reports, more studious, thorough, and thoughtful than the casual sources the *Post* reporter cited, that had painted the Texas testing program in a more positive light. No mention was made of any of them in the *Post* article.

Texas's scores on the neutral, common National Assessment of Educational Progress (NAEP) were used by the *Post's* reporter as a benchmark to prove that the "achievement gap" between minority and white students had not, in fact, been narrowing, as scores on the Texas tests alone would indicate. Much later, it was mentioned that average NAEP scores for all Texas students had been rising since the Texas testing program was introduced, corroborating that, on average, Texas students were learning more. But, the reporter quickly dismissed the NAEP scores in this case as insignificant, and again brought up the problem that the "achievement gap" really is not narrowing as Texas officials say.[4]

Six paragraphs in the beginning of the article were devoted to criticisms from three of the reporter's "experts" before it is mentioned, in a parenthesis in paragraph 28, that all three were paid witnesses in a failed lawsuit to stop the testing program by alleging ethnic bias. The judge did not find these people's arguments credible, but the *Post* reporter accepts them as truth. Indeed, all the critics in the article are given the label "expert" whereas none of the test's defenders are.

The *Post* article on testing in Texas was a tawdry exercise for a media outlet with pretensions for objectivity. But, we all make mistakes. A newspaper can rectify a mistake-prone or one-sided story by printing letters and op-ed pieces that correct the mistakes or present the other side of the story. I sent the *Post* a letter and I know of others who also sent letters. None were printed. A few days after the story, the *Post* published an editorial entitled, "Don't Flinch on Standards," reiterating their steadfast and uncompromising support of state high-stakes testing programs.

"The Downside of High-Stakes Tests," According to the Washington Post

It seems intuitively sensible that dropouts would increase with the implementation of high-stakes tests, until one thinks about it a bit. U.S. schools have had high dropout rates, over 50 percent in some areas, whether or not there were high-stakes tests. Students drop out from boredom, pregnancy, to work, or for a variety of other reasons. Moreover, most states that have implemented high-stakes tests have gone overboard to help students pass, with tutoring, Saturday classes, extra summer school. In some cases, in high-stakes testing states, students who fall behind are getting help for the first time. When there was no testing requirement, there was no obligation for the schools to help them. With the testing requirement, there is.

So, really, it can go either way. Introducing high-stakes testing could increase the dropout rate, it could decrease it, or it could have minimal effect.

To hear most journalists tell it, however, high-stakes testing always increases the dropout rate. Along with many other newspapers, the *Washington Post* published an article during the 2000 presidential campaign asserting that the Texas Assessment of Academic Skills had increased the dropout rate in Texas. (Mathews 2000) In fact, it had not. But, the *Post* was using testing critic Walter Haney's unique personal definition of "dropout" without explanation.

Again, Haney defined anyone who does not graduate "on time" as a dropout. If a student missed a month of school because she was sick, then attended summer school after the 12th grade, and graduated in August, she was a "dropout" by Haney's definition...even though she had never actually dropped out of school. Texas also happens to retain a significant number of below-grade-level students in grade 9 (just before the high school graduation test in grade 10). Most of these students do eventually graduate. Most of these students never drop out of school. Nonetheless, Haney calls them "dropouts," if they were retained in grade 9, since they did not graduate when they were "supposed to" according to Haney.

The *Post* published a chart purporting to show a decline in the proportion of students graduating in Texas throughout the 1990s, the period of the TAAS. The label inside the graph reads "Percentage of Texas ninth-graders who reached 12th grade." That title was erroneous. A correct title would have been "...who reached 12th grade exactly 3 years later (and not a day late!)." The title of the section of the article with the graphic reads, "The Link Between Testing and Dropouts." That, too, was erroneous, as most of the students who do not graduate "on time" do, in fact, graduate and do not, in fact, drop out.

Only in the *Post* caption was the description of the information technically accurate: "Boston College professor Walt Haney compared the number of 12th-graders in a particular year with the number of ninth-graders three years earlier." Alas, that is not a measure of dropouts.

Television Coverage of Testing

The Tiffany Television Network on Testing

Once, while watching the television program *CBS Sunday Morning*, I heard the announcer mention they would do a segment on standardized testing the following week. Curious to know who *CBS Sunday Morning* was interviewing and what they intended to use for source material, I telephoned, and left a message. The young assistant producer who returned the telephone call asked immediately, "Who do you work for? Who's paying you?" Not sure what she meant but, assuming that she assumed I must have been working for some interest group (I was not), I hesitated in responding. Then, she accused me of "being defensive" while she was only asking "a simple question."

She then recounted several "facts" that she had recently learned regarding the great scandal of standardized testing, all of which were wrong. I never did get my questions answered, as she interrupted me each time I tried to ask one, but I did manage to leave the impression that I thought there was another side to the story.

To that she responded, "How did you do on standardized tests?" Again, this is a rhetorical device used by some journalists to shame testing supporters. The thinking is: those who "do well on tests" and who also wish to impose testing on others who "do not do well on tests" are probably motivated by self-interest and self-validation. Thus, anyone who "does well on tests" is suspect as an advocate for testing, whereas those who "do well on tests," but are still willing to speak out against them, may be considered unselfish altruists.

The tenor of the *CBS Sunday Morning* segment on testing was predictable. Below, I summarize three recent *CBS News* stories on standardized testing: the aforementioned, a *60 Minutes* episode broadcast during the 2000 presidential campaign, and another campaign story from a regular CBS News broadcast.

CBS Sunday Morning: "Put to the Test" (April 1, 2001)

Subject matter:	Massachusetts state testing
	The Scholastic Assessment Test (SAT)
Advocates against testing	Walter Haney, Education Professor
(35 lines in the transcript)	Paul Wellstone, U.S. Senator
	Richard Atkinson, President of U. California
	FairTest spokesperson
Advocates for testing	George W. Bush (video clip)
(12 lines in transcript)	Matt Gandal, V.P. of Achieve

Prejudicing the jury:	Matt Gandal is from Achieve, a "business-backed organization"
	A FairTest spokesperson is presented as a "parent."
	Education professor, again, is presented as unbiased, objective, and not self-interested.
Preconceived bias and unsupported assertions (from reporter's statements):	"Some people would say what you're really doing, when it comes down to it, is teaching to the test."
False or misleading "facts" (from reporter's statements):	"America's children, among the most tested in the world..."
	[regarding the SAT] "And don't tell it to their parents, who shelled out hundreds, sometimes thousands of dollars on tutors and prep courses."
	"...some states today are saying one test will decide whether you're going to graduate from high school."
Tabloid sensationalism:	Interview with Walt Haney, with drawings he asked children to make of their feelings about tests, showing one drawing with horns.

Notes:
- Several students also were interviewed; all critical of or opposed to standardized testing.
- The education professor alone had more air time than all the testing defenders combined.
- In fact, American students are among the least tested in the industrialized world. The source of CBS's "fact" declaring the opposite is not listed in the transcript.
- Only some, not all, parents "shell out hundreds of dollars" for test prep courses and they do it spite of the research evidence that these courses do little good.
- Reporter parrots the silly, but very successful concept of "teaching to the test." It is not mentioned that these same testing opponents criticize the SAT and some other tests not aligned to particular curricula for just the opposite reason—one cannot "teach to them."
- There are, in fact, no U.S. states that use a single test to decide whether or not a student graduates from high school.

60 Minutes: "Testing, Testing, Testing" (September 10, 2000)

Subject matter:	State standardized tests in Texas and Massachusetts
Advocates against testing (78 lines in the transcript)	Linda McNeil, Education Professor
	4 teachers
Advocates for testing (22 lines in transcript)	George W. Bush (video clip)
	1 school principal
	Rod Paige, Houston school superintendent

Prejudicing the jury:	Rod Paige labelled "a Bush campaign supporter."
	Education professor presented as unbiased, objective, and not self-interested.
Preconceived bias and unsupported assertions (from reporter's statements):	"All over Texas, principals and teachers are acting less like educators, and more like cheerleaders."
	"Practice for the test, critics say, is crowding out real teaching."
	"Parents can protest and teachers can complain, but so long as the public and the politicians demand accountability, or at least what passes for it..."
False or misleading "facts" (from reporters' statements):	...one-fourth of the African-American and Latino students in our state repeat ninth grade - "That's one of the highest minority repeat rates in the country."
Tabloid sensationalism:	Young boy standing in front of school is crying. Why? [reporter] "...it's the TAAS [the Texas test] that's making you nervous. I'm sorry."

Notes

- The education professor alone had more air time than all testing defenders combined.
- CBS reporter parrots the notion of testing opponents that tests and preparing for tests are activities separate from and not related to "education" or "real learning."
- It is true that Texas has one of the highest grade repetition rates in the country for ninth grade. But, that status exists only for ninth grade. Look at any other grade, or look at the average of all grades, and Texas has a below average repetition rate and a very low repetition rate compared to other states with high proportions of minority students.

CBS News: Campaign 2000: **"Texas: Miracle or Mirage" (October 24, 2000)**

Subject matter:	The "October Surprise" Rand report criticizing Texas's test
Advocates against testing (34 lines in transcript)	Stephen Klein (CRESST): 7 lines
	James A. Thomson: 5 lines
	Rand report (excerpts): 22 lines
Advocates for testing (11 lines in transcript)	George W. Bush: 4 lines
	Bush "Campaign": 7 lines
Prejudicing the jury:	Bush and the Bush campaign are portrayed as cynical and self-interested manipulators of information.
	Rand researchers are portrayed as forthright, well-intentioned, reputable, honest, independent, and dispassionate scientists.

Preconceived bias and unsupported assertions (from reporter's statements):	Bush: "bragged" and "boasts" Rand: "...the nonpartisan Rand Corp." and "Appreciative of the power of the Rand name the Bush campaign tried to spin the paper as the views of a few rogue researchers."
False or misleading "facts" (from reporters' statements):	"...major improvements by Texas students in tests administered by the state are not reflected in national exams given to the same youngsters." "...when they compared the results of national reading and math tests to state test results in the same subjects, researchers found a 'striking' gap in average scores between whites and students of color." "Texas students don't exceed national norms."
Tabloid sensationalism:	Rand study: "a stink bomb [for] Bush's campaign," "may give Bush a black eye," "more than a bad hair day for Bush," "red meat for [opposing candidate Al] Gore's ad men," "Gore may finally have something he can pin on Bush"

Notes

- It was not mentioned that these particular researchers at the Rand Corporation worked on two large federal contracts in danger of elimination if Bush was elected.
- It was not mentioned that other researchers at the Rand Corporation, with no such conflicts of interest, had earlier published better studies praising the Texas testing program.
- Contrary to the Rand report's claims, Texas students' test scores improved not only on Texas's tests, but also on the National Assessment of Educational Progress (NAEP), over the same time period. Indeed, the Texas gains on the NAEP were the second strongest of any state in the 1990s.
- It is not mentioned that despite the "striking gap" between ethnic groups in test performance (which is hardly unique to Texas), Texas' minority student test scores had increased substantially during the period of Texas's testing program.
- While it is true that Texas students' academic achievement does not exceed national norms, they used to be near the bottom. Texas's students have improved their achievement more than all but one other state in the 1990s.
- No testing experts were interviewed to counter the Rand report's claims, implying that all testing experts would agree with these Rand researchers. They certainly would not.

Public Broadcasting's Merrow Report on Standardized Testing: Can Education Journalism Get Any Worse?

Once, in a radio interview, Public Broadcasting's John Merrow said that he understands education issues, in part, because he has an education school degree. It shows. "Testing Our Schools," a documentary broadcast in the *Frontline* series first in spring 2002, tells a story strictly by the (education establishment) book. Here is how the issue of standardized testing gets presented when bound by that book:

- Who supports standardized testing? Answer: politicians and businesspeople. "Testing Our Schools" proves this, since all the testing supporters on the show are from these two groups.
- What do testing experts think about standardized testing? Answer: They oppose using standardized tests in anything like the way they are being used in states today and how they would be used under President Bush's plan. "Testing Our Schools" proves this, since all the testing experts on the show express this point of view.
- Are there any testing experts who disagree with them? Answer: No. "Testing Our Schools" proves this, since no experts with a contrary point of view appear on the show. Remember, only politicians and businesspeople support testing, and "most" of them "are dirt-ignorant regarding what these tests should and [should] not be used for."
- What about commercial test developers? Surely they must support the use of the high-stakes tests they sell? Answer: No, they do not; not even them; they think that standardized tests should not be used for high-stakes purposes. "Testing Our Schools" proves this since the two experts on the show who work in test development say so.
- What about your average, typical classroom teachers; don't some of them support the use of high-stakes standardized tests? Answer: Some of them just seem to be going along with what they are supposed to do, but the most articulate among them—those who seem to have given the issue a lot of thought and developed well-formed opinions—are very much opposed. "Testing Our Schools" proves this, since the teachers on the show expressing the most articulate and well-thought-out arguments vehemently oppose testing.
- What about the general public and parents; don't they support standardized testing? Answer: Maybe, but only to the extent that they have been duped by politicians and businesspeople. Besides, the general public has a far too simplistic an understanding of the topic and they "read too much into test scores." Standardized testing is very complicated, you see, and it takes experts—usually education school professors—to understand and explain it properly. We should do what the mainstream education school professors tell us to do; they know best.

Using the show's transcript, I count up the lines allocated to all sides in the debate:

Interviewees: Expert Testing Opponents	Lines in transcript	Interviewees: Politician/Business Defenders	Lines in transcript
James Popham, ed. professor	34	David Driscoll (Massachusetts)	18
Bill Schmidt, ed. professor[5]	19	Jeff Nellhaus (Massachusetts)	12
George Madaus, ed. professor	18	Rod Paige (federal government)	8
Audrey Qualls, Iowa Test	16	Bill Bosher (Virginia)	7
Ted Sizer, ed. professor	12	Lou Gerstner (IBM)	6
Michael Kirst, ed. professor[5]	12		
TOTAL	111	TOTAL	51

My accounting above indicates that testing opponents got more time to talk—twice as much time. But, the counts should be qualified in three respects. First, Merrow did happen to pick politicians and a businessperson who are extremely well informed on the topic of testing. In my opinion, they did an excellent job in "Testing Our Schools." As is so often the case in U.S. media treatment of the testing issue, however, the politicians went first and the experts got to respond, and not vice versa. Done this way, of course, the experts can say anything they please, since no retort is allowed. "Testing Our Schools" did give Driscoll and Nellhaus a small amount of time to respond to some of the experts' assertions, however, and that was crucial toward giving the show a tiny hint of balance. Moreover, Paige was sharp enough in the tiny amount of time allotted to him to anticipate what opponents' arguments would be.

The second reason my counts in the table above should be qualified has to do with time "allotted" in the show to politicians and businesspersons in video clips. At the beginning of "Testing Our Schools," the audience is shown clips of George W. Bush (10 lines), H. Ross Perot (3 lines), Lou Gerstner (4 lines), Pete Wilson (2 lines), and Gray Davis (3 lines). Some of the clips reveal innocuous content (e.g., Wilson signing a bill, Davis awarding a plaque, Bush in a classroom photo shoot). The clips were meant to set the stage for the debate in "Testing Our Schools"; they were not part of the debate. None of the five public officials featured in the video clips were given any chance on the show to respond to the specific criticisms of the experts interviewed on the show.

Third, the line counts for the interviewees should be qualified because they do not include time Merrow allotted to the "ringers" he had on his show. At least two, probably four, and perhaps more of those presented on "Testing Our Schools" as average, ordinary, just-happened-to-run-into-them, they-could-be-your-own-child's teachers and principals on the show are experienced anti-testing activists, affiliated with well-known anti-testing organizations and events (e.g., Linda Nathan [seven lines], Judi Hirsch [13 lines], Steven Weinberg [17 lines]).

Naturally, "Testing Our Schools" also repeats many of the contradictions, false facts and fallacies that have inundated those of us who are regularly exposed to anti-testing rhetoric.

Contradictions: "Testing Our Schools" asserted all of the following:

- These tests are too difficult and produce failures, dropouts, and demoralized students.
- These standardized tests are too easy; creative, higher-order instruction has been replaced or dumbed down to the low level of these simple tests, that could be passed by 5th graders.

- For the sake of clarity and fairness, academic standards, course work, textbooks, instruction, and tests should all be consistent and operate from the same play book.
- Teachers must be allowed to tailor instruction uniquely to each class, indeed, to each individual student. Teachers are intelligent craftpersons who should be granted creative license to choose appropriate course content and instructional styles, and not be bound by standards and norms.

- High-stakes standardized tests are bad for all the reasons stated above.
- Students consider tests without stakes to be meaningless, and make no effort on them.

False Facts: Also to be found in the transcript of "Testing Our Schools," are the following "facts," all of which are untrue:

- "One test" is being used to "determine the outcome of twelve years of schooling, decide who gets a diploma and who gets nothing." Other measures, such as grades and teacher recommendations, are not being used in graduation decisions in high-stakes testing states.
- A student can get partial credit on a test with open-ended questions, but not on a test with multiple-choice format.
- One can figure out the correct answers on multiple-choice tests without knowing the topic or solving the problem, just through "plugging in" answers or "manipulation." Students can get high scores on these tests without understanding the subject matter.
- "Test preparation" is unrelated to learning and instruction and, indeed, may be antithetical. Indeed, "tests" are unrelated to subject matter and may be antithetical.
- Standardized tests are discriminatory; students from poor backgrounds cannot do well on them.
- "We don't need tests to tell us who's having a hard time and who's having trouble in school."
- High-stakes standardized tests are purely a "bottom line" business solution applied to a very different type of organization—schools. The idea

started with a businessperson in Texas, H. Ross Perot. [by implication... No other country on earth used high-stakes standardized tests before Perot suggested the concept]

- Curriculum standards are being decided by "a small group of people, people you can't get at, people who say there's one answer.... We have to have a dialogue about what [to teach]... We don't go there." [contradicted by show itself, in visiting a Virginia standards-drafting meeting]
- [Also, a school in California was teaching subject matter a grade level too late, in the grade just above the one where the state tested that material. Obviously, this is unfair, but the show implies that such a situation is: the fault of the test or of the state, and not that school's fault; and inevitable in any school in an environment of high-stakes testing.]

Comparing to perfection instead of to the actual alternatives to tests: As usual, "Testing Our Schools" judges standardized tests against a standard of perfection instead of against the actual, available alternatives. The available alternatives (e.g., grade-point averages, teacher evaluations, classroom tests) are replete with problems and fare worse by comparison to perfection than standardized tests do, but are given scrutiny by education journalists only rarely. Never does one find an education journalist who puts all the available alternatives in the balance together at the same time before making judgments regarding the quality of each.

- "The tests turn out to have mistakes."
- "There's whole types of intelligence that you're not measuring."
- Standardized test scores "contain a margin of error."

The one-sided slant of "Testing Our Schools" was no accident. Granted, I am not capable of reading the minds of John Merrow or his producer and, thus, cannot truly know what their motives were. The evidence to support the assertion that the show had a deliberate intent is this—few, if any, of those interviewed on the show expressed points of view that were not known to the show's producers beforehand. The show presented several individuals as ordinary teachers and principals the camera crew just happened to find at the average, typical schools they just happened to visit. None of the show's school visits were accidental, though, they were selected.

The *Merrow Report* picked teachers and principals who had already expressed themselves publicly, either through the activities of anti-testing organizations or in earlier work done by other journalists.[6] For example, members of the anti-testing advocacy groups, California Resisters, Bay Area Resisters, and the California Coalition for Authentic Reform in Education were interviewed previously by writers for the *San Francisco Chronicle, Sacramento Bee,* and *Atlantic Monthly* (but still presented on Merrow's Testing Our Schools as average, ordinary teachers they just happened to find that day) (California

Teachers Association 2001; M. May 2001; Schrag 2000) The Boston Arts Academy just happens to have as its school principal a widely known author and outspoken opponent of high-stakes standardized testing (presented on the show as nothing more than an ordinary school principal they found by chance) (see, for example, Nathan 2000).

John Merrow may be more propagandist than journalist.[7] When a caller to a radio talk show suggested, very mildly, that he thought Merrow might be biased (*Washington Post On Line*), Merrow responded:

> Am I biased? I think I bring a lot of background knowledge to this issue after 26 years of reporting, teaching at three different levels, and a doctorate in education and social policy from Harvard.... Thomas Griffith, a *Time* editor for many years, wrote "The relationship between a journalist's beliefs and his reporting is something like that of a juror's desire to reach an impartial verdict. Jurors are not required to be empty minds, free of past experience or views; what is properly demanded of them is a readiness to put prejudices and uncorroborated impressions aside in considering the evidence before them. As much is asked of the journalist."

Worldwide Web Coverage of Standardized Testing

The distortion in favor of the status quo on the topic of testing is lopsided even on the Worldwide Web. For example, a search using the Google search engine in October 2001, with the instructions, "FairTest" AND (test OR tests OR testing), retrieved 4,500 links. Similarly, the research group, CRESST, whose work is overwhelmingly opposed to the use of high-stakes standardized testing, garnered 3,500 links. No groups with sympathetic views toward testing could even remotely approach those numbers.

I also ran searches using this same format on each of the individual names of testing experts that I had used in the Dow Jones Interactive Search through the print media. Once again, as can be seen in Figure 6.2, testing opponents get more attention.

Among individuals, testing critics Howard Gardner, Alfie Kohn, Linda Darling-Hammond, Bob Chase, Richard Atkinson, and Jonathan Kozol stand out, with over 1,000 links each. Indeed, Howard Gardner's name retrieved over 8,000 links. Defenders of testing in this stratosphere of Web linkage, with over 1,000 links, are E. D. Hirsch, the Core Knowledge founder (who is, really, very critical of some types of standardized testing [i.e., portfolios and performance tests]), Diane Ravitch, and Chester Finn, Jr. Indeed, Hirsch, Finn, and Ravitch alone account for three-quarters of all testing defender links. Testing opponents Gardner, Kohn, Darling-Hammond, Chase, and Atkinson alone account for as many hits as all 26 testing defenders.

With the exception of Kohn, however, none of the testing experts up in the stratosphere of Web coverage are testing specialists. Rather, they are education experts who often express opinions about testing or who mention tests or

Figure 6.2
Number of "Hits" for Names of Certain Testing Experts at Web Sites
Pertaining to the Issue of Standardized Testing

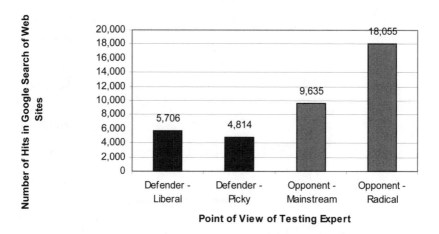

test results within the context of other education issues. Take away these non-testing-specialist high outliers who skew the counts—Gardner, Darling-Hammond, Chase, Atkinson, and Kozol on the opponents side (number of hits—15,800) and the five most popular experts on the defenders side (Hirsch, Ravitch, Finn, Walberg, and Sanders ; number of hits—8,147)—and the slant in favor of testing opponents appears even more dramatic. Testing opponents get more exposure, and the more extreme the opposition the greater the amount (see Figure 6.3).

In the troposphere of Web linkage, with over 200 links, one finds mostly testing opponents (Deborah Meier [850], Monty Neill [644], Susan Ohanian [589], Peter Sacks [450], Robert Schaeffer [344], Lorrie Shepard [434], Gerald Bracey [594], Walt Haney [391], Paul Houston [350], George Madaus [261], Linda McNeil [298], Peter Schrag [900], Jay P. Heubert [209], Stephen Klein [338], Brian Stecher [224], Eva Baker [467], Nicholas Lemann [396], Robert Linn [598], and Daniel Koretz [254]). To counter these 19 testing opponents, one finds five testing defenders in the troposphere of Web linkage—William Sanders (386), Herbert Walberg (511), Dale Ballou (223), Michael Podgursky (311), and Nancy Cole (254).

Down in the mesosphere of Web linkage, between 100 and 200 Google links, testing defenders finally outnumber testing opponents (opponents: Robert Hauser [199]; defenders: Matt Gandal [123], John Bishop [173], George Cunningham [158], Mark Musick [135]; and Gene Bottoms [198]).

On the ground, under the stratosphere, troposphere, and mesosphere of Web linkage, one finds only testing defenders (Robert Costrell (24); Katy Haycock (15); Amy Wilkins (99); Bella Rosenberg (99); Gregory Cizek (94);

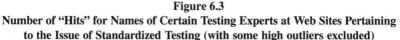

Figure 6.3
Number of "Hits" for Names of Certain Testing Experts at Web Sites Pertaining to the Issue of Standardized Testing (with some high outliers excluded)

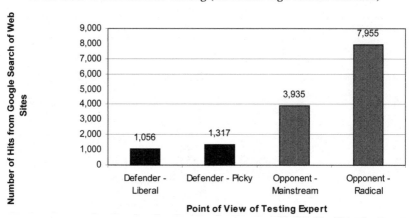

Robert Schwartz (92); Michael Kean (63); Barbara Lerner (49); Bill Mehrens (34); Robert Murray (63); Richard Phelps (37); Susan Phillips (81); and Ron Hambleton (48). Actually, there are other testing defenders who, perhaps foolishly, still believe that major public policy issues should be decided in the careful, rigorous, environment of scientific journals, so they publish their work in those journals. Most of these folks cannot be found on the Web at all.

Why is linkage on the Web so one-sided? In part, it may be because many education producer groups list only those sources who share their point of view (or, to be more exact, the side of the issue favored by the leadership of each organization). Pick most any of the many education administrator associations and look at their websites. One is likely to find many links to "research" on testing, but virtually all of it will be from only one side of the issue.

This crude censorship stands in stark contrast to the behavior of the organizations on the other side of the issue, who defend the use of testing, and to that of organizations of testing professionals. One will find both sides of the story at the Websites of the National Association of Testing Directors or the Educational Testing Service, for example. Indeed, if anything, the NATD and ETS websites will lead one to more anti-testing documents than pro-testing documents. Moreover, one will hear both sides of the story at conferences of the Association of American Publishers—School Division (i.e., the commercial test developers). The test publishers, often portrayed as greedy, opportunistic demons by testing opponents, go out of their way to make certain that all sides are allowed to speak at their conferences and on their websites.

For contrast, go to the websites of the American Association of School Administrators (AASA), the National Association of Secondary School Principals (NASSP), the National Education Association (NEA), the National School Boards Association (NSBA), the American Association for Supervision and Curriculum Development (ASCD), or most of the curriculum-specific professional organizations (e.g., NCTM, NCTE, NCSS, etc.) and you will find an unvaried diet of anti-testing propaganda. Dozens of the largest and most influential U.S. education organizations outwardly profess to support democracy, free speech, open discussion, and critical, creative, and higher-order thinking. Yet, in the effect of their actions, much of their behavior mimics that of authoritarian, doctrinaire, intolerant cults. Their members simply are not allowed exposure to "aberrant" points of view.

As if the censorship within the education organizations was not bad enough, it would seem that testing opponents have also assumed control of most Web directories on the topic of standardized testing. For those of you still unfamiliar with the workings of the Worldwide Web, the two most important facilities in the Web are "portals" and "search engines." There is so much information available in the Web that one can not begin to digest it without a search engine to cull the mass of information to meet one's specific needs. "Portals" are entry, or connection, points. Popular portals include: America Online (AOL), Yahoo!, Lycos, MSN, CompuServe, Juno, and so on. Popular search engines include: Google, FAST, Northern Light, Alta Vista, HotBot, and so on.

As essential as they are, portals and search engines are only means to an end. They only help get you to where you want to go; in and of themselves, they have no "content." "Directories" have lots of content. They are, in a sense, the Worldwide Web version of encyclopedias, and they are still in the process of being built. Given how important they are, we should probably be concerned about the character of the one who, in particular, is building them.

Consider the two most important directories on the issue of "standardized testing" within the Open Directory Project, which maintains the directories used by dozens of search engines. One of them until recently was managed by a testing professional and she provided links to many organizations and publications on all sides of the issue. It was reached through the logical path: Reference > Education > Standardized Testing. The other was managed by a schoolteacher with an attitude, and he provided over 40 links, all but a few of them exclusively to the most extreme anti-testing groups and publications. His directory was reached through a different logical path: Society > Issues > Education > Standardized Testing.

An Encounter with the Politburo of the Peoples' Republic of the Web

The Worldwide Web is supposed to make the world more democratic, by making more information available to more people more easily. That assumes, of course, that information is disseminated throughout the Web in a fair, open, democratic, or, at least, random way. Is it?

Most Web search engines contain reference directories and these directories provide much of the content that is on the Web. Since there are so many different search engines, the existence of all these directories would seem to support the democratizing hypothesis. Unfortunately, there are, essentially, only three sets of reference directories, and the vast majority of search engines use one of the three. Yahoo! has built its own set of directories. LookSmart has one that is used by a half dozen search engines; an entry in the LookSmart directories costs money though, so that set of directories is pretty limited. That leaves the directory that is used by hundreds of other search engines worldwide, including Google, Lycos, Netscape, InfoSeek, Northern Light, and many others. It is the "Open Directory Project," run by volunteer editors. Apparently, it was originally started by Netscape. Using volunteer editors, of course, helps keep costs down. Its folklore about itself is that it is "open," and "democratic"—the "Republic of the Web." "Humans do it better," is another one of its slogans.

Being an editor, however, requires some work and some diligence. Who is willing to take that on for no pay? Certainly, there are those who wish to facilitate open and informed discussion, and they become editors in the interest of pursuing the avowed goals of the Open Directory Project. Unfortunately, there also exist totalitarian wannabees who seek to ensure that the public only gets to hear the arguments on the side of a topic that they personally prefer. Either one of these types of people can volunteer to be an Open Directory editor. Do some surfing yourself through the Open Directory Project's massive list of directories and you will find both kinds of directories-ones that make an effort at balance, and others that represent completely one-sided advocacy listings.

Sure, the Open Directory Project has "Editor's Guidelines" and, though the emphasis on balanced coverage is not nearly as emphatic as I think it should be, it is still clearly there. But, that has not prevented biased directory editing, nor could it if editors with a bias have somehow convinced themselves that they are open-minded.

For several years, Web searchers interested in the topic of standardized testing were misled because the Open Directory Project directory (Society > Issues > Education > Standardized Testing) was controlled by anti-testing advocates. Almost all of its links went to organizations and articles on only one side of the issue, and the extreme end of that side to boot. Even the descriptions of those links were more boosterism and advertisement than informational. The most extreme, unrestrained, and vitriolic anti-testing organization in the United States was uniquely labeled a "cool site" and "editor's choice" and, so, placed at the top and in bold letters.

I have copied the directory in compacted form into an endnote, so that you can judge for yourself.[8] It was copied out of the Lycos search engine (on August 12, 2001) and has 45 links. All but a few of the 45 links lead one to groups or documents that are clearly anti-testing.

To be complete, it must be added that the directory included a few links to organizations sympathetic to testing. If one followed those particular links, however, one discovered that they carried you not to those organizations' main websites, but uniquely to single documents critical of testing (see, for example, the ETS and ERIC links). Indeed, the directory consisted almost entirely of links to individual documents—to "dead ends," severely limiting any researcher's options, rather than to websites that offered many documents or still more links, websites that expanded a researcher's options and information. The directory was very "directive."[9] This directory's editors were not at all interested in broadening a user's horizons. Rather, they had found the truth, and they were solely interested in leading one to it.

I, and undoubtedly others, complained via the available public conduits about the slant of this directory, but to no avail. So, naturally, when I saw the editorship open up in the summer of 2001, I applied for it, frankly asserting why I wanted to be the editor, and my application was accepted, much to my surprise. Either the "Open Directory Project" really was democratic, in keeping with its self-image, or nobody was paying attention and any bum off the street could have become editor. Surely, the former explanation made more sense.

I spent most of a weekend during summer vacation editing the directory, I thought the work was so important. I changed the protocols so that no sites were given priority (no "cool sites"), no site got more than two lines of description, and the language describing each site was neutralized (no advertising). Most of these changes were made to bring the directory into conformity with the very explicit instructions in the Open Directory's Editor's Guidelines about how directories should be laid out. I also added a lot of links, including some to organizations whose work I strongly disagree with, because they were, nonetheless, organizations that any researcher on the topic should be aware of.

It did not take long before I received a message. The message was not sent to me directly; it was imbedded in a screen that blocked my path into the editor's domain. Someone had been watching what I was doing and was not pleased. He blocked my access to the directory so that I could make no more changes. His name was "SFJohnson."[10]

Who was "SFJohnson?" He just happened to be one of the two editors responsible for the directory as it had been, with its 45 anti-testing links and the extremist group FairTest as the "editor's pick" and "cool site." (The other editor responsible for the directory as it had been, "noonenj,"[11] continues to edit other directories, including those covering bilingual education.) SFJohnson also was a "meta-editor," one with more power than an ordinary editor like me.

I had made many changes to the directory, but he remarked on only one of them. I had "un-cooled" the link to FairTest, so that it was no longer the "editor's choice." I had also reduced the amount of verbiage describing it so that it fit in just two lines, as the Open Directory Editor's Guidelines requires. He strongly suggested that I put that extra verbiage back in and that I "re-cool" FairTest. He was genuinely, though probably not to his own knowledge, ordering me to violate the Open Directory Editor's Guidelines.

I thought I had already thoroughly explained my reasons for "un-cooling" FairTest in the editor's notes that accompany any directory change—I had argued that "cooling" any site for a topic as controversial as standardized testing was tantamount to taking sides and telling the public what to think. Besides, the Open Directory Project's Editor's Guidelines define a "cool site" to be "the most definitive site on a subject...the best site in the category" and only an advocate on one side of the issue, and a very extreme one at that, could describe FairTest's site that way. I thought that there should be no "cool" sites, in keeping with the Open Directory's philosophy of neutrality. I was happy to discuss the issue further with him, but I certainly did not agree with his suggestion.

I was being naïve. In fact, despite all of SFJohnson's diplomatic-sounding rhetoric, he had, in fact, given me no choice. I would do what he wished, or I would not be allowed back into the collective. I tried pointing-and-clicking at several places on the screen, but could not get out of the screen or respond to his message except, apparently, via one particular button. The only button allowing me continued access as an editor (and the possibility of communicating to any other editors besides him via the editors' forums) was the "AGREE" button. SFJohnson did not try to communicate with me via an interactive mode. He made no attempt to engage me in a discussion. I was given no option, if I wished to continue editing, other than to agree with him. Welcome to the "Peoples' Republic of the Web."

I tried several more times over the course of the next week to figure out a way to respond to the lock-out in a way other than by agreeing with the meta-editor's "suggestions." Nothing worked. Finally, I protested at the main public Open Directory feedback site and requested an arbiter or a hearing. I heard nothing back. After another week or so, I sent an e-mail directly to SFJohnson requesting an arbiter or a hearing. After a few more weeks, he replied, completely ignoring my request for an arbiter or a hearing. Here is what he wrote:

> ...the idea is to build a comprehensive collection of sites covering Standardized Testing Issues. This means including some sites you agree with and some you don't. Based on what could be learned about you, I and others are concerned that pro-testing [sic] issue sites might not get added as long as you are editor in this area.

Of course, I do not know if he really did talk to anyone else. And I heard from no one else, despite repeated requests. SFJohnson apparently did not much appreciate what I had done as editor. So he did some investigating of my personal background and decided to accuse me of a "conflict of interest," which violates Open Directory guidelines, and is cause for removing an editor. As evidence that I had a conflict of interest, he pointed to the "Test Bashing Series" I wrote for EducationNews.org in the year 2000 (for which I was paid nothing).[12] The "conflict of interest" provisions in the guidelines have to do with commercial ties (of which I had none), and are meant to prevent those with a financial interest in doing so from removing competitors' websites from a directory to their own commercial advantage. I had not removed anyone's websites and I had no commercial ties but, so what? I behaved in an "aberrant" manner, therefore it was necessary to eject me from the collective.

Not only had I not removed any anti-testing groups from the directory (unless one wants to count eliminating a duplicate link), I added several.[13] Moreover, I did not remove SFJohnson's beloved FairTest; I just "un-cooled" it. I also added a dozen or so sites that represent broad ranges of perspectives, neutral, or balanced points of view.[14] With the possible exceptions of a link to the Texas Education Agency and, at most, a couple of now-dead links, no sites that could arguably be considered neutral or balanced existed in the directory before I became editor. Finally, I also added several sites that represented pro-testing points of view.[15] Arguably, only three such sites had existed in the directory before, two extremely brief Texas newspaper notes of statements made by George W. Bush and one link that most likely was a mistake.[16]

So SFJohnson removed me as an editor allegedly because I had a conflict of interest and a bias. Note that he thinks the previous two editors of the Standardized Testing directory, one of which was him, had no bias, and both continue as editors. I took my own stroll back through the Open Directory Guidelines and found half a dozen provisions that SFJohnson has violated, having to do with balancing the offerings in a directory, how listings should be short, concise, and neutral, procedures for communicating with other editors, and so on. Yet he and the equally authoritarian "noonenj" continue as editors. Why?

Because the "Republic of the Web" is not run in a fashion even remotely republican. It is run more like the old Soviet Politburo. Who got in there first has the most power and, as long as you do not tread on the turf (the directories) of other editors, they will probably leave you alone to run yours as you please. Otherwise, power is strictly hierarchical and there are no elections, just "selections" and "removals," which can be arbitrary. Yes, all are equal in the Peoples' Republic of the Web, but some are more equal than others. A wide range of perspectives in a directory is called bias. An exclusive offering of sites at one extreme end of the spectrum of opinion is called "balance," if the "meta-editor" says so. A possible or potential bias is not acceptable. A demonstrated, proven bias is fine. How many fingers do you see, Winston?

The Open Directory wants to be the most comprehensive directory in the world. Given how it is run, there seems absolutely no possibility of that. The

Open Directory also claims the ambition to be the largest Internet-based directory of information in the world. Heaven help us if they should succeed.

Only One Side Gets to Link-Censorship at Yahoo!

The first of the major Internet Search Engines, Yahoo!, has by now developed quite a large set of reference directories. I list the contents, as of September 16, 2001, of the directory Education > Standards and Testing > High Stakes Testing in compacted form in an endnote.[17] For those readers unfamiliar with these particular links, I invite you to investigate them yourselves. You will find an unadulterated, one-sided diet of misinformation from groups opposed to standardized testing. There are dozens of other links available on the topic that could provide balance to this list, but Yahoo! refused to list any of them.

I contacted Yahoo! on a few occasions over the course of a year, complaining about the bias in this directory and other Yahoo! directories on testing, and offered suggestions for additional links that could help to balance its extreme one-sidedness. All correspondence was ignored, and no changes were made.

The Education "Trade" Press

Editorial Projects in Education (EPE) publishes *Education Week* and *Teacher Magazine. Education Week* (*EdWeek*) is considered by most to be the main "industry trade paper" and, indeed, calls itself "Education's Newspaper of Record." It is a frequent point of debate among its critics, however, what *EdWeek* means by "Education" in that phrase—is it education writ large, or is *EdWeek* an advocacy paper for those institutions and individuals vested in the current public education system and structure.

Education's "Newspaper of Record" on High-Stakes Testing, Part 1

Guess who wrote the words below:[18]

> Of all the school reform ideas circulating today, high-stakes student testing has to be about the worst. Unfortunately, instead of slowing down and reassessing the use of these tests, more and more states seem determined to make them the engine of their school-improvement strategies. Apparently they would rather risk a public backlash than be perceived as "backsliding."
>
> Those who push for high-stakes testing contend that the threat of severe penalties pressures students and teachers to improve performance. Schools are doing poorly, they imply, because students and teachers are not working hard enough. This argument brushes aside decades of research that links poor performance to the way schools are organized, operated, governed, and funded. It also ignores the impact that poverty and discrimination have on student performance.

The two paragraphs above are filled with the standard premise and argument of testing opponents on education school faculty and in some well-known advocacy groups. There is a call for more "research" before standardized testing is administered for high-stakes and, presumably, the research will be conducted by testing's opponents, with predictable results. It is assumed that the alleged "backlash" against testing is derived from widespread and new public opposition rather than the activities of a few small pressure groups that have long opposed testing. The writer adds the now all-too-familiar charge that supporters see high-stakes testing as a "silver bullet" cum "quick fix" cum "cheap fix" without identifying any testing supporters who are really so narrow-minded, probably because there are few or none. Finally, the writer cites "the research" which purports to show that poor student performance has nothing to do with what and how students are taught. If even half of the research conducted by the more radical constructivists and egalitarians (hereafter, "utopians," for short) whom he trusts was any good, I might agree with him.

The words above were written in a *Teacher Magazine* editorial by the long-time editor of its sister publication, *Education Week*. It would not be so distressing to see such bias if these were just any old publications. Unfortunately, Editorial Projects in Education (EPE), the parent group of the two publications, has a very strong presence in education "trade" journalism. Many ostensibly objective, nonpartisan organizations use EPE as their source of allegedly objective information on education stories. Many ordinary newspapers link to EPE as a source and reference for their coverage of education issues.

Here are some further accusations of high-stakes testing from the editorial written by this high official at "Education's Newspaper of Record" along with my responses:

1. "States are using standardized test scores as the single measure to determine whether a student passes or graduates, which is stupid and unfair."

No, they are not. Students are given several to many chances to pass these high school exit exams. Moreover, these exams are typically set at a middle-school level of difficulty, or lower, and untimed. Most parents do not want their children to leave high school before they have mastered the basic core subjects at a 6th- or 7th-grade level of difficulty.

Moreover, exit exam requirements are no different from any other high school completion requirement. If a state requires that students complete four levels of English to graduate, no student can graduate without passing four levels of English. If a student fails a senior-level English course, she does not graduate. And, ultimately, at the margin, she can fail simply for not passing an end-of-semester exam in any level of English, by just one question. What is true for English is true for any other graduation requirement, from passing grades in four levels of Physical Education courses to completion of minimum amounts of community service time in some states.

2. The editor writes: "Many middle and high school students-especially those in the most disadvantaged neighborhoods-do not read well and have not had an opportunity to learn the material required to meet the standards set for them....the teachers generally assigned to the most at-risk students are those least prepared for the task [to teach to standards]."

Whose fault is it that students do not have an opportunity to learn required material? Whose fault is it that some teachers are unprepared to do their jobs? Whose fault is it that the least-prepared teachers end up with the most at-risk students? If the editor would like to support genuine solutions to those problems, he will face the vested interests in public education who will oppose him. Tests did not cause these problems.

3. The editor describes multiple-choice test items as "primitive."

Contemporary multiple-choice tests are the most technically advanced and reliable (i.e., fair) type of standardized test in the world. It is open-ended format tests that are "old-tech." Mind you, that does not make open-ended tests all bad. Both types of tests have advantages and disadvantages, but the alleged disadvantages of multiple-choice tests have been way overblown and their advantages largely ignored.

4. According to the editor, "...high-stakes tests (along with grade-specific standards) actually reduce flexibility and emphasize even more the lock step process of schooling."

"Flexibility" has its limits as a beneficial force. Yes, indeed, teachers need flexibility in addressing the learning needs of their students. But, contrary to the rhetoric of the utopians, no teachers other than home schoolers can feasibly adapt every lesson to each individual student. Besides, standardized tests do not dictate instructional technique, they require the mastery of certain knowledge. Teachers and students are free to master that knowledge in any manner that works best for them.

5. The editor claims: "Many states use 'off-the-shelf' standardized tests that are not aligned with the standards and curricula they've installed in schools. In some cases, high stakes are attached to norm-referenced tests, which rank students according to the performances of their peers, not to any academic benchmark. How logical is that?"

I agree that it is not fair to make high-stakes decisions about students based on tests that are not matched to a required curriculum. I do not agree that "many" states are following such a practice; moreover, the one or two that have did so only while they were in the process of constructing high-stakes tests aligned to their standards.

> 6. The editor asserts: "Many organizations and individuals are working hard to fulfill the enormous potential of standards-based reform. It would be a pity to let high-stakes testing derail the movement now."

It is unfortunate that EPE is not one of those organizations. By portraying external measures as antagonistic to "standards-based reform," EPE plays right into the hands of the vested interests who tolerate only that "reform" that they can control. That is reform in name only.

Education's "Newspaper of Record" on High-Stakes Testing, Part 2

Guess who wrote the words below:[19]

> America's obsession with standardized tests is about to become even more intense....The foolish emphasis we put on testing is expensive, unnecessary, and probably harmful to millions of children.... Despite warnings from testing experts and educators that important decisions should not be based on a single measure, 17 states now require high school students to pass an exit exam to graduate, and at least seven more plan to do so.
>   Standardized tests have too many deficiencies to be the determining factor in assessing student achievement. But the most egregious flaw is that they don't address the qualities that most parents want their children to have—such as the skills and attitudes needed to continue learning on their own and to be good citizens, productive citizens, and fulfilled human beings. Parents want their kids to develop virtues and values that we can all agree on, like diligence, honesty, tolerance, fairness, and compassion.

The person writing the passage above is the same as before-the main man at Editorial Projects in Education, publisher of "Education's Newspaper of Record," *Education Week*. Despite what he says, when parents have been allowed to speak for themselves, instead of through an educator-interpreter, they have said that they want schools to, first and foremost, teach the basic skills (i.e., subject matter, such as reading, writing, and arithmetic) (Johnson and Immerwahr 1994). In addition to misrepresenting parents' preferences, the writer employs pejorative language (e.g., "obsession with standardized tests," "foolish emphasis") and proffers several false facts. Again, I respond:

- There exists no state where high school graduation is determined "by a single measure."
- Not all "testing experts and educators" are opposed to high-stakes standardized testing. Such an assertion represents self-serving wishful thinking.
- If anything, the existence of high-stakes standardized tests probably encourages diligence, fulfillment, productivity, and the skills and attitudes

needed to continue learning on one's own. Certainly, there is no evidence that a lack of standardized testing does so.

- There is no reason to believe that the existence of standardized testing is antithetical to the existence of honesty, tolerance, fairness, and compassion.

This *EdWeek* publisher wants our schools to teach moral virtues. Many parents might well wonder if our schools should attempt to take on that enormous responsibility if they are not capable of or willing to fulfill their most basic functions—teaching our students to read, write, and subtract.

The astute journalist Joanne Jacobs (2002) wrote a short critique of the *EdWeek* publisher's article excerpted above. In it, she said:

> Most parents do want their children to be fulfilled human beings. But they don't want the public schools to be judging their kids on level of fulfillment. On the other hand, they do think it's the school's job to teach reading, writing, history and science, and they'd like to know if their kids are learning those subjects.... Some years ago, I was invited to talk to a committee at a school district considering a change in its graduation requirements. A parent asked if I thought they should require that students demonstrate good character, emotional well-being and a propensity for "life-long learning" in order to earn a diploma. After all, these are qualities we want in our young people.
>
> I said, "Imagine a straight A student who's a nasty, mixed-up kid. Imagine yourself denying him a diploma on the grounds that he hasn't met your character or emotional health requirements. Do you really want to do that? Imagine a student who's learned nothing in 13 years of education. What makes you think she'll become a life-long learner in the future?"
>
> The district put all the blather in its mission statement, and stuck with academic graduation requirements.

Incidentally, *Education Week's* publisher recently wrote yet another editorial recommending the elimination of homework. [In sum, he wants no external testing, no high-stakes testing, and no homework.] His argument? Homework deprives students of the opportunity to pursue more edifying activities, such as: visiting museums, reading novels, learning to play a musical instrument, and taking up arts and crafts hobbies. He assumes, of course, that it is homework that is keeping our youngsters from pursuing those other, admittedly wonderful activities (Wolk 2002b).

Brand Loyalty—CRESST and Other Favorite Education Week Sources of Expertise

Education Week's website contains an imbedded search engine capable of accessing most of its stories dating back to 1981.[20] I used this search engine to learn *Education Week's* sources on testing issues over the past two decades. I searched for people, using all variations of their names, counting how many times each individual was represented by either: (1) quotation or interview; (2) reference to their research or activities; or (3) Op/Ed or letter to the editor.

When *Education Week* reporters write a story on standardized testing, whom do they call for expert commentary?...whose work do they read? There are many possibilities open to them, of course. The National Council on Measurement in Education (NCME), perhaps the primary professional organization of educational testing researchers, alone has over a thousand members. Another thousand or so testing professionals and research experts work in the test development industry, in university psychology, economics, or sociology departments, in consulting firms, and elsewhere.

There are many, many measurement experts that *Education Week* reporters could call. Whom do they call? As it turns out, very few of them. Dozens of the world's foremost experts and researchers on educational testing have never been contacted by *Education Week* reporters.

Education Week's favorite place to call is the Center for Research on Evaluation, Standards, and Student Testing (CRESST). Counting just ten of the researchers at CRESST who tend to make statements on questions of public policy, 93 *Education Week* articles have included their quotes, 16 articles have discussed their research without quoting them, and 3 times these CRESST researchers have written Op/Ed pieces or letters to the editor. That is well over 100 articles featuring these ten researchers on a testing topic. And that does not include researchers affiliated with the National Research Council's Center for Education, which maintains an incestuous relationship with CRESST, and produces virtually identical reports. Counting them would add another five quotations/interviews. CRESST and *Education Week* officials, of course, would assert that CRESST does objective, neutral, and balanced research. My response would be: No, it does not.[21]

Education Week's second most favorite place to call is the National Center for Fair and Open Testing (FairTest), the most extreme and strident of the anti-testing organizations. FairTest officials have been quoted in *Education Week* 51 times. Another 3 times, their "research" was referred to without any quotes in *EdWeek*, and FairTest officials have published 24 opinion pieces in *Education Week*.

Another favorite place for *EdWeek* reporters to call is the Center for the Study of Testing, Evaluation, and Educational Policy (CSTEEP) at Boston College.[22] Two testing opponents there have been quoted in 18 *Education Week* articles, their research has been referred to without quotation another 3 times, and one of them once published an opinion piece in *Education Week*.

Even independent anti-testing gadfly Alfie Kohn alone has been quoted or interviewed in 15 different articles and represented in 5 opinion pieces on testing in *Education Week*. One of the articles was a full-length, several page biographical story. Of course, that's not the end of it. Other testing opponents are frequently contacted by *EdWeek* reporters, too. Howard Gardner and Linda

Darling-Hammond, for example, have been quoted in 18 different articles on testing, referred to in three other pieces on testing, and wrote three opinion pieces on testing.

So prominent testing opponents receive many telephone calls from *Education Week* reporters. What about prominent experts on student testing who have broader views and cannot be relied upon to oppose high-stakes standardized testing? As already mentioned, there are thousands of educational testing researchers, so how to find a feasible comparison group? Here is one— among the past 21 years of annually elected presidents of the National Council on Educational Measurement (NCME). No one could argue with any credibility that these individuals are not recognized as experts in their profession.

NCME is an organization that welcomes all comers. One can find in NCME avid opponents of standardized testing, along with strong standardized-testing proponents. We know that *Education Week* reporters talk to the former; do they also talk to the latter?

I conducted a similar type of search through the past two decades of *Education Week* articles, looking for any word from or mention of these 21 individuals in the *EdWeek* archives. I count total "mentions" in two decades of *Education Week* publications—any article in which an individual is mentioned by a direct quote or a reference to research, or the individual himself writes a letter to the editor or an Op/Ed piece.

The five past NCME presidents who are directors or affiliates of the anti-testing organizations CRESST and CSTEEP are mentioned 3, 6, 11, 23, and 30 times, for an average of 14.6 mentions. Another past president, who also happens to have been a strong, outspoken opponent of high-stakes standardized testing and one of two recipients of a CRESST Distinguished Achievement Award, was mentioned 7 times (the average for these six past presidents is 13.3). The majority of these contacts were initiated by Education Week reporters, soliciting "expert" commentary on some testing policy issue.

Of the other NCME past presidents, seven have never been mentioned in *Education Week* publications, while they were presidents or at any other time, and another six have only 1 or 2 mentions. All these individuals are world-famous scholars and among the most highly respected in their profession. Perhaps it goes without saying that, on balance, these 13 individuals have more favorable attitudes toward standardized test use than do the six prominent testing opponents who are so popular with *Education Week* reporters.[23] The average number of mentions for these 13 other NCME past presidents is 0.6 (see Figure 6.4).

Gratefully, for the sake of some balance, two new advocacy groups have been formed just within the past few years that both have favorable views on standardized testing and get some telephone calls from *Education Week* reporters. They are Achieve, founded by governors and business executives as

Figure 6.4
Whom Do *Education Week* Reporters Call for Testing
Expertise Among former NCME Presidents?

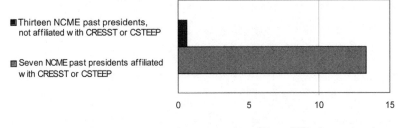

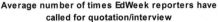

Average number of times EdWeek reporters have
called for quotation/interview

an outgrowth of one of the national Education Summits, and the Education Trust, formed by higher education interests and foundations as an advocacy group for high standards among poor and minority children. Prior to these groups' formations, the American Federation of Teachers (AFT) was probably the only large group advocating testing that got much attention from the press. *Education Week* has not given these three groups anything close to the amount of attention it bestows on anti-testing groups, but it is better than nothing. Still, it seems sad that experts who can counter the point of view of the vested interests on an issue must form an advocacy organization in order to get journalists' attention. Moreover, as thoughtful and knowledgeable as Achieve and the Education Trust happen to be, these two groups do not represent the range of opinion among testing advocates; far from it.

All told, whom do *Education Week* reporters call when they want research expertise? Using the same group of 26 opponents and 26 defenders used above, a search on all of the names in Education Week's archives reveals this view of the universe of testing expertise (see table 6.2).

When *Education Week* reporters desire what they believe to be genuine, research-based expertise on testing, overwhelmingly they call testing opponents for an interview or quotation. With the single exception of Williams Sanders, the value-added testing expert, *EdWeek* reporters almost completely ignore those testing researchers who might have something more positive to say about testing and who might counter the assertions of the testing opponents with whom they speak.

As far as *Education Week* is concerned there are few serious researchers who support the use of testing under current circumstances. This matches the education establishment's view of things. Only politicians, businesspeople, and naive advocates support testing. Those who really understand the issue—the objective, independent scientists—oppose the use of high-stakes

Table 6.2
Who Ya Gonna Call?—*Education Week*'s Preferred Expertise on Testing

Advocacy groups (experts) / individual advocates	Defenders of testing	Opponents of testing
	Achieve (Schwartz, Gandal**); **Ed. Trust** (Wilkins*, Haycock*); **Assn. American Publishers** (Kean); **Southern Regional Education Board** (SREB) (Musick***, Bottoms)	**FairTest** (Neill***, Schaeffer*);
	Chester Finn, Diane Ravitch**	Alfie Kohn*, Gerald Bracey, Deborah Meier
Research groups (experts) / individual researchers		**CRESST** (Baker**, Linn**, Koretz***, Shepard***, Klein, Stecher); **National Research Council, Center for Education** (Hauser); **CSTEEP (Boston College)** (Madaus*, Haney*);
	William Sanders	Howard Gardner*, Linda Darling-Hammond,**

Note: all those whose names are mentioned had 5 or more quotations/interviews on testing stories in *Education Week*, 1981-2001.

* 15 or more quotations/interviews

** 25 or more quotations/interviews

*** 35 or more quotations/interviews

standardized tests. Or, rather, they support these tests, really; it is just that the standards they would require and the restrictions they would impose on such tests would make them infeasible.

Mind you, there do exist groups sponsoring researchers willing to find results favorable toward testing policies (e.g., the Education Consumers Consultants Network [ECCN], the Thomas P. Fordham Foundation, the Center for Advanced Research in Human Resources [CAHRS] at Cornell University), but *Education Week* reporters seldom call the testing experts affiliated with these groups.[24] Moreover, these groups are vastly outmatched in resources by comparison with the taxpayer-funded CRESST and NRC, and the foundation-funded FairTest and CSTEEP.

Counting up the total "mentions" across two decades of *Education Week* articles on testing (i.e., interviews/quotations + references to research or activity + Op/Eds or letters to the editor) the anti-testing group, CRESST, alone, has gotten more attention from *EdWeek* reporters on the topic of testing (N = 205) than have all the experts in either testing defender group. Table 6.3 shows how the counts sum up.

In Figure 6.5 I have placed the *Education Week* counts into the same format used earlier for the Dow Jones Interactive and Google search counts.

At first glance, the relative weight given the two sides seems less lopsided in the *Education Week* counts than it did in the Dow Jones Interactive Search of 550 print media or the Google search of sites on the Worldwide Web. But, consider that well over half of the Liberal Defender count can be attributed to quotes from Mark Musick, Diane Ravitch, Chester Finn, and Ron Hambleton in their capacity as officials serving on national boards (the National Assessment Governing Board (NAGB) for all four of them, and the boards of Presi-

Table 6.3
**Testing Experts in *Education Week*, by Type of
Expert and Type of Mention: 1981-2001**

	Total Mentions	Quotations / Interviews	References to Research or Activities	Op/Ed or Letter to the Editor
Members of groups				
Defenders of testing (6 groups)*	222	182	7	33
Opponents of testing (6 groups)**	402	305	54	43
Independent researchers or advocates				
Defenders of testing	140	75	32	33
Opponents of testing	219	74	44	101
TOTALS				
Defenders of testing	362	257	39	66
Opponents of testing	621	379	98	144

* Testing experts at the Education Consumers Consultants Network (ECCN), the American Federation of Teachers (AFT), Achieve, the Education Trust, the Southern Regional Education Board (SREB), and the Association of American Publishers-School Division (AAP).

** Testing experts at the National Center for Fair and Open Testing (FairTest), the Center for Research on Evaluation, Standards and Student Testing (CRESST), the National Research Council's Center for Education, CSTEEP at Boston College), the National Education Association, and the National Board for Professional Teaching Standards (NBPTS).

Figure 6.5

Number of "Mentions" for Names of Certain Testing Experts in *Education Week* Stories about Testing: 1981-2001

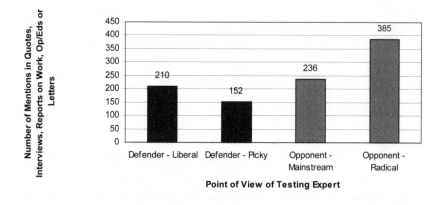

dent Clinton's proposed Voluntary National Tests (VNT) and the elder President Bush's National Council on Education Standards and Testing (NCEST) for Chester Finn. Take away these quotes, which are unique to the group of Liberal Defenders, and Figure 6.5 would resemble the earlier ones.

When test defenders are simply so important that *EdWeek* cannot avoid calling them if they want a story (e.g., the stellar administrator Musick was chairperson of NAGB for many years) they call them. Seldom do *Education Week* reporters contact Liberal Defenders to comment on general or state testing policy issues, or research-based or methodological issues. When *Education Week* reporters have a choice, they call testing opponents.

I also looked at *Education Week's* website in fall 2000, during the presidential campaign, at its "Assessment" reference section, where they recommended websites and documents as sources on the testing issue. There were links to the three most prominent anti-testing groups-CRESST, FairTest, and the Boston College group. Another link took you to a report edited by one of CRESST's directors. Another took you to a report written by one of CRESST's chief researchers, also of Boston College. Another link took you to the Educational Testing Service (ETS) website, but exclusively to a single report called "Too much testing of the wrong kind and too little of the right kind," which is, true to its title, critical of most current standardized testing programs.

Were there also links at *EdWeek's* website to reports or groups with more favorable views toward testing? No, none.

Finally, I should acknowledge that I can examine *EdWeek's* coverage in detail because they have such a great search engine. Its chief rival in the education trade press, *Education Daily*, does not have nearly as good a search capability, so I could not check on them as thoroughly. My general impression, however, is that *EdDaily*'s coverage of testing and other education issues is even more slanted toward the vested interests than *EdWeek*'s.

Consider the October 2002 edition of *Education Daily*'s new spinoff newsletter, *Education Assessment Insider*, which includes representatives from CRESST and FairTest on its editorial board. The issue includes a story entitled, "Survey Says...Public Backs Testing, Opposes High Stakes." claiming that a Public Agenda poll found "fully 75 percent of parents, 89 percent of teachers, and 81 percent of employers...said it 'would be wrong to use the results of just one test to decide whether a student gets promoted or graduates."

The *Ed Daily* writers neglected to mention that:

- no U.S. state makes graduation decisions based on a single test administration; and
- the overwhelming majority of the public, parents, and students—as represented in Public Agenda's polls—support high-stakes testing.

The Education Press's Cop-Out on Testing—The Education Writers' Association

There is a single organization that claims to represent the interests of all journalists who write on education issues, the Education Writers' Association (EWA). I decided to examine their website, in the same manner as any journalist might who was looking for background information on the topic of standardized testing. Below, I describe what I found in fall 2000, in the heat of a presidential campaign in which high-stakes standardized testing was a major issue.

In the "Hot Topics" section was a subsection on testing that contained 26 paragraphs. About half were factual or neutral to any testing debate, but the rest were not. Those paragraphs featured quotes from commentators and presentations of opinion. Ten paragraphs were devoted to the anti-testing point of view, while just two offered a pro-testing viewpoint.[25] In the same subsection was a page devoted to an alleged anti-testing "backlash" organized by independent local groups of students and parents, which the EWA accepted as a fact, rather than as a ruse mostly promoted by the same old anti-testing organizations ("grassroots organizations are rising up against tests").[26]

A rather revealing box aligned to the left of the main text section on testing bore a large, bold title, "Web Sources," and links to five organizations. Any reporter only looking at this, by far the longest text section devoted to the testing issue, would be presented only with these links as source references. Among the five were two organizations-the Education Commission of the States (ECS) and Catalyst for Chicago Education Reform—for whom testing is just one of many topics they consider. The remaining three links in the box were for websites of well-financed, high-profile organizations that concern themselves only with testing. They also happen to be the three most prominent anti-testing advocacy groups in the country (FairTest, CRESST [UCLA], and CSTEEP [Boston College]). Any reporter looking only at the main text section on testing at EWA's website would have these three sources recommended as contacts.

In the "New Research" section of the EWA's website were listed two sources, a Harvard Graduate School of Education conference transcript and a primer on testing written by Gerald Bracey for the American Youth Policy Forum. The transcript features the comments of three staunch opponents of high-stakes testing (Angela Valenzuela, Ted Sizer, and Linda Nathan) and the SAT critic, Nicholas Lemann. For his part, no argument is possible that could portray Gerald Bracey as neutral.

So there you have it. In the heat of the presidential campaign, the EWA website gave prime time to pretty much the whole range of anti-testing opponents. Between the "Hot Topics" and "New Research" sections, 13 testing opponents, including all of the most extreme ones, were featured. How many commentators were represented who would argue that testing may not be so horrible and terrible and, by gosh, may actually have some benefits? Just two, the AFT and me.

Our country boasts the most knowledgeable psychometricians in the world. Other countries look to the U.S. for expertise and are starting to adopt the advanced technical methods developed here (yes, multiple-choice tests). Do U.S. journalists talk to these, the world's most knowledgeable testing experts? With the exception of the small proportion of them who share the extremists' anti-testing viewpoint, generally they do not.

In response to an earlier criticism of her organization's coverage of testing, the EWA's president wrote (incidentally, an Education Week editor said, more or less, the same thing):

> The irony, of course, is that the opponents of testing that [I accused] EWA of being biased toward complained about just the opposite— that we represent the proponents of testing too often in our work."

Indeed, some testing opponents would rather EWA did not mention the proponents or the neutrals at all, which it has come very close to doing at its website. Some of the anti-testing organizations have a great deal of money and other resources available to them. They have the time to troll the Web and check on every education site to see if it is presenting their propaganda and, likewise, not presenting any opposing views. And, there are many websites that purport to represent all research on testing but provide links exclusively to anti-testing groups.[27]

All should realize that the debate on testing (high-stakes testing, that is) is not limited to a world of tweed jackets, sweet-smelling pipes, and green quadrangles where nice, earnest professors have polite disagreements with each other. It is part of a war for the control of our country's schools, being fought by the insiders against outsiders. The booty is our children's futures. The stakes are enormous. The question is: Is the EWA up to covering a war, or not? If it is, it should know what the fight is about, who the combatants are on both sides, and it should spend some time with both sides. Currently, it does not.

How Easy is It to Manipulate Education Journalists?

"Spinning" Journalists around the Poll, Part 1

As part of their effort to manufacture a "backlash" against standardized testing, some vested interest groups conducted their own public opinion polls in the year 2000. The Association of American School Administrators' (AASA) poll described in my introduction-with a paltry response rate; only one weekend of telephone calls; no published methodology data; crude, untested, misleading questions; conducted by an inexpensive "quick and dirty" political polling outfit-was one of them.

Here is the task facing the AASA: the public is strongly supportive of testing, whereas the AASA is strongly opposed to external evaluation of the schools. But, we live in a democracy and the public's opinion is supposed to matter in the public schools. So, how to get the public to say they are opposed to standardized testing when, actually, they are not?

Here is an appropriate "spin cycle" for a situation like this: Conduct a poll, but write the questions yourself in a fashion that will lead to the answers you want. Reveal only those results that fall in your favor, and hide the rest. Manipulate the numbers and the wordings so that the results sound like they are in your favor even when they are not. Do not allow the public access to any of the details of how the poll was conducted; do not publish a methodology report.

The AASA did all this. First, they actually conducted two surveys, the extremely crude, short, brief, and simplistic poll conducted by the political polling firm Luntz/Lazlo with biased questions,[28] and focus groups that delved much deeper into public preferences for various possible school reforms. If you dig, you can find the documents for the focus groups, but the AASA did not publicize them, perhaps because the results were not much to their liking.[29]

After the AASA poll was completed, the association's president proclaimed tests to be: "unreliable, unrealistic, and unfair;" "imprecise;" and "invalid for...high-stakes decisions such as promotion or graduation." They: "measure factoids" "distort" and "narrow" curriculum and "cannot reliably measure problem solving." Their effect on instruction is to "narrow" it; turn teachers into "drill sergeants;" "taint the atmosphere;" and promote "memorization and repetition" (Houston 2000).

Given that all other responsible public opinion surveys on the subject, going back thirty years, and for a year after, found quite different results; given the AASA's obvious self-interest in opposing testing; and given its president's rather unrestrained rhetoric, one would think journalists would be skeptical of his story.

They were not. The several who covered the story covered it in a way that must have pleased the AASA. There was no mention of the "other" AASA survey finding that over two-thirds of respondents thought statewide standardized tests would improve the public schools. Some news stories just copied the AASA press release. Here is *Education Week*'s take on the story (Olson 2000a):

> A recent poll suggests that the public may be uneasy with the growing emphasis on using standardized tests to make important educational decisions about students.
>
> The bipartisan poll [30], released last month by the American Association of School Administrators, found that a majority of voters responding disagreed with the idea that a single test can accurately measure students' progress for a school year. Nearly half did not agree that students should repeat a grade if they failed a state exam.
>
> The results are somewhat similar to those from a recent poll of parents.

The same *Education Week* reporter wrote a story a few weeks later covering another poll sponsored by the Association of American Publishers, the trade organization representing most standardized test developers/publishers (Olson 2000b). The AAP conducted a much more substantial survey over the course of three months, achieved a far higher response rate, and released more substantial results, which were supportive of standardized testing.

How did the *EdWeek* reporter handle the story? To be blunt, she made it sound like they were the odd guys out and that their results should be considered in the light of their self interest.

Here is the lead paragraph:

> Several public opinion polls released this summer have suggested that parents and other voters oppose using tests to make high-stakes decisions about students, such as whether they can graduate or advance to the next grade. Now, a new poll released by the Association of American Publishers, the national trade association for the U.S. publishing industry, while not addressing the issue of high-stakes testing, suggests that parents value the information that standardized tests provide.

It is certainly fair to note the AAP's self-interest in the issue but, by contrast, the same reporter had labeled the AASA poll "a bipartisan poll." Moreover, with the AASA poll, she wrote the "results" as if they were facts, even though she largely just copied verbiage from the AASA press release verbatim. For the AAP story, however, all results were written in quotes from AAP officials, as if to imply that they were just opinions.

I wrote to the *EdWeek* reporter asking her what the other "several public opinion polls released this summer" were to which she was referring to. I never received a reply. Other than the bogus "bipartisan" poll done for the AASA by Luntz/Lazlo, all the public opinion surveys conducted in the year 2000 of which I am aware showed overwhelming support for high-stakes standardized testing. Those surveys include the focus groups study done for AASA, a Harris Interactive poll sponsored by the ASCD, a SmarterKids.com survey, and a Public Agenda poll conducted in the fall. Only the press releases of some of these organizations showed a backlash.

"Spinning" journalists around the Poll, Part 2

Another large group of school administrators, the Association for Supervision and Curriculum Development (ASCD) sponsored another survey on the public's opinions on testing shortly after the AASA did theirs. The ASCD, however, chose the more reputable Harris Interactive, the firm originally founded by Louis Harris, legendary in the old days for being the most patient and thorough of the pollsters for hire.

Harris Interactive conducted a more responsible survey, as one can discern from reading their methodology report, available to anyone right off the Web. Harris chose to focus solely on public school parents—those with the most at stake with high-stakes testing in the public schools (i.e., their own progeny may be held back if they fail). Indeed, vested interest research groups such as the National Research Council and CRESST have been telling journalists for a while now (and journalists, generally, have believed them) that the public, really, only likes the concept of high-stakes testing. When their own kids are threatened, they'll change their minds soon enough, won't they (Olson 2000a; Hoff 2000a, 2000b)?[31]

Have public school parents changed their minds? What did Harris find? "Over half of respondents from both high-stakes (51%) and non-high-stakes (56%) states indicated that they support the purpose of their state's educational assessments as they understand them. The remaining respondents were split evenly between not supporting the purpose of their state's assessment, and not being sure whether they did or did not support it."

So, more than twice as many supportive than not, among parents whose children are directly affected. Parents in states with high-stakes tests were then asked to "indicate how much they agreed or disagreed with each of a series of statements regarding state-mandated educational assessments." They were presented a multiple-choice response scale ranging from 1, disagree strongly, to 5, agree strongly, with 3 being neutral.

1. "State-mandated educational assessments are relevant and meaningful for my child's education." (44 percent agree; 33 percent disagree)
2. "Results of state-mandated educational assessments should be used when making a decision about whether a child is allowed to progress to the next higher grade." (42 percent agree; 40 percent disagree)
3. "Results of state-mandated educational assessments should be used to determine whether a student is qualified to graduate from high school." (51 percent agree; 38 percent disagree)
4. "School accreditation should be determined in part by results of state-mandated educational assessments." (51 percent agree; 29 percent disagree)
5. "My public school district adequately prepares children for my state's mandatory educational assessments." (50 percent agree; 20 percent disagree)
6. "Some academic skill areas are being overlooked as a result of preparing students to take state-mandated educational assessments." (57 percent agree; 13 percent disagree)
7. "Schools are neglecting some enrichment education areas, such as the arts, team learning, and science projects, because they're not evaluated in those areas." (57 percent agree; 18 percent disagree)

For those of you speed reading, here's a summary: A majority of public school parents with an opinion think that state-mandated standardized tests are valuable. Overwhelming majorities feel that students (i.e., their own children) should have to pass a high-stakes state-mandated test to graduate and that a school's accreditation should be decided by their students' performance on those tests. Parents with an opinion were evenly divided about using high-stakes tests for grade-level promotion decisions. Overwhelming majorities also thought that high-stakes testing was narrowing the curriculum to the basics. Note, however, that they were not asked whether they thought that was a good or bad thing.

Overall, any objective observer would have to admit that the survey uncovered a ringing endorsement for high-stakes testing within the very demographic subgroup that was supposed to be most strongly against it. The only genuine equivocation had to do with using state-mandated high-stakes tests in single grade-level promotion decisions and, perhaps, with the curricular focus on basic subject matter.

Not to be discouraged, the ASCD "spun" the Harris poll results in a manner more to their liking. In so doing, they took advantage of Harris Interactive's responsible behavior. Responsible researchers, after all, tend to produce voluminous, carefully worded, heavy-on-the-details methodology reports. Journalists with a deadline do not have the time to read them; and many would probably not understand them even if they had the time.

A group that desires to purchase objective information from a survey organization will pay that organization to do its work and then let that organization handle the work from that point on, right through the dissemination of the findings. Public Agenda's surveys, for example, are like this—handled from start to finish by Public Agenda. Public Agenda writes the reports, its personnel give talks at conferences, and Public Agenda writes the press releases that advertise its work.

With the Harris survey of parents' attitudes toward high-stakes standardized testing, the ASCD itself wrote the press release, and it wrote a doozy. "Among the survey findings regarding parents' views," from the ASCD survey:

- Half are unsure of or do not know what the state standardized tests measure.
- Overall, parents do not feel informed about standardized assessment tests nor equipped to help their children prepare for them.
- A majority do not believe mandated state testing is a true or valid measurement of what their children have learned.
- Nearly half find inconsistencies between their children's standardized test results and their report cards.
- More than half believe some academic skills and areas of enrichment are being neglected as a result of the emphasis on state-mandated assessment.
- Overwhelmingly, parents believe that additional preparation outside of school would help their children's performance on state-mandated tests.
- Only a small percentage of parents suggest that classroom work and grades should be included as part of any state-mandated assessment.
- Approximately half disagree or are undecided about whether these tests should determine promotion or graduation.

Is the ASCD referring to the same Harris Interactive survey described earlier? Yes and no. The ASCD managed, through judicious information selection and organization, to create survey results that exposed a strong endorsement of high-stakes testing sound like they had found just the opposite. The main results-overwhelming support among public school parents for state-mandated, high-stakes testing, and using it to deny children graduation and schools accreditation-were buried at the back of the press release and, even then, at the end of a paragraph and, even then, described in a hedging manner. Here is the paragraph (7th paragraph, after the highlights):

> Most respondents believe the purpose of educational assessment is to assess both the child's and the school's performance. Although more than half of the parents from both high-stakes (51 percent) and non-high-stakes (56 percent) states support this purpose, the remainder are split evenly between not supporting the purpose of their state's assessments or being undecided.

Moreover, when it served ASCD's purpose, it would add the neutral responses (do not know, no opinion) to their side of an issue. "Half are unsure or do not know what their state educational assessments measure" could have been described more straightforwardly as: 50 percent know what their state educational assessments measure; 23 percent do not know; and 27 percent are not sure.

The ASCD might also have mentioned that more parents might actually know what their state standardized tests measure than understand what their children's grades measure. Indeed, the ASCD might have mentioned that if parents cannot understand what state assessments measure, that really is the fault, first and foremost, of those who have direct responsibility for communicating this information to students and parents. Who are these people? Why, they are school administrators and guidance counselors—ASCD members, in other words.

The ASCD press release was a snow job. Results the organization did not like were ignored or covered up. Results the organization wanted, but did not get, were manufactured. Was the ASCD's snow job successful? Yes. Several journalists covered the story and the ASCD must have been very pleased with the result: the pro-testing survey results ignored in the ASCD press release were ignored in the news stories as well; journalists emphasized issues in pretty much the same order as the ASCD press release did; and the neutral or don't know responses were used to optimal effect (they counted on the anti-testing side!).

The Education Commission of the States—Allegedly Bipartisan: Is It Unbiased?

One place U.S. journalists often call for information on education issues is the Education Commission of the States (ECS). They call under the assumption that they will obtain unbiased and accurate information on education issues. In the United States, the states are primarily responsible for formulating education policy and implementing education programs. ECS staffers, charged with informing politicians of both political parties and a wide range of political persuasions in the states, are expected to know all sides of the issues on which they specialize and keep our elected representatives up to speed. If there was any organization in the country from which one should expect to find balanced, objective coverage of the issue of standardized testing, this would be it.

For whatever reason, unfortunately, the ECS tends to present vested-interest orthodoxy as if it were unbiased, objective truth. In the year 2000, for example, ECS fell for the ruse of anti-testing groups that a nationwide groundswell of "independent, grassroots, parents'" organizations had risen up in opposition to high-stakes testing. ECS declared the "anti-testing backlash" to be a fact.[32] Some ECS staffers also retain a devout faith in the cardinal tenets of the anti-testing canon: informing journalists that "teaching to the test," "narrowing the curriculum," and other familiar political slogans, indeed, represent very serious genuine problems to which we must attend.

In defense of ECS, it is not a large organization and it has the full menu of education issues on its plate, not just testing. Indeed, there are really only one or two staffers at ECS at any given time who specialize in testing issues and programs and only several others who even know testing issues tangentially. Unfortunately, in an effort to beef up their standardized testing expertise, ECS entered into an exclusive research alliance with the country's premier anti-testing group, the Center for Research on Evaluation, Standards and Student Testing (CRESST), at UCLA's Education School. ECS now presents CRESST researchers, of all people, to our state and local policymakers as the oracles of objectivity regarding research on standardized testing. CRESST represents in real life the figurative "wolf in sheep's clothing." Is the ECS biased against education consumers? ...or, are ECS staffers simply naïve?[33] (Olson 2000d)

In Table 6.4, I list the citations from an ECS primer on assessment. This listing speaks for itself. The ECS is well aware of the resources and arguments of testing opponents and close to completely ignorant of any resources or arguments on the other side of the issue. This publication is meant to provide ECS's clients-our country's thousands of state-level elected officials-with

Table 6.4
Your Tax Dollars at Work—Resources cited in *The Progress of Education Reform 1999-2001: Assessment,* Education Commission of the States, Vol. 1, No. 6, March-April 2000

	Pro-testing links	Anti-testing links
"Resources" (i.e., links to publications)	1. Fordham Foundation report defending testing	1. National Research Council *High-Stakes* book order site 2. CRESST report objecting to the use of high-stakes tests 3. Boston College (CSTEEP) report against high-stakes tests 4. Teachers College (Columbia U.) report criticizing high-stakes test use 5. Report opposing use of test scores to judge schools, by Cross-City Campaign (Chicago)
"Other Useful Web Sites" Testing)		1. CRESST (Center for Research on Evaluation, Standards and Student 2. FairTest (National Center for Fair and Open Testing) 3. MALDEF (Mexican-American Legal Defense and Educational Fund

objective, balanced coverage of the issue. After all, these clients have been elected to represent the interests of all U.S. citizens, not just those few who benefit from the current governance structure of public education. Instead, this document attempts to indoctrinate these public servants in whom American citizens have put their trust with the self-serving arguments of public education's comfortable and wealthy vested interests.

Journalist's Coverage of Testing: Why Does Only One Side Get to Talk?

Why is media coverage of testing so one-sided? I am not intimately familiar with journalists' motivation and preferences. Therefore, I asked several education journalists, including a few I think do a poor job of covering the topic of testing (though, I did not tell them that). I also read the report of a survey of education journalists, education providers, and the public about education journalism from the ever-dependable Public Agenda, which was conducted in cooperation with the Education Writers Association (Public Agenda 1997). Based on these sources, and my own direct, and usually frustrating, experiences in dealing with journalists, I offer these speculative explanations for media coverage of testing below.

Frankly, I just wanted to get some handle on this perplexing problem, because I was at a loss to explain it. I could not understand how, given journalists' high-minded goals and codes of ethics, the coverage of the testing issue could be so slanted to favor the vested interests. The suggestions I heard were quite revealing. Some of the journalists I contacted were reluctant to "talk out of school," others were remarkably open about what they perceived to be their profession's shortcomings.

Journalists Want to Be "Liberals"

Accusations abound of a "liberal bias" in news coverage in the United States, and some studies have been conducted affirming the accusation[34] (see, for example, Goldberg 1996; Bartley 2000). Perhaps so many journalists see themselves as "liberals" because they wish to fight for the powerless and the downtrodden, represent the public interest against special interest, and give voice to those who have few resources with which to project their opinion.

The testing issue offers a magnificent opportunity to a journalist with these goals, in my opinion. A system is in place that benefits a relatively tiny proportion of the population vested in it that profits from it; everyone else in our society is worse off. The public, which overwhelmingly endorses a change in the status quo, is disparaged by the special interests as ignorant. The public's elected representatives, when they attempt to represent the popular will, are characterized by the vested interests as sleazy, venal, and corrupt. Furthermore, the vested interests eschew an ethic of public service, even though their salaries are paid by the taxpayers, and they are paid to care responsibly for the taxpayers' children. Unlike all the rest of us who work for a living in the United States, these coddled special interests say that they cannot and should not be held accountable for how they do their work because their performance is immeasurable (or, only they, themselves, can measure it properly).

Why would not any liberal muckraking journalist want to take on this challenge? Why have most education journalists, instead, chosen to side with the bad guys? Apparently, many education journalists have naively fallen for the ruse that by opposing standardized testing they are somehow being "liberal" and siding with poor kids against mean authoritarians and corporations.

Only Problems are News

If things are OK, it is not news. Nobody wants to hear it. It's not interesting. There's also no "policy issue" in play if things are okay. So, there's no news story if testing is fine; there is only a news story if testing is not fine. (This concept could also explain why the same journalists and media outlets, who liberally take the U.S. public education system to task for its lack of standards and poor performance relative to other countries, excoriate it again when it tries to address those problems, as other countries do, with a rigorous system of measurement.)

The public respondents in Public Agenda's survey of education news coverage (1997: 11-17) felt that education journalists dwelt too much on bad news and too little on substantive issues, too much on problems and too little on solutions. Ironically, among 16 areas of education Public Agenda suggested for generatingmore news stories, the largest majority of the public (77 percent) chose "raising academic standards."

Cannot Afford to Alienate Primary Sources

Much, as it is said, a war journalist cannot afford to alienate the military—or she will not be allowed near the battle front to get a story—an education journalist perhaps cannot afford to alienate the vested interests in public education. Aggressive anti-testers control the most important sources of stories on testing. They include the National Research Council, CRESST, several administrators' associations, and the American Educational Research Association, for example. State the obvious—that they are biased or they have a self-interest in opposing testing—and their news tips may go to other journalists instead.

Eighty-one percent of the education journalists in Public Agenda's survey (1997: 20) admitted that there was "a lot/some truth" to the public's negative perception that they were "too dependent on school officials for information."

Cannot Afford to Alienate Readers

Those media outlets exclusively devoted to education—the education trade press—serve a clientele made up largely of individuals vested in the current system of public education. Many of those individuals would prefer not to have their performance measured, thank you. Moreover, few of these individuals are exposed to anything besides anti-testing arguments at their association conferences, on their websites, and in their organization's magazines. If a trade paper were even to give those on the other side of the issue a platform, in the interest of balance, it could be seen by some as blasphemy and disloyalty. Many mainstream media outlets, unfortunately, rely on the education trade press for their stories, and assume that they are objective and unbiased.

Time and Resource Constraints

There is only so much time in the day and so much money in the budget. A reporter assigned a story when he arrives in the morning may have only until the end of the day to complete it. Obviously, convenience is going to determine the nature of the story to some degree. The vested interests tend to have the resources and organization to make a harried reporter's work easier. They can hire full-time public relations staff, build and maintain a websites, produce "research" reports quickly and post them at their websites, build and maintain data banks of contacts and other resources that will represent their point of view.

According to Public Agenda (1997: 6), 85 percent of the educators in their sample of superintendents and teachers have contacted the press (once or more) regarding education issues. That seems a phenomenal figure-education providers are extraordinarily active in their efforts to influence the press. By contrast 63 percent of the public has never contacted a local media organization about education. With education providers so readily available and eager to provide source material, and knowledgeable education consumers not so available, a passive journalist is likely to write stories from the provider point of view.

Space Limitations

Space and time are scarce commodities. Those who take a lot of space or time to explain complicated topics may well get bumped in favor of those who take up little space or time to explain complicated topics.

Journalists Trust Each Other (maybe too much)

Journalist have a very high opinion of the work they do—that's why they work in journalism. They tend to believe that journalists try hard to be objective, maintain high ethical standards, and produce the best quality work they can. This would explain why so many journalists accept other journalists' work without question and without checking. It also helps explain why one biased and erroneous story can get repeated, with only nominal changes, in dozens of media outlets throughout the United States.

New technologies seem only to have made the problem worse. A reporter assigned to do a story on testing when she arrives in the morning can, within minutes, pull up testing stories already written by other reporters throughout the United States. Our reporter need simply copy other reporters' stories—not word-for-word, mind you—but with the same assumptions, slant, "facts," and "experts" interviewed.

"Established Groups" Provide Credibility

With every testing story, a journalist has the opportunity to talk to an ordinary researcher, who might actually say something nice about testing, or someone from a prestigious, nationally known educational testing research center, whom, it so happens, will strongly oppose testing. One of these anti-testing research centers, CRESST, is funded by taxpayers, though you certainly would not surmise that given their devotion to their profession's own self-interest. Another of these centers consists of nothing more than a few anti-testing professors, and a few staff, at a single university. But, it calls itself, humbly, the National Board on Educational Testing Policy (NBETP). There is nothing "national" about them (and nothing balanced about their work). For the journalist, however, it may not matter if the quality of their work is poor or if their work is biased. Their organization names sound authoritative!

Journalists Have No Memory

Journalists cover "what's happening now" and every day has a new story. After awhile, journalists forget what they wrote in the past. Or, perhaps what they wrote in the past does not matter because that was then and this is now. There is virtually no evidence in testing news stories from the past couple of years to indicate that reporters remember the origins of the new testing requirements-that they are connected to the preceding movement to set academic standards. Most journalists now seem to accept testing opponents' incredible assertions that standards are new and imposed by mean politicians. In fact, standards in most states were developed over a several-year period (in the 1990s in most states), either with considerable public input and review or directly by citizens' committees, and journalists emphatically supported them.

A lack of memory would also explain why some anti-testing advocates take no risk in producing dishonest and fraudulent research, and why so much of it surfaces in the public domain. A researcher found fudging numbers, doctoring data, or making up facts one day can make new claims tomorrow and still be accepted by journalists at face value.

Journalists Do Not Read Journals

Perhaps it is an outcome of journalists' time and resource constraint problem that journalists do not read professional journals. Granted, much of the highest quality research is written in technical language that only the most extraordinary journalist could understand. But, not all of it is. NCME's journal *Educational Measurement: Issues and Practice (EM:IP)*, for example, often features very accessible articles written in plain English. It is rare that a journalist, even in the education trade press, looks at any of them, however.

New technologies seem only to have exacerbated the problem of source information bias. Most refereed professional journals still require payment from subscribers, which requires payment, ordering, and waiting. Why would any journalist be bothered with that when gobs of "research" are available freely on the Web with just a point and click. Research easily available on the Web, of course, tends not to be research refereed by rigorous, unbiased, and objective journals but, rather, research produced by those with the money to freely produce the research that promotes their interests. Since there is so much research available on the Worldwide Web, it must cover the territory. Right?

Wrong. The Web has served to make more junk and biased research more widely available and, of course, vested interest advocates have more resources and motivation to put such up on the Web.

What You See is What There is

Journalists cover "live" news-what is visible, not hidden-action, not inaction. This may be why journalists are prone to report a "growing movement of parents against testing" when they see a dozen or so folks with placards at a protest against testing in front of a state capitol building, despite the fact than an overwhelming majority of parents in reliable polls claim to support standardized testing with high stakes. This habit may also explain why some journalists cite as evidence for a "new movement" against testing the activities of anti-testing advocates who have been active for many years-because these journalists just started looking at the topic and did not notice these people before...because they were not looking before.

Many journalists exhibit a tendency-very annoying to us statisticians-to glibly assume that whatever they see is a representative sample of what there is. All the stories they see on testing must validly represent all the stories there are. All the "experts" they have read and interviewed must represent all the "experts" there are. The students and parents they read about protesting against testing must represent all students and all parents. Furthermore, many journalists seem to assume that the two sides in the testing debate are evenly matched and, so, the fact that anti-testing advocacy is more prominent must mean it is superior.

Education is a Low Status Beat

Outside the media outlets devoted exclusively to education, education stories are typically given to the youngest, least seasoned (and, perhaps, least skeptical) reporters. Experienced reporters prefer the more high-profile and glamorous beats, such as the military, crime, diplomacy, business, and sports.

Many Education Journalists are Education School Graduates Themselves

Some education journalists were indoctrinated in the philosophy and rhetoric of the vested interests firsthand in education school and are no more independent, objective observers of the education scene than a hired public relations firm would be.

The Huge Advantage of the Vested Interests in Educational Testing Debates

On the topic of education, U.S. journalists, unfortunately, have left the side with the money and the organization determine the debate. CRESST receives millions of dollars a year from the federal government. If you count the National Research Council's Board on Testing and Assessment, which might as well be considered a CRESST subsidiary given its common personnel, its wholesale (and virtually exclusive) reliance on CRESST "research," and its common benefactor, there's another million dollars a year at a minimum. The anti-testers at Boston College's CSTEEP have a $1 million grant from the Ford Foundation. FairTest gets a half million a year from The Ford and Joyce Foundations alone, and still more from nice, well-intentioned, but very misguided church groups.

Anti-testing groups can put a face on their research in every media market in the country, particularly at state and regional meetings of school administrator associations and in the many thousands of "professional development workshops" teachers are required to attend at the taxpayers' expense. Some of the most prominent (and most loose with the truth) anti-testing advocates make their livelihoods on this "rubber chicken" circuit, appearing regularly throughout the country presenting their views on standardized testing and the "truth about American education" in general. These "gadflies" are readily available for interviews with the local press.

Representatives of the education consumers' interests, by contrast, do not have such reach or the resources to attain it. Essentially, education consumers' groups have no money at all. The coffers of the education producer groups are limitless by comparison.

Furthermore, testing opponents have many more numerous opportunities to disseminate their writings than do testing defenders. Those who work at taxpayer-funded research centers have the taxpayer bankrolling their report production, their website maintenance, and their marketing. Those testing opponents who do not may still be very welcome among book publishers who sell to the huge education provider community. Alfie Kohn can write pretty much anything he pleases, and does, and commands a high sales volume. Education school professors assign his books for their courses. Other educators may take solace from his writings that their franchise is vigorously defended. Ironically, some of the same corporations that develop and sell standardized tests for profit also publish the most vitriolic anti-testing screeds.

Furthermore, testing opponents have the money and infrastructure necessary for coddling journalists. The education press can call FairTest, CSTEEP, and CRESST and get their calls returned right away because these organizations pay full-time staffers to handle press relations.

Good reporting is surely about working hard, writing well, and establishing contacts but, just as surely, it must also be about knowing the agenda and resources of every source. Without that knowledge, stories can be lopsided. On issues where all sides have equal amounts of money and organization, it might not matter. But, on issues where the sources on one side have money and organization behind them, and the sources on the other side do not, it could matter.

One such lopsided issue area is education research, as most of it is conducted by graduates and professors of education schools, who have a vested interest in maintaining the current governance structure of U.S. public education. On two issues in particular-school choice and "high-stakes" student testing-self-interest seems to wholly define the debate. Perhaps that is because these two issues threaten the very stability of the education research establishment. Without standardized testing, no one can know how our schools are performing. So long as no one knows, few will protest. So long as no one protests, educators will be held to no standards. Held to no standards, educators can do as they please.

Most people, in the end, defend their self-interests, either because they sincerely believe their interests are good for everyone else, or because they worry about keeping their jobs and getting their kids through college. There are some courageous education professors who would like to speak out against the education research establishment, but are afraid to. Afraid of having their papers rejected at journals. Afraid of being denied tenure or promotion. Afraid of being compared to the racists and elitists in the 1920s and 1930s who wished to misuse standardized tests to uphold their perverted theories. Afraid of the inquisition. The education press could talk to them anonymously, but they do not.

Moreover, not all testing experts are education professors. There are in fact hundreds of qualified testing experts working for national, state, or local agencies (not to mention the experts working for organizations that develop tests under contract to governments). But, they are contractually and ethically restricted from expressing their views regarding testing policy. The education press could talk to them anonymously, but they do not.

When Journalists Side with the "Little Guy" and the "Public Interest"

There are some issues, or at least there were in the past, on which journalists would side with the common folk against the power of huge professional associations. One such example is provided by the celebrated attempt, in the 1980s, of the American Medical Association to ban Federal Trade Commission (FTC) oversight of its members' activities. Briefly, the AMA and its allies were so rich and influential that it attempted, essentially, to monopolize the provision of all medical care in the United States (e.g., freeze out lower cost and more accessible midwives, nurse practitioners, chiropractors, psychologists, optometrists, psychiatric social workers, and other competitors), and set legally enforceable (and very high) price levels for their services.

The FTC had been intervening in AMA activities because some of them were clearly anti-competitive and illegal. Medical doctors who combined their practices with those of lower cost health practitioners, for example, in some cases had their licenses revoked, even though such activity was perfectly legal. The FTC cited many instances where organized groups of medical doctors acted to artificially and illegally restrain trade in health services, restrict entry of competitors into local markets for health services, and mandate price levels for services.[35]

Skeptics suggested that the AMA's motive in stopping the FTC was to stifle competition and raise prices (and their salaries), but that is not how the AMA described it. In the process of their lobbying effort, the AMA used many of the same arguments we hear today from the vested interests in public education in their opposition to external, high-stakes standardized testing. It would seem that economists may be correct when they argue that monopoly power behaves in fairly predictable ways. Examples of AMA assertions made at the time include:

- Only M.Ds are qualified to judge the quality of medical care;
- Only M.Ds can properly assess the performance of other M.Ds;
- M.Ds must be allowed to practice their craft flexibly and creatively;
- If is impossible to know how to do a medical procedure beforehand-each case is different-so one cannot judge its quality in any standardized way; and

- The AMA believes that the American people do not want a government bureaucracy interfering with the cost and quality of their personal medical care.

Supporting the AMA legislation were organizations representing doctors, dentists, and veterinarians. By some estimates, the AMA and the American Dental Association alone donated over $2.8 million to Congresspersons during the 97th session of Congress. But each of these groups' state affiliates were also free to form their own political action committees and make contributions (as many of them, in fact, did).[36]

The primary opponents of the bill, represented by N-CAP (the Nurses Coalition for Action in Politics), mustered less than $0.1 million in campaign donations for the 97th Congress. Some individual state medical groups made larger total campaign contributions to Congress. Add in the contributions of other opponent groups—chiropractors, pychologists, and optometrists—and the total contributions of the AMA bill's primary opponents was still less than $0.2 million. A spokesperson for the American Psychological Association asserted before Congress:

> The economic power of the AMA and its multimillion-dollar political action committee cannot, currently, be even approached by organized psychology's resources.... Therefore, as antitrust efforts continue, non-physicians need the assistance and the leadership of agencies such as the Federal Trade Commission.

Quite in contrast to the behavior of the press on education issues today, however, most journalists then sided with the underdogs, and against the AMA. The FTC's own tally of editorial opinion on the AMA's bill was: 154 for the FTC and 0 for the AMA. In another stark contrast, Ralph Nader's organization, Congress Watch, also sided against the AMA.[37]

The end game was joined at 6 a.m. after an all-night session of a lame-duck Congress on December 17, 1982, after almost a year's deliberations and preliminary votes, overwhelmingly in the AMA's favor. In a stirring denunciation of the AMA and special interest groups in general, the sleepless Senator Warren Rudman (R, NH) rose to say:

> I noticed something very interesting in the last week. For the first time in 20 years doctors are making house calls. They made house calls in the Dirksen [Senate] Office Building....They made house calls in the Russell [Senate] Office Building. They are so concerned about our health that the reception room is packed with them. As they trudge down the steps, discouraged and disheartened because we did the right thing, as they get into their Mercedes and Porsches and drive back to their suites in the Madison, let us give the American people a break. Let us regulate those things which need regulation. Let us regulate anti-competitive practices. Mr. President, I do not get excited by my own rhetoric. I get excited when I see someone attempting to perform a frontal lobotomy on the free-enterprise system, which is precisely what is going on here. (Pertschuk 1986: 84)

The AMA's attempt to exempt itself from "external" regulation eventually failed, but only because of the virtually unanimous opposition of the country's journalists and the heroic efforts of some public interest groups and at least one senator, Warren Rudman. Why cannot the public have journalists on its side in the debate over standardized testing?

Many education leaders insist that teachers deserve the same level of respect, pay, and professional independence as doctors and lawyers and, if they got it, most of our country's education problems would be solved. They tend not to mention the trade-offs that these other professions have made in order to maintain their higher status and salaries. Doctors, dentists, and lawyers, for example, are not simply given a captive group of clients as public school teachers are; if their clients do not like their work's quality, outcome, or price, they may well go to someone else. Moreover, these higher-paid professionals are subject to malpractice lawsuits and so must purchase insurance and can lose their license for poor quality work, whereas most teachers can only be fired for irresponsible conduct that bears no relationship to their instructional abilities.

Finally, these supporters of higher status and pay for teachers do not seem to realize that other professionals are subject to regulatory oversight, as the example of the AMA and the Federal Trade Commission above illustrates, must adhere to tightly specified professional codes of conduct, and must obey the laws of their state. They are not free to do whatever they please in the practice of their craft. Linda Darling-Hammond, a strong opponent of high-stakes standardized testing and the main inspiration behind the teaching profession's most prominent current efforts to raise its pay and status, insists that teachers should be unencumbered in managing their classrooms as befits the unique individual character of each class. Teachers who attempt to adhere to legally mandated rules and schedules specifying the order and pace of a standardized curriculum, she suggests, may be committing "malpractice" (Darling-Hammond 2002).

Not All Journalists Do Biased Work

I would be irresponsible if in my zeal to document the prevailing bias against standardized testing among journalists I did not mention that a small proportion of journalists do make some effort at writing balanced stories on testing. Some wise, experienced journalists who present balanced coverage on education issues that one can trust include Jimmy Kilpatrick of EducationNews.org; Gail Chaddock and her colleagues at the *Christian Science Monitor*; Bill Kurtis of the Arts & Entertainment Channel's *Investigative Reports*; the free-lance investigative reporter Nicholas Stix; Danny Glover of SpeakOut.com; the editors of *The Washington Monthly*; Joanne Jacobs in California; Elinor Burkett; Tim Chavez and Diane Long in Tennessee; Susan

Laccetti Meyers in Georgia; Robert Holland in Virginia; Larry Parker in Washington, D.C.; Ana Veciana-Suarez in Florida; and Steve Blow in Texas. I apologize to those special others whose names I have not mentioned here.

Media Bias on testing: What It means for Our country

Cynthia Crossen's survey of media coverage of research led her to the conclusion that journalist's ethical standards regarding their sources' conflicts of interest are simplistic and biased (1994):

> Of the three conflicts of interest inherent in research—the sponsor's, the researcher's and the media's-only one, the sponsor's, is usually noted in news reports of studies, surveys, and polls.... [but] Self-interested researchers are just as intelligent as their colleagues, and just as articulate and persuasive. (p. 226)
>
> The psychology of researchers themselves—mostly without reflection or self-awareness-has undergone a profound change...and many researchers' ethical standards have drifted from the scientist's toward the lobbyist's. Researchers have almost given up on the quaint notion that there is any such thing as "fact" or "objectivity." (p. 17)

The notion of special interests influencing political policy is not new. Our country's founding fathers were astutely aware of the problem; that is why they crafted a "separation of powers," "checks and balances," protections for minorities against majority domination, and so on. Even with all of our political system's protection against special interest control, however, powerful interests still can throw their weight around to good effect.

Not only do the producer groups vested in the current public education system (i.e., teachers' unions, administrator associations, education professors) have an enormous amount of money, they have huge memberships. Moreover, those members are scattered throughout the country, in each and every congressional district. They are organized, they lobby, they get out the vote, and they make campaign donations on a massive scale.

For education consumers, by contrast, there exist some organizations, but their numbers are fewer, and they certainly have no money with which to make campaign donations.

When degrees of influence are this dramatically asymmetrical, our society relies on a free and independent press to help provide the weaker party a platform. It is sad for our country that on many education issues, including standardized testing, the press has chosen to side with the powerful against the weak. Instead of contributing to a reasoned and rational public debate on an important issue, the press seems to do its best to stifle debate. As Crossen asserts (p.7):

I worry about the thoughtless and growing abuse of research.... without research we can trust, we will never understand our world.

I am hardly the only U.S. citizen discontent with the quality of education journalism, however. Public Agenda (1997: 9, 12) reports that 50 percent of parents rate the quality of local newspaper education coverage only fair or poor (and only 22 percent rely on it for useful information about their schools), and think even less of that from national newspapers and television. Despite the efforts of the vested interests, moreover, public support for testing seems to be holding up, even after a multi-year onslaught of virtually unanimous opposition to testing in the press.

Thank goodness for freedom of thought.

Notes

1. The National Council for Measurement in Education (NCME), for example, divides its research among three publications: a methodology journal that few journalists could understand; another entitled *Educational Measurement: Issues and Practice* (EM:IP), most of whose articles are accessible to the layperson; and a newsletter, all of whose articles are accessible. Yet, I have never witnessed a general media story on educational testing (and only rarely in media outlets exclusively devoted to education, either) that cited an article from these publications of the country's main professional association of educational testing researchers.

2. One method the association used for fudging the numbers was to combine the responses from the "don't know," "undecided," and "no response" categories with the responses they favored.

3. To be complete, I must mention that a few of those I classify as testing opponents do, in fact, support the use of some current, feasible external high-stakes exams. Nicholas Lemann, for example, supports the use of the ACT and state curriculum-based exams. All the attention he gets from the press, however, is devoted to his opposition to the SAT. So, in the matter of the news articles surveyed here, he is a steadfast opponent. Richard Atkinson, president of the University of California, shares a similar point of view. For another example, Linda Darling-Hammond fiercely opposes some types of testing—high-stakes student tests and high-stakes tests of teachers on subject matter—while she advocates medium stakes teacher entrance tests based on pedagogical knowledge.

4. The *Post* reporter also neglected to mention that, regardless of whatever may have been happening with the "achievement gap," Texas's minority students' scores on the NAEP had been increasing since the Texas testing program was introduced, along with the overall Texas student average. This suggests that minority students were learning more as a result of the Texas testing program, a concrete accomplishment that will improve their lives.

5. To the extent that I am familiar with the writings of Bill Schmidt and Michael Kirst, I do not believe that they can be pigeonholed as opponents of high-stakes testing. Indeed, Bill Schmidt serves as an advisor to the pro-testing advocacy group, Achieve. But, Kirst's few statements in "Testing Our Schools" were certainly critical of California's testing program, and Schmidt's statements on the show were certainly critical of something. Schmidt spoke about the lack of coherence among standards, textbooks, instruction, and test content. In other contexts, these arguments could be used to support the use of high-stakes standardized testing. If you watch "Testing Our Schools," however, I believe you will agree that his comments

were meant (by the editor, if not him) to criticize the manner in which current and future testing programs are and will be set up.

6. Henrico County, Virginia's schools, its superintendent, and the teachers at its Baker Elementary School, for example, had been visited earlier by the authors of a National Education Goals Panel report on standardized testing (National Education Goals Panel 2000). The Spotsylvania County, Virginia School District offices and the teachers at Courtland High School had been visited earlier by a writer for the *Education Week* newspaper (Portner 2000).

7. In other venues, Merrow personally rails against high-stakes tests by: endorsing the use of portfolios and performances to replace traditional standardized tests; claiming that states are not now using multiple measures for graduation; asserting that high-stakes standardized testing causes cheating ("The pressure is just too intense when everything hangs on one test."); characterizing our elected representatives as ignorant and uncaring about education; claiming that standards are better when they are few and terse, and openly encouraging his listeners on a radio talk show to become involved in anti-testing advocacy organizations.

8. The "unbiased" Open Directory "Society/Issues/Education/Standardized Testing," as edited by "SFJohnson" and "noonenj": "WEBSITES: (1) National Center for Fair and Open Testing—The nation's only nonprofit advocacy organization dedicated to preventing the misuse of standardized tests. Offers a quarterly newsletter, fact sheets and other resources. (2) "Brouhaha on National School Testing"—Most American parents are being told by local schools that their children rank "above average" in both reading and math. *Christian Science Monitor*. (3) "Bush Must Share Glory of Rising TAAS Scores"—Reforms helping today's at-risk students began years before the governor took office. Austin 360. (4) "Bush Praises Local Districts' Use of TAAS for Promotion"—Bush said he appreciates local school districts using the power of local control to address the problem of social promotions. *Lubbock Online*. (5) "Bush's 'Texas miracle' in schools? TAAS tells"— Gains on TAAS are not paralleled in other measures of student achievement. *Capitol Alert*. (6) "Cheating Teacher Skews Schools' Test Scores"—The unfair help given to students has forced Lawrence, Kansas school officials to ask the state Department of Education to throw out the results from the Iowa Reading Test taken in April 1998. (7) "College Drops SAT Requirements"—Dickinson College dropped SAT requirements and SAT scores went up. Op Ed piece in *New York Times*. (8) *Combating Standards and Standardized Testing*—Stop the continued push for more standardized testing to raise standards. (9) Consortium for Equity Standards and Testing—Focuses attention on how educational standards, assessments, and tests can be used more fairly. Presents issues, documents, links, and citations related to fairness in testing practices. (10) Division of Student Assessment— Texas Education Agency official site. Information on the TAAS and end-of-course examinations. (11) *Frontline: Secrets of the SAT*—Looks at standardized tests and examines the national obsession over them. (12) *High Stakes: Testing for Tracking, Promotion, and Graduation*—A study of the uses and effects of high-stakes testing, by the Committee on Appropriate Test Use, National Research Council. (13) "High TAAS Scores Nothing to Cheer About?"—As TAAS scores continue to rise, the percentage of Texas students who require remediation in college has grown, and Texas SAT scores remain below the national average. (14) IRA— *High-Stakes Assessments in Reading*—Summary of a position statement of the International Reading Association. The full text of the paper is available in PDF format. (15) *Is There Too Much Testing in American Schools?*—From the Educational Testing Service. (16) "Kentucky School Testing Simplified"—State's 14-

year shape-up plan called CATS. *Cincinnati Enquirer.* (17) "Lawmaker Wants TAAS Testing to Include Special Ed Students"—A Houston legislator has filed a bill that would require all state school districts to include most special education students in the TAAS. *Lubbock Online.* (18) "Minority Groups Seek to Stop Achievement Testing"—A key Texas case goes to trial as minority groups seek to stop a school reform trend. *U.S. News & World Report.* (19) NAEYC Position Statement: Standardized Testing of Young Children—Summary of National Association for the Education of Young Children's position statement, adopted in November 1987. Full text available in PDF format. (20) "National School Testing"—Oklahoma governor Frank Keating says, "President Clinton's plans for national school testing are seriously flawed." (21) "NCTE Moves to Present Own Voice on High-Stakes Testing"—Members of the National Council of Teachers of English pass a resolution to encourage continued research regarding the political, educational, and social impact of high-stakes testing. (22) "New York Cheating Teachers"—NPR—Teacher and school evaluations are often tied to such test scores. RealAudio. (23) "Ohio Proficiency Testing Examined"—An examination of the results of Ohio's proficiency tests, finding evidence of socioeconomic bias. (24) "On Standardized Testing"—While standardized tests are problematic at all ages and levels of schooling, they are especially questionable in primary grades. *ERIC Digest,* 1991. (25) "Pass or Fail?"—Does testing unfairly discriminate against minorities? The case of *GI Forum, et al. v. Texas* is being closely watched by educators nationwide. *Law News Network.* (26) "Proficiency Tests Score Unfairly"—Allegations of bias in Ohio. Reinventing Assessment—"Too Much Testing of the Wrong Kind; Too Little of the Right Kind in K-12 Education." (27) "San Francisco School Tests"—NPR—A San Francisco School Board decision to defy the state law that requires all students to take standardized tests in English only. RealAudio. (28) "Scans: Real Tests for Real Kids"—*Wired News*: Canadian educational software developer Gerry Morgan may have found a way to assess qualities such as creativity, insight, and teamwork. (29) "Schools Panel Recommends Longer Year, Tougher Testing"—Recommendations for school improvement in Iowa. (30) "Standardized Test Scores"-NPR—A growing number of parents who are complaining that the use of standardized tests to promote or hold back students in public schools is unfair. RealAudio. (31) "State Idea to Expand TAAS Testing Unfair"—*High Wired.net* student opinion. (32) Student Assessment and Testing—Northwest Regional Educational Laboratory Equity Center position paper. (33) "Study Says Law Erases Link Between Schools' Wealth, TAAS Results"—Texas's share-the-wealth school finance law has erased the link between a school district's wealth and how well its students perform on the academic skills test, according to a new Texas A&M study. *Dallas Morning News.* (34) "TAAS Cheating"-NPR—Several schools officials in Texas caught manipulating school testing data to improve their schools' rankings. Requires RealAudio player. (35) "TAAS Provides Needed Accountability"—*Amarillo Globe-News Opinion.* (36) Test Usage Information Links—Research, articles, and information about high stakes tests and their misuse. (37) *Testing in American Schools: Asking the Right Questions*—These new approaches are attractive, but inevitably carry some drawbacks. Complete article available in PDF format. (38) *The Harmful Impact of the TAAS System of Testing in Texas*—TAAS testing is reducing the quality and quantity of education offered to the children of Texas, especially poor and minority youth. Civil Rights Project at Harvard University. (39) *The TAAS Test*—Issues page from the Parents' Coalition of Texas. (40) "Too Good To Be True--New Orleans Schools Test Results"—Scores and testing practices raise suspicions of experts. Special report by the *Times-Picayune*. (41) "Virginia School Tests"—NPR—The reaction in Virginia to the state's efforts to connect test scores to school accreditation. RealAudio. (42) *What Do Test Scores in Texas Tell Us*—Rand Corporation's study of the Texas Assessment of Academic Skills (TAAS) test scores in Texas. Includes link to Rand Corp. press release and Rand CEO's statement. (43) *What You Can Do To Fight Standardized Tests*—by Alfie Kohn. Sixteen ways to express your opinion of standardized tests. PDF format. (44) *Why Testing Experts Hate Testing*— The strengths and weaknesses of standardized testing and ways of improving it. (45) *Why the Testing Craze Won't Fix Our Schools*—A collection of articles examining the use of proficiency tests. *Rethinking Schools*, Spring 1999."

9. The directory was also filled with a good deal of junk—some links were, in fact, duplicates that led one to the same document, but at two different websites; some were little more than random personal thoughts from someone who did not know much about the topic, but had read a few things and had opinions (against testing, of course). Dozens of the most important sites in the country for the topic—on all sides of the issue—were not even listed.

10. Not his real name.

11. Not his real name.

12. There is no denying, of course, that I have opinions about standardized testing, mostly concerning what I perceive to be biased research by self-interested groups and one-sided coverage in the media (and by the Open Directory Project). I made no attempt to cover this up when I applied to be an Open Directory editor. In my application, I had specifically mentioned that I had spent much of my spare time the past couple of years fighting one-sided coverage of the issue. I bluntly asserted the reason I wanted to edit the Standardized Testing directory to be my conviction that it was very biased. I submitted as one of three proposed links that I would add to the directory that to the *Test Bashing Series* itself. Under these conditions, I was accepted as an editor.

    Still, I was not willing to assume the editorship until after I had reviewed all the guidelines, and could assure myself that I was qualified and could abide by them. The Open Directory Editor's Guidelines are fairly explicit in asserting that they welcome advocates as editors, as advocates are often very well-informed people in their field. No editor, however, is to use his preferences to bias or restrict the offerings in their directory.

13. (e.g., CRESST, Boston College's NBETP, the NRC's Board of Testing and Assessment, SCAM in Massachusetts, the Massachusetts Teachers Association).

14. (e.g., ERIC/AE, ECS, ETS' series of essays from invited critics, the Buros Institute, NATD, NCME, AFT).

15. (e.g., Achieve, The Education Trust, my *Test Bashing Series*).

16. To the Fordham Foundation's *Why Testing Experts Hate Testing*, which, because of its title, has been misinterpreted by several anti-testing groups to be sympathetic to their cause.

17. "Site Listings: (1) American Educational Research Association: *High-Stakes Testing in PreK-12 Education*—position statement. (2) FairTest: National Center for Fair & Open Testing—nonprofit advocacy organization for fair, open, and educationally relevant tests. (3) *High-Stakes Testing: Opportunities and Risks for Students of Color, English-Language Learners, and Students with Disabilities*—complete text of a paper by Jay P. Heubert. (4) International Reading Association: *High Stakes Testing in Reading*—position paper. In PDF format. (5) National Education Association: *High Stakes Testing*—details the organization's positions on the issue. (6) *Use of Tests as Part of High-Stakes Decision-Making*

for Students—archived report from the U.S. Department of Education's Office for Civil Rights."

18. R. A. Wolk, "Crash Test," *Teacher Magazine*, October 2000.
19. R. A. Wolk, "Multiple Measures," *Teacher Magazine*, April 2002.
20. The search engine is basic, and literal—if you want to find all the instances of a person's name, for example, you must use all possible variations of the person's name that might have been used at any point (e.g., with and without a middle initial or nickname).
21. In twenty years of taxpayer funding, CRESST has produced over 500 reports. Some of them are purely technical or otherwise just informational. Those that front onto policy issues, however, are uniformly opposed to high-stakes, large-scale standardized testing. That opposition ranges from polemical rants to the standard finesse of "more research is needed" (presumably, conducted by them) before we should use standardized tests with stakes. Any reader is welcome to look for that CRESST report among the several hundreds that made an effort to estimate, or even simply consider, the benefits of testing. Any reader is welcome to look for that CRESST report among the several hundreds that considered the drawbacks of the alternatives to standardized tests, such as grade point averages. I have not been able to locate any such reports.
22. Here, I am counting only two individuals who tend to oppose standardized testing in rather unrestrained terms, and not other researchers in CSTEEP, such as those who worked on the Third International Mathematics and Science Study.
23. There remain two more past presidents who might be called special cases. One was the director of a state assessment program and his name was mentioned in four *Education Week* stories about the administration of that particular program. Another became a high official at the Educational Testing Service (ETS) and, eventually, president of ETS. She was not mentioned in any *Education Week* stories on testing while she was president of NCME, only years later after she became an ETS spokesperson. All told, her name was mentioned 17 times over two decades. Only four of those mentions concerned testing policy issues, however; the other stories were mundane, having to do with a job appointment, career milestone, or note on a new ETS product or contract.
24. Conversely, there are several organizations with anti-testing positions whose spokespersons have been quoted or interviewed in *Education Week* five or more times and, thus, would be eligible for entry into the upper-right cell in the table of anti-testing advocates. Moreover, there are at least several individual testing opponents who also have been interviewed five or more times. But, I am keeping with my restriction of comparing equal numbers of opponents and defenders (26 of each), even though the list of opponents to whom *Education Week* pays attention is much longer than the list of defenders.
25. Representing the anti-testing point of view were the usual coterie of advocates and education professors: the National Center for Fair and Open Testing (FairTest), Alfie Kohn, Peter Sacks, Deborah Meier, the National Center for Restructuring Education, two Latino civil rights groups, and professors Robert Linn and Robert Hauser. Representing an opposing viewpoint were the American Federation of Teachers (AFT) and me.
26. At the same time, one could, in fact, find most of those "independent grassroots organizations" on FairTest's website, where one would also notice that most of the leaders of these "independent grassroots organizations" worked for FairTest. One needed only compile a list of the leaders of all these "independent grassroots organizations" and then look at a list of FairTest's state coordinators. One can also

find some of the documents that FairTest and these "independent grassroots organizations" use to harass state and local testing directors and misinform the public. The documents look very much alike, like maybe they have not "risen up" so "independently" after all.

27. I think it would be a terrible policy for EWA to use testing opponents' complaints, or my complaints for that matter, as benchmarks to judge the balance of its coverage, however. I am reminded of the story of the opportunist who sues someone he does not like on a phony charge in a court with a lazy judge. The judge does not want to make the effort to weigh the evidence and so just splits the difference. The opportunist gets half of what he sued for. So, he sues again on a phony charge and asks for even more. Again, he gets half of what he asked for.

28. I must confess that I do not know exactly how the questions were worded in the ephemeral Luntz/Lazlo poll as I was unable to obtain them or any methodology report, despite my request. I have made a consistent study over several years of public opinion surveys on the topic of standardized testing and have never before been refused such basic information.

29. In the unpublicized AASA survey, 68 percent of parents asserted that "implementing a statewide student standards test [was] likely to improve public schools." Fifty-nine percent of parents asserted that "high test scores" was "one of the most [or] very important attributes of a good school." The focus groups revealed other proposed reforms to be more popular than standardized tests, but the most popular of all, such as "removing disruptive students" and "higher teacher standards" are opposed by the AASA, too.

The AASA press release implies that the first question posed was something like: "Can a student's progress for one school year be accurately summarized by a single standardized test?" The majority purportedly disagreed with the statement. Second question: "Should students be kept back a grade if they fail to achieve a passing score on a statewide standardized test?" A slight majority purportedly disagreed. Third question: "When you took a standardized test, did the score accurately reflect what you knew about the subject being tested?" Here, a majority purportedly agreed that the scores did accurately reflect their knowledge. Fourth question: "Do standardized test scores accurately reflect what children know about the subject being tested?" Now, a majority disagrees.

How does one reconcile the different responses to questions 3 and 4? Standardized tests used to be OK, but now they are not? By the way, this is it. These four questions are the poll. Can you imagine a pollster calling you up on a weekend and popping just these four questions at you out of the blue?

The questions are vague, ambiguous, and crudely worded. There are many different standardized tests; which ones are they talking about? The first question implies that it is common to judge a student's progress for a year based on a single standardized test. Outside of Advanced Placement exams, which are hugely popular, and their equivalents in honors courses in New York State and California, there are few places where this situation occurs.

There are many states, however, that administer high-stakes tests covering the basic subjects at about a 7th-grade level of difficulty as a requirement for high school graduation. They are, essentially, basic literacy tests. But, all states with such tests give students many chances to pass these tests—typically several chances each year to pass until 12th grade and even more after that if the student still has not passed. Moreover, in most cases, the tests are not timed; students have all day to complete sections that average 45 minutes to 1 hour completion times.

30. No political parties had anything to do with the poll. Its "bipartisan" label derives from the fact that the polling firm conducting the poll, like many political polling firms, is run by one pollster who works largely for Democratic Party clients and one pollster who works largely for Republican Party clients. The "bipartisanship" refers to just two people; it is an advertising slogan, for sale to anyone willing to pay for it.

31. There have been several opinion polls conducted with parents that asked them how they would feel about high-stakes standardized testing if their own children were held back because of poor performance on them. Overwhelmingly, parents have said they are still in favor of high-stakes standardized testing. Indeed, all the reliable evidence shows that parents are stronger advocates of high-stakes testing than non-parents are, and many testing experts know this. *Education Week*, however, asked the question of testing experts at CRESST and the National Research Council who either purposely ignored all the evidence, or did not care about it.

32. To its credit, however, ECS did promote some discussion of the issue, and invited Deborah Wadworth, of Public Agenda, to appear on a panel at an ECS conference. Wadworth declared the "backlash" theory to have no evidential foundation.

33. ECS practices other behaviors, too, that do not seem very "balanced." ECS staff write a monthly column in the magazine *Phi Delta Kappan*, the most strident education publication in the United States defending the education status quo. ECS also sends out daily press clippings from *Education Week*, the flagship publication of an organization openly opposed to the use of high-stakes standardized tests.

34. For example, a Roper-Freedom Forum survey a decade ago found that 89 percent of the Washington press corps claimed to have voted Democratic for president in the 1992 general election and only 7 percent Republican (Bartley 2000).

35. Some examples cited by the FTC:

- The FTC charged that the American Society of Anesthesiologists kept prices artificially high by forcing anesthesiologists—through its ethical code—to bill patients separately for each service performed. Their code essentially made salaried employment "unethical."

- The FTC charged the Michigan State Medical Society with threatening to boycott the state Blue Cross/Blue Shield and Medicaid plans in order to gain fee increases.

- When a regional medical center in West Texas that lacked an obstetrician tried to recruit one-80 percent of the county's mothers were forced to give birth elsewhere—the town's five doctors protested. They claimed that the plan to put the new doctor on salary amounted to "socialized medicine." The five doctors wrote the new recruit threatening to bar him from the local medical society if he came. He stayed away. They also threatened the hospital administration with a boycott if the deal went through. The FTC learned of the doctors' behavior and charged them with illegal restraint of trade.

- The FTC fought the efforts of medical groups to enforce "relative value scales" for physician fees on the grounds that these documents were thinly disguised price-fixing agreements.

- The FTC enjoined M.D.s from boycotting emergency rooms that recruit lower cost physicians.

- The FTC investigated complaints of denial of malpractice insurance to physicians who provide back-up services for nurse-midwives.

- The FTC investigated complaints that rural health clinics in Alabama were forced to close because they were run by nurse-practitioners, not doctors.

- An FTC order prohibited a local medical society from keeping its members from advertising to senior citizens that they accept Medicare as payment in full.

36. According to Public Citizen's Congress Watch, 213 of the 219 House co-sponsors had received campaign contributions from the AMA and the ADA—$2.3 million between January 1, 1979, when lobbying for the antitrust exemption first began, and July 30, 1982. American Medical PAC (AMPAC) alone gave $1.7 million to candidates in the 1982 election campaign, more than any other PAC, according to Common Cause.

37. The former FTC chairman, Michael Pertschuk, and others have argued that rich and powerful special interests have more influence in Congress when their issues are complicated, obscure, and not covered by the press. Conversely, they argue, the more public visibility an issue receives, the more likely Congress is to vote for the public, not special, interests. Indeed, some statistical tests support this hypothesis in specific reference to the progress of AMA-supported bills in this era in Congress (see Phelps 2001i).

7

The Fruits of Victory (Benefits of Testing)

Most of the overwrought characterizations of test "misuse" have been addressed in previous chapters. In this chapter, I summarize and explain the results of research on the benefits of standardized testing, particularly high-stakes standardized testing.

Those who do research on the benefits of standardized tests do not find benefits to be ubiquitous, however. They find benefits to testing in some situations and not in others. The next chapter will address some of the legitimate drawbacks and limitations to the use of standardized tests.

Testing is Beneficial Because People Want It

A democrat might argue that it does not matter if the "experts" disagree about the benefits of standardized testing. After all, the public, in overwhelming proportion, wants standardized testing, preferably with high stakes. Is not the public entitled to what it wants in the *public* schools? Besides, what constitutes a benefit? A benefit, or "good" in economists' lingo, is nothing more than something people want.

Still, testing's popularity begs the question of *why* the public favors standardized testing. It is probably safe to assume that the American public would not want to use a technology on its own children that it judged to be harmful or worthless. But, virtually all adults have had a good deal of personal experience with standardized tests, high-stakes tests, and most of the genuine alternatives. American adults have quite a lot of direct experience from which to judge the relative merits of all the various options for measuring student achievement.

Is the judgment of the American people not to be trusted? Many inside public education's aristocracy seem to think so and sometimes say so. Many educators opposed to testing either do not care what the public wants, or they do not respect it. They either ignore public opinion, or they attempt to manufacture their own public opinion, as was shown in the previous chapter.

Prevailing in the public domain against a policy that the public clearly favors requires tenacity and persistence—a protracted propaganda effort. Propaganda has two prominent features: restricting the dissemination of contradictory evidence and alternative points of view; and repetition. In combination, these features can convince an audience of the opposite of the truth.

The "Thin" Evidence for Testing's Benefits

Some prominent testing opponents, who know better, like to tell journalists that research demonstrating testing benefits does not exist or, if it exists, it is only marginal work done by those ever-present "right-wing ideologues." In a typical *Education Week* story on standardized testing in which, true to form, CRESST researchers were consulted for the final word on the matter, the journalist wrote: "...all of the researchers interviewed agreed with FairTest's contention that research evidence supporting the use of high-stakes tests as a means of improving schools is thin." "All of the researchers" *she chose* to interview agreed, that is (Viadero 1998).

When not simply ignored, solid research with inconvenient or politically "incorrect" results can be dismissed by one of at least two other methods. If a researcher is so prominent that she cannot just be ignored, her research may be submerged in a sea of "correct" research. One recently published collection of research articles on standardized testing research, for example, includes an article by John Bishop, the most prominent economist studying the empirical evidence of high-stakes testings' benefits, sandwiched in between several other articles, all written by testing opponents. A naive reader might jump to the conclusion that "most of the research," if not quite all of it, finds standardized testing to be a bad thing (Orfield and Kornhaber 2000).

Another method for dismissing "politically incorrect" research on standardized testing, other than ignoring it, is through condescension. Here, for example, is how Henry Levin, the "court economist" of public education's royal house, dismisses the findings of standardized testing's benefits from thirty years' work and, literally, thousands of research studies conducted by industrial/organizational psychologists, among them the world's foremost scholars in the field.[1]

Researchers who assume [strong] productivity implications [to the use of standardized testing]...use studies by industrial psychologists to buttress their claims (Bishop 1989). However...disinterested appraisals of the research on the predictive validity of test scores conclude that there is only a very modest connection between test scores and productivity ratings by supervisors (Hartigan and Wigdor 1989). Indeed, an overall summary of the potential economic gains from using test scores for employment selection suggests that the economic claims of industrial psychologists are flawed and highly exaggerated. (H. Levin 2000)

Levin dismisses out-of-hand an abundance of empirical evidence accumulated by thousands of industrial/organizational (I/O) psychologists based on two pieces of argument. First, he, Henry Levin, wrote an article critical of their research. Second, one "disinterested" National Research Council (NRC) panel wrote a report critical of their research.[2] Unfortunately, much mainstream education research is written in this fashion, more as propaganda than research. And, it is anything but "disinterested."

From the National Research Council's organizational twin on testing policy matters, the Center for Research on Evaluation, Standards and Student Testing (CRESST), Daniel Koretz (1996) chimed in tune:

> Despite the long history of assessment-based accountability, hard evidence about its effects is surprisingly sparse, and the little evidence that is available is not encouraging.... The large positive effects assumed by advocates...are often not substantiated by hard evidence...

Essentially, these mainstream education researchers dismiss out of hand the relevance of any research not done by them, for example, at CRESST or the NRC. When willing to recognize that the "hard evidence" for testing's benefits is actually fairly abundant, they will dismiss its quality in the typical fashion—saying test scores as predictors are not perfect, without saying that they are often better than any single alternative, and almost always better than the alternative of not considering test scores at all (for example, see Levin 1998).

Honest, trusting souls can be taken in by propaganda, however. William Mehrens, a competent, thoughtful, and objective testing and measurement professor from Michigan State, delivered a presidential address to the National Council of Measurement in Education (NCME) several years ago on the topic of standardized testing's effects. The written version of his talk has over sixty footnotes and his talk seems exhaustive of the topic. He delivered the address that way, too, as if he felt that he had looked at the sum total of what we know about testing's effects (Mehrens 1998).

The picture he saw did not look pretty. Standardized testing, particularly when it had high stakes, seemed to do more harm than good.

As conscientious and responsible as Mehrens' review of the literature was, however, it was also extremely narrow. Among the over-sixty citations one can find zero from economists' studies, zero from the studies of industrial/organizational psychologists, and zero from research outside the United States. Moreover, he apparently did not know about other studies conducted by education researchers which found testing's effects to be net positive, perhaps because, given the direction of their results, they have not been widely disseminated in the education community.

Most of his attention, in fact, focused on the many testing program evaluations conducted by a single organization, the Center for Research on Evaluation, Standards, and Student Testing (CRESST). If that single organization provided a representative sample of research in the field, and sponsored unbiased work, Mehrens' focus on their products might have been valid. But, unbeknownst to Mehrens, looking through CRESST's publication list for evidence of testing's benefits was akin to looking among the Vatican's publications for evidence to support atheism.

As narrowly focused as Mehrens' review was, it was, nonetheless, enlightening in its exposition of the range, character, and persistence of *anti-testing* research. Many studies he reviewed found that the introduction of a standardized testing program had no effect on how teachers taught, and that was usually considered to be a slam on the testing program, which had promised a change/improvement in how teachers' taught. Just as many other studies, however, found that the introduction of a standardized testing program did affect how teachers taught, and that was usually considered to be a bad thing, too, because that meant teachers were teaching to the test, narrowing the curriculum, "corrupting" the pure, natural order...and so on. No matter what the change was, or if there was no change at all, the end result was considered bad. Standardized tests are bad, no matter what they do, even if they do nothing at all.

Mehrens' review reveals something else—a myopic focus on educators' happiness. Most of the testing program evaluations conducted by mainstream education researchers employ teachers' utopian wish-list for what they personally prefer to do in the classroom as the benchmark against which testing program effects are measured. If an English teacher prefers to teach a literature course using certain books he, personally, prefers, and the state standards, and the standards-based tests, call for a different set of books, many evaluators would call the testing program a failure, simply because the teacher does not like it. The teacher must do something that, left alone to do whatever he pleased, he would not have to do. The standards and tests are said to "inhibit creativity," "stifle innovation," "deskill teachers," and "stunt teachers' pursuit of best practice." If teachers do not like a testing program, for any reason whatsoever, it is no good.

Moreover, virtually all of these testing program evaluations are conducted just after a new testing program has been implemented, when teachers are most likely to resent the change and disruption. Talk to a teacher in a system that has had a test for twenty years and adapted to it, and the opinion might be different.

Note, however, that astonishingly few of the studies conducted by mainstream education researchers make an effort to determine if a testing program has improved productivity or student learning. Even fewer make any effort to learn the reaction of public education's financiers and consumers (i.e., taxpayers, parents, employers, students). Most testing program evaluations are conducted as if the only aspect that matters is whether or not teachers and administrators—those who are getting paid to serve the public's needs—are happy with it. In what other field of endeavor, would the wishes and welfare of the funders and consumers be considered close to irrelevant?

What if a testing program increased student learning and improved educational productivity substantially? First, the standard evaluation conducted by mainstream education researchers is not even equipped to find this result, so it would be ignored. Second, mainstream education research, in the United States anyway, would still find a bad result if the teachers did not also like the testing program.

A consumer advocate or an economist might conclude that teachers who do not like such a successful testing program may be ill-suited to the job and, perhaps, they should pursue another profession where they can be more productive. Mainstream education research is more likely to recommend dropping the testing program.

Despite the fact that some testing opponents have done their best to hide or suppress it, a cornucopia of empirical and logical evidence for high-stakes testing's benefits does exist, and some of it is summarized below. Much of the work, not surprisingly, has been conducted by researchers in fields outside education schools, such as economics, psychology, and sociology. Testing research in mainstream education circles seems fixated on finding costs to and problems with testing, both real and (mostly) imagined.

International "Natural Experiments" in Test Dropping and Reintroduction

Many in the United States tend to think of the youth-oriented "movements" of the 1960s and 1970s as a U.S. phenomenon. But, they were not exclusive to the U.S. These youth movements may have been supported, in part, by the new prosperity throughout Europe and North America which allowed youth more free time and longer school careers, as well as by the "baby boom" cohort bulge which, though not as large as in the U.S., existed in other postwar societies, too.

One common theme of the times was a rejection of restrictions, structures, and rules in favor of an eagerness to experiment with greater freedoms. In some countries, this included dropping some standardized test requirements. This phenomenon of test-dropping in the 1960s and early 1970s is unfamiliar to many Americans because we had little previous history of high-stakes standardized testing.

It was expected that this relaxation in testing requirements would be permanent. But, in many countries, it was not. Gradually, steadily, the test requirements have returned and, indeed, additional new tests have been added. The trend since the mid-1970s across the industrialized world has been strong and clear—countries are adding tests, at all levels, and the variety of test types is broadening. Moreover, as they learn the technology, other countries are adding multiple-choice formats to their tests.

The 1960s and 1970s effort in test-dropping turned out, in retrospect, to be just another social experiment—another social experiment that failed. The countries, states, and provinces that reintroduced tests after having dropped them tell a consistent story: after the standardized testing was dropped, academic standards declined, students studied less and took their studies less seriously, curricula became muddled and incoherent, and selection and promotion decisions became subjective and arbitrary.

This story that one hears to explain why testing requirements were reintroduced is similar whether one is in France, British Columbia, the Netherlands, Sweden, Alberta, Scotland, Germany, New Brunswick, England and Wales, Ontario, Portugal, China, or Newfoundland. These countries, provinces, or states did not reintroduce systemwide high-stakes testing requirements on a whim. Commissions were formed, studies were conducted, researchers were called, public and expert opinion was collected, and much consideration was applied to the issue. Their conclusions: based on experience both with them and without them, it was apparent that high-stakes standardized tests produced positive net benefits and represented a clear public good (Phelps 2000g).

Indeed, a similar story unfolded in Eastern Europe and the countries of the former Soviet Union. With political liberalization, some countries dropped standards, and then saw a decline in student effort and achievement. Now, they are reintroducing testing requirements (Phelps 2000g). Moreover, according to Heyneman and Ransom (1990), experiments with test-dropping have hardly been limited to Western countries:

> ...Newly independent countries sometimes considered testing an unwanted colonial legacy, irrelevant for building new national identities. In some countries such as Tanzania and the People's Republic of China, education officials replaced standardized tests with school-based assessments and experimented with other criteria for selection and certification such as political attitudes or quotas based on socioeconomic, geographic, and ethnic origins or on gender. Unforeseen problems arose. With school-based assessments it is difficult to ensure that all teachers are judging on the same criteria. Since parents judge teachers on their ability to get their children ahead, teachers tend to inflate grades. Judging a child's potential on political attitudes is not reliable since attitudes can be faked. Though quotas are sometimes necessary to ensure equal utilization of facilities, making selection decisions solely on ethnic or geographic criteria can lead to abuse and can also create resentment among groups not selected. However, whether criteria are academic or political, the need for some fair and efficient mechanism to recognize and reward ability is indisputable.

Other countries do much more high-stakes testing than we do and have for decades. Why would they if testing were not beneficial? Is it plausible to assume that they are all misguided and that we alone know the true path?

In a study of curriculum and instruction systems across thirty countries that participated in the Third International Mathematics and Science Study (TIMSS), a strong relationship was found between the number of decision points—high-stakes selection points—which serve as quality controls and student performance on the TIMSS 8th-grade mathematics exam. The more high-stakes selection points, the better the country performance (see Table 7.1). Decision points consist of tests required for entrance to or exit from a level of education, selection to curricular tracks or ability groups, teacher test requirements, and so on (Phelps 2001e).

Table 7.1
Summary of Decision Point Information

	Top Performing Countries (mean)	Bottom Performing Countries (mean)	United States
Systemwide Measures			
Number of decision points	13.88	4.42	6
Retention in Grade			
Percent Retained (grades 7 and 8)	2.34	6.34	1.65

Figure 7.1 contrasts the top- and bottom-performing groups of countries (the United States fits neatly into the bottom group) on the relationship between their number of systemwide decision points and average percent of correct answers on the 7th- and 8th-grade level TIMSS tests. The scatterplot implies a positive relationship between more quality control measures enforced (i.e., decision points) and higher test scores (the Pearson product-moment correlation is 0.78).

It would appear that:

- Top performing countries use more systemwide quality control measures. The U.S. number lies in-between the averages of the top and bottom performers, but is closer to the bottom.
- The bottom performers show higher rates of retention in grade, perhaps as a substitute for the systemwide measures they lack.
- The United States is low on all summary statistics—closer to the bottom performers on systemwide measures and lower than both top and bottom performing countries in its rate of grade retention.

Controlling for country wealth, with average test scores and numbers of decision points divided by GDP per capita, produces Figure 7.2. It suggests an exponential relationship between quality control and student achievement; after a certain critical mass of quality control measures are implemented, student achievement can really take off.

Figure 7.1
Average TIMSS Score and Number of Quality Control
Measures Used, by Country

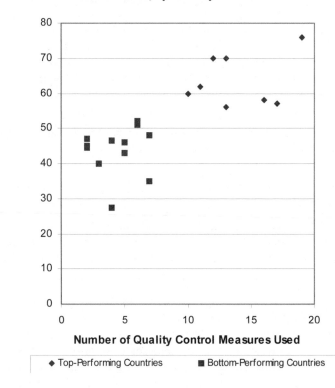

Why does the United States incorporate fewer quality control measures than other countries? It may have something to do with the greater degree to which our education system is decentralized and localized. The fact that U.S. education provider groups are far larger, and perhaps more politically powerful as a result, might also be relevant.

The Need for Tests is Obvious

As Robert Holland puts it, standardized tests are "indispensable." How else would we know how our children are achieving? How else would we know how our schools and teachers are performing? (Holland 2001). Even the most virulent opponents of standardized testing cite research that employs standardized test scores as outcome measures. Indeed, virtually all studies of educational achievement, numbering in the several thousands, use standardized test scores as their outcome measures. This represents an im-

Figure 7.2
Average TIMSS Score and Number of Quality Control Measures Used
(each adjusted by GDP/capita), by Country

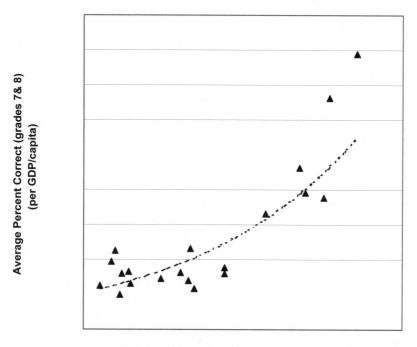

Average Percent Correct (grades 7& 8)
(per GDP/capita)

Number of Quality Control Measures Used (per GDP/capita)

plicit acknowledgment that other common measures of achievement, such as course grades and grade-point averages, are too unreliable to be trusted as outcome measures.

Why not trust research that uses local measures, such as student grade-point averages, as outcome measures? Grade-point averages (and class ranks) are norm-referenced measures, normed at the school level. Pretty much every school, no matter what its standards, no matter what the effort of its students, no matter what the difficulty of its course offerings, awards some As and some Cs. The fact that a student has accumulated a high grade-point average is a strong indicator of only one thing—probably that student is a high achiever by comparison with her peers, at that particular school. But even that is not a certainty. Schools and teachers also vary in the range of grades they award. Some schools with low standards and low student and teacher effort, award a high proportion of As, whereas other schools, with high standards, and high student and teacher effort, award a low proportion of As.

Outside of education, we rely on tests in just about every aspect of our lives, and those tests range widely in their reliability and validity. Blood tests for one's cholesterol level, for example, are notoriously unreliable. That is why doctors recommend taking them more than once. But, no doctors recommend avoiding them altogether. Adults with high levels of cholesterol have a higher proclivity to heart attack, and preventive measures can be taken to minimize the risk. Thus, knowing, or simply suspecting, that an adult has a high cholesterol level is important to that person's medical diagnosis.

Are tests of academic knowledge and ability less reliable and valid than cholesterol tests? No; actually they are far better. And, in those aspects of our society where it really matters to us directly in profound and dramatic ways, how willing would we be to throw out "high stakes" standardized tests and rely just on grade-point averages? If there were a poll tomorrow, what proportion of the U.S. population would vote to eliminate high-stakes standardized entrance examinations for doctors, lawyers, pharmacists, physical therapists, clinical psychologists, and accountants?

We all know that only a small proportion of the general population would vote for such a proposition. The overwhelming majority of the U.S. population desires checks, balances, and quality control. What, then, is the inherent, structural difference in the content and method of those high-stakes standardized tests we all want given to our future doctors, lawyers, and accountants, and those high-stakes standardized tests given to our school students?

In fact, there is none. If one is opposed to high-stakes standardized testing of school students, based on the most popular arguments raised against them, one should logically be just as opposed to the high-stakes standardized tests given to doctors, lawyers, and accountants. They all have the same "problems," "flaws" (i.e., deviations from absolute perfection), and "unintended consequences" that critics attach to standardized tests in education. So, should we get rid of all of these tests and measurements? ...medical tests; professional licensing tests; and how about measurements of weight, volume, size, or value in the trade of billions of goods while we're at it?

Most of the attacks on student testing, indeed, are attacks on measurement—of any kind—or, more specifically, any measurement made by groups "external" to the group being measured. Should the sellers of goods and services in the marketplace be the only ones allowed to measure the dimensions or quality or those goods and services?

The Benefits of Testing are Just Common Sense

Types of Testing Benefits

Distilled to the most rudimentary elements, the benefits of standardized testing accrue mainly in four categories—information, motivation, organizational clarity, and goodwill. That represents quite a thorough distillation. Information alone takes several different forms, for several different audiences. Test results can measure the achievement of an individual student. They can describe the performance of a teacher, a curriculum, a textbook, a school, a program, a district, or a state policy. Moreover, test results can inform one or more among many parties—parents, voters, employers, higher education institutions, other schools, state departments of education, and so on.

Perhaps the simplest, and least disputed, beneficial *information* use of standardized tests is in *diagnosis.* Test results can pinpoint a student's academic strengths and weaknesses, areas that need work, and areas of particular promise. Test scores provide a measurement tool for judging the effectiveness of preexisting or proposed school programs. Test results inform teachers, schools, and school systems about their curricular and instructional strengths and weaknesses. That may lead to a better alignment of curriculum with instruction, a benefit often enumerated by teachers and administrators in evaluations of testing programs.

Information benefits can also be associated with *accountability.* Information can be used by higher-level school system administrators to make judgments about performance at the school or school district level and to make changes to increase efficiency. In an environment of school choice (e.g., school districts with open enrollment), information about school performance can help parent-student school shoppers to make a more informed selection.

Finally, information benefits can be found through *signaling, screening,* and *credentialing.* College admissions counselors and employers can make a more informed decision about applicants' academic achievement with test scores than they can without. Colleges, for example, use measures of *predictive validity* (correlation coefficient of entrance test score with college achievement) to justify requiring applicants to submit scores from college admissions tests (ACT or SAT). Measures of *allocative efficiency* (efficient sorting of applicants to organizations) are more difficult to measure, but are relevant benefits as well.

Finally, we may have reached the point in the United States where standardized tests provide the only pure measure of subject-matter mastery. Some critics charge that, for some time now, education schools have encouraged teachers to grade students using a cornucopia of criteria that includes perceived persistence or effort; perceived level of handicap due to background, participation or enthusiasm; and perceived need. Subject matter mastery is just one, and often not the most important factor, considered in calculating a student's course grade. If standardized tests are, indeed, the *only* trustworthy measure of academic achievement, can our society afford not to use them? External standardized tests may be the only reliable source of information on education performance not controlled by individuals or groups with an incentive to suppress it.

Even teachers who endeavor to grade their students on the basis of academic achievement are unlikely to have received more than cursory training in testing and measurement. Those who criticize standardized tests for their alleged imperfections of structure and content seldom mention that standardized tests are written, tested, and retested by large groups of Ph.D.s with highly technical training in testing and measurement.

Of the four main categories above, information is arguably the only one common to educational tests whether or not they have "stakes," and whether or not they are conducted "internally" or "externally." The other categories—motivation, organizational clarity and efficiency, and goodwill—are unlikely to exist when tests "do not count."

Motivation may not be an end in itself, but can lead to desirable behaviors, such as a student paying greater attention in class and studying more which, in turn, leads to the accumulation of more knowledge and skill. Like information, motivation can affect many different parties to the educational enterprise and provide benefits to various different types of recipients. Motivational effects are manifest when rewards or punishments are provided (or imposed upon) students, teachers, administrators, schools, districts, programs, service providers, politicians, or even parents. The beneficial effects of motivated efforts can accrue to any of the parties above, employers, higher education institutions, or society in general.

Just one example of the *organizational clarity or efficiency benefit* of standardized testing is provided by the testimony of teachers in many states, provinces, and countries who participate in test development, administration, and scoring. Overwhelmingly, they assert that the experience helps them as instructors. After struggling, along with other teachers and testing experts, to design and score assessments fairly, they understand better how their students might misunderstand concepts and how they might better explain the concepts. Moreover, they can much more efficiently align their own instructional program with state standards after undergoing a deep immersion into the state standards (see, for example, General Accounting Office 1993a, 1993b; Heyneman and Ransom 1990; Anderson, Muir, Bateson, Blackmore, Rogers 1990; Stake and Theobold 1991; Achieve 2001; Lumley and Yen 2001; Johnson, Treisman, and Fuller 2000; Stone 1999; Goldberg and Roswell 1999; Din 1996; Schafer, Hultgren, Hawley, Abrams, Seubert, Mazzoni 1997; Corbett and Wilson 1991; Ferrara, Willhoft, Seburn, Slaughter Stevenson 1991; Bond and Cohen 1991; Abar 1996).

The economist John Bishop, for another example, argues that it is illogical and counterproductive to insist that a teacher be both a "coach" and a "judge." The teacher is a coach when she helps a student to succeed, a judge when she grades a student's test and decides that the student should not be promoted to the next grade. By Bishop's theory, this dual role puts the teacher in a moral dilemma which is often resolved only through social promotion. Most teachers would rather be coaches than judges and, so, promote students to the next level even when they are not ready. After a few years of social promotion, unfortunately, students may be so far behind that they are unable to succeed by any objective standard. They may become disillusioned, give up trying, and drop out. Bishop argues for external high-stakes testing as a means to free each teacher to be a coach the student can trust to help him meet the challenge of the examination which is "external" to both of them.

Finally, "external" measures, such as systemwide standardized test scores, serve as a check on other measures of performance (psychometricians label this phenomenon generally "restriction of range"). To fully appreciate the benefits of organizational clarity and efficiency that external standardized testing can provide, one must imagine a society without standardized testing. What, for instance, might happen to grade inflation if there were no standardized test scores to which one could compare the grades? How much effort would students, teachers, and administrators make to improve achievement if there were no standardized tests with which to check their progress?

The final general category of benefit cited above—*goodwill*—is certainly the most often overlooked, and the most difficult to measure. The public pays for the public schools and hands over responsibility for its children's welfare to the public school authorities for substantial periods of time. The public in a democratic society has a right to objective, impartial information about the performance of the public schools' main function—the academic achievement of their children. Classroom grades are unreliable and often invalid sources of such information. Standardized tests, when they are used validly, provide far more reliable and trustworthy information.

Examples of goodwill include: renewed public confidence in the school system; public faith that the schools are working to uphold standards; and peace of mind that teachers and school administrators might gain in the wake of the new parental and public trust. Students have also reported in some surveys feelings of genuine achievement and accomplishment when they pass important, meaningful tests.

The Testing Benefit Process

Let us summarize the above section on testing benefits simply. Standardized tests can be instrumental in starting the benefit process. For one or more reasons—like motivation or organizational clarity—students learn more with testing programs in place than they otherwise would. This increase in knowledge and skills represents a potential benefit. It remains only *potentially* a benefit until it is actually used.

When the increased knowledge and skills are used, they produce a benefit. The actualized benefit takes the form of work that is of higher quality than it otherwise would be; work of equal quality that is completed in less time than it otherwise would be; the completion of work that would otherwise not even be possible, and so on.

Standardized tests can also be instrumental in completing the benefit process. Potential benefits can be transformed into actualized benefits by identifying those individuals who possess the increased knowledge and skills, or the type of knowledge and skills they have. This identification function can help the individual with the increased knowledge and skills—she can offer her test results as evidence to a potential employer or higher education institution of the increased knowledge and skills she possesses and get the job she wants. Likewise, the identification function can serve the employer or institution—they can select the applicant with the higher level of knowledge and skills from among their pool of applicants and thereby "capture" the benefit of the increased knowledge and skills for themselves.

Economists use terms such as "signaling," "screening," and "credentialing" to label the processes by which individuals with superior knowledge and skills are found. Psychologists use the more general term, "selection," as well as others to identify various permutations of the selection process.

Who "captures" the benefit?...the individual with the potential, or the employer or institution that selects him? It depends on who is in the better competitive position. If, for example, there are many job applicants and few jobs available, the employers should be able to minimize their salary offers to just the best applicants, thus capturing the benefits for their firms. It would be fair to say, however, that the individuals with the higher level of knowledge and skill "capture" some job security. That is, they do obtain a job, unlike their less skilled counterparts.

Conversely, if there are many jobs and few applicants, the applicants should be able to bid up the salary offers, and the applicants with the extra knowledge and skill should be able to bid up the salary offers to the point where they can capture most of the benefit.

How Testing Benefits are Measured

Measuring the benefits of testing may seem to present something of a conundrum. After all, virtually all studies of student achievement use standardized tests as their outcome measure. So, how can one determine if student achievement has been improved by the existence of a testing program? One cannot use a test to judge the effects of the same test without critics, inevitably, arguing that "teaching to the test" will explain the result.

Controlled experiments of testing's effects are conducted by two different methods. The first is to "treat" the experimental group with tests that count throughout a semester or year while, at the same time, the control group is not tested and receives further instruction. Then the groups are compared afterwards according to some outcome measure or measures.

The second method has two groups of students following the same curriculum, but one group faces a high-stakes examination at the end of their program and, for the other group—the control group—the same test has no stakes. The experimental group may be told, for example, that they will be paid a sum of money, or given a prize, based on their test results, while the control is told that there is no connection between their test results and any reward. Many experiments like these have been conducted on a small scale (see, for example, Tuckman 1994; Brown and Walberg 1993; Jones 1993; Engeland 1995; Tuchman and Trimble 1997; Wolf and Smith 1995; Khalaf and Hanna 1992; or Cameron and Pierce 1994). Typically, these studies are conducted outside regular school processes. These controlled experiments, with students randomly assigned to groups, always find significantly greater average effort and achievement in the experimental group—the one taking more tests or tests with "stakes."

Some testing opponents might still argue that "teaching to the test" was the probable cause of the experimental group's success. Indeed, some of these critics years ago set up a different kind of "quasi-experiment." They administered another, different standardized test to two groups of students—one group from a high-stakes testing school district and another group from a no-stakes testing school district. Their hypothesis was that the high-stakes district students should be able to perform better on the other, different standardized test if the high-stakes environment had motivated them toward greater achievement. In other words, if the students learned anything more than how to take the particular test administered in their high-stakes school district, that increased knowledge should be "generalizable" (i.e., it should be detected by higher scores in the other, different test).

Such a study was conducted several years ago with some unrevealed tests at an unrevealed location by some well-known critics of high-stakes testing, all of them members of CRESST (Linn 2000). These researchers found no evidence of generalizability, and asserted that high-stakes testing seemed only to produce "teaching to the test" and "narrowed curriculum" with no actual increase in learning overall. This single study has spawned dozens of articles, citations, and claims of proof that high-stakes testing has no benefits, and may do harm. Typically, when the study is mentioned, no mention is also made of the dozens of other studies of similar structure that achieved contradictory results.

The skeptical reader might also notice the catch-22. Some of the same critics who argue that tests must be well-aligned to a curriculum in order to be valid, will howl "narrowing the curriculum" when scores increase on an aligned test, but not on an unaligned test. There is no justifiable reason why one should expect student test scores on a test not aligned to their curriculum to increase over time. Nor is there anything sacrosanct about the other, un-aligned test used in the CRESST researchers' study. One would not expect student scores to increase on a plumbers' test after they had taken an electri-cians' course, either. But, one would be worried if their scores on an electri-cians' test did not improve.

Thus, one way researchers measure a benefit of improved student achieve-ment with high-stakes testing programs is to compare the performance of those students to that of students from other jurisdictions, that have no high-stakes testing programs, on a separate, unrelated examination that has *similar* content. Dozens of studies of this type have been conducted, by researchers not affiliated with CRESST, which have found positive results (see, for ex-ample, any of several Bishop studies; Woessman 2000; Grissmer and Flanagan 1998; or Phelps 2001e).

Other studies detecting benefits to high-stakes standardized testing, simi-lar in the aspect that students from high-stakes testing jurisdictions were compared to students from no-stakes testing jurisdictions, have used out-come measures other than a separate test. Some popular outcome measures used include average wages after high school or after college; high school persistence or graduation; college matriculation, persistence or performance; and job performance (see, for example, several Bishop studies; Graham and Husted 1993; Jacobson 1992).

Still other testing benefits studies have employed other research methods, such as surveys, focus groups, benefit-cost analysis, or case studies.

Table 7.2 provides a sample of the many studies that have found ben-efits to standardized testing and, particularly, high-stakes standardized testing.

Table 7.2 provides only a morsel from the complete diet of testing benefit studies. Had I, for just one example, decided to include excerpts from thirty years of industrial/organizational psychologists' studies of the benefits of tests in job selection (both for employers and employees), Table 7.2 could have run to hundreds of pages.

In order to be concise, I eliminated from inclusion the largest swaths of ground in the field of testing benefit research. Among the other categories of research with a substantial quantity of empirical research on the benefits of testing, and particularly high-stakes testing, are:

- *Most poll and survey results* from the last thirty years which have consis-tently found overwhelming support for high-stakes standardized student

Table 7.2
Some of the Studies Finding Benefits to Testing

Author, Year	Data Source	Benefits Found	Negative Effects Not Found	Method
International Studies				
Phelps, 2001	TIMSS, 100+ other studies	quality control, improved coordination & achievement	higher retention rates	comparison groups evaluation, case studies
Woessman, 2000	TIMSS micro data, OECD indicators	improved achievement		robust linear regression (cross sectional)
Bishop, 1999	TIMSS, dozens of other studies	improved achievement; more student and teacher effort	curricular narrowing, low-level instruction	multiple regression (cross sectional)
Mullis, 1997	TIMSS	improved achievement	n/a	exploratory data analysis
Bishop, 1994	IAEP (Canada)	improved achievement	curricular narrowing	multiple regression (cross sectional)
Wedman, 1994	Sweden	"second chance" options, alternative paths	n/a	n/a
Bishop, 1993	U.K., French, Dutch, U.S. documents	improved achievement	curricular narrowing, low-level instruction	case studies
G.A.O., 1993 (1)	Canadian Provinces	improved coordination, quality control, teacher development	teacher dis-satisfaction	meta-analysis, surveys, case studies, interviews
Bishop, 1993	IAEP	improved achievement	curricular narrowing	multiple regression (cross sectional)
Bishop, 1993	IEA-Reading	improved achievement	n/a	multiple regression (cross sectional)
Calder, 1991	Alberta, Canada	improved motivation, achievement, curricular alignment	teacher, student opposition	surveys
Anderson, Muir, Bateson, Blackmore, Rogers, 1990	British Columbia, Canada	greater student effort, morale and involvement, improved achievement	curriculum narrowing, low-level instruction	mixed-mode with surveys
Heyneman, Ransom, 1990	World Bank countries	improved coordination, quality control, predictive validity		case studies
Heyneman, 1987	World Bank countries	clarity, reliability, comparability, adjustment to growth		program review

Table 7.2 (cont.)

Boissiere, Knight, Sabot, 1985	East Africa, test scores and wages later	predictive validity	n/a	multiple regression (longitudinal)
Wesdorp, 1983	Netherlands, national exams	curricular/instructional alignment	n/a	survey
U.S. National Studies				
Dee, 2002	Census 5% sample (PUMS)	increased wages and hiring (but, increased dropouts, too)		multiple regression (longitudinal)
Grissmer, 2000	State NAEP	improved achievement	higher dropout rates	multiple regression (longitudinal)
Antonnucci, 1999	State NAEP and administrative records	quality control, improved coordination & achievement		comparison groups evaluation, case studies
Betts, 1998	U.S.	improved achievement		multiple regression (longitudinal)
Bishop, 1998	New York & North Carolina	improved achievement	n/a	multiple regression (cross sectional)
Aber, 1996	U.S.	"second chance" options, alternative paths	n/a	compendium
Phelps, 1994	U.S.	improved achievement, predictive validity, allocative efficiency	high cost, high burden	benefit-cost analysis
Frederiksen, 1994	U.S. states	improved achievement		pre-post & control group comparison
Graham, Husted, Bishop, 1993	SAT by state	improved achievement	higher dropout rates	multiple regression (cross sectional)
Bishop, 1992	U.S.	predictive validity, allocative efficiency; improved wages, job stability & performance	n/a	multiple regression (longitudinal)
Jacobson, 1992	U.S. states (NLS)	improved achievement for lowest achievers	higher dropout rate	multiple regression (longitudinal) re: minimum comp.
Stake, Theobold, 1991	7 U.S. states	greater student effort, improved coordination and quality control	curricular narrowing low-level instruction	surveys
Bishop, 1989	U.S.	improved achievement, job performance & stability, wages	n/a	multiple regression (longitudinal)
Chai, Woehlke 1979	review of 18 studies	predictive validity of ESL tests	n/a	meta-analysis

Table 7.2 (cont.)

U.S. state studies				
Yearwood, 2002	Texas	predictive validity of state test for African Americans		multiple regression
S.R.E.B., Bradby, Dykman, 2002	Southern States	quality control, improved coordination & achievement		pre-post comparisons
Dougherty, Collins 2002	Texas	curricular alignment, implementation of school-level diagnosis		survey
Jerald (Business Roundtable), 2001	Texas	improved achievement	more dropouts, fewer grads	literature review, data analysis
Achieve, 2001	Massachusetts	quality control, improved coordination, curricular, instructional clarity, focus	n/a	program evaluation, content analysis
Lumley, Yen, 2001	Pennsylvania	increased curricular focus, motivation		teacher survey
Toenjes, Dworkin, Lorence, Hill, 2001	Texas	generalizability	more dropouts, fewer grads	data analysis, critique of literature
Johnson, Treisman, Fuller, 2000	Texas	improved achievement, curricular alignment & focus, improved diagnosis, greater motivation, clarity	counter-productive consequences not preventable	literature review and data analyses
Massachusetts Finance Office, 2000	Massachusetts	improved achievement		multiple regression
Phelps, 2000	Texas	generalizability	more dropouts, SD and LEP exclusions; fewer grads	literature review, administrative records
Goldberg, Roswell, 1999	Maryland	improved coordination, quality control, teacher development	teacher dis-satisfaction	case study
Sanders, J., 1999	Tennessee	improved achievement, especially for lower 50 percent of students		multiple regressions of 4th, 5th grade teacher effect scores on their students' 9th grade test scores
Grissmer, Flanagan, 1998	NAEP, Texas & North Carolina	improved achievement	n/a	multiple regression (longitudinal)
Firestone, Mayrowetz, Fairman, 1998	Maine, Maryland	improved curriculum alignment, organizational clarity and focus		case studies, administrative records, surveys
Schafer, Hultgren, Hawley, Abrams, Seubert, Mazzoni, 1997	Maryland	improved achievement, information, organizational clarity and focus	n/a	multiple regressions (cross-sectional)
		alignment of curriculum,		teacher and principal

Table 7.2 (cont.)

Din, 1996	Kentucky	instruction, planning with tests		surveys
Clotfelter, Ladd, 1996	South Carolina	improved achievement		multiple regressions
Abar, 1996	Massachusetts	quality control; curricular, instructional alignment		interviews, survey
Sanders, Horn, 1995; Stone 1999	Tennessee	quality control of instruction; classroom diagnosis	n/a	multiple regression (longitudinal)
Jett, Schafer, 1993	Maryland	curricular/instructional alignment	teacher dis-satisfaction	teacher survey
G.A.O., 1993 (2)	U.S. states & districts	quality control, accountability, diagnosis		surveys re: net benefits
Rudger, 1991	Texas	improved achievement (but not for advanced students)		pre-post comparisons
Wilson, Corbett, 1991	Maryland & Pennsylvania	curricular, instructional clarity and focus, improved student diagnosis, achievement		teacher and administrator surveys
Ferrara, Willhoft, Seburn, Slaughter, Stevenson, 1991	Maryland	curricular and instructional clarity and focus	teacher dis-satisfaction	survey
Bond, Cohen, 1991	Indiana	curricular and instructional clarity and focus	curricular narrowing	survey
Glasnapp, Poggio, Miller, 1991	Kansas	accountability, greater student effort, diagnosis	curricular narrowing	survey
Lerner, 1990	New Jersey	improved achievement, especially among weakest students		pre-post test
Ligon, Johnstone, Brightman, Davis, et al., 1990	Texas	improved achievement and quality control (but not for advanced students)		pre-post comparisons
Delong, 1990	California	quality control; curricular, instructional alignment, improved achievement		survey of district administrators
Grulick, 1986	South Carolina	allocative efficiency of placement tests		meta-analysis, multiple regression
Schlawin, 1981	New York	curricular and instructional alignment		surveys, interviews
Most California postsecondary institutions, 1980s and 1990s	California	predictive validity of placement tests		multiple regression

Table 7.2 (cont.)

Local Studies				
Roderick, Engel, 2001	Chicago	improved achievement, effort & support for low-achieving students	higher rates of retention	surveys re: minimum comp.
Hannaway, McKay, 2001	Houston - (TAAS and Stanford 9)	improved achievement	lack of generalizability	multiple regression (longitudinal)
Atria, 1999	Chicago	quality control; curricular, instructional alignment	teacher dissatisfaction	teacher survey
Ladd, 1999	Dallas	increased achievement, motivation		multiple regression (cross-sectional)
Schleisman, 1999	Minneapolis	improved focus on & achievement of at-risk students		structured interviews
S.R.E.B., 1998	Hoke County, NC, and other Southern districts	improved rates of achievement, enrollment, further education	increased dropouts	case studies
Neville, 1998	Chicago	quality control; curricular, instructional alignment	teacher dissatisfaction	case studies, interviews, surveys
Webster, Mendro, Orsak, Weerasinghe, Bembry, 1997	Dallas	quality control of instruction; classroom diagnosis		multiple regression (longitudinal)
Psacharopoulos, Velez, 1993	Bogota, Columbia	predictive validity & allocative efficiency; improved wages, job stability & performance	higher retention rates	multiple regression (longitudinal)
Rodgers, et al. 1991	Austin, TX	improved achievement (but not for advanced students)		pre-post comparision
Mangino, Babcock, 1986	Austin, TX	improved achievement, especially among weakest students		pre-post comparision
Theoretical Models or Experiments				
O'Neil, 1998	n/a	improved clarity, focus, achievement in writing with reliable standardized testing	n/a	literature review, historical analysis
Tuckman, Trimble, 1997	n/a	increased motivation and long-term increase in achievement due to frequent testing	n/a	controlled experiment
Betts, 1996	n/a	increased wages later	n/a	n/a
Webb, 1996	n/a	improved diagnosis, coordination, achievement with job profiling assessments	n/a	feedback loop process between employees in filed and students
Sommanathan, 1996	n/a	lack of standards leads to greater wage inequality later on	n/a	n/a

Table 7.2 (cont.)

Costrell, 1995	n/a	increased motivation and more information	n/a	n/a
Wolf, Smith, 1995	n/a	testing increases performance & motivation (& anxiety)	n/a	controlled experiment
Egeland, 1995	n/a	improved motivation, achievement	outcome differences by gender, attitudes toward science	controlled experiment (3 groups: control, Hawthorne, treatment)
Tuckman, 1994	n/a	increased motivation, improved achievement	n/a	controlled experiment
Costrell, 1994	n/a	increased motivation and more information	n/a	n/a
Jones, 1993	"second chance" of final exam to improve course grades	increased motivation, persistence, and attitudes; reduced gender, racial gaps	n/a	controlled experiment
Costrell, 1993	n/a	improved achievement in college	n/a	n/a
Brown, Walberg, 1993	n/a	increased motivation	n/a	controlled experiment
Khalaf, Hanna, 1992	n/a	improved achievement	n/a	controlled experiment
Becker, Rosen, 1990	n/a	increased motivation and more information	n/a	n/a
Bishop, 1989	n/a	increased motivation, predictive validity / allocative efficiency	n/a	n/a
Kang, 1985	n/a	increased motivation and more information	n/a	n/a
Weiss, 1983	n/a	increased allocative efficiency	n/a	n/a
Stiglitz, 1975	n/a	increased allocative efficiency	n/a	n/a
Studies with results that dispute alleged drawbacks of testing				
Assn. American Publishers, 2001	U.S.		public opposition to testing	poll, literature review
Business Roundtable, 2001	U.S.		public opposition to testing	poll
Public Agenda, 2000	U.S.		public opposition to testing	poll, focus groups, meta analysis

Table 7.2 (cont.)

Phelps, 2000	OECD countries	quality control, curricular and instructional clarity, accountability, diagnosis	trend away from testing overseas	literature review, meta-analysis
Phelps, 2000	U.S. states and districts	n/a	excessive cost	surveys, literature review
Phelps, 1998	U.S.	quality control, curricular and instructional clarity, accountability, diagnosis	public opposition to testing	literature review, meta-analysis
Mayer, 1997	U.S.	multiple-choice tests serve traditional and progressive methods equally well	M-C tests undermine NCTM standards	growth curves with comparison groups
Phelps, 1997	U.S. states and districts	n/a	too much testing	surveys, literature review
Phelps, 1996	13 countries & U.S.	quality control, improved coordination, curricular and instructional clarity and focus, diagnosis	too much testing in U.S.	surveys, literature review
Walberg, et al. 1994	U.S.	little evidence for superiority of constructivists' tests	inferiority of traditional test types	literature review
G.A.O., 1993 (2)	U.S. states and districts	quality control, curricular and instructional clarity, accountability, diagnosis	excessive cost, quantity	surveys
Teacher Tests				
Ballou, Podgursky,	U.S. states	improved *student* achievement	n/a	meta-analyses
Phelps, 1996	Texas	improved instruction, higher teacher wages	teacher dis-satisfaction	benefit-cost analysis
Ferguson, 1991	Texas	improved *student* achievement	n/a	multiple regression
Solmon, Fagnano, 1990	Texas	improved achievement, reduced dropouts, higher wages, job stability & performance	n/a	benefit-cost analysis
Some Essays on the Consequences of *not* testing				
Popham, 1987	Frary, 1982	Ebel, 1981	Finscher, 1978	

testing among the general public, employers, teachers, students, parents, and other groups. Many of these surveys have asked respondents to specify testing's benefits. It can probably go without saying that, given the strong support for testing, most believe the net benefits to be positive. Moreover, all but the youngest students possess a considerable familiarity with standardized testing—enough from which to directly judge its merits (see, for example, Phelps 1998b).

- With a few exceptions, *studies conducted in other countries* that would require translation and studies conducted by or for other countries' governments that found positive net benefits to high-stakes standardized testing.
- *Studies of the predictive validity and/or allocative efficiency of U.S. college admissions tests*, such as the SAT and ACT. There are several dozen such studies (see, for example, Willingham, Lewis, Morgan, and Ramist 1990).
- With only several of the most easily obtainable studies excepted, *program evaluations of testing programs*, many of them conducted by or for state or local education agencies in the United States.
- The hundreds of more general *studies conducted by economists, psychologists, and others of the positive motivational effect of "extrinsic rewards,"* such as good or passing grades or test scores, selection to advanced programs, academic awards, and so on (see, for example, Cameron and Pierce 1994; Freeman 1994).
- Industrial/Organizational (a.k.a., personnel) psychologists' *studies of the relative advantages of the use of various types of tests compared to other measures commonly available to employees or employers in job selection.* These studies number in the thousands.[3]

Focus on Three Types of Testing Benefits

As I do not have the space to go into the detail of even a small portion of the many studies of testing benefits, I focus on three types of benefits: greater effort due to the motivation of incentives, predictive validity, and allocative efficiency. The first is probably easily understandable by all; the latter two will be explained in due course.

(1) *Incentive effects.* In some testing program evaluations, students report feeling a greater motivation to learn and an increased sense of responsibility. High-stakes tests may provide an incentive for the students to work harder, by giving them a clear target, a "punishment" worth avoiding or a "reward" worth pursuing, and, the Cornell economist John Bishop would argue, "signaling" to them that society considers academic achievement important. Teachers and students report that students spend more time doing homework and pay better attention in class in the face of high-stakes external tests. Bishop argues, moreover, that the incentives affect the behavior not only of students, but parents, teachers, administrators, and others as well.

Bishop is not the only researcher to have conducted controlled studies of the incentive benefits of testing systems with stakes, but he has been the most persistent and thorough. Most of his testing studies involve using a neutral large-scale assessment—usually one without any stakes—and comparing the performance on that assessment of students from jurisdictions with high-stakes testing systems to those from jurisdictions without high-stakes testing systems. On national assessments, like the National Assessment of Educational Progress, he compares students from testing and non-testing states (as David Grissmer and Ann Flanagan [1998] have also done). Likewise, with the SAT (as Graham and Husted [1993] have also done). On international assessments, like the Third International Mathematics and Science Study, Bishop compares students from testing and non-testing countries (as Woessman 2000; Phelps2001e; and Mullis 1997a have also done). Likewise, with the International Assessment of Educational Progress (IAEP) and the International Reading Literacy Study (IRLS).

Bishop measures incentive effects broadly, as the increased productivity and earnings of workers over their lifetimes, that they gain from the increased academic achievement, induced by the incentives of the high-stakes tests. These incentive effects are so strong, moreover, that he can detect them in a several year "backwash" at grade levels well below those of the high-stakes exams. For example, he has looked at the test scores of 8th graders in both the International Assessment of Educational Progress (IAEP) and in the Third International Mathematics and Science Study (TIMSS) and compared the test performance of students in states, provinces, or countries with high-stakes examination systems to those in states, provinces, or countries without. The students in places with high-stakes exams do better in 8th grade, even if the high-stakes exam might be in 12th or 13th grade.

The incentive effects that Bishop picks up in his regression studies are increases in knowledge and skills (economists would say "human capital accumulation") caused by students studying more, paying better attention in class, and taking tougher courses, in a high-stakes testing environment.[4]

Since test scores, Bishop argues, can signal academic achievement to employers, employers should pay a premium for job applicants with higher test scores, and graduates would reap some of the benefits of their own human capital accumulation. There would be efficiency gains for society, too, because employers for whom academic achievement mattered more would, presumably, be willing to pay more for it. The match between job-seeking and hiring would, then, become more efficient (Bishop 1996b, 1995b, 1989a).

Clearly, information and incentive benefits cannot be precisely separated. Bishop's studies may be picking up the results of some information benefits (e.g., organizational clarity), too. For example, teachers in British Columbia, Maryland, Massachusetts, Kansas, Pennsylvania, and Texas have reported that external, high-stakes tests help them coordinate better with other teachers and common standards, understand their students' performance better, and so on (see, for example, Anderson et al. 1990; Goldberg and Roswell 1999; Achieve 2001; Lumley and Yen 2001; Glassnap, Poggio, and Miller 1991; Johnson, Treisman, and Fuller 2000). Local school district administrators reported in a 1991 GAO survey that external, high-stakes tests gave them information useful for student and curriculum diagnosis (U.S. GAO 1993b).

These survey respondents claimed that information from the tests helped instruction. If instruction was improved, it only stands to reason that students' learning increased.

Bishop argues that tests as incentives are only fully effective if they are curriculum-based, rather than "aptitude" tests or achievement tests that are only vaguely related to the school curriculum. If students do not see that studying school subjects can get them a higher score on an exit exam, they may see little purpose to studying more than they would in the absence if an exit exam (Bishop 1995b: 31-32; 1989b: 9-10; 1988b: 408-421; see also Jencks and Crouse 1982).

Bishop, then, distinguishes the high-stakes examination programs he thinks can be effective from all others, calls them Curriculum-based External Exit Examination Systems (CBEEES), and ascribes to them certain characteristics. They: (1) produce signals of student accomplishment that have real consequences for the student; (2) define achievement relative to an external standard, not relative to other students in the classroom or the school; (3) are organized by discipline and keyed to the content of specific course sequences; (4) signal multiple levels of achievement in the subject; (5) cover almost all secondary school students; and (6) assess what students studying a subject are expected to know or be able to do.

New York State. Until recently, New York State was the only one among all the U.S. states with curriculum-based graduation examinations with some level of stakes attached for students at all achievement levels. The Regents examination system was far more than just a single minimum competency exam. Bishop cites results obtained by Graham and Husted (1993) which compared Scholastic Assessment Test (SAT) scores of New York students to those of students from other states in which the SAT is the predominant college admissions test, controlling for background factors in 1991.

New Yorkers performed significantly better on the SAT (particularly the math portion) than students of the same race and social background living in other states. The differential between New York State's SAT mean and the prediction for New York based on outcomes of the other 26 states was about 20 percent of a standard deviation or about 75 percent of a grade level equivalent (Bishop 1995a: 14-15) (see Table 7.2). It is unfortunate, in Bishop's opinion, that New York State employers tended to ignore Regents' exam information in hiring decisions (Bishop 1994a: 10-11).

Canada. In 1991, only some Canadian provinces—Alberta, British Columbia, New Brunswick, Newfoundland, and Québec—had curriculum-based exit examinations, whereas the others did not. Bishop tested several hypotheses using the student-level data from the 1991 International Assessment of Educational Progress (IAEP), which included representative samples of 13-year-olds from each Canadian province. Holding background variables constant, students from provinces with high-stakes curriculum-based exit exams performed better on the IAEP than did their colleagues from non-exam provinces. The difference was 23 percent of a standard deviation in mathematics and 18 percent of a standard deviation in science (Bishop 1995a: 15-16; 1994a).

Bishop's analysis also found that examination systems had pervasive effects on school administrators, teachers, and parents. In the provinces with external exams, *schools* were significantly more likely to: employ specialist teachers in math and science; employ teachers who had studied subject in college; have high quality science labs; schedule extra hours of math and science instruction; assign more homework in math, in science and other subjects; have students do or watch experiments in science class; and schedule frequent tests in math and science class (Bishop 1994a: 23-26).

In the provinces with external exams, *teachers* were significantly more likely to: give more homework; cover more difficult material; schedule more quizzes and tests; reduce the time students spend doing group problem solving; increase the time students work alone; and schedule more experiments in science class (Bishop 1994a: 22, 25-26). In the provinces with external exams, *students* were significantly more likely to: watch less television (40 percent less), report that their parents want them to do well in exam subjects (4 to 6 percentage points more likely) and talk to them about what they are learning in school, read more for pleasure, and choose educational programs when they did watch television (Bishop 1994a: 21-22, 25-26).

Countries Participating in the IAEP. Bishop also compared average student performance on the International Assessment of Educational Progress (IAEP) between countries with CBEEE systems and countries without.[5] For mathematics, the difference was highly significant and quite large, roughly equivalent to the average increase in achievement of two U.S. grade levels[6] (see Table 7.2). CBEEEs had a smaller non-significant effect on science achievement. East Asian students scored significantly higher than students in Europe and North America in both subjects.

Countries Participating in the TIMSS. The Third International Mathematics and Science Study (TIMSS) administered mathematics and science tests and background questionnaires to 7th and 8th graders in about 40 countries in 1994-95.[7] Bishop gleaned information about the nature of secondary-level exit examinations for each country from comparative education studies, education encyclopedias, and embassy personnel interviews. He classified 21 national school systems as having curriculum-based exit examinations in both subjects. Three countries had them in math but not science. Five countries had them in some states but not in others. The results indicated that TIMSS test scores were significantly higher in more developed nations, East Asian nations, and in nations with a CBEEE system. Bishop's findings in the TIMSS data have since been corroborated by Woessman (2000) and Phelps (2001e).

Ludger Woessman of the Kiel Institute of World Economics conducted what may be the largest and broadest study of educational efficiency ever. He used micro-level (i.e., student level) data from the TIMSS, controlled for the effects of the various hierarchical levels (i.e., individual student, classroom/ teacher, school, state) and even added important information from data sources other than the TIMSS, such as from the annual education indicators study of the Organisation for Co-operation and Development (OECD). Woessman's study could be much more sensitive to correlations and effects because he employed so much more detail; most studies with the international test databases before his used only aggregate data (i.e., one data point for each country)[8] (Woessman 2000, 2001).

He found several factors to have a significant positive effect on achievement: school autonomy over staffing and operations; public funding of private schools; and centralized budgets, curricula, and examinations. He found organized labor's influence to have a significant negative effect, and aggregate spending levels to have no effect.

About half the countries included in Woessman's analysis used some kind of centralized (i.e., external) examinations. All other factors held equal, students from countries with external examination systems scored significantly higher in mathematics and also higher, though not to the level of statistical significance, in science.[9] Moreover, the stronger the link between mathematics examinations and the mathematics curriculum, the higher the academic achievement in math.

Woessman (2001) hypothesizes the causal effect of external examinations on student achievement:

> ...centralized exams make it obvious whether it is the student or the teacher who is to blame. This reduces the teachers' leeway and creates incentives to use resources more effectively. It makes the whole system transparent: parents can assess the performance of children, teachers, and schools; heads of schools can assess the performance of teachers; and the government and administration can assess the performance of different schools.

> Centralized exams also alter the incentive structure for students by making their performance more transparent to employers and advanced educational institutions. Their rewards for learning thus should grow and become more visible. Without external assessments, students in a class looking to maximize their joint welfare will encourage one another not to study very hard. Centralized exams render this strategy

futile. All in all, given this analysis, we should expect centralized exams to boost student performance.

The Effect of External Exams on Earnings. To estimate the size of the benefit in terms of lifetime wage earnings of the higher student achievement in jurisdictions with CBEEES, Bishop looked to six different longitudinal studies that had calculated the ratio between grade-level-equivalent differences in student achievement and lifetime earnings.[10] With these ratios, he could estimate net present values (NPVs)—the estimated value in current dollars of current and future income – of the difference in achievement made by the effects of high-stakes testing programs[11] (see Table 7.3).

The incentive benefits, measured in dollars, are positive in all cases, and substantial. The median effect is about $13,000 *per subject area*; this is the size of the benefit accruing over the lifetime of an individual student fortunate enough to attend school in a jurisdiction with a curriculum-based exter-

Table 7.3
Bishop's Estimates of the Impact of Curricular-Based External Examination Systems on Student Outcomes, by Type of Outcome and Study

	Difference (in grade-level-equivalent units)	Difference (in net present value) in 1993 dollars*
IAEP (Canada): High-stakes testing provinces vs. others	.75 (math) .67 (science)	$13,370 $11,940
IRLS: High-stakes testing countries vs. others	1.0 (reading)	$17,830
SAT: New York State vs. rest of U.S.	.75 (verbal + math)	$13,370
AEP: High-stakes testing countries vs. others	2.0 (math) .7 (science)	$35,650 $12,480
NAEP: New York and North Carolina vs. other states	0.4 (math) 0.5 (science) 0.7 (reading)	$ 7,130 $ 8,915 $12,480
TIMSS: High-stakes testing countries vs. others	.9 (math) 1.3 (science)	$16,040 $23,170

* Based on male-female average, averaged across six longitudinal studies, cited in Bishop 1995, Table 2, counting only general academic achievement, not accounting for technical abilities.

IAEP: International Assessment of Educational Progress 1991

IRLS: International Reading Literacy Study 1993

SAT: Scholastic Assessment Test, annual

NAEP: National Assessment of Educational Progress, various years

TIMSS: Third International Mathematics and Science Study 1995

nal examination system. To appreciate the potential magnitude of the benefits, one needs to multiply by the number of students who potentially can benefit, and over time. The U.S. student population currently exceeds 50 million. If they could all benefit, the total gain to society could exceed $650 billion, for the current 12-year-wide cohort of elementary and secondary students. Add future cohorts, or the over billion students overseas, and the incentive benefit amount mushrooms.

One could also then multiply by the number of subject areas that would be included in any comprehensive, multiple-subject, high-stakes examination to arrive at a benefit estimate on the order of tens of trillions of dollars for the current cohort of U.S. students alone. This is a very rough estimate, of course, that counts all benefits independently. In fact, there is likely considerable overlap in the incentive effect across subject areas, meaning that one should not expect the full effect of several single subject-area tests in a single several-subject examination. Nonetheless, one can see that the incentive benefits of external, high-stakes examinations have the potential to be enormous.

(2) (3) *Information Benefits—Predictive Validity and Allocative Efficiency.* The concepts of predictive validity and allocative efficiency were briefly introduced in an earlier chapter, in the section on the Scholastic Assessment Test (SAT). Here, I discuss the same concepts in the context of the enormous body of work conducted by Industrial/Organizational (i.e., personnel) psychologists on "test utility" (i.e., test benefits) over the past century.

Allocative efficiency is a measure of the quality of the "match" between job applicants and the jobs they get, or of student applicants and the schools that accept them. *Predictive validity* is a measure of how well test scores correlate with (i.e., "predict") some future performance. The SAT and ACT are designed to predict, when considered with other measures, a student's first-year academic performance in college. For a century, personnel psychologists have studied the predictive validity of various measures commonly available to employers in hiring new employees. There are a variety of such measures available—the traditional interview, highly structured interviews, recommendations, amount of education, job tryouts, even graphology.

Personnel psychologists have now conducted over a thousand controlled studies of the predictive validity of various hiring methods, singly or in combinations. The conclusions are clear. For hiring employees without previous experience in a particular job, the single best predictor of future job performance is a score on a test of general mental ability (GMA), an aptitude test or a very general achievement test. The best overall combination of two predictive measures is a GMA and some measure of integrity or conscientiousness, including a simple paper and pencil test of integrity. The GMA measures a person's foundation of knowledge and skill, as well as his ability to learn more quickly. The integrity test measures how devoted the employee will be to doing the job he agrees to do.

Based on their review of many studies and meta-studies, Schmidt and Hunter (1998) list several other reasons for granting general mental ability tests a special place:

- GMAs have the highest validity and lowest cost of all procedures that can be used for any and all jobs, at all levels of employment. Meta-analyses show predictive validities ranging from .58 for professional-managerial jobs to .23 for completely unskilled jobs. For the broad middle level (62% of all jobs in the U.S.), predictive validity is .51.
- The research evidence for the validity of GMAs is the best developed of that for all selection measures commonly used by employers.
- GMAs are also the best available predictors of job-related learning (i.e., hires with high GMAs tend to be the best workers to start with, but also the best and fastest learners on the job). No other measure comes close.
- The theoretical foundation for general mental ability is stronger than that for other measures commonly used in hiring.

Psychologists theorize that the level of knowledge and skill indicated by the results of a general mental ability test represent two things: the level of achievement attained by an individual, her accomplishment, as it were; and the foundation level of knowledge and skill upon which the individual has to draw in approaching challenges in a new job—the larger the foundation, the larger the amount of knowledge, skill, and experience that can be brought to bear. New employees with higher GMA scores should be quicker learners, by this theory, and the empirical evidence supports it.

Table 7.4 lists the predictive validity coefficients of various methods used to screen hires, singly and in combination with another method.

Why Do Employers Not Use Test Information Like Colleges Do?

The correct answer to the question could be simple: many jurisdictions have no external testing; many employers do not know about the tests in jurisdictions that do; there are too many achievement tests and that confuses employers; and little effort has been made anywhere to introduce testing programs to employers.

It is, perhaps, impossible to know what it would take to get U.S. employers to use test information like colleges use the ACT and the SAT. It appears that employers do not use state- or provincial-level test information in New York State or British Columbia, for example. But, we really do not fully know why (Bishop 1994a: 11; Anderson et al. 1990).

Schmidt, Hunter, Bishop, and others argue that the U.S. economy would reap sizable benefits if employers would only use measures of educational achievement in their hiring and salary decisions. Currently, they really do not have very good measures at their disposal. High school transcripts are unreli-

Table 7.4a
Predictive Validity for Overall Job Performance of General Mental Ability Scores Combined with a Second Predictor Using (Standardized) Multiple Regression

	Validity (r)	Multiple R	Validity Gain from Adding Supplement	Percent Increase in Validity	Standardized Regression Weights	
					GMA	Supplement
1. General Mental Ability (GMA) Tests	.51					
2. Work Sample Tests*	.54	.63	.12	24%	.36	.41
3. Integrity Tests	.41	.65	.14	27%	.51	.41
Conscientiousness Tests	.31	.60	.09	18%	.51	.31
4. Employment Interviews (Structured)	.51	.65	.14	27%	.41	.41
Employment Interviews (Unstructured)	.38	.58	.07	14%	.44	.27
5. Job Knowledge Tests	.48	.58	.07	14%	.36	.31
6. Job Tryout Procedure	.44	.58	.07	14%	.40	.20
7. Peer Ratings	.49	.58	.07	14%	.35	.31
8. T&E Behavioral Consistency Model	.45	.58	.07	14%	.39	.31
9. Reference Checks	.26	.57	.06	12%	.51	.26
10. Job Experience (Years)	.18	.54	.03	6%	.51	.18
11. Biographical Data Measures	.35	.52	.01	2%	.45	.13
12. Assessment Centers	.36	.52	.01	2%	.44	.14
13. T&E Point Method	.11	.52	.01	2%	.39	.29
14. Years of Education	.10	.52	.01	2%	.51	.10
15. Interests	.10	.52	.01	2%	.51	.10
16. Graphology	.02	.51	.00	0%	.51	.02
17. Age	-.01	.51	.00	0%	.51	-.01

* Involve performing some of the work of the job. Can only be done by those with experience in the job.

SOURCE: Schmidt, Frank L. and Hunter, John E. 1998. "The Validity and Utility of Selection Methods in Personnel Psychology: Practical and Theoretical Implication of 85 Years of Research Findings," *Personnel Psychology*, v. 51, Table 1, p. 265. Copyright © 1998 by the American Psychological Association. Adapted with permission.

Table 7.4b
**Predictive Validity for Overall Performance in Job Training Programs of
General Mental Ability Scores Combined with a Second Predictor Using
(Standardized) Multiple Regression**

	Validity (r)	Multiple R	Validity Gain from Adding Supplement	Percent Increase in Validity	Standardized Regression Weights	
					GMA	Supplement
1. General Mental Ability (GMA) Tests	.56					
2. Integrity Tests	.38	.67	.11	20%	.56	.38
Conscientiousness Tests	.30	.65	.09	16%	.56	.30
3. Employment Interviews	.35	.60	.04	7%	.51	.23
4. Peer Ratings	.36	.57	.01	1.4%	.51	.11
5. Reference Checks	.23	.61	.05	9%	.56	.23
6. Job Experience (Years)	.01	.56	.00	0%	.56	.01
7. Biographical Data Measures	.30	.56	.00	0%	.55	.03
8. Years of Education	.20	.60	.04	7%	.56	.20
9. Interests	.18	.59	.03	5%	.56	.18

SOURCE: Schmidt, Frank L. and Hunter, John E. 1998. "The Validity and Utility of
Selection Methods in Personnel Psychology: Practical and Theoretical Implication of 85
Years of Research Findings," *Personnel Psychology*, v. 51, Table 2, p. 266. Copyright ©
1998 by the American Psychological Association. Adapted with permission.

able and, studies have found that high schools tend to be slow, or reluctant, to
provide them, anyway. Some employers use aptitude tests that they administer themselves and, an abundance of evidence shows, those employers who
do not would be wise to do so...or, wise to convince their state governments to
institute testing programs whose results they would use.

   Employers in some other countries use educational test scores in their
hiring decisions, perhaps because the tests have existed for a generation or
more, are well publicized, and well understood. Examining the characteristics of the ACT and SAT that make them useful to college admissions counse-

lors might also help us understand how test scores could be useful to employers:

- they are extremely inexpensive—they actually cost the colleges nothing, but even if the colleges paid for them, their costs are close to negligible at $25 a student;
- they are national tests that put all applicants on a single scale that measures a fairly comprehensive set of basic skills. The scale is not perfect but, for its cost, it is hugely descriptive. The admissions counselor can break out two (on the SAT) or several (on the ACT) scales, but all applicants can be compared on just one, combined score.[12]

If U.S. employers were to use test scores, say to the same degree that university admissions counselors do, would the information benefits to employers be on the same scale as those to university admissions counselors? On the one hand, the predictive validity coefficients from psychologists' workplace studies are actually higher than those estimated in college-admissions studies. On the other hand, employers typically have access to less other information about the job applicant than college admissions counselors have about their applicants. Moreover, they seem to use even less of what is available. Frank Schmidt and John Hunter conclude that employers tend to use just two or three predictive measures when hiring job applicants, even though they would benefit from using more (Schmidt and Hunter 1998).

Colleges have access and consider all those sources of information about the applicant listed in the NACAC table, such as GPA, recommendations, extracurricular activities, personal statement, and so on. Few employers even look at the high school GPA, or are given it even when they request it. Most hiring decisions are made based on little more than recommendations from previous employment, if any, the possession, or lack thereof, of a high school diploma, and the superficial impression made during the job interview. By comparison with the sophisticated admissions process of colleges, most employers are flying blind.

The Debate over Expanded Use of the General Aptitude Test Battery

It seems tempting that a fairly standard general achievement or aptitude test could offer much of the predictive power to employers that the ACT or SAT offers to college admissions counselors. Indeed, it would probably offer more predictive power, if employers would use it. Raising the subject, however, begs the question: Which test would they use?

In the 1980s, it was proposed that the federal government's General Aptitude Test Battery (GATB) might be used for the purpose. It seems fairly appropriate. The GATB is used to screen and place job applicants for the enormous labor pool of the U.S. federal government. The federal government, naturally, has had an interest in knowing how useful the GATB was. The main criterion used for judging the success of the test has been its predictive validity. Several hundreds of predictive validity studies had been performed on data sets incorporating GATB scores, usually correlated with one or more of a variety of outcomes measures—job performance measured somehow (by a variety of types of supervisor ratings, output-per-time period for jobs where that is possible, promotions, earnings increases, and so on) (for example, see Boudreau, 1988: 84-116, for an annotated listing of hundreds of studies).

As John Bishop asserted:

> ...a large body of research suggests that the cognitive subtests of the GATB are valid predictors of job performance in many private sector jobs (Hunter 1983). This research implies that it is in the private interest of individual companies to use these tests for selection....the true effect is...likely to be about 2 or 3 percent of compensation or between $60 and $90 billion per year. Thus, the sorting benefits of greater use of the GATB in selection decisions are quite substantial. (Bishop 1989a: 20-21)

Dividing Bishop's estimated effect by the number of workers involved produces an *annual* benefit of $850 to $1,250 per worker. Using the same assumptions as before (see Table 7.3) for calculating the present value (baseline at age 18 and, thus, a 45-year working life, and a 5 percent real discount rate) produces a range of present values between about $16,000 and $23,000. By comparison with a cost of less than $50 per worker for a test, the benefits loom enormous. Hunter claimed benefits on a similar scale (Hunter 1983).

John E. Hunter and his frequent collaborator, Frank L. Schmidt, carried out much of the work on "utility" estimation of the GATB over the course of a couple of decades. They made use of a rather straightforward utility formula for calculating the economic benefits of personnel selection tests. Cronbach created the formula in its first, nascent form, but Brogden is credited with developing the original formula widely put to practical use in validity studies (Hartigan and Wigdor 1989: 235-236).

In the late 1980s, the U.S. Department of Labor considered providing the federal government's General Aptitude Test Battery (GATB), which is used for hiring in federal jobs, to local employment offices for use in hiring outside the federal government. The test would have been made available to job applicants who wished to take it, and test results would have been made available to employers who wished to review them. The Labor Department asked the Board on Testing and Assessment at the National Research Council to review the question.

Their report is extraordinary. In the face of overwhelming evidence to the contrary, the Board declared the following: there was only negligible evidence to support the predictive power of the GATB, and tests in general provided few benefits in personnel selection. Their conclusions were reached through tortuous illogic and contradiction, and possibly a judicious selection of both committee members and research sources (see Phelps 1999a).

For example, not one of the hundreds of academic psychologists who studied personnel selection was invited to participate in writing the report, whereas several education professors who were well-known opponents of high-stakes testing were.[13] Several personnel psychologists intimately familiar with the research belonged to a "liaison group," and their names were listed in the final report, but they were never consulted. Moreover, only one of the thousands of empirical studies on personnel selection was discussed, a single one of Hunter and Schmidt's many studies.[14]

The Board dismissed the benefits of hiring better qualified applicants for jobs by arguing that if an applicant was rejected for one job, the applicant would simply find another somewhere else in the labor market, as all are employed somewhere. The U.S. labor market is a zero-sum game and all workers are employed somewhere in the economy. (No matter that the other job might be less well-paid, in an undesirable field or location, part time, temporary, or even nonexistent. In the view of the report, "unemployment is a job.")

The Board continued with the astounding contradiction that, whereas selection benefits should be considered nonexistent because all jobs can be considered equivalent, general tests, like the GATB, cannot be any good as predictors because these tests do not account for the unique character of every job.

The committee criticized the validity studies on the GATB in several ways, driving down the predictive validity coefficient through a variety of rationales. Some of their criticisms of past studies were valid, but had already been addressed through the natural progress of research in the more recent studies in the academic literature of applied psychology. In the report chapter on predictive validity, the Committee conceded a general, average predictive validity of about 0.22, half the level of the highest, unadjusted predictive validity claimed for the GATB—still enormous by comparison with the meager cost of a standardized test[15] (Hartigan and Wigdor 1989: 134-171).

The Zero-Sum Labor Market Argument

Regarding unsuccessful job applicants, the National Research Council Committee asserts:

> ...even if they score low on the test, they will get to work, and their productivity must be allowed for.... The economy as a whole is very much like a single employer who must accept all workers. All workers must be employed.... If a firm uses tests to identify the able and if the firm can be selective, then it can improve the quality of its work force. The economy as a whole cannot; the economy as a whole must employ the labor force as a whole. Testing can increase aggregate productivity only if there are gains to be made from matching people to jobs...utility analysis cannot be applied

to the economy as a whole because the economy as a whole cannot have a selection ratio of much less than 100 percent." (Hartigan and Wigdor 1989: 241-242)

The zero-sum labor market argument, however, is erroneous, if not downright silly. First, there are the unemployed, comprising about 5 percent of the labor force. The Committee cites the fact that the unemployment *rate* is fairly stable over time as evidence that the unemployed population is stable (Hartigan and Wigdor 1989: 235-248). While the *rate* may vary only within a narrow band, the labor market churns people through the ranks of the officially and unofficially unemployed, in and out, over and over again. There is an incessant rearrangement of chairs among the unemployed and marginally employed.

Using figures from the Bureau of Labor Statistics for the average duration of unemployment within the year 1995 (16.6 weeks), and the monthly average number unemployed (seasonally adjusted) for 1995 (7.4 million), one can estimate the number of "spells" of unemployment for 1995 at 23.2 million. At first thought, one might think this to be the number of persons who are unemployed at some time during the year. While the estimate probably brings us close to that number, the estimate probably also subsumes a small number of spells that are shared by individuals. In other words, some persons may have more than one spell of unemployment in a year. If there were no cases like this, and there probably are not many, 17.5 percent of the labor force would fit in the category of unemployed at some time during the year (U.S. BLS 1995).

Second, another average 3.3 percent of the labor force in 1995 were "economic part-time" employees. That is, they wanted to work full time, but could not find full-time employment. There is no average duration figure with which to calculate the number of persons who go through "economic part-time" spells during the year. We have to settle for this lower-bound number for the number of workers who are at some time during the year forced to accept part-time employment when they would prefer full-time employment. Add this 3.3 percent to the 17.5 percent who are unemployed at some time during the year and one calculates a proportion of the labor force close to 21 percent (U.S. BLS 1997).

Third, there remain "contingent workers," whose number is very difficult to estimate. Anne E. Polivka, in the *Monthly Labor Review* (Polivka 1996), calculates three estimates for the size of this population. They range from 2.7 million workers who are in jobs for less than one year and expect the jobs to last no longer than one year more (estimate 1) to 6.0 million workers who do not expect their jobs to last. If we subtract the subpopulation of persons classified as "independent contractors or self-employed" from estimate 3, for the reason that those people have chosen a necessarily contingent occupation, I calculate 5.3 million workers who believe their jobs are temporary. That total comprises 4.0 percent of the labor force (Polivka 1996).

Add these three subpopulations of the labor force together—unemployed at some time during the year, economic part-time, and contingent workers—one arrives at a proportion of the labor force unemployed or precariously employed of 25 percent.

And that is just the labor force. An estimated 8.6 percent of persons out of the labor force would like to be employed but are not because they have quit looking out of discouragement for their prospects, they are currently in school, perhaps to learn some skills that will help them get a job, or for various other reasons. For example, there exist many parents who have made the decision that one of them will work and one of them will stay home and raise the children and manage the household. Which one works? If the couple has chosen the one with the best prospects in the labor market, they have made a decision to capture selection benefits.

Finally, there remain some working-age adults with jobs they do not like or that are not in their chosen line of work. They are "underemployed" or "misemployed."

The zero-sum labor force argument used by the National Research Council assumed that if a worker did not get selected for a job, she would get selected for a different job. They also implicitly assumed that the other job would be equivalent in the most important ways to the job she did not get. That assumption is untenable. The person not selected for the first job could end up unemployed ($p=.175$), or unwillingly working part time ($p=.033$), or working in contingent employment ($p=.04$). But, even those three possibilities do not cover the gamut. There is a high possibility that the person rejected for the first job could end up in a different job that is not in her field, or her occupation, or that uses her skills or training.

Testing for the Purpose of a "Second Chance" or "Placing Out"

Any employer who hires applicants with superior knowledge and skills saves time and money later on. That is because the superior applicants are more likely, everything else being equal, to produce more work, work of higher quality, and take less time to train, on average, than the other applicants. If a test tells the employer who the superior applicants are, the employer can benefit from the information.

Similarly, the information benefits of testing can be clearly seen in situations where passing a test saves the test-taker the time and money that would otherwise be needed for a classroom course. If one can prove that one knows the relevant subject matter by passing a test, one should not need to sit through a time-consuming and costly classroom course to prove one's knowledge (and for which there is likely a similar test at the end).

This is the principle behind "placing out" of education completion or credentialing requirements. It is similar in principle to the "second chance"

exams that are common in Europe. Some graduates on a certain higher education or career path, decide, after they have tried it for a while that they do not
like it. In order to get a "second chance" at retraining for a different career
path, they may study for a while and pass a test, without having to go through
and entire level of education over again (see Aber 1996; DAEU 1996; Jones
1993; Wedman 1994).

Summing up. In the end, the NRC Board still conceded a substantial part of
the benefits, but did not add them up in its report. Hunter and Schmidt had
estimated a potential annual benefit to the U.S. economy of $80 billion a year
(in 1980 dollars). Taking just the one-fourth to one-half that the antagonistic
NRC Board would concede, $20 to $40 billion a year still represents a substantial benefit to society. Using Bishop's net present value assumptions (see
Table 7.3), it amounts to an annual benefit (in 1993 dollars) of $300 to $500
per worker, and a range of present values between $5,000 and $8,000 per
worker. Again, by comparison with a cost of less than $50 per worker for a test,
the benefits still loom enormous.

Add to those benefits the *incentive* benefits estimated above of around
$13,000 per person per subject area and one arrives at a extremely conserva-
tive estimate of about $20,000 in net present value per worker in U.S. society.
Tell the U.S. public, already strongly in favor of high-stakes testing, of these
available benefits available from improved efficiency in education and human resource management—incentives, predictive validity, allocative efficiency—and their support could only increase.

Reconciling Benefits and Costs

As for the costs of high-stakes external tests, two distinctly different situations apply:

- The GAO (1993b) estimated *all-inclusive, stand-alone marginal costs* of
  large-scale, systemwide tests, costs portending in a situation where the
  tests had to be administered independent of any school system structure or
  schedule, say during the summer months and by hired personnel. The SAT,
  ACT, and AP exams are administered this way. The costs for the average
  state in the relevant GAO study sample of 6 states (with 11 performance-
  based tests, and 6 multiple-choice tests) are listed in Table 7.5.
- Recalculating the GAO study's estimates under two reasonable assumptions: (1) that the tests, as is usually the case, would be administered during the
  regular school year, using regular school personnel, and would be integral
  parts of the school system curricular and instructional plan; and (2) that
  the tests would be used in many school districts to replace, rather than
  supplement, some preexisting test. These adjustments are made explicit
  for a generic systemwide test and for the two most common test formats
  in Table 7.6.

Cumulative Effect of the Two Adjustments to Cost Estimates

Assuming a regular school year test administration and the effects of test replacement in response to testing mandates causes a proportionately large reduction in marginal testing cost estimates from the all-inclusive, stand-alone cost estimates of the GAO study (see Table 7.5). The marginal cost of a state-mandated test becomes only $5 on average, $11 if it is a performance test and only $2 if it is a multiple-choice test. Far from being the hugely expensive enterprise that some testing critics claim for it, standardized test-

Table 7.5

Average All-Inclusive, Stand-Alone per-Student Costs of Two Test Types in States Having Both

Cost factors	Type of test	
	Multiple-choice	Performance-based
Start-up development	$2	$10
Annual costs*	16	33

* Includes ongoing, recurring development costs

Source: U.S. GAO 1993b: 43.

Table 7.6

Average Marginal Cost per Student of Systemwide Testing in the United States with Adjustments, by Type of Test

	All system-wide tests	Sample of 11 state multi-subject performance tests	Sample of 6 state multiple-choice tests in those same states
All-inclusive, stand-alone marginal cost	$15	$33	$16
...minus 46 percent adjustment for regular school year administration	-7	-15	-7
...minus adjustment for replacement of preexisting tests (42, 37, and 74 percent)	-6	-12	-12
Marginal cost after adjustments*	$5	$11	$2

* The difference is less than the sum of the two adjustments because the two subtractions are made cumulatively.

ing is not very expensive by most standards. Even under the rather unrealistic assumptions of the GAO study's upper-bound estimates, systemwide tests impose a time and cost burden, as one state testing director put it, "on a par with field trips."

Comparing to Benefits

By contrast with the estimates above of the per-student incentive effects of graduation exit exams—around $13,000 *per subject area*—and information effects, under extremely conservative assumptions, of $5,000 to $8,000, testing costs are puny. $20,000 is manifold larger than $2, $5, or $11, giving a benefit-cost ratio of over 2,000 to 1. Even assuming all-inclusive, stand-alone costs, as in the GAO study, of $16 to $33 for the average state test, the benefit-cost ratio is over 600:1. Even if one agrees with the National Research Council arguments against information benefits (I don't), total testing benefits vastly outweigh the costs. The benefits can be so high because they affect a large number of people and they produce lasting and cumulative effects. Meanwhile, the testing costs are low and incurred only once or a few times.

Are Not U.S. Students Already Too Busy, Though?

Calculating Slack Capacity in Students' Schedules: Valuing Students' Time

Some advocates for high-stakes testing assert that it induces students to pay better attention in class and to spend more of their non-school time studying. Evaluations of the reintroduction of Canadian provincial high-stakes examinations, in British Columbia and Alberta, for example, revealed that students took more responsibility for their studies and spent more time studying.

In his excellent study of the value of homework, the economist Julian Betts estimates that the gain in increased mathematics achievement from doing more homework, which subsequently leads to increased lifetime earnings, more than compensates for the "loss" of time devoted to other activities. To calculate that value of the foregone other activities, Betts uses an average weekly wage rate for part-time workers with little experience, the kind of wage that teenagers might have. He multiplies that rate by a number of foregone hours per week and compares it to the increase in lifetime earnings produced by an increase in the same number of hours per week spent doing homework[16] (Betts 1998: 21-35).

Betts realizes perfectly well that if a student decides to study X number of hours per week more than in the past, the X hours may not all come from time that was formerly spent in wage employment. Indeed, it is not necessarily the case that any time in wage employment would be sacrificed with some teenagers, particularly those younger than age 15, the age by which half of all students are in the labor force at least some time during the year. The teenager might, instead, sacrifice some time socializing, watching television, doing chores around the house, or anything else. Most likely, the teenager would sacrifice some time from several other activities and not just one.

Betts is valuing each teenager's time at the part-time wage rate because as well as he can tell, that is how teenagers value it. He assumes that teenagers are not working part-time just to "get enough" money to operate a parent's car and socialize, but that they set a labor/leisure ratio just like adults do: incorporating expenditure requirements for all their needs; fully informed about the impact of their choices on their future earnings; and calculating that impact with a reasonable value for the discount rate.[17]

How reasonable are these assumptions? For example, teenagers are notorious for not seeing the long-term implications of their behavior and for undervaluing long-term benefits—they have not experienced what it is like to be an unemployed or underemployed adult. They do not know the long-term costs or benefits because they have not experienced either. They just do not know, so they cannot value their choices properly. Besides, as John Bishop argues, the signal we give them, absent high-stakes exit exams, is that school work is not very important.

Another consideration is that only relatively older students partake in wage employment; most teenagers younger than age 16 do not. Are we to assume that younger teens who do not work for wages value their free time at zero? What of, say, 9-year-olds? While it is true that they are legally prohibited by law from wage employment, are we to speculate on what their wages would be absent child labor laws in order to calculate the proper value of their free time? We cannot assume that their time in wage employment would be equivalent to that of 16-year-olds; they are far less skilled and less physically able.

If we accept that child labor laws exist and that we adults are responsible for minors, perhaps we should value the free time of elementary and secondary school students differently than we do that of adults. Perhaps we should incorporate our superior adult knowledge of the long-term impact of their time use choices. That is the way the law would have it, after all; until teenagers are 18 years old, we adults, as parents, get to decide how much time they spend in wage employment. How many parents would insist or allow their children to work at Burger King if they knew that more studying was essential for passing a junior or senior high school exit exam?

Lawrence Steinberg reviewed the literature on the academic effect of students' use of out-of-school time, focusing particularly on after-school employment, "cocurricular" participation (i.e., extracurricular school activities), and leisure. He notes that while some believe that work experience "will reinforce skills acquired in school. Unfortunately, studies of how adolescents actually spend their time on the job indicate that opportunities to use school-taught skills are quite rare. The typical adolescent spends almost no job time in activities involving reading, writing, or performing calculations—three job tasks that might enhance school performance"[18] (Steinberg 1993: 35-40).

Steinberg argues that the problem affects everyone, not just the working students:

> Widespread student employment lowers teachers' expectations for their students, leading to less assigned homework and the increased use of class time for what would otherwise be out-of-school assignments. Teachers are forced to adapt expectations and standards for students who are overly committed to working...

A simple crosstabulation of data from the National Education Longitudinal Study of 1988: First Follow-up Student Survey shows student grades in science rising with larger amounts of time spent on homework or cocurricular activities and smaller amounts of time spent watching TV or in outside employment. Average sophomore hours spent watching TV and working in wage employment (about 27 per week), however, exceeded those spent on homework or in cocurricular activities (about 10) even among students with A averages in science. Among students with D averages in science the former activities dwarfed the latter activities by about 33 hours to (Ingels, et al. 1995, Table 3.8 and Figure 3.3).

Steinberg continues "...poor students are relatively more likely to work, but working long hours leads to their further disengagement from school." The poor students, however, may seek wage employment in order to help their families meet their basic needs. For middle-class adolescents, wage employment generates income used for current leisure consumption. One could argue, further, that not only are the middle-class students making poor use of their time by taking on part-time jobs, they are taking away low and unskilled employment opportunities from unemployed, poorly educated, and unskilled adults who qualify for no other kind of employment (Steinberg 1993: 35-40).

U.S. adolescents are not the only ones engaged in non-apprenticeship-related wage employment while in school. Higher proportions of 16-19-year-old Canadians, Danes, and Dutch in 1994 were. About the same proportion of Australians as Americans were (about 19 percent). In nine other countries surveyed, however, the proportions were smaller, in most cases far smaller. Less than 5 percent of 16-19-year-olds in Greece, Italy, Spain, Portugal, Belgium, Ireland, Luxembourg, and France participated in non-apprenticeship-related wage employment while enrolled in school (Organisation for Economic Co-operation and Development 1996: 44-47) What are the 16-19-year-old students in those latter eight countries doing with their extra 15 hours a week? They might be using at least some of it to study.

Evidence for Slack Capacity in U.S. Students' Schedules

International comparisons. How do U.S. students compare with their international counterparts in other aspects of time use? The recent Third International Mathematics and Science study surveyed and tested students at about the 8th-grade and 4th-grade levels. At the 8th-grade level, 39 countries reported test and background survey data. The four major uses of out-of-school time are TV watching, playing or socializing with friends, playing sports, and studying. U.S. 8th-graders rank tied for 13th in the world in socializing time, tied for 10th in TV-watching time, and 1st out of 39 countries (and 15 percent higher than any other country) in time devoted to sports. Interestingly, 8th graders in many other countries *say* that it is important to be good at sports, they just do not spend as much time on it. As for studying, U.S. 8th graders were tied with 3 other countries for 27th place (out of 38) (Beaton et. al. 1996a, Tables 4.7 and 4.8; 1996b, Tables 4.7 and 4.8).

The rankings are slightly less discouraging for the United States in 4th grade. Our students were tied with 3 other countries for 10th (out of 25 countries) in time spent socializing. They were tied with 2 other countries for 6th in TV watching. They fell to second, behind Israel, in the amount of time devoted to sports. As for studying, U.S. 4th graders were about average, tied with 2 other countries for 12th place (out of 24 countries reporting) (see Martin et al. 1999, or Mullis et al. 1997, Tables 4.9 and 4.10).

The differences in out-of-school time use seem to have a distinct regional caste. Eighth-grade students in East Asian countries spend a greater than average amount of time studying and watching TV and less time socializing and playing sports. Students in large Western European countries spend the least amount of time watching TV, but a greater than average amount of time studying and socializing. Students in Eastern European countries spend as much time as U.S. watching TV and socializing, but more time studying and less time playing sports. U.S. students spent the most time playing sports, more time watching TV or socializing than students in East Asia or Western Europe, and less time studying than anyone (Beaton et al. 1996a, Tables 4.7 and 4.8; 1996b, Tables 4.7 and 4.8). (See Table 7.7).

Evidence from time diary studies. There is evidence to suggest that even the U.S. students' poor showing in study time might be too high. In the book, *Time for Life*, authors John P. Robinson and Geoffrey Godbey describe studies of Americans' use of time that are based on detailed time diaries. The authors assert that keeping daily, detailed time diaries is the most reliable method for learning how people use their time. Recall, they claim is just not as reliable (Robinson and Godbey 1997: 209-215).

In two time diary studies of 6-11-year-olds—one done nationally with a low response rate and the other done in California with a far better response rate—youngsters claimed to spend 1.7 or 2.2 hours studying *per week*, far

Table 7.7
Average 8th-Grade Student Report of Hours per Day Spent on Various
Activities, by Activity and World Region, 1994

Region/Country	Average number of hours per day devoted to...			
	Sports	Watching TV	Playing or socializing with friends	Studying
USA	2.2	2.6	2.5	2.3
East Asia (N=5)	0.9	2.4	1.3	3.1
Large Western Europe (N=4)	1.6	2.0	2.4	2.8
East Europe (N=7)	1.6	2.6	2.5	2.9

Source: Third International Mathematics and Science Study, 1994.

less than 4th graders claimed in the TIMSS (2.9 hours *per day*). If we assume that the time diary studies are counting the entire year, including school vacation times, we should make a school-year adjustment to the estimate (by doubling it), to about 4 hours per week. It still seems unimpressive, and small by comparison with the U.S. time estimates in the TIMSS. Estimates between the time diaries and the TIMSS were similar for time devoted to playing sports or socializing. Estimates for TV-watching time, however, were somewhat higher in the time diary studies (at 15.6 or 21 hours *per week*, versus 2 hours *per day*[19] (see Martin et al. 1999, or Mullis et al. 1997, Tables 4.9 and 4.10).

If Robinson and Godbey are correct about the superior reliability of time diary estimates, U.S. students do not spend even as much as the relatively small amount of time studying as they claimed in the TIMSS. The TIMSS results placed U.S. students in about the middle of the range for study time among 4th graders. If that estimate really was a five-fold exaggeration, however, and we assume that students from other countries in the TIMSS were not making similar exaggerations, U.S. 4th graders would place dead last in the amount of time they devote to study.

Student time use choices at the margin. A Chrysler Corporation Foundation/Peter D. Hart survey in August 1993 asked students what they would do with their time if they magically had an extra hour in every day. Half said that they would spend the time with friends, while another quarter said that they would play sports. Another 10 percent would listen to music or watch TV. Another 12 percent would read a book or magazine. That leaves not many votes for more time on homework (Chrysler Learning Connection 1993: 3-4).

Unless there is something in the basic physiology of U.S. students that is different from their counterparts overseas, it would appear that U.S. students are spending more of their time in unproductive activities and less of their time in productive activities associated with long-term personal success and societal benefit. That is how they choose to spend their time, and the exhortations of grown-ups that it would be good for them do not seem to be sufficient to motivate them to study more. Our students are wasting time.[20]

Put another way, there appears to be slack capacity available in the schedules of U.S. students. This slack capacity is large and could absorb more academic or academically related activity. The students and society would benefit from the increased academic achievement and higher skill levels of this absorption. From a net benefit perspective, absorption of beneficial activity into slack capacity is attractive because it would produce windfall gains. For example, if U.S. 8th graders watched as little TV as they do in Western Europe, and played sports and socialized as little as they do in East Asia, they could more than double the amount of time they now devote to studying.

Evidence for Slack Capacity in Student Attention and Motivation

Students' attention in the classroom is certainly more difficult to measure than student time on homework, but Bishop cites a series of studies done by Frederick, Fischer, Goodlad, Klein, Tyle, and Wright, and Frederick, Walberg, and Rasher that attempted such estimates:

> Studies of time use and time-on-task show that students actively engage in a learning activity for only about half the time they are in high school. A study of schools in Chicago found that public school with high-achieving students averaged about 75% of class time for actual instruction; for schools with low achieving student, the average was 51% of class time.... Other studies have found that for reading and math instruction the average engagement rate is about 75.... Overall, [researchers] have estimated 46.5% of the potential learning time was lost due to absence, lateness, and inattention." (Bishop 1989b: 6)

Adding estimates for student time in school and time studying at home and comparing them to estimates of student time watching TV, Bishop concluded that the average U.S. student spends more time watching TV than involved in learning activity of any kind, regardless of the level of engagement.

Notes

1.   Henry Levin is one of the few education professors with economics training, and is, as often as not, at odds in his interpretation of reality with those economists who are not education professors, that being the overwhelming majority of them, of course. Levin serves a crucial role in the preservation of the public education status quo. Because many of the most compelling arguments for radical change in the

U.S. education system are essentially economists' arguments, Henry Levin is often trotted out by public education's aristocracy to present the point of view of an astute economist who just happens to sincerely disagree with any and all criticism of the status quo. Levin has been used to hold the line on a variety of threatening issues—choice, vouchers, privatization, funding, and, now, even testing.

2. The quality of work conducted by the National Research Council's Center for Education and the "disinterested" panels it assembles will be discussed in more detail later in the chapterin previous chapters but, just to remind the reader of one among several revealing facts: not one of hundreds of academic psychologists expert in personnel selection research was invited to participate in this particular study, whereas several education professors who were well-known, and outspoken, opponents of high-stakes testing were.

3. See, for example: (1) Frank L. Schmidt and John E. Hunter (1998), "The Validity and Utility of Selection Methods in Personnel Psychology: Practical and Theoretical Implication of 85 Years of Research Findings," *Personnel Psychology*, V. 51; (2) John E. Hunter and Ronda F. Hunter (1984), "Validity and Utility of Alternative Predictors of Job Performance," *Psychological Bulletin*, Vol. 96, No. 1; (3) John W. Boudreau (1988), "Utility Analysis for Decisions in Human Resource Management," Working Paper #88-21, School of Industrial and Labor Relations, Cornell University; (4) John Bishop (1988a), "The Economics of Employment Testing," Working Paper #88-14, School of Industrial and Labor Relations, Center for Advanced Human Resource Studies, Cornell University; (5) Neal Schmitt, Richard Z. Gooding, Raymond D. Noe, and Michael Kirsch (1984), "Meta-Analysis of Validity Studies Published Between 1964 and 1982 and the Investigation of Study Characteristics," *Personnel Psychology*, Vol. 37, No. 3; (6) John E. Hunter and Frank L. Schmidt (1982), "Fitting People to Jobs: The Impact of Personnel Selection on National Productivity," in Marvin D. Dunnette and Edwin A. Fleishman, eds. *Human Performance and Productivity: Volume 1—Human Capability Assessment*, Hillsdale, NJ, Lawrence Erlbaum Associates.

4. Unfortunately for most students in most of the U.S. states without meaningful high-stakes testing requirements, the benefit of their working hard in school is completely absorbed by employers. Employers who do not have access to test scores, and do not use, cannot use, or cannot obtain high school transcripts, have no information about job applicants' academic performance. Thus, academic performance is no better than a random variable in predicting job performance. Employers will strike it lucky if they happen to hire an employee who was a good student, and unlucky if they happen to hire an employee who was a bad student (Bishop, 1988b: 417-421, or 1996b).

5. The average percent of test items correct (adjusted for guessing) for students was regressed on a set of available control variables from the background questionnaires and aggregate information for each country.

6. Since the U.S. standard deviation was 26.8 percentage points in mathematics, the CBEEE effect on math was more than one-half of a U.S. standard deviation or about 2 U.S. grade level equivalents.

7. The mean 7th and 8th grade science and mathematics test scores were regressed on per capita gross domestic product for 1987 and 1990 deflated by a purchasing power parity price index, a dummy for East Asian nation and a dummy for CBEEEs. Adjustments were also made for age differences across the student samples for each country.

8. He included data from 39 countries in all, though data were not available from all 39 countries for each and every factor he employed in his analysis.

9. Woessman offers two hypotheses for the weaker result in science—fewer countries participated, so he had less data to work with, and science may be less amenable to standardization than mathematics.
10. Including the Panel Study of Income Dynamics (1989), the National Adult Literacy Survey (1994), the National Longitudinal Survey of Youth, 1981-85 and 1990 cohorts (both 1994), Maier and Grafton study of military (1994), and a Bishop study using a General Aptitude Test Battery follow-up sample. The first four studies calculated long-term earnings and productivity effects of a one grade-level-equivalent increment in a general aptitude test taken in the base year holding years of schooling fixed. The last two studies made the same calculation holding years of schooling and type of job fixed.
11. Bishop's baseline assumptions in calculating net present values were: assume 18 years of age in the base year, a 45-year working life, a 5 percent discount rate, and values in 1992-93 dollars.
12. Those who desire perfect fairness may howl at this, but if selection decisions are going to be made, the choices have to be based on something, and admissions counselors do not have access to perfect information. The only available alternative is much worse—much less information.
13. It has been asserted to me that at least two of the Committee members were fairly expert in I/O psychology even though they were not employed in academe at the time, nor specialists in test utility. That seems a feeble defense to me. The education professors had no background whatsoever in test utility studies and little familiarity with the literature, and there were five of them, easily enough to outvote the psychologists. Moreover, if this were a legitimate defense, I would want to see the National Research Council do the converse, say, for panels on educational testing. They do not. Their panels on educational testing are dominated by education professors—education professors who are outspoken opponents of high-stakes testing. Indeed, for the most part, the NRC gets researchers from CRESST to form its testing panels and so it should be no surprise that the NRC reports are full of citations to CRESST reports and articles written by CRESST authors.
14. The NRC Board also refused to consider some of the most basic and relevant evidence pertaining to personnel testing issues, such as: the ways in which the Hunter and Schmidt estimates of utility *underestimated* the benefits of testing; the true magnitude of the effect of range restriction on the utility estimates (for which the Board refused to correct); the true value of average interrater reliability of .50 (they assumed .80, thus under correcting for criterion unreliability); and (pertaining to the NRC assertion that Hunter and Schmidt did not adjust their estimates for the time value of money, incremental validity, or what have you) the substantial research in personnel psychology that has explicitly considered all those issues
15. The National Research Council Committee also attempted to diminish the purported economic benefits to testing of allocative efficiency, or job-matching. They chopped down a Hunter and Schmidt estimate of the annual benefits of 1.6 to 4 percent of GNP to just 1 percent, under the assumption that all employers would not use tests like the GATB to select employees or use the test optimally. (Hartigan and Wigdor, pp.243-246). But, capturing even just 1 percent of the GDP's worth of potential benefits would be large, far larger than the meager cost of administering a test. In an economy of $8 trillion GDP, 1 percent is $80 billion. That's not nothing.
16. As difficult as it may be for non-economists to believe, economists may be the most democratic of social scientists. They resist, for example, passing judgment on the value of how people choose to spend their time and they try to value it as people

themselves value it. Wage rates are good proxies for that value because it is not unreasonable to presume that, at the margin, an extra hour worked would be remunerated at something close to the regular hourly wage rate and one less hour worked would represent an hour's less remuneration. If someone is willing to forego an hour's pay, she is, essentially, paying her employer an hour's wage to let her do something else.

17. Even if all these assumptions were true, some economists would quibble with Betts setting students' leisure time equal in value to their work time. Transportation economists doing "modal choice" studies have found that most people do not value their non-work time as much as they do their work time. They believe this because they have calculated when individuals are willing to switch to a faster or slower means of public or private transportation to the workplace or other location, relative to the increase or decrease in cost. It is a consensus among transportation economists to value people's off-hours at *half* their wage rate in benefit-cost studies. Some think off-hours should be valued at an even lower rate than that. If Julian Betts had valued teenagers non-school time at half their part-time wage rate, his net benefits from doing homework would have loomed even larger (see Mohring or Hensher and Truong).

18. According to Steinberg: "...after-school employment does little to enhance school performance...research consistently finds that school grades and school engagement are substantially lower among students who work long hours. Studies do indicate that disenchantment with school may impel students into part-time jobs, but longitudinal follow-ups over time find that working further exacerbates alienation...an important threshold in studies of student employment is about 20 hours per week, with the most substantial negative effect on school performance and engagement appearing among youngsters working more than this amount of time. Work in small doses—less than 10 hours weekly—does not seem to hurt school performance. Bear in mind, however, that nearly half of all high school seniors work in excess of 20 hours weekly. ...students who work a great deal are absent from school more often, are less involved in school-sponsored activities, and report enjoying school less than their peers."

19. Robinson and Godbey also assert that U.S. adolescents "get 5-10 more hours of sleep a week than those in the working-age population, which may be beyond what is biologically necessary" (Robinson and Godbey, 1997: 215).

20. Essentially, it appears that we are letting our young do what they wish with their time, instead of directing them to allocate it in ways we think would be best. We abnegate our responsibility. John Bishop argues that it is not enough to tell them we think that they should study more, we have to demonstrate that we really mean it by rewarding it and giving them goals and targets to direct their efforts.

8

The Spoils of War
(Valid Concerns about Testing)

Standardized tests are not perfect and neither are the human beings who develop, administer, or score them. Unfortunately, the fog of criticism is so dense, and the obfuscation of testing opponents so intense, that the legitimate, reasonable criticisms of testing become obscured by the illegitimate and unreasonable. The resulting confusion can stunt the policymaking process. A policymaker who is not expert in the topic must choose from a plethora of criticisms and concerns, some of them contradictory. Up until now, this book has focused on revealing the fraudulent criticisms. This chapter focuses on those issues the public really should be worried about in making decisions on testing programs.

Standardized tests do not produce benefits just by the fact of their being used. Humans administer standardized tests, and humans are capable of using them in ways that do little good, or even harm. Testing opponents promote the notion that such is inevitably the case, but it is not. Perhaps the most important finding of research on the benefits of testing over the past two decades has been that high-stakes tests can hold back achievement as well as accelerate it. This does not happen in the way most testing opponents would assert, however.

The "Single Target" of Performance Problem

High-stakes standardized tests offer targets of performance. Ideally, the target is set above a group of students' untested level of achievement and, through hard work, study, and a focus on the target, the students increase their level of achievement. However, students vary in ability, achievement, focus, motivation, and persistence. Some start school at higher academic achievement levels than others (perhaps because they had parents who taught them to read early and gave them books). Some students learn at different rates or with differing ease. Some students like doing academic work more than others do. Finally, some students simply work harder than others.

Setting just one target for students who are at widely ranging achievement levels is problematic. Setting that one target above the top of the range may make it impossible to reach for students at the lower end of the range, and discourage them. Setting the one target just above the low end of the range, as is commonly done in U.S. states, provides the low-achievers a reachable target, but may condemn the higher achievers to boredom. These low-target exams, often called "minimum-competency" exams, can therefore serve to slow achievement for some students while they accelerate it for others (see, for example, Hernstein and Murray 1992; Ligon 1990; Rodgers 1991).

Jonathan Jacobson's (1992) study examined the effect of 1980s-era minimum-competency tests on academic achievement and young adult earnings. He used data from the National Education Longitudinal Study (NELS), which consists of a panel group questionnaire with an achievement test imbedded. He compared the most recent average NELS achievement test scores and subsequent respondent earnings between those individuals who had attended high school in minimum-competency test states and those who had not.

As expected, he found that the lowest-achieving students were, indeed, made better off in the minimum-competency test states. Both their average test scores and their average level of earnings were substantially higher than those of their counterparts, the lowest-achieving students from non-test states. This was encouraging. However, he also found that the other students, particularly the middle-achieving ones, in the minimum-competency testing states ended up worse off. Their average NELS achievement test scores and their subsequent average earnings were lower than those for their counterparts, the middle-achieving students from non-test states.

It is easy to speculate about what might have happened to produce these results. In test states where the only threshold to exceed was that at the minimum level of achievement, substantial effort focused on that level. Perhaps schools and teachers kept themselves so busy making sure the lowest-achieving students got over the minimum-competency threshold that they neglected the middle-achieving students and the curriculum and instruction that they needed.

Two years earlier, economists William Becker and Sherwin Rosen (1990) had anticipated Jacobson's findings through mathematical modeling. They asserted that high-stakes tests clearly would be beneficial, but recommended multiple thresholds for achievement—multiple targets—in order to give all students at all levels of preparation a target within range of their capabilities.

Unfortunately, some testing programs still exist that seem to provide schools with direct incentives to hold high-achieving students back. In jurisdictions where schools as a whole are judged on the basis of student performance on tests only in a few grade levels or only a few subject areas, schools can increase their average scores by retaining high-achieving students with their age-level peers rather than letting them advance a grade, or by making them take courses in basic subject matter they have already mastered. Keeping the higher-achieving students in the pool of test takers can help to raise the average scores.

The differential effect may help explain why some civil rights groups strongly support minimum-competency testing (particularly when, as in Texas, schools are required to report achievement progress by ethnic group), while parents of "gifted and talented" children often strongly oppose them. From the perspective of the former groups, these tests pull achievement standards up. From the perspective of the latter groups, these tests pull achievement standards down.

More common is the phenomenon suggested by Jacobson's study of extra resources flowing to low-achieving students while middle-achieving students get neglected. The highest-achieving, or gifted and talented students may be protected from adverse effect when resources and standards are directed toward low-achieving students. They may have access to course work with independent curricula (e.g., honors courses, magnet schools, Advanced Placement courses, International Baccalaureate programs). They may also be more highly motivated, with the ability to learn largely on their own, or have parents who are more active and assertive in promoting their children's interests.

There are two solutions to the "single target" problem, one passive and one active. The passive solution is currently used in many U.S. states. Essentially, it involves letting individual students take the minimum-competency test early in their school careers and, once they pass it, they are allowed to move on. If the test is "high-stakes" only for the individual student, there is no incentive for anyone to hold the student back, that is, to prevent her from taking accelerated course work from then on. Some states allow students to attempt the state minimum-competency exam that is required for high school graduation as early as 6th grade. First attempts in 7th, 8th, or 9th grades are common across the states.

The "active" solution to the "single target" problem, and the solution that promises greater overall benefits, is to offer multiple targets. This is often called the "European system" because most European countries have such high-stakes examination systems. New York has stood out historically as the one U.S. state that has long had a "multiple target" examination system, with its Regents "Competency" exams and Regents "Honors" exams. The former has been required for high school graduation with a "regular" diploma, while the latter was required for graduation with an "honors" diploma.

It is one of the great ironies of education policy that largely socialist Europe has no qualms about offering different educational programs to different students, based on student choice and demonstrated ability, whereas, in the more libertarian United States, many professional educators insist on a single program for all students which, critics would argue, inevitably produces a low-level program.

European examination systems exist in a variety that reflects the educational programs offered. Students are differentiated by curricular emphasis and by ability levels, and so are their high-stakes examinations. This differentiation starts at the lower secondary (i.e., middle school) level in most European countries, but exists in all of them by the upper secondary level. Students attend schools with vastly different occupational orientations—typically vocational-technical, general, or advanced academic. The advanced academic schools prepare their students for university. The general schools prepare their students for the working world or for advanced technical training. The vocational-technical schools prepare their students for direct entry into a skilled trade. Typically, all three types of schools require the passage of an exit examination for a diploma. In the case of the vocational-technical schools, there may be no school exit exam, but the graduates must eventually pass a certification examination in their chosen profession, one that may be written jointly by the employers and skilled tradespersons of that industry. Some of these certification exams can be very tough.

Status quo apologists for the one-size-fits-all U.S. curriculum often label the European system as "elitist" and our system as a more "democratic" "second chance" system. Those labels, however, are somewhat behind the times. The European systems are less restrictive in entry to the upper academic levels now than they used to be. Moreover, most countries now offer bridge programs in which students who followed, say, a vocational track in school, but discover after some experience that they do not like the occupations possible for them, can take courses in preparation for entry to university or advanced technical programs. Typically, these bridge programs are free of charge.

If the one-size-fits-all U.S. curriculum is neither less elitist nor more conducive to "second chances," how is it superior? It is not, really. A Swiss, German, Danish, or Austrian student who enters a vocational-technical track at the lower secondary level and finishes his school career by passing the industry-guild certification examination as a machinist enters an elite of the world's most skilled (and most highly paid) craftspersons. A vocational-technical student in the United States, by contrast, is almost certainly stigmatized by a curriculum with a reputation as a "dumping ground," and may receive only low-quality training, with out-of-date equipment, for low-level jobs.

Giving students multiple high-quality options and multiple targets gives them multiple opportunities to succeed.

Still, testing programs must be built up piece-by-piece. Testing programs are complicated. It is difficult enough to introduce just one new test into a school system every few years. Most states start with the "floor"—the minimum-competency exam—set at a low level of difficulty that all students must pass. If they stop there, however, they are likely to slow the high-achieving students down at the same time they pull the low-achieving students up. Higher targets must be put in place, too.

Some testing opponents, however, like to focus only on minimum-competency tests and the low *average* improvement in achievement they induce. See, they say, tests do as much harm as good, so we should get rid of all high-stakes testing. They wish to destroy the building after only the foundation has been laid by arguing that it does not keep out the rain.

Plans for multiple examination systems across U.S. states come in some variety. Some states favor the traditional New York State model of two- or three-levels of academic difficulty, the top level offering an "honors" diploma; some states allow commercially available "honors" examinations (e.g., Advanced Placement (AP) exams; the International Baccalaureate exam) to serve the same purpose. Other states plan to offer curricular choice—students must pass a minimum number of advanced subject-area examinations in order to graduate (or, graduate with honors), but the student can choose the subject areas she prefers. A few states have attempted to offer separate examination options for vocational-technical students but have encountered a good bit of resistance.

Tests Can Be No Better Than the Curriculum Standards on Which They Are Based

Again, the primary problem with a single target of performance is that it must necessarily be low and, set low, it may slow the progress of higher-achieving students. The same can happen, however, if the curriculum standards on which a testing system is based are inferior at all levels.

Many would be surprised to learn that some strong proponents of higher standards and challenging curricula are opponents of high-stakes tests. They worry that required tests based on low-level standards will serve the function of fixing those low standards in place. Consider the type of parent who highly values education with high standards and a strong academic focus. They may have changed their residence when their eldest child approached school age in order to live in a school district with high standards and a focus on academics. They may pay the extra hundreds or thousands of dollars a year required to send their children to private or parochial school. It may have come at some sacrifice, but these parents were able to provide the quality education they wanted for their children. If the state then requires common standards, curriculum, and tests, odds are that their children will be worse, not better, off academically.

To those viewing the standards wars from the outside, the debate can often sound confusing, because each side asserts that the other's curriculum is "low level" (e.g., phonics supporters consider whole language to represent a "dumbing down" of the curriculum, while whole language advocates say the same about phonics). Regardless, the general principle is correct—no standards-based test, no matter how much care and effort is put into writing it, can salvage bad curricular standards. If the test is aligned to the standards, as it must be in order to be a fair high-stakes test, those standards must be of good quality for the test to be of good quality.

Profound disputes over curriculum and instruction are the major reason high-stakes state tests can vary so widely in character. Take the neighboring states of Maryland and Virginia, for example. Maryland's School Performance Assessment Program (MSPAP) incorporated test administrations at three different grade levels and performance carried consequences for schools. The test was entirely "performance-based," had no multiple-choice items, and even included group work and "hands-on" demonstrations. It emphasized "process" more than any state educational test to date. (I use the past tense because the MSPAP is now being phased out.) Virginia's Standards of Learning examinations (SOLs), by contrast, are more traditionally administered, more content-oriented, have a large proportion of multiple-choice items, and are completed in their entirety by individual students.

Different theories as to what should be taught in our schools and how it should be taught underlay the development of the Maryland and Virginia examination programs. Sure, different theories of assessment were also involved, but those assessment theories tend to be inextricably tied to the different curriculum and instruction theories. Only the most extreme testing opponents opposed both the Maryland and Virginia tests. Most mainstream or "progressive" educators tended to like Maryland's. "Traditionalists" and other critics of current mainstream U.S. education theories tended to prefer Virginia's.

Likewise on the West Coast, anyone new to the education debates might find it confusing to learn that some of the strongest supporters of California's high-stakes testing system are also some of the strongest opponents of Oregon and Washington State's high-stakes testing systems, and vice versa.[1] The difference is in how the two testing systems relate to differences in curriculum and instruction theories, first, and differences in the theories of assessment that derive from them, second.

Implementation Issues

Even if one assumes that, say, the French examination system is worth emulating, a U.S. state with no testing program cannot replicate the French examination system overnight. As economists would say, any large-scale technological innovation can only succeed with the help of many supportive technologies. The enviable French examination system is supported by a relatively uniform curriculum development system, which is managed by university subject-area experts. This developed curriculum buttresses several to many (in vocational areas) curricular tracks that students can follow. The several (to many) different types of examinations are all administered under high-stakes conditions. Students are given multiple opportunities to pass the examination of their choice, and they are given substantial help in the form of further classes and tutoring, to pass the examinations of their choice. But, they must pass before they can go on, to university, polytechnic, or a specialized trade. They are given every reasonable aid to succeed but, in the end, they must know the basic subject matter of their chosen path, or they will not be allowed to proceed at taxpayers' expense.

Take a U.S. state with little to no examination system that decides it wants to adopt the French system. What would that require? There are two general issues involved in building an examination system: sequencing and structuring.

Sequencing is the more straightforward. Implementation of tests that are linked to state standards and carry consequences for students, teachers, or schools cannot be treated cavalierly. It takes time and care. The standards must be in place first, and taught to, before students can fairly be tested according to those standards. New tests then need to be piloted (i.e., "field tested"), to iron out the inevitable kinks and set baselines for performance. Only after all that is accomplished, which can take a few years, are new high-stakes examinations actually employed.

Adoption of a minimum-competency exam brings a state only to the edge of an examination system like one finds in France, however. There, minimum-competency examinations are given at the end of lower secondary school (i.e., junior high school) and passage is required before a student can move on to upper secondary (i.e., high school) or specialized vocational schools. The students who advance through this next level of education in France will have chosen a curricular specialization (e.g., natural sciences, languages, philosophy and humanities, physical sciences and mathematics, technology, or any number of vocational specializations) and then face a very tough exit examination of a type and level of difficulty that scarcely exists in the United States. The closest equivalents would be in those schools offering the International Baccalaureate. An ambitious American student could simulate an equivalent program by taking *several* Advanced Placement (AP) examinations, except that she will graduate from high school whether or not she scores highly on the AP exams.

Some U.S. states (e.g., Virginia, Michigan, Alabama) are attempting to build something like this structure by requiring passage of a certain number of student-selected advanced-level end-of-course examinations in high school.[2] Generally, however, the basic-skills, or minimum-competency examinations are put in place first and only after they have become established are the advanced-course systems implemented. The step-by-step process is necessary not only because tests are complicated and must be implemented with care, but because, in the best testing systems, the tests fit together in an integrated whole. Integration is easier to accomplish when the tests are implemented one at a time.

Another aspect of sequencing concerns the difficulty level of the examinations. Some U.S. states have constructed high quality examinations that match the reasonable standards they developed through the democratic process, only to discover, during tests, that few of their students could pass the examinations. Any state in which the majority of students fail a test required for graduation only one year after all students graduated (when there was no test), may face a public uproar.

Generally, there exist two possible solutions: start easy and gradually ratchet up the level of difficulty of the examination over time (i.e., "raise the bar"). Though some critics assert that the "ratcheting up" has not occurred in Texas, this gradual approach was the original plan in both Texas and in North Carolina.

The other possible solution is to not compromise on the difficulty level, but provide an extraordinary level and array of publicly funded assistance to students to help them pass the examinations. This was the strategy adopted in Massachusetts, apparently with great success. Massachusetts' elected officials, however, bore an extraordinary level and array of invective from testing opponents (including one state-teacher union) while they stood firm on the standards. The Massachusetts strategy is not for the thin-skinned or faint of heart.

Behind any sequencing strategy is a concern about the political durability of a testing program. If the first test in a multi-test system is implemented badly, the other tests may never be implemented at all. The result could be a no-test system or a system entirely dependent on nothing but a minimum-competency test—a "single target" system with all the problems described above.

Structuring is more varied and complicated than sequencing and will not be covered thoroughly here, just illustrated with a few examples. One aspect of structuring has already been described—the character of the testing *system*. In other countries with well-developed testing systems, one tends to find two general types that are distinguishable by their relative degree of curricular specialization or "branching."

The French example above describes a very high degree of curricular branching or tracking, common to the European "continental" system. Starting at the end of primary school, or perhaps even before, students are tracked into different types of schools according to ability level and personal and parental choice of curricular focus. The degree of branching only increases at the end of lower secondary school and during upper secondary school. It is a continual process of searching and sorting that takes place over several years. But, in the end, no matter in which branch a student finds himself, he faces a pretty tough exam and must pass it in order to graduate. That includes the students in specialized vocational tracks, who will face pretty tough exams they must pass if they want to go on to technical institutes, engineering polytechnics, or into high-skilled trade apprenticeships.

If there is an alternative to this system, it is the traditional "two-tiered" British system which offers very general curricula well into high school, but at two levels of difficulty—the "O," or ordinary level, and "A," or advanced level.[3] New York State, with its Regents Examination and Regents Honors Examination could be said to offer this model.

Aside from the portfolio of tests themselves, the *incentives* tied to the tests can be structured in a wide variety of ways. The tests may have stakes for students, teachers, administrators, schools, or any combination thereof. The stakes may be low, medium, or high. The stakes may portend negative consequences (e.g., retention in grade, denial of promotion) or positive consequences (e.g., scholarship money for college, reward money for school). The traditional incentive structures in other countries have concentrated on negative consequences for students—i.e., a student does not proceed in the direction she would like if she does not pass the required examination.

U.S. states, however, have become quite innovative and varied in setting up incentive structures. One of the more celebrated criticisms of incentive structures that seemed patently unfair involved financial rewards to schools in North Carolina, Texas, and California—incentive structures that were the model incorporated into early versions of the "adequate yearly progress" provision of the Bush Administration's proposed No Child Left Behind legislation.

As shown by state researchers in Texas and modeled by Kane, Staiger, and Geppert, basing rewards on individual schools' average performances on individual grade-level tests can be fraught with statistical complications and unfairness (Kane, Staiger, & Geppert 2002). The basic problem relates to the nature of a grade within a school as a statistical unit. These statistical units come in a wide variety of sizes and character and are hardly self-contained and immutable. Students are not fixed in place, so neither are "classes" within schools. The character of the student population in a school's 5th grade can be strikingly different from the character of the same school's 6th grade depending on: which families moved in or out of the school's territorial boundary; whether the boundary stayed the same or changed; which students were promoted and which ones retained in grade; which disabled students are included in the test administration and which are not; the state of the job market for the students' parents one year compared to other years; and so on.

Moreover, as Kane, Staiger, and Geppert point out, the volatility is greater the smaller the school. The addition or deletion of just a few exceptionally high achievers or exceptionally low achievers will leverage much larger swings in average test scores in small schools than in large schools. This statistical behavior can bestow more rewards to smaller schools, with their higher volatility in average test scores from year to year and grade to grade, in states that reward proportionally large improvements in average scores. Conversely, the same statistical phenomenon would bestow more punishments to smaller schools in states that sanction proportionally large declines in average scores.

For testing opponents, such research provides more evidence "proving" that high-stakes standardized tests should be banned. For testing supporters, such research helps guide public servants toward improving the system, and, in fact, that is fairly easily done.

Oversight

Few independent observers would disagree that state administrators and elected officials have more incentive toward transparency and full disclosure of student achievement than do local school officials. Nonetheless, state officials' objectivity can be compromised, too, particularly if they have campaigned on a promise of improving education. Even with tests administered under fair, consistent, and secure conditions, average test scores can rise over time for reasons other than an improvement in student knowledge and skills.

All the while that Texas state administrators and politicians have been beaten up by education insiders and journalists for allegedly imposing tough, draconian testing requirements, some advocates for high standards were accusing the state of making the Texas Assessment of Academic Skills (TAAS) easier over time, presumably so that average scores would rise, whether or not student achievement was actually improving. The fact that Texas' scores on the independent NAEP also rose in the 1990s strongly suggests that educational achievement has, indeed, been improving in Texas.

But, the high standards critics have offered some fairly compelling evidence that Texas' assessments have actually gotten easier over time (see, for example, Patterson 2002; Clopton, Bishop and Klein 1999; Stotsky 2000; American Federation of Teachers 1999; Elliot and Bryant 2002).

To some skeptics, such evidence of still-too-frequent political compromises that with the quality of state tests, suggests that test administration must be done by an independent group–independent of both education provider groups and state government. The debate over proper oversight should continue to be rather prominent over the next several years and could lead to some interesting proposals for new governance structures over testing. Some have suggested that every state needs a bipartisan oversight body similar in structure to the National Assessment Governing Board (NAGB), that oversees the National Assessment of Educational Progress (NAEP). NAGB membership, according to its own rules, must represent various populations (e.g., politicians, psychometricians), and individuals serve for staggered terms, appointed by different administrations.

Test Anxiety

Finally, to be fair, one must admit that some students' test performance can be debilitated by test anxiety. But, getting rid of all high-stakes standardized testing is only one solution to that problem. Others involve dealing directly with those students' anxiety and attempting to resolve it. Likely, tests are not the only thing in life that make them anxious.

Still other solutions can be found in the testing program itself. Ironically, the more familiar tests and testing are, the less likely they are to make students anxious. Frequent testing promotes familiarity. Familiar test formats do, too. When students encounter test content they have studied and test structure that is familiar, they are less likely to be anxious. The best solution to the problem of test anxiety may be to test far more frequently.

Notes

1. California has adopted standards and tests much like Virginia's—detailed, specific, and otherwise "traditional," whereas Oregon and Washington State's standards and tests are more "progressive" and "constructivist."
2. Standardized end-of-course (EOC) exams certainly meet all of John Bishop's requirements for curriculum-based external exit exams, if they have high-stakes. The curriculum and the incentives could not be clearer. The actors responding to those incentives—the particular students and particular teacher—could not be clearer, either.
3. England and Wales changed their examination system about a decade ago such that there are now three examinations: the traditional A levels; the GCSE, which replaces the traditional O levels; and the AS exams.

9

The Agony of Defeat
(The Consequences of Losing the War: The
Alternatives to Standardized Testing)

Of all the many fallacies testing opponents hold dear, one stands out as primary. Critics do not compare standardized testing to available alternatives but, rather, to an unattainable utopian perfection. Neither standardized tests nor the manner in which they are administered will ever be perfect. But, the alternatives to standardized testing are far from perfect, too.

The most prominent available alternative to standardized testing is a system of social promotion with many levels of nominally the same subject matter taught in high school, ranging from classes for the self-motivated kids to those for the kids who quit trying years before, and whom the system has ignored ever since[1] (see also Chaney and Burgdorf 1997; Hoffer 1997). Too often, the result is a system that graduates functional illiterates.

Another available alternative to high-stakes standardized testing is the large-scale institution of remedial programs in colleges, to compensate for the degradation of instruction in the elementary and secondary schools (see, for example, Breneman, Haarlow, Costrell, Ponitz, and Steinberg 1998; Greene 2000b; U.S. Department of Education 1996).

Another available alternative to high-stakes standardized testing is an absence of reliable information of student performance anywhere outside a student's own school district. As long ago as the early 1960s, the economist Burton Weisbrod (1964) discovered that, on average, only 10 percent of a school district's graduates end up working within the geographic confines of their school district as working adults. Given the arbitrary and idiosyncratic character of high school graduation credentials, the overwhelming majority of employers (90 percent by Weisbrod's estimate) had little clue as to the skills and academic achievements of their job applicants, based on school district transcripts (that is, in those odd cases where it was even possible for an employer to obtain a school district transcript within an appropriate period of time). Unless employers tested their job applicants themselves, as many chose to do, they could not determine an applicant's level of academic achievement.

Still another available alternative to high-stakes standardized testing is a school culture in which students are routinely passed and graduated whether or not they earn it, and the few teachers brave enough to assign failing grades may well have their marks erased and changed by school administrators, thus allowing failing students to graduate and controversy to be avoided. In high schools where any student can pass courses and graduate despite doing little work, other students, and their parents, will assume that they, too, can pressure school administrators for selfish advantage. Behind-the-scenes prerogatives become the implicit academic standards (see, for example, Blum 2002; V. Johnson 2002; Perera 2002; *USA Today* 2001; Wyatt 2001)

The *available* alternatives to standardized testing, it turns out, contain most of the same problems that testing opponents ascribe, rightly or wrongly, to standardized testing.

Eliminating *high-stakes* standardized testing would increase our reliance on teacher grading and testing. Are teacher evaluations free from all the complaints listed in the anti-testing canon? Of course not. Individual teachers can narrow the curriculum to that which they personally prefer. Grades are susceptible to inflation with ordinary teachers, as students get to know a teacher better and learn his idiosyncrasies and how to manipulate his opinion. That is, students can hike their grades for reasons unrelated to academic achievement by gaming a teacher's system.[2] A teacher's grades and test scores are far more likely to be idiosyncratic and non-generalizable than any standardized tests'[3] (see, for example, Mathews 2001a).

Moreover, teacher-made tests are not necessarily any better supplied with "higher order thinking" exercises than are standardized tests. Nonetheless, test critics would rid us of all high-stakes standardized tests and have us rely solely on teacher evaluations of student progress and performance. How reliable are those evaluations?

Not very. There are a number of problems with a reliance on teacher evaluations, according to research on the topic. Teachers tend to consider "nearly everything" when assigning marks, including student class participation, perceived effort, progress over the period of the course, and comportment, according to Gregory Cizek. Actual achievement in mastering the subject matter is just one among many factors. Indeed, many teachers express a clear preference for non-cognitive outcomes such as "group interaction, effort, and participation" as more important than averaging tests and quiz scores (Cizek 1995, 1996; Cizek, Fitzgerald, and Rachor 1995/1996; see also Waltman and Frisbee 1994; McMillan 2001; Stiggins, Frisbee, and Griswold 1989; Stone 1995; Brookhart 1993; Boothroyd 1992; McMorris and Boothroyd 1992). It's not so much what you know, it's how you act. Being enthusiastic and group-oriented gets you into the audience for TV game shows and, apparently, also gets you better grades in school.

Some critics charge that education schools promote this behavior by denouncing the assignment of grades for subject-matter mastery as onerous and discriminatory, and encouraging prospective teachers to adjust their evaluations based on their perceptions of students' socioeconomic background (for example, see Kramer 1991: 32-35). One study of teacher grading practices discovered that 66 percent of teachers feel that their perception of a student's ability should be taken into consideration in awarding the final grade (Frary, Cross, and Weber 1993). Parents of students who assume that their children's grades represent subject matter mastery might be very surprised.

Given that most teachers have had little to no training in testing and measurement, it is not clear that their testing and grading practices would be of high quality even if they focused only on subject matter mastery, as parents would like them to. As Greg Cizek (2000) writes:

> ... one strains the gnat in objecting to the characteristics of high-stakes tests, when the characteristics of those tests are compared to what a child will likely experience in his or her classroom the other 176 days of the school year. This point should cause all those genuinely committed to fair testing to refocus their attention on classroom assessment. Decades of evidence have been amassed to support the contention that the quality of teacher-made tests pales compared to more rigorously developed, large-scale counterparts. Such evidence begins with the classic studies of teachers' grading practice by Starch and Elliot (1912, 1913a, 1913b) and continues with more recent studies which document that weaknesses in typical classroom assessment practices have persisted (see, for example, Carter 1984; Gullickson & Ellwein 1985). It is not an overstatement to say that, at least on the grounds of technical quality, the typical high-stakes, state-mandated test that a student takes will—by far—be the best assessment that student will see all year." [see also Jozefowicz, Koeppen, Case et al. 2002]

The actual alternative to standardized testing is an absence of standardized curriculum and instructional practice (because they would be unenforceable). If the curriculum is not tested, we cannot know if any of it works. Without standardized tests, no one outside the classroom can reliably gauge student progress. No district or state superintendent. No governor. No taxpayer. No parent. No student. Each has to accept only whatever each teacher says and, without standardized tests, no teacher has any point of comparison, either.

Without common, enforceable standards, there may be no good way to affect performance systemwide other than through high-stakes standardized tests (as in the Netherlands, for example). Without either common standards or high-stakes standardized tests, there may be no effective way *at all* to monitor performance systemwide. Some U.S. teachers may be doing a wonderful job in their totally customized classes, but some may be doing an awful job. How is one to know or tell which? In the United States, one must hope that teachers will face down the natural incentives of their students, parents, schools, and themselves to avoid accountability by holding themselves and their students to high standards of performance. One must also hope that teachers will know how.

Standardized Tests versus the Actual Alternatives

Judging standardized tests against a benchmark of utopian perfection that does and can not exist, means standardized tests always look bad. How would testing critics' accusations look compared to the actual, available alternatives? The table below provides a glimpse.

Common Standards and Tests	Teachers/Schools do as they Wish
Teaching to the Test	
Testing opponents repeatedly assert that teachers will teach the material that will be on a test. But, if the tests are high-stakes, and they are kept behind lock and key until the day of the test administration, how can teachers know what material will be on the test, except in the most general terms?	Teachers always "teach to" something. If they are not "teaching to" a required curriculum that is covered in a standardized test, what are they teaching to? ...and why should we be so sure that it is better than teaching the required curriculum? In the absence of common standards and standardized tests, teachers still teach to something, but that something is arbitrary; it is whatever the teacher himself personally prefers to teach. And, why should the taxpayers pay for that?
Narrowing the Curriculum	
Common standards and tests do involve a prescribed curriculum. It is a curriculum, however, that has been chosen through a public process, based on public wishes, not one chosen at whim by an individual classroom teacher based on personal preferences. As there are only so many hours in a day and so many days in a year, it is not possible that a common curriculum has any less content than a teacher-arbitrary curriculum. Common standards do not reduce the amount of instructional time. If, when common standards are imposed, a teacher must drop a certain topic or unit, she is also, at the same time, adding a different topic or unit not used before.	What teachers and schools do in the classroom absent any adherence to common standards is not necessarily any "broader" than what happens with common standards. Indeed, it is likely to be "narrower" as it is determined by nothing more than one individual's personal preferences. Nor is it necessarily any better, more profound, or more beneficial to the students. It's merely more arbitrary.

Cheating by Students	
Cheating is far easier to prevent and detect with standardized tests. Different forms can be used in the same classroom making copying unrewarding. Computer programs can be run after the fact that look for telltale patterns.	Cheating in regular classroom work has become epidemic. The overwhelming majority of students admit to cheating in polls. Teachers and schools are ill-equipped to monitor or detect most cheating. Meanwhile, the Internet makes cheating far easier than it used to be.

Cheating by Teachers	
The fact that cheating by teachers on high-stakes standardized tests is well publicized is testament to how easily that cheating can be detected.	Testing opponents argue that teachers have an incentive to cheat on high-stakes tests and no incentive to cheat otherwise. Nonsense. Social promotion and grade inflation provide the contrary evidence. The majority of teachers admit in surveys that they feel overwhelming pressure to promote students they feel they should not and to give better grades than students deserve.

Preferred Instructional Methods	
Testing critics claim that what happens in the classroom absent standardized testing is wonderful (rich, innovative curriculum; the joy and magic of learning, and so on).	But, they provide no evidence of any of their claims. We are left with no choice but to take their word on it.

Opposition to Norm-Referenced Tests	
Testing critics excoriate the use of norm-referenced standardized tests as unfair (i.e., it is unfair to simply rank kids, rather than measure them against standards).	But, they would have us rely on grade-point-averages, which are norm-referenced measures, normed at the school level

Preference for Teacher-Made Classroom Testing	
Standardized tests are developed by cadres of technicians with Ph.D.s in testing and measurement. The most capable measurement experts in the world work in North America developing standardized tests.	Few teachers have had anything more than a cursory exposure to testing and measurement training, if they have had any whatsoever. But, standardized testing critics would have us rely exclusively on the performance measurements of these individuals with no training in measurement.

The Perils of Portfolios and Other "Authentic" Attractions

Some prominent testing opponents tell journalists that they are supporters of high-stakes standardized tests, but only if those tests are "authentic" and/ or "portfolios." Proponents of authentic instruction and authentic assessment promote the image of naturalness in education. Instruction should be as much like "real life" as possible; to do otherwise would be "artificial." Authentic instruction typically employs "hands-on" lessons, or uses materials in demonstrations, as in a teacher conducting a science experiment in front of a classroom. Authentic assessment, to use a similar example, might consist of students, one-by-one, or in groups, conducting laboratory experiments and getting scored on their "performance."

Most certificate tests for the skilled trades are "authentic"–a student must "show" that she knows how to wire a circuit box or edge a banister molding by actually doing it. Proponents of authentic assessment will often use the example of a pilot's test to press their point. After all, who would want to be a passenger in an airplane piloted by someone who had never before flown a plane, but had done very well on a paper-and-pencil exam about piloting?

Having said all that, the analogy does not necessarily translate all that well to regular K-12 education for the most part. True, a laboratory experiment may be a more authentic representation of what a scientist does than filling in a paper-and-pencil test is. And, authentic test advocates use this argument to press their case that more or all tests should be authentic. But, we do not teach science in elementary school because we want *all* our students to become scientists and, truthfully, only a very tiny proportion of them can or will become scientists. We do, however, want all of them to accumulate a substantial body of knowledge about science, a body of knowledge sizable enough that it becomes usable in decision-making–in making home health-care decisions, doing home construction projects, or even deciding if one wishes to pursue a career in science.

The question of knowledge accumulation leads naturally to a directly related issue—how time-consuming both authentic instruction and authentic assessment are. Some high school science classes that emphasize authentic instruction and assessment consist of class after class of experimentation. Each class involves the students setting up the equipment, conducting the experiment, and then discussing the results independent of any prompting from the teacher.

No one can deny that such a class format can be beneficial to students' learning. But, authentic instruction can be expensive, and it is very time-consuming. It can take an entire class to learn one or a few simple points that the teacher, alternatively, can just tell the students in a minute or two. If authentic instruction were to completely replace traditional instruction, inevitably, students would be able to accumulate only a tiny proportion of the factual knowledge they can otherwise amass. Even if the radical constructivists are correct in their assertion that a point learned through authentic learning is more durably learned than one learned by simply being told (believe it if you want, I don't)...if it takes 100 times longer to teach a student a simple point "authentically," how cost-effective is the authentic method of learning?

With authentic *assessment* in particular, there can be huge reliability and fairness problems. It can take several days of a teacher observing individual students in succession conducting a single hands-on science experiment just to determine how well each of them knows just one or a few points of information. In a paper-and-pencil objective test, all students may be posed hundreds of questions within a couple of hours, simultaneously, and with just one or two teachers as test monitors.

We all still want the pilot of the plane we fly to have taken an authentic assessment, however. But, traditionally, most societies have structured their education systems so that students *accumulate* as much knowledge as is possible, first. Then, after the students have narrowed the focus of their career track, and only then, do they undertake authentic instruction and authentic assessment. There are three reasons for structuring things this way:

1. authentic instruction/assessment is relatively *very* expensive;
2. it takes far more time in authentic instruction/assessment to cover the same amount of material as can be covered with traditional instruction and paper-and-pencil standardized tests; and
3. some authentic instruction/assessment is simply impossible to implement on a large scale.

As a society, we simply cannot afford to provide all our high school students with authentic flying lessons. But, that is no justification for not teaching our students the basic aerodynamic concepts of lift, drag, and thrust. For the very few students who, in the end, choose to be pilots for a living, instead of one of the thousands of other occupations available to them, our society does make the investment in authentic instruction and assessment.

Portfolios are collections of authentic work, specifically a student's best or favorite work. Portfolios are popular with radical constructivists enamored with the idea of *naturalness* in education. They may consist of any type of work–writings, drawings, dances, or even an arithmetic assignment done well. Unfortunately, portfolios are notoriously difficult to score in a consistent, standardized manner. Moreover, they are open invitations to cheating. If a student turns in a portfolio for a statewide, standardized assessment, who is to know if the essay enclosed is written by that student, or her mother, or by someone in New Zealand who posted it on the Internet. (see Cizek 1991; Gearhart and Herman 1996).

Traditionally, grading portfolios has been the preferred method of judging performance in the arts and architecture. And, judging performance in those fields is notoriously subjective, personal, and prone to passing fads and fashions. These fields use portfolios because they have little alternative. There is simply no better, more reliable method for judging performance.

There is, however, a very high-quality alternative for judging performance in mastering the basic academic subject matter in our elementary and secondary schools. This alternative is far more reliable and objective than portfolio analysis. This alternative is called the standardized test.

Part of the strength of standardized tests is that they do *not* mimic classroom activity, as portfolios are meant to. Standardized tests measure performance and knowledge accumulation in a manner that is useful, different from all the alternatives, and complementary to that already available. The more like ordinary classroom activity we make standardized tests, the less useful they become.

Holding Our Children Hostage

It will not have escaped the notice of some insightful readers that most of the negative "unintended consequences" of external standardized testing are entirely under educators' own control. *Educators* tell us that high-stakes testing will induce *educators* to cheat. *Educators* tell us these tests will induce *educators* to "teach to the test" and "narrow the curriculum" (and that these are bad practices). *Educators* tell us that *educators* will dumb-down the curriculum, practice rote instruction, and write meaningless test score reports for public consumption. (These testing critics also expect us to assume that these unfortunate practices do not occur in the absence of external testing.)

It may remind one of the silly and time-worn joke set in a doctor's office where the visitor says, "Doctor, it hurts when I do this," and the doctor replies, "Then, don't do that." If educators believe the practices mentioned above should be stopped, it is entirely within their power to stop them.

Instead, testing critics inside the education establishment tell us that they simply cannot be trusted to behave professionally, responsibly, or ethically if the public insists on employing quality control in the public schools. The critics insist that we leave them completely free to spend our tax dollars and treat our children as only they know best.

Notes

1.   For example, according to Jeff Moss, the associate school superintendent for the Hoke County, North Carolina schools, before accountability reforms, "We had seven levels of instruction for a subject matter, such as seven levels of biology, seven levels of English One, which ranged from remedial to honors or college

preparatory. So the teacher expectation was such that if I labeled you a basic student I needed to put you in basic English and not require much from you." See Molpus.

2. Indeed, "gaming"—behavior that improves one's grade but is not necessarily related to mastery of the academic subject matter—is probably a larger factor in boosting grade point averages than it is in boosting standardized test scores. Teachers are human, and humans cannot be perfect graders, perfect test developers, perfectly fair, or immune to manipulation. Teachers and schools can be "gamed" just as standardized tests can be gamed. This, by the way, is no different than with most of life's tasks. Every system has its structure and standards and much of life is about learning them. Gaming methods only go so far, though; students who did not show up for English class in high school and skipped Algebra and Geometry will not produce a stellar performance on the ACT or SAT after merely having attended a Stanley Kaplan course.

3. For a comprehensive overview of the quality and reliability of teacher evaluations of student achievement, see Stiggins and Conklin 1992.

Appendix
An Anti-Testing Vocabulary

As the empirical research evidence does not work for them, testing opponents have built a vocabulary to suit their needs. Their vocabulary is misleading when used in the public domain, but...that may be its purpose. Testing opponents take common, ordinary words and give them alternate definitions. They then use those words in the public domain, leaving the public to think they are using the common, ordinary definition, when they are not. "Rote Recall," for example, is used to describe the response to *any* test item with a multiple-choice response format, no matter how complex the question or complicated the process required to get from the question to the correct answer.

Much anti-testing "research" amounts to little more than name-calling. Some tracts hundreds of pages long consist of nothing more than the use of ill-sounding words to describe standardized testing and good-sounding words to describe its absence. They contain no data, no analysis, just rhetoric. But it is called research. Below, I list some of the terms used, and attempt to explain them.

The reader should realize, however, that anti-testing vocabulary, as large as it is, comprises merely a subset of a much larger "insiders" vocabulary that pervades all of U.S. education. The Texas Education Consumers Association (TECA) has performed a public service by reproducing much of E. D. Hirsch's "Critical Guide to Educational Terms and Phrases" from his book, *The Schools We Need & Why We Don't Have Them*, and posting it (http://www.math.nyu.edu/mfdd/braams/nychold/hirsch-termin.html) (see also Raimi 2000; Wolff 2002).

Here is how TECA introduces Hirsch's vocabulary list:

"Education Terminology Every Parent Must Understand"

Teachers and administrators use jargon which is sometimes unfamiliar to parents. When faced with strange jargon, parents are reluctant to ask questions or debate educators for fear of sounding ignorant. When parents do gather the courage to argue, educators sometimes use their jargon against us. For example, if you were to express a desire for traditional teaching methods, the teacher may use pejorative terminology to thwart your complaints. You may be told that traditional education is "just" drill and kill or rote-learning. The implication is that *you* are misguided, ignorant of children's developmental processes, and perhaps even mean-spirited. Then the teacher tells you: "We are a child-centered school, so we do not use those old-fashioned methods anymore because research has shown that our child-friendly methods are better."

This use of jargon implies that the teacher cares more about your child's education than you do. After all, the teacher has been trained to use the most progressive methods available, so his or her knowledge on this subject shouldn't be questioned. What the teacher neglects to tell you is that the "research" she refers to is not necessarily supported by mainstream scientific inquiry (i.e., published in scientific journals within a specific discipline such as psychology).

By using terminology that has either negative- or positive-sounding connotations, educators can succeed in silencing your opposition, simply because you don't understand the meaning of the words and phrases. Therefore, you should arrive at the teacher conference knowing the language teachers speak, just as you would have to do if you visited a foreign country.

An Anti-Testing Vocabulary

Authentic Teaching—(see Real Learning).

Better Tests—Usually, testing opponents mean tests without stakes for anyone—teacher, student, school, school system—because stakes "corrupt" the natural learning process. They also usually mean classroom testing only, and classroom tests without any multiple-choice test items.

Cheap Fix—(see Silver Bullet).

Complex Topics—That which is taught in the absence of common academic standards and high-stakes standardized tests (see also Real Learning).

Corruption—Based on the assumption that whatever happens in the classroom absent any "outside" influence is natural and ideal, any deviation from what a teacher is "naturally" inclined to do is labeled a "corruption." Since standardized tests hold teachers to following common standards, the tests induce teachers to change (i.e., "corrupt") their behavior from what it would be in the natural ideal. By this definition, *any* teacher behavior in the absence of standards is "uncorrupted." This could include discussing yesterday's television shows or basketball game or any of a teacher's pet topics. Any instruction related to academic standards, however, is "corruption" unless it is instruction a teacher would "normally" have pursued absent common standards. In a system where every teacher has been free to structure classes any way they please, the adoption of common standards is likely to lead to a large amount of corruption (see also Pollution).

Creative, Productive Learning Environments—(see Real Learning).

Craze, the Testing—The act of administering external, standardized tests.

Cure-All, Ultimate—(see Silver Bullet).

Curriculum Distortion—(see Real Leaning).

De-Democratizing—(see Democratic).

Democratic (decision-making, discourse, control, etc.) in education—Letting the "professionals" make education policy decisions. Testing opponents argue that any outside influence on what a public school on its own "naturally" desires to do impedes "democracy." Opponents of common academic standards and standardized tests like to paint a picture of much student and parent involvement in every aspect of school operations, including the academic content in each classroom. Only in other contexts will they admit the minimal level of parent involvement in school activities, or the virtual absence of any parent involvement in choosing course content (textbook publishers choose course content absent common standards). Interestingly, most testing opponents define school choice—the process of allowing students and parents to choose the school they believe to be most appropriate to their needs and preferences—as "anti-democratic." School choice is described with words and phrases such as "corporate," "market-driven," and "treating schools like products on a shelf."

De-Professionalization of Teaching—(see De-Skilling).

De-Skilling—This term means close to the opposite of what most would probably think it means. Most people think of the term "skill" to mean the mastery of a routine or technique, as in: fighter pilots and surgeons are highly skilled professionals who have spent many hours practicing their routines and techniques. Many testing opponents think of a teacher's "skill" to mean something close to the opposite of that. In their preferred philosophy of radical constructivism, a good teacher does not provide knowledge or "instruct" students. Rather, a good teacher is a "facilitator" (i.e., a "guide on the side" and not a "sage on the stage") who helps each student "construct" his or her own knowledge. A good teacher, then, in their view, does not employ instructional techniques or routines, because a good teacher does not "instruct" at all. Because teachers under pressure to improve student achievement (in the face of standardized tests, for example) tend to use methods that work best to improve student achievement...and because those methods tend to be teacher-centered and not student-centered (i.e., not "constructivist") ...standardized tests cause teachers to be "de-skilled." Again, the decades worth of evidence from randomized experiments, showing that instructional techniques with highly structured lessons and lots of drill and practice significantly improve student achievement, while radical constructivist techniques do not, is either discounted or ignored by testing opponents (see also Rich Curriculum).

Drills—Any instruction that takes place in classrooms where common academic standards and high-stakes standardized tests have influence. The fact that many teachers in environments with high-stakes tests still use Socratic methods (e.g., class discussion, question-and-answer format) is defined to not exist. Again, the decades worth of evidence from randomized experiments, showing that instructional techniques with highly structured lessons and lots of drill and practice more reliably improve student achievement than radical constructivist techniques, is either discounted or ignored by testing opponents.

Drill-and-Kill—(see Drills).

Expert, Testing—Someone who opposes testing. Usually an education school professor.

Higher-Order Thinking—A grab-bag of cognitive processes alleged to be related to creativity, such as lateral thinking and meta-analysis. It is sometimes alleged that standardized tests cannot test higher-order thinking. More often, it is alleged that standardized tests with multiple-choice response formats cannot test higher-order thinking (but open-ended response formats can). Some famous higher-order thinkers: Albert Einstein, Walter Mitty (see also Rote Recall).

How Children Learn, What We Know About—(see Real Learning).

Independent Researchers—Testing opponents who are, in most cases, education professors with much to gain personally from an absence of high-stakes standardized tests (e.g., they can teach and research anything they please without regard to improving student achievement), claim that they are "independent researchers." Further, they claim that testing advocates, whom they allege to be "politicians," are not "independent" because they have a self-interest in misleading the public about the state of our public schools in order to win votes.

Innovative—Is what you like, and is always good, no matter what the consequences.

Integrate Concepts and Topics—Allegedly, standardized testing makes it impossible to integrate concepts and topics (see also Real Learning).

Lake Wobegon—Phrase to describe test-score inflation (in Lake Wobegon, "all the children are above average"). Refers to a phenomenon in the 1980s where, after a number of years of use, the average student score on a certain commercial standardized test was above average in every state using the test. The causes included: schools reusing old copies of the same version of the test (with which teachers had become familiar); the test publisher waiting too long before "renorming" the test; and the fact that student achievement really was improving throughout the 1980s. The test administration problems that contributed to the Lake Wobegon effect are easily controlled and not relevant to the conditions under which current state standards-based high-stakes tests are administered. Testing opponents, however, want us to believe that the Lake Wobegon effect is inevitable to any standardized test use, uncontrollable, and will always be us.

Legislated Learning—Academic standards.

Mania, Testing—The act of administering external, standardized tests.

Meaningful Forms of Assessment—(see Better Tests).

Multiple Intelligences—Posits the truism that different people have different intellectual strengths and may learn best in different ways. The current guru of this line of thought, Howard Gardner, an avid opponent of high-stakes standardized testing, asserts that there are more than several different kinds of "intelligences," and by emphasizing one or the other in our standardized tests, we are being unfair to the others. Most standardized tests, Gardner asserts, focus on logic and analysis and neglect other intelligences, perfectly legitimate in their own right, such as the "kinetic" intelligence of dancers. Ending this bias toward logic and analysis and giving equal time to each of the other "intelligences" might, indeed, help to alleviate our American society's oversupply of mathematicians, scientists, and engineers, and satisfy its shortage of artists, dancers, and athletes.

Narrowing the Curriculum—Test critics often accuse high-stakes tests of "narrowing the curriculum," but only the amount of instructional time available can narrow it. There is only so much instructional time available and choices must be made as to how it is used. If the critics intend to continue asserting that non-tested subjects are being dropped, they should show evidence that *student requirements* for taking music, art, language, or other nontested subjects are being dropped. Some critics claim that a narrowing of curriculum occurs in the primary grades, where individual teachers are responsible for all subjects, and so could, on their own, spend less time on, say, music and art to the benefit of the more frequently tested subjects. In principal, a school system could implement high-stakes tests in art, music, language, and civics, too, or in any other subject considered important. Attaching high-stakes to tests in some subjects and not others would be interpreted by most as a signal that the former subjects are considered to be more important. Likely, more effort will be expended in teaching the former subjects as a result among teachers, like those at the primary level, who have a choice of emphasis. In those cases where the students are, indeed, woefully deficient in basic skills and need extra instructional time devoted to them, however, probably few parents would object. Primary school students may need to establish a foundation in reading, writing, and arithmetic before they can learn any-thing else well later on. Poll results show clearly that the public wants stu-dents to master the basics skills first, before they go on to explore the rest of the possible curriculum. If that means they must spend more time on the basics, so be it.

Obsession, Test—The act of administering external, standardized tests.

One Size Fits All—Phrase used to criticize any effort to standardize curricu-lum or instruction, and often used in anti-testing tracts. Note that the phrase is not used in conjunction with discussions of public education governance or ability grouping. The same folks rabidly against the "standardizing" aspect of testing seem perfectly happy with a "one size fits all" public education system and grade progression. Indeed, to propose otherwise is attacked as elitist. (Thus, the phrase is used hypocritically as well as fallaciously. The fallacy is that standardized tests do not impose "one size" on any student's learning or thinking. A student can arrive at an answer to a test question any way she wishes to. It is the subject matter itself that imposes "one size" on the material. Unless, of course, one wants to argue that every student has a right to create his or her own rules of mathematics and English grammar, and should only be judged by his or her own, unique, individualized subject matter.)

Perverse Effects—(see Unintended Consequences).

Political Not Educational, Standardized Testing is...—Most testing oppo-nents ignore the cornucopia of evidence for standardized testing's benefits and public popularity—they simply talk and write as if they do not exist, as their existence is extremely inconvenient to their arguments. The mass of evidence of standardized testing's benefits tends to exist outside of some education professors' research world—in psychology and economics papers and articles, for example. Certainly, education professors who are testing opponents do not spend their time looking for standardized testing's ben-efits. Given the myopic insistence on no evidence of benefits, then, testing opponents argue that the only reason for having high-stakes standardized testing is "political"—"politicians," they argue, have a self-interest in mis-leading the public about the state of our public schools in order to win votes. Standardized tests, then, are solely a "political" devise whose purpose is to make the public schools look bad; standardized tests have no educational purpose whatsoever, according to them.

Pollution—Similar to the concept of "corruption," the term "pollution" is used more commonly to apply to test scores. Based, again, on the assumption that whatever happens in the classroom absent standardized testing is natural and ideal, any deviation from what a teacher is "naturally" inclined to do is judged to be wrong. The practices of "teaching to the test," "narrowing the curriculum," and the like, caused by standardized tests, allegedly result in test scores that are "polluted."

Problem-Solving—Just another phrase for responses to open-ended test items. By definition, any test item with a multiple-choice response format cannot involve problem-solving. So, for example, finding the answer to the test item—"How many cubic centimeters are contained in a box 2 meters wide by 3 meters long by 4 meters tall? (a) 23.4 thousand (b) 24 million (c) 0. 24 (d) 24 (e) none of the above"—cannot involve "problem solving" because the response format is multiple choice. If the response format were open-ended (i.e., just a blank space on the test sheet), it could involve "problem solving."

Quality of What is Taught, Decline in the...—(see Real Learning).

Quick Fix—(see Silver Bullet).

Real Education—(see Real Learning).

Real Learning—Many, if not most, testing opponents are believers in radical constructivist philosophy, despite the weak evidence that radical constructivist teaching methods improve student achievement. They prefer teaching methods where each student "constructs" his or her own knowledge in his or her own personal way without "interference" from the teacher. They claim that students only "really learn" if they "construct their own knowledge." Thus, "teacher-centered" classrooms, where teachers give students information, cannot induce "real learning." Because teachers under pressure to improve student achievement (in the face of standardized tests, for example) tend to use the methods that work best to improve student achievement...and because those methods tend to be teacher-centered and not student-centered...standardized tests impede "real learning."

Real Teaching—Any teaching that occurs in the absence of standardized testing.

Rich Curriculum—Defined to be any academic content used in the absence of standardized testing. Most testing opponents like to argue that, in the absence of enforced common academic standards, each teacher is using his or her own professional judgment to devise a unique curriculum crafted to the unique needs of each unique student in each unique classroom. That is the radical constructivist ideal. They fail to mention, as most teachers would tell, that this ideal is physically impossible to implement. No human teacher is capable of doing all the work this ideal requires, and no classroom can possibly be managed in the manner the ideal requires. In other contexts, these testing opponents will acknowledge that, in the absence of enforced common academic standards, the vast majority of teachers use the curriculum plan of the textbooks they have chosen or been assigned and do not craft individual learning plans for each student and create new curriculum every day that is tailored to those plans. Interestingly, most of the same critics who argue for adapting instruction uniquely to each unique student oppose ability grouping, which combines students in a way that makes a teacher's instructional focus much easier.

Rote Memorization—(related to Rote Recall and Drills).

Rote Recall—What a student does in responding to any test item in objective response format (e.g., multiple-choice or fill-in-the-blank), no matter how complex the cognitive processing required to get from the question to the correct answer. In a presidential speech at an annual meeting of the American Educational Research Association, for example, a leading testing opponent offered this test item as an example of one that required "rote recall:" "James had 5 cents. He earned 13 cents more and then bought a top for 10 cents. How much money did he have left? *Answer:*_____ " Most people would think that "rote recall" means a regurgitation of a memorized fact. By that common definition, this question could only demand rote recall if it and its correct answer had been memorized. Short of that, the average student would need to do some calculation, and some cognitive processing that incorporated learned procedures, in order to find the correct answer. Is the misleading way in which testing opponents use the term designed to misrepresent the content of standardized tests to the public? That's my guess.

Silver Bullet—Anti-testing researchers often claim that testing advocates believe high-stakes standardized tests are a.... I have read probably over a thousand articles and essays on testing policy at this point, and I have yet to read any testing advocate claim that high-stakes testing alone will solve all our country's education problems.

Special Interest Groups—Alleged to be business groups only. It is not entertained as possible that testing opponents could represent special interests. They identify themselves as "independent" researchers. It is also usually not mentioned by testing opponents that the overwhelming majority of the public, of parents, of students, and, with certain exceptions, of teachers, want common academic standards and high-stakes standardized tests.

Teaching to the Test—Usually means any instruction on subject matter that is covered by a test. Generally, testing opponents' cry of "teaching to the test" is obfuscation. Teaching to the test is only a problem when students are tested on material they have not been taught. When students are tested on material they have been taught, any teacher not teaching to the test is behaving irresponsibly. It may be for this reason that, despite testing opponents' (largely successful) efforts to convince journalists that teaching to the test is a horrible practice, parents continue to tell pollsters that, of course, they want their students' teachers to teach to the test. Opponents' arguments beg the question: Would they prefer a test so obscure in structure and content that teachers cannot help students prepare for it?

Test Preparation—Defined to mean *any* instruction related to the content of a standardized test. In states with common academic standards and high-stakes tests aligned to those standards, all instruction will be related to the content of the tests. Thus, by testing opponents' definition, all instruction is bad, inferior to the natural instruction or, rather, "construction" of knowledge they allege takes place in classrooms unaffected by standardized tests.

Test-Prep Materials—*Any* instructional materials used in classrooms influenced by standardized testing.

Test-Score Inflation—(see Lake Wobegon).

Unintended Consequences—Just another way of saying that standardized tests are not perfect instruments of social engineering (e.g., students who score poorly might get hurt feelings, or be held back a grade). Everybody who has ever attended school, however, knows this already. Testing opponents take the concept a bit further in two respects: in their idealization of the "natural" education process in which teachers and schools are left alone to do whatever they please; and in their insistence that standardized tests should not be allowed in use until they are perfect and have no "unintended consequences."

Validity—"Validity" is a term commonly used by testing experts that relates to the degree a test score represents what it is supposed to represent. The SAT and ACT, for example, are supposed to help predict academic performance in the first year of college, so students' scores on those tests should be well-correlated with their grades from their first year at college. High school exit exams are, usually, supposed to represent student mastery of the academic material covered in the high school years. Many new types of "validities" have proliferated in recent years, however, and some testing opponents have invented validities that tests they do not like are certain to fail.

Glossary

Achievement Test

A test designed to measure a person's knowledge, understanding, or accomplishment in a certain subject area, or the degree to which a person possesses a certain skill. Achievement tests should be distinguished from aptitude tests, which attempt to estimate future performance.

Aptitude Test

A test that assesses knowledge and skills from a very broad, general domain. It is theorized (and empirical evidence seems to support the theory) that the larger one's foundation of knowledge of skill, the greater the potential is for learning more, as most new knowledge is built as an extension on top of that already known.

Assessment

Generally refers to large-scale, systemwide measurement programs for pupil diagnosis, program evaluation, accountability, resource allocation, or teacher evaluation.

Criterion-Referenced Test

A test that allows its users to interpret scores in relationship to a functional performance level. Criterion-referenced measures provide information as to the degree of competence attained by a particular student, without reference to the performance of others.

Constructivists, Radical

"Constructivists" believe that learners "construct" knowledge in their own way from their own set of "found materials" in their memory. Most educators believe that there is something to the notion of constructivism, and any teacher using what used to be called the Socratic Method (a question-and-answer technique) is practicing it to some degree. "Radical constructivists" believe that it is the *only* proper, legitimate, durable, or acceptable method of learning and it should be adopted as the exclusive form of instruction in our public schools. They believe in "student-centered" learning, *construction* as a complete replacement for *instruction*. They may express outrage at any use of such traditional instructional methods as teacher lectures, memorization, review, drills, and most "teacher-centered" structured forms of instruction.

Radical constructivists tend to oppose school practices that they think "fix" behavior. They see standardizing curricula and instructional practice as restricting teacher behavior and multiple-choice standardized tests as shackling student responses to problems.

Egalitarians, Radical

Most of us are "egalitarians" to some degree. That is, we believe that people should be treated equally in certain circumstances. The most popular and celebrated form of equality in the United States is "equality of opportunity," which spawns such aphorisms as the "level playing field" and an "equal chance." *Radical* egalitarians want there to be an equality of *outcomes* as well as opportunity—the score at the end of the game played on the level playing field should always be a tie.

Some radical egalitarians believe that basing selection decisions on test scores rewards students who work harder, and that isn't "fair" to the other students. Others argue that work has nothing to do with it, as student achievement is determined exclusively by parents' income and level of education, and predestined before the first day of kindergarten. And so test scores merely reinforced the social class structure.

High-Stakes Test

A test that is used to determine promotion, retention, or graduation. "High-stakes" tests and tests used for "student-level accountability" are often considered synonymous. "Medium- or low-stakes" tests are terms often used when test results are used *in combination with* other criteria in diploma decisions.

Minimum-Competency Test

Generally, a high-stakes test set at a low level of difficulty. Many current state tests required for graduation are minimum-competency tests, set at a 7th- or 8th-grade level of difficulty, with several opportunities to pass, over a several-year period. Often, these tests are untimed, "power tests."

Norm-Referenced Test

A test that shows a person's relative standing along a continuum of attainment in comparison to the performance of other people in a specified group, such as test-takers of a certain age or group.

Performance-Based Test

A test that measures ability by assessing open-ended responses or by asking a person to complete a task. Also known as alternative assessment, constructed response, or task performance, performance-based tests require the respondent to produce a response, or demonstrate a skill or procedure. Examples include answering an open-ended question, conversing in a foreign language, solving a mathematics problem while showing all calculations, writing an essay on a given topic, or designing a science experiment.

Reliability

The reliability of a test refers to the degree to which test results are consistent across test administrations. Individual student scores are reliable if the same student gives the same answers to the same questions asked at different points in time. Test reliability can also be measured at the classroom, school, or district level. Tests tend to be reliable if their questions are clear and focused, and unreliable if their questions are vague, contradictory, or confusing. Reliability can be measured rather precisely.

Representative Sample

A sample is a subgroup of a population. A sample is representative if it accurately reflects the character of the population in those aspects under study.

Standardized Test

A test is standardized if it is given in identical form and at the same time to students in more than one school, and all the results are marked in the same way. Tests scored by machine-reading of student marks in answer "bubbles" are not the only type of standardized test. Tests with open-ended essay questions and other kinds of performance-based tests can be standardized, too, if the conditions of administration and scoring are common and carefully controlled across schools.

Validity

The validity of a test refers to the degree to which it measures what it is designed to measure. There are several kinds of validity. Curricular validity, for example, would be strong if a test contained questions based on the content of the curriculum, and weak if a test contained questions not based on the content of the curriculum. Predictive validity would be strong if an individual's test score accurately forecasted some other event, such as the likelihood of graduating or succeeding in a particular endeavor. Unlike reliability, validity is difficult to measure precisely.

References

Abar, Sylvia H. 1996. "The Perceived Influences that Prompt Teachers to Initiate Changes in Curriculum and Instruction." Ed.D diss., University of Massachusetts.

Aber, Joanne. 1996. *Getting a College Degree Fast: Testing Out & Other Accredited Short Cuts*. New York: Prometheus Books. (ERIC: ED401780)

Achieve, Inc. 2001. *Measuring Up: A Report on Education Standards and Assessments for Massachusetts*, October.

American Federation of Teachers. 1994. *Valuable Views: A Public Opinion Research Report on the Views of AFT Teachers on Professional Issues*. Washington, DC.

American Federation of Teachers. 1995a. *Defining World Class Standards*. Washington, DC.

American Federation of Teachers. 1995b. *Making Standards Matter: A Fifty-State Progress Report on Efforts to Raise Academic Standards*. Washington, DC.

American Federation of Teachers. 1996. "A System of High Standards: What We Mean and Why We Need It." *American Educator* (spring).

American Federation of Teachers. 1999. *Setting Higher Sights: A Need for More Demanding Assessments for U.S. Eighth Graders*. Washington, DC.

Anderson, John. O., Walter Muir, David J. Bateson, David Blackmore, and W. Todd Rogers. 1990. *The Impact of Provincial Examinations on Education in British Columbia: General Report*. British Columbia Ministry of Education, March 30.

Apple, Michael W. 1990. *Ideology and Curriculum*. New York: Routledge.

ASCD 2000. "National Survey Gauges Parent Perceptions of State-Mandated, Standardized Tests." Alexandria, VA, June 13.

Banerji, Madhabi. 2000. "Designing District-level Classroom Assessment Systems." Paper presented at the annual meeting of the American Educational Research Association, New Orleans, LA, April.

Bartley, Robert L. 2000. "The Press Pack: News by Stereotype." *Wall Street Journal*, September 11, A45.

Barton, Paul E. 1999. *Too Much Testing of the Wrong Kind: Too Little of the Right Kind in K-12 Education*. Policy Information Center, Educational Testing Service, Princeton, NJ, March.

Beaton, Albert E. 1996. *Mathematics Achievement in the Middle School Years: IEA's Third International Mathematics and Science Study*. Chestnut Hill: Boston College.

Beaudry, Jeff. 2000. "The Positive Effects of Administrators and Teachers on Classroom Assessment Practices and Student Achievement." Paper presented at the annual meeting of the American Educational Research Association, New Orleans, LA, April.

Becker, Betsy Jane. 1990. "Coaching for the Scholastic Aptitude Test: Further synthesis and appraisal." *Review of Educational Research*, Vol. 60, No. 3 (fall): 373-417.

Becker, William, and Rosen, Sherwin. 1990. "The Learning Effect of Assessment and Evaluation in High School." Economics Research Center, NORC Discussion Paper #7, June.

Bennett, Randy E., Donald A. Rock, and Minhwei Wang. 1991. "Equivalence and Free-Response and Multiple-Choice Items." *Journal of Educational Measurement*, Vol. 28, No. 1 (spring): 77-92

Betts, Julian R. 1998. "The Impact of Educational Standards on the Level and Distribution of Earnings." Department of Economics, University of California, San Diego, mimeo.

Betts, Julian R., and Robert M. Costrell. 2001. "Incentives and Equity under Standards-Based Reform," in Diane Ravitch, ed. *Brookings Papers on Education Policy*, Washington, DC.

Bishop, John H. 1988a. "The Economics of Employment Testing," Working Paper #88-14. Cornell University, School of Industrial and Labor Relations, Center for Advanced Human Resource Studies.

Bishop, John H. 1988b. "Employment Testing and Incentives to Learn," *Journal of Vocational Behavior*, Vol. 33: 404-423.

Bishop, John H. 1989a. "Incentives for Learning: Why American High School Students Compare So Poorly to Their Counterparts Overseas," Working Paper #89-09. Cornell University School of Industrial and Labor Relations.

Bishop, John H. 1989b. "Why the Apathy in American High Schools?" *Educational Researcher*, Vol. 18, No. 1 (January–February): 6-10.

Bishop, John H. 1991. "A Program of Research on the Role of Employer Training in Ameliorating Skill Shortages and Enhancing Productivity and Competitiveness." Philadelphia: University of Pennsylvania, National Center on the Educational Quality of the Workforce, November 19.

Bishop, John H. 1994a. "Impact of Curriculum-Based Examinations on Learning in Canadian Secondary Schools," Working Paper #94-30, Center for Advanced Human Resource Studies, New York State School of Industrial and Labor Relations, Cornell University, Ithaca, NY, December.

Bishop, John H. 1994b. "Impacts of School Organization and Signaling on Incentives to Learn in France, The Netherlands, England, Scotland, and the United States," Working Paper #94-30. Center for Advanced Human Resource Studies, New York State School of Industrial and Labor Relations, Cornell University, Ithaca, NY, December.

Bishop, John H. 1994c. "Schooling, Learning and Worker Productivity," in Rita Asplund, ed. *Human Capital Creation in an Economic Perspective*. Helsinki: Physica-Verlag.

Bishop, John H. 1995a. "Education Quality and the Economy." Paper presented at the Seventh International Conference on Socio-Economics of the Society for the Advancement of Socio-Economics, Arlington, VA, April 8.

Bishop, John H. 1995b. "Improving Education: How Large are the Benefits? How Can It Be Done Efficiently?" Testimony presented at a hearing entitled, "Education's Impact on Economic Competitiveness," before the Senate Subcommittee on Education, Arts, and Humanities, Committee on Labor and Human Resources of the United States Senate, Thursday, February 2.

Bishop, John H. 1995c. "The Power of External Standards." *American Educator* (fall).

Bishop, John H. 1996. "Signaling the Competencies of High School Students to Employers," in Lauren B. Resnick and John G. Wirt, eds. *Linking School and Work: Roles for Standards and Assessment*. San Francisco: Jossey-Bass.

Bishop, John H. 1997a. "The Effect of Curriculum-Based Exit Exam Systems on Student Achievement," Working Paper #97-15. Cornell University, School of Industrial and Labor Relations, Center for Human Resource Studies.

Bishop, John H. 1997b. "The Effect of National Standard and Curriculum-Based Exams on Achievement," Working Paper #97-01. Cornell University, School of Industrial and Labor Relations, Center for Human Resource Studies.

Bishop, John H. 1999a. "Are National Exit Examinations Important for Educational Efficiency?" *Swedish Economic Policy Review*.

Bishop, John H. 1999b. "Nerd Harassment, Incentives, School Priorities, and Learning," in Susan Mayer and Paul Peterson, eds. *Earning and Learning*. Washington, DC: Brookings Institution.

Bishop, John H. 2000. "Diplomas for Learning: Not for Seat Time." *Economics of Education Review* (summer).

Bishop, John H. 2001. "International Evidence on the Effects of External Exams," in *Why do Students Learn More When Achievement is Examined Externally?* in *Education Next* (winter).

Bishop, John H., F. Mane, M. Bishop, and J. Moriarty. 2001. "The Role of End-of-Course Exams and Minimum Competency Exams in Standards-Based Reforms," in Diane Ravitch, ed. *Brookings Papers on Education Policy*, Washington, DC.

Black, Lisa. 2001. "Parents Fault Way Schools Grade Kids." *Chicago Tribune*, August 27.

Blum, Justin 2002. "Grade Changes Found at Top D.C. School: Teacher's Discoveries at Wilson High Prompt Investigation." *Washington Post*, June 9, C01.

Bobrow, Jerry. 1994. *Cliffs SAT I Preparation Guide*. Lincoln, NE: Cliffs Notes.

Bond, Linda A., and Darla A. Cohen. 1991. "The Early Impact of Indiana Statewide Testing for Educational Progress on Local Education Agencies," in Rita G. O'Sullivan and Robert E. Stake, eds. *Advances in Program Evaluation*, Vol. 1, Part B. Greenwich, CT: JAI Press.

Boothroyd, Roger A. et al. 1992. "What Do Teachers Know about Measurement and How Did They Find Out?" Paper presented at the Annual Meeting of the National Council on Measurement in Education, San Francisco, CA, April.

Boser, Ulrich. 2000. "States Face Limited Choices in Assessment Market." *Education Week*, March 8.

Boudreau, John W. 1983. "Economic Considerations in Estimating the Utility of Human Resource Productivity Improvement Programs." *Personnel Management*, No. 36.

Boudreau, John W., and Sara L. Rynes. 1985. "Role of Recruitment in Staffing Utility Analysis." *Journal of Applied Psychology*, Vol. 70, No. 2: 354-366.

Boudreau, John W. 1988. "Utility Analysis for Decisions in Human Resource Management," Working Paper #88-21. New York State School of Industrial and Labor Relations, Cornell University, December.

Bracey, Gerald W. 1989. "The $150 Million Redundancy." *Phi Delta Kappan*, 70(9), May: 698-702.

Breneman, David W., William N. Haarlow, Robert M. Costrell, David H. Ponitz, and Laurence Steinberg. 1998. "Remediation in Higher Education: A Symposium." Thomas P. Fordham Foundation, July.

Briggs, Derek C. 2001. "The Effect of Admissions Test Preparation." *Chance* (winter).

Bridgeman, Brent. 1991. "Essays and Multiple-Choice Tests as Predictors of College Freshman GPA." *Research in Higher Education*, Vol. 32, No. 2 (June): 319-32.

Bridgeman, Brent, Laura McCamley-Jenkins, and Nancy Ervine. 2000. *Predictions of Freshman Grade-Point Average from the Revised and Recentered SAT I: Reasoning Test*. Report No. 2000-1. New York: College Entrance Examination Board.

Brogden, Hubert E. 1959. "Efficiency of Classification as a Function of Number of Jobs, Per Cent Rejected, and the Validity and Intercorrelation of Job Performance Estimates." *Educational and Psychological Measurement*, Vol.19, No. 2.

Brookhart, Susan M. 1993. "Teachers' Grading Practices: Meaning and Values." *Journal of Educational Measurement*, Vol. 30, No. 2 (summer).

Brown, Steven M., and Herbert J. Walberg. 1993. "Motivational Effects on Test Scores of Elementary Students. *Journal of Educational Research*, Vol. 86, No. 3 (January-February): 133-36.

Business Roundtable. 2001. *Assessing and Addressing the "Testing Backlash."* Washington, DC: Author.

California Teachers Association. 2001. "High Stakes are for Tomatoes, Say Resisters." *California Educator*, Vol. 5, No. 5 (February).

Camara, Wayne. 2001. "Is Commercial Coaching for the SAT I Worth the Money?" CollegeBoard.

Cameron, Judy and W. David Pierce. 1994. "Reinforcement, Reward, and Intrinsic and Extrinsic Motivation: A Meta-Analysis." *Review of Educational Research*, Vol. 64, No. 3(fall): 363-423.

Cameron, Judy, and W. David Pierce. 1996. "The Debate about Rewards and Intrinsic Motivation: Protests and Accusations Do Not Alter the Results." *Review of Educational Research*, Vol. 66, No. 1 (spring): 39-51.

Cannell, John J. 1987. *Nationally Normed Elementary Achievement Testing in America's Public Schools: How All Fifty States are Above the National Average* (2nd ed.). Daniels, WV: Friends for Education.

Carnine, Douglas. 2000. Why Education Experts Resist Effective Practices. Thomas P. Fordham Foundation, Washington, DC. (http://www.edexcellence.net/library/carnine.html), April.

Carter, Kathy. 1984. "Do Teachers Understand Principles for Writing Tests? *Journal of Teacher Education,* 35(6): 57-60.

Caterall, James. 1990. *Estimating the Costs and Benefits of Large-Scale Assessments: Lessons from Recent Research.* CSE Technical Report 319, CRESST/UCLA, November.

Celubuski, Carin, Elizabeth Farris, and Shelley Burns. 1998. *Status of Education Reform in Public Elementary and Secondary Schools: Principals' Perspectives.* National Center for Education Statistics, Statistical Analysis Report, May.

Chaney, Bradford, and Kenneth Burgdorf. 1997. "Influencing Achievement Through High School Graduation Requirements." *Educational Evaluation and Policy Analysis*, Vol. 19, No. 3 (fall).

Chrysler Learning Connection and Peter D. Hart Associates. 1993. "National Survey of American Youth," August.

Cizek, Gregory J. 1990. "The Case Against the SAT," book review. *Educational and Psychological Measurement*, 50(3) (autumn):705.

Cizek, Gregory J. 1991. "Confusion Effusion: A Rejoinder to Wiggins." *Phi Delta Kappan*, Vol. 73, No. 2 (October): 150–153.

Cizek, Gregory J. 1994. "In Defense of the Test." *The American Psychologist,* Vol. 49, No. 6: 525-526.

Cizek, Gregory J. 1995. "Further Investigation of Teachers' Assessment Practices." Paper presented at the Annual Meeting of the American Educational Research Association, San Francisco, April.

Cizek, Gregory J. 1996. "Grades: The Final Frontier in Assessment Reform." *NASSP Bulletin*, December.

Cizek, Gregory J. 1999. *Cheating on Tests: How to Do It, Detect It, and Prevent It.* Mahwah, NJ: Lawrence Erlbaum Associates.

Cizek, Gregory J. 2000. "Pockets of Resistance in the Assessment Revolution." *Educational Measurement: Issues and Practice,* Vol. 19, No. 2 (summer).

Cizek, Gregory J. 2002. "More Unintended Consequences of High-Stakes Testing." *Educational Measurement: Issues and Practice,* Vol. 21, No. 1 (winter).

Cizek, Gregory J., Shawn M. Fitzgerald, and Robert E. Rachor. 1995/1996. "Teachers' Assessment Practices: Preparation, Isolation, and the Kitchen Sink." *Educational Assessment*, Vol. 3, No. 2: 159-179.

Clarke, Marguerite, George Madus, Catherine Horn, and Miguel Ramos. 2001. *The Marketplace for Educational Testing*. The National Board on Educational Testing and Public Policy, Vol. 2, No. 3, April.

Clopton, Paul, Wayne Bishop,and David Klein. 1999. *Statewide Mathematics Assessment in Texas*. Mathematically Correct. (http://www.mathematicallycorrect.com/lonestar.htm).

Clotfelter, Charles T., and Helen F. Ladd. 1996. "Recognizing and Rewarding Success in Public Schools," in H. F. Ladd, ed. *Holding Schools Accountable: Performance-Based Reform in Education*. Washington, DC: Brookings Institution.

Cohen, S. Alan, and Joan S. Hyman. 1991. "Can Fantasies Become Facts?" *Educational Measurement: Issues and Practice*, (spring): 20-23

Cole, Nancy, and Warren Willingham. 1997. *Gender and Fair Assessment*. Princeton, NJ: ETS.

College Entrance Examination Board. 1988. *Guide to the College Board Validity Study Service*. New York, Author.

Corbett, H. Dickson, and Bruce L. Wilson. 1991. *Testing, Reform, and Rebellion*. Norwood, NJ: Ablex.

Costrell, Robert M. 1993. "An Economic Analysis of College Admission Standards." *Education Economics*, Vol. 1, No. 3.

Costrell, Robert M. 1993. "Can National Educational Standards Raise Welfare." Mimeo. November.

Costrell, Robert M. 1994. "A Simple Model of Educational Standards." *American Economic Review*, Vol. 84, No. 4 (September): 956-971.

Coulson, Andrew J. 1999. *Market Education: The Unknown History*. New Brunswick, NJ: Transaction Publishers.

Crossen, Cynthia. 1994. *Tainted Truth: The Manipulation of Fact in America*. New York: Touchstone.

Cutler, William W. III. 2000. *Parents and Schools: The 150-Year Struggle for Control of American Education*. Chicago: University of Chicago Press.

DAEU: le diplome de la seconde chance. 1996. *Le Monde de l'Education* 241 (October): 81-84.

Darling-Hammond, Linda. 2002. "Emerging Issues in Teacher Performance Assessment." Talk delivered at Princeton, NJ, October 30.

DerSimonian and Laird. 1983. "Evaluating the Effect of Coaching on SAT Scores: A Meta-Analysis." *Harvard Educational Review* 53: 1-5.

Din, Feng S. 1996. "The Impact of Kentucky State Testing on Educational Practices in Kentucky Public Schools." Paper presented at the Annual Meeting of the Eastern Educational Research Association, Cambridge, MA, February (ERIC: ED405352).

Driesler, Stephen D. 2001. "Whiplash from Backlash? The Truth about Public Support for Testing." *Newsletter of the National Council on Measurement in Education*, September.

Durham, Gisele. 2000. "Study Finds Lying, Cheating in Teens." Associated Press, October 16.

Ebel, Robert L. 1961. "Must All Tests Be Valid?" *American Psychologist*, Vol. 16: 640-647.

Ebel, Robert L. 1981. "The Social Consequences of Not Testing," in William B. Schrader, ed. *Admissions Testing and the Public Interest*. New Directions for Testing and Measurement. San Francisco: Jossey-Bass, November 9.

Eckstein, Max A., and Harold J. Noah. 1993. *Secondary School Examinations: International Perspectives on Policies and Practice.* New Haven, CT: Yale University Press.

Education Daily. 1998. "Diversity Takes Back Seat to Standards in New Poll," July 30, pp. 3,4.

Education Week. 1992. "By All Measures: 8 Questions: On Cost, Impact, The Politics of Who Chooses," June 17.

Education Week on the Web. 1997. "News in Brief: Test Violations Uncovered," August 6, p. 5.

Educational Measurement: Issues and Practice. 1988. Summer.

Egeland, Paul Charles. 1995. "The Effect of Authentic Assessments on Fifth-Grade Student Science Achievement and Attitudes." Ed.D diss., Northern Illinois University.

Elliott, Janet, and Bryant Saletheia. 2002. "With Scoring Standards Lowered, More Passing TAAS." *Houston Chronicle*, May 16.

Erickson, Judith B. 1991. *Indiana Youth Poll: Youths' Views of High School Life.* Indianapolis: Indiana Youth Institute.

Erickson, Judith B. 1992. *Indiana Youth Poll: Youths' Views of Life Beyond High School.* Indianapolis: Indiana Youth Institute.

FairTest. 1997. "How the States Scored," and "Vermont," *FairTest Examiner,* summer, p.1, and pp.1-3,

FairTest. 1998. "Testing Our Children: Introduction." Cambridge: Author, p.2.

FairTest 2001. "The SAT: Questions and Answers." Cambridge: Author, last updated August 28.

Farkus, Steve, Jean Johnson, Will Friedman, Ali Bers, and Chris Perry. 1996. *Given the Circumstances: Teachers Talk About Public Education Today.* New York: Public Agenda.

Farkus, Steve, Jean Johnson, and Ann Duffet. 1997. *Different Drummers: How Teachers of Teachers View Public Education.* New York: Public Agenda.

Farkus, Steve, Jean Johnson, John Immerwahr, and Joanna McHugh. 1998. *Time to Move On: African-American and White Parents Set an Agenda for Public Schools.* New York: Public Agenda.

Feinberg, Lawrence. 1990. "Multiple-Choice and Its Critics: Are the 'Alternatives' Any Better?" *The College Board Review*, No. 157 (fall): 13-17, 30-31.

Ferguson, Ronald F. 1991. "Paying for Public Education: New Evidence on How and Why Money Matters." *Harvard Journal on Legislation* 28(2): 465-498.

Ferrara, Steven, Joseph Willhoft, Carolyn Seburn, Frank Slaughter, and Jose Stevenson. 1991. "Local Assessments Designed to Parallel Statewide Minimum Competency Tests: Benefits and Drawbacks," in Rita G. O'Sullivan and Robert E. Stake, eds. *Advances in Program Evaluation: Effects of Mandated Assessment on Teaching.* Greenwich, CT: JAI Press.

Fincher, Cameron. 1978. "Beyond Bakke: The Positive Benefits of Testing," Paper presented at a Seminar for State Leaders in Postsecondary Education, New Orleans, LA, October.

Finn, Chester E., Jr. 1991. *We Must Take Charge: Our Schools and Our Future.* New York: Free Press.

Fiske, Edward B. 1989. "Questioning an American Rite of Passage: How valuable is the S.A.T.?" *New York Times*, January 18, B10.

Frary, Robert B. 1982. "Social Consequences of Not Testing." *New Directions for Testing and Measurement*, No. 16 (December): 147-52.

Frary, Robert B., Lawrence H. Cross, Larry J. Weber. 1993. "Testing and Grading Practices and Opinions of Secondary School Teachers of Academic Subjects: Implications for Instruction in Measurement." *Educational Measurement: Issues and Practice*, Vol. 12, No. 3: 23+.

Fredericksen, Norman. 1994. *The Influence of Minimum Competency Tests on Teaching and Learning*. Princeton, NJ: Educational Testing Service.

Freeman, Kirk Alan. 1994. "Effect of Selected Student Incentives on Average Daily Attendance Rates, Student Dropout Rates and Academic Performance in Indiana Senior High Schools." Ph.D diss., Indiana State University.

Gearhart, Meryl, and Herman, Joan L. 1996. "Portfolio Assessment: Whose Work Is It?" *Evaluation Comment*, CSE, CRESST, winter.

Gevirtz, Leslie. 2001. "More College Students Drop Out than Graduate." Reuters News Service, August 15.

Glasnapp, Douglas R., John P. Poggio, and M. David Miller. 1991. "Impact of a 'Low Stakes' State Minimum Competency Testing Program on Policy, Attitudes, and Achievement," in Rita G. O'Sullivan and Robert E. Stake, eds. *Advances in Program Evaluation: Effects of Mandated Assessment on Teaching*. Greenwich, CT: JAI Press.

Goldberg, Bernard. 2002. *Bias: A CBS Insider Exposes How the Media Distort the News*. Washington, DC: Regnery.

Goldberg, Debbie. 1996. "Buying a Better Score." *Washington Post Education Review*, October 27, p. 21.

Goldberg, Debbie. 1996. "Putting the SAT to the Test." *Washington Post Education Review*, October 27, pp. 20-21.

Goldberg, Gail, and B. S. Roswell. 1999/2000. "From Perception to Practice: The Impact of Teachers' Scoring Experience on Performance-Based Instruction and Classroom Assessment." *Educational Assessment*, 6(4): 257-290.

Graham, Amy, and Thomas Husted. 1993. "Understanding State Variation in SAT Scores." *Economics of Education Review*, Vol. 12, No. 3: 197-202.

Gray, C. Boyden, and Evan J. Kemp, Jr. 1993. "Flunking Testing: Is Too Much Fairness Unfair to School Kids?" *Washington Post*, September 19, C3.

Greene, Jay. 2000a. "Texas Education Miracle No Mirage." *City Journal*. New York: Manhattan Institute.

Greene, Jay P. 2000b. *The Cost of Remedial Education: How Much Michigan Pays When Students Fail to Learn Basic Skills*. Midland, MI: Mackinac Center for Public Policy, September.

Griffin, Bryan W., and Mark H. Heidorn. 1996. "An Examination of the Relationship Between Minimum Competency Test Performance and Dropping Out of High School." *Educational Evaluation and Policy Analysis*, Vol. 18, No. 3 (fall): 243-252.

Grissmer, David, and Ann Flanagan. 1998. *Exploring Rapid Score Gains in Texas and North Carolina*. RAND National Education Goals Panel, Washington, DC, November.

Grissmer, David W., Ann Flanagan, Jennifer Kawata, Stephanie Williamson. 2000. *Improving Student Achievement: What NAEP State Test Scores Tell Us*. RAND, July.

Gross, Martin L. 1999. *The Conspiracy of Ignorance: The Failure of American Public Schools*. New York: Harper Collins.

Gullickson, Arlen R., and Ellwein, Mary C. 1985. "Post-hoc Analysis of Teacher-Made Tests: The Goodness of Fit between Prescription and Practice. *Educational Measurement: Issues and Practice,* 4(1): 15-18.

Haladyna, T. H., N. S., Haas, and S. B. Nolan. 1989. *Test Score Pollution* (Technical Report 89-1. Phoenix: Arizona State University West

Haney, Walter M. 2000. "The Myth of the Texas Miracle in Education." *Education Policy Analysis Archives*, Vol. 8, No. 41 (http://olam.ed.asu.edu/epaa/v8n41).

Haney, Walter M., George F. Madaus, and Robert Lyons. 1993. *The Fractured Marketplace for Standardized Testing*. Boston: Kluwer.

Hannaway, Jane, and Shannon McKay. 2001. "School Accountability and Student Achievement: The Case of Houston." *Education Next* (fall).

Hartigan, John A., and Alexandra K. Wigdor. 1989. *Fairness in Employment Testing: Validity Generalization, Minority Issues, and the General Aptitude Test Battery*. Washington, DC: National Academy Press.

Hensher, David A., and Truong P. Truong. 1985. "Valuation of Travel Time Savings: A Direct Experimental Approach." *Journal of Transport Economics and Policy*, Vol. 19, No. 3 (September): 237-262.

Hernstein, R. J., and Charles Murray. 1992. "But We're Ignoring Gifted Kids: Those Low SAT Scores Reflect Too Many Years of 'Dumbing Down,'" *Washington Post*, February 2.

Heubert, Jay P., and Robert P. Hauser, eds. 1999. *High-Stakes: Testing for Tracking, Promotion, and Graduation*. Washington, DC: National Research Council.

Heyneman, Stephen P., and Angela W. Ransom. 1990. "Using Examinations and Testing to Improve Educational Quality," World Bank. *Educational Policy* 4, No. 3: 177-192.

Heyneman, Stephen P. 1987. *Uses of Examinations in Developing Countries: Selection, Research, and Education Sector Management*, Seminar Paper No. 36. Economic Development Institute, The World Bank

Hill, Paul T., and Mary Beth Celio. 1998. *Fixing Urban Schools*. Washington, DC: Brookings Institution.

Hills, John R. 1991. "Apathy toward Testing and Grading." *Phi Delta Kappan*, 72, 540-545.

Hirsch, E. D., Jr. 1996. *The Schools We Need & Why We Don't Have Them*. New York: Doubleday.

Hoff, David J. 2000a. "Testing Foes Hope to Stoke Middle-Class Ire." *Education Week*, March 22.

Hoff, David J. 2000b. "Polls Dispute a 'Backlash' to Standards." *Education Week*, October 11.

Hoffer, Thomas B. 1997. "High School Graduation Requirements: Effects on Dropping Out and Student Achievement." *Teachers College Record*, Vol. 98, No. 4 (summer).

Holland, Robert. 2001. *Indispensable Tests: How a Value-Added Approach to School Testing Could Identify and Bolster Exceptional Teaching*. Arlington, VA: Lexington Institute, December.

Horatio Alger Association. 1996. *The Mood of American Youth, 1996*. Alexandria, VA: Author.

Houston, Paul. 2000. "Side Effects of High Stakes Tests." *Washington Times*, July 3.

Hunter, John E., and Frank L. Schmidt. 1982. "Fitting People to Jobs: The Impact of Personnel Selection on National Productivity," in Marvin D. Dunnette and Edwin A. Fleishman, eds. *Human Performance and Productivity: Volume 1—Human Capability Assessment*. Hillsdale, NJ: Lawrence Erlbaum Associates.

Hunter, John E. 1983. *The Economic Benefits of Personnel Selection Using Ability Tests: A State of the Art Review Including a Detailed Analysis of the Dollar Benefit of U.S. Employment Service Placements and a Critique of the Low-Cutoff Method of Test Use*. USES Test Research Report No. 47. Washington, DC: Employment and Training Administration (DOL).

Hunter, John E. 1983. *Test Validation for 12,000 Jobs: An Application of Job Classification and Validity Generalization Analysis to the General Aptitude Test Battery*. Washington, DC: U.S. Employment Service, Department of Labor.

Hunter, John E., and Frank L. Schmidt. 1983. "Quantifying the Effects of Psychological Interventions on Employee Job Performance and Work-Force Productivity." *American Psychologist*, April, 473-478.

Hunter, John E., and R. F. Hunter. 1984. "Validity and Utility of Alternative Predictors of Job Performance." *Psychological Bulletin*, Vol. 96, No. 1.

Impara, James C., and Barbara S. Plake. 1996. "Professional Development in Student Assessment for Educational Administrators." *Educational Measurement: Issues and Practice,* 15(2): 14-20.

Ingels, Steven J., Barbara L. Schneider, Leslie A. Scott, Stephen B. Plank, and Shi-Chang Wu. 1995. *A Profile of the American High School Sophomore in 1990.* Washington, DC: National Center for Education Statistics, U.S. Education Department.

Jacob, Brian A. 2001. "Getting Tough?" *Educational Evaluation and Policy Analysis* (fall).

Jacobs, Joanne. 2002. "Tests of Character." ReadJacobs.com and FoxNews.com, April 8.

Jacobson, Jonathan E. 1992. "Mandatory Testing Requirements and Pupil Achievement." Mimeo. Massachusetts Institute of Technology, October 29.

Jaeger, Richard M. 1991. "Legislative Perspectives on Statewide Testing," in "Accountability as a Reform Strategy." *Phi Delta Kappan*, November.

Jencks, Christopher, and J. Crouse. 1982. "Aptitude vs. Achievement: Should We Replace the SAT?" *Public Interest*, No. 67 (spring).

Jerald, Craig D. 2001. *Real Results, Remaining Challenges: The Story of Texas Education Reform.* The Business Roundtable, Washington, DC.

Jett, Daniel L., and William D. Schafer. 1993. "High School Teachers' Attitudes toward a Statewide High Stakes Student Performance Assessment." Paper presented at the Annual Meeting of the American Educational Research Association, Atlanta, April.

Johnson, Jean, and John Immerwahr. 1994. *First Things First: What Americans Expect from the Public Schools*. New York: Public Agenda.

Johnson, Jean, Steve Farkas, Will Friedman, John Immerwahr, and Ali Bers. 1995. *Assignment Incomplete: The Unfinished Business of Education Reform.* New York: Public Agenda.

Johnson, Jean, Steve Farkas, Ali Bers, Will Friedman, and Ann Duffett. 1997. *Getting By: What American Teenagers Really Think about Their Schools*. New York: Public Agenda.

Johnson, Jean, with Ann Duffett. 1999. *Standards and Accountability: Where the Public Stands: A Report from Public Agenda for the 1999 National Education Summit*. Public Agenda, September 30.

Jones, Jean Birkhead. 1993. "Effects of the Use of Altered Testing/Grading Method on the Retention and Success of Students Enrolled in College Mathematics." Ed.D. diss., East Texas State University.

Johnson, Joseph F., Uri Treisman, and Ed Fuller. 2000. "Testing in Texas." *School Administrator*, Vol. 57 No. 11 (December): 20-24, 26.

Johnson, Valen E. 2002. "An A Is an A Is an A.... And That's the Problem." *New York Times*, April 14.

Jozefowicz, Ralph F., B. M. Koeppen, S. Case et al. 2002. "The Quality of In-House Medical School Examinations." *Academic Medicine*, Vol. 77, 156-161.

Kane, Thomas J., Douglas O. Staiger, and J. Geppert. 2002. "Randomly Accountable." *Education Next* (spring).

Kang, Suk. 1985. "A Formal Model of School Reward Systems," in John H. Bishop, ed. *Incentives, Learning, and Employability.* Ohio State University, National Center for Research in Vocational Education.

Kaufman, P., Kwon, J., Klein, S., and Chapman, C. 1999. *Dropout Rates in the United States: 1998*. Washington, DC: U.S. Education Department, National Center for Education Statistics.

Kellaghan, Thomas, George F. Madaus, and Anastasia Raczek. 1996. *The Use of External Examinations to Improve Students Learning*. Washington, DC: American Educational Research Association.

Khalaf, Abdulkhalig S. S., and Gerald S. Hanna. 1992. "The Impact of Classroom Testing Frequency on High School Students' Achievement." *Contemporary Educational Psychology*, Vol. 17, No. 1(January): 71-77.

Kiesler, Charles A. 1998. "On SAT Cause and Effect." *Education Week*, May 13, p. 43.

Klein, Stephen P., Laura S. Hamilton, Daniel F. McCaffrey, and Brian M. Stecher. 2000. *What Do Test Scores in Texas Tell Us?* Santa Monica, CA: RAND Education.

Koretz, Daniel et al. 1992. *The Reliability of Scores from the 1992 Vermont Portfolio Assessment Program*. Technical Report No. 355, Los Angeles: CRESST, December.

Koretz, Daniel. 1996. "Using Student Assessments for Educational Accountability," in E. A. Hanushek and D. W. Jorgenson, eds. *Improving America's Schools: The Role of Incentives*. Washington, DC: National Academy Press.

Kozloff, Martin A. "Constructivism in Education: Sophistry for a New Age." Mimeo. May 1998.

Kramer, Rita. 1991. *Ed School Follies*. New York: Free Press.

Kuhs, T., A. Porter, R. Floden, D. Freeman, W. Schmidt, and J. Schwille. 1985. "Differences Among Teachers in their Use of Curriculum-Embedded Tests." *The Elementary School Journal*, Vol. 86, No. 2: 141-153.

Kulik, James A., Bangert-Drowns, Robert L., and Kulik. 1984. "Effectiveness of Coaching for Aptitude Tests." *Psychological Bulletin* 95: 179-188.

Lee, Jaekyung. 1997. "Multilevel Linkings between State Policies and Educational Outcomes: An Evaluation of Standards-Based Education Reform in the United States." Ph.D diss., University of Chicago.

Lemann, Nicholas. 1999. *The Big Test*. New York: Farrar, Straus, and Giroux.

Lerner, Barbara. 1990. "Good News About American Education." *Commentary*, Vol. 91, No. 3 (March).

Levin, Henry. 1994. "Can Education Do It Alone?" *Economics of Education Review*, Vol. 13, No. 2 (June): 99.

Levin, Henry. 2000. "High Stakes Testing and Economic Productivity," in Orfield, Gary and M. Kornhaber, eds. *Raising Standards or Raising Barriers? Inequality and High Stakes Testing in Public Education*. New York: Century Foundation.

Ligon, Glynn et al. 1990. "Statewide Testing in Texas." A Symposium presented at the Annual Meeting of the Southwest Educational Research Association, Austin, Texas, January 25-27.

Lindsay, Drew. 2000. "CON-Test." *Education Week on the Web*, April 5.

Lindsay, Drew. 2001. "Against the Establishment: Father of the SOLs." *Washington Post*, November 11, W24.

Linn, Robert L. 1995. *Assessment-Based Reform: Challenges to Educational Measurement*. William H. Angoff Memorial Lecture Series, Educational Testing Service, Princeton, New Jersey, August.

Linn, Robert L. 2000. "Assessment and Accountability." CRESST, November 1998, or *Education Researcher*, January.

Lumley, Dale R., and Wenfan Yen. 2001. "The Impact of State Mandated, Large-Scale Writing Assessment Policies in Pennsylvania." Paper presented at the Annual Meeting of the American Educational Research Association Seattle, April.

Madaus, George F. 1991. "The Effects of Important Test on Students: Implications for a National Examination System." *Phi Delta Kappan*. November.

Madaus, George F., and Thomas Kellaghan. 1991. "Student Examination Systems in the European Community: Lessons for the United States." Contractor report submitted to the Office of Technology Assessment, Washington, DC, June.

Mangino, Evangelina, and Marilyn A. Babcock. 1986. "Minimum Competency Testing: Helpful or Harmful for High Level Skills." Paper presented at the annual meeting of the American Educational Research Association, San Francisco.

Manzo, Kathleen Kennedy. 1997. "North Carolina Consensus Pushes for New Set of Reforms." *Education Week on the Web*, April 9.

Maroon, Suzy. 1997. "Measuring Success in School," [letter to the editor]. *Washington Post*, August 30, A26.

Martin, Michael O., Ina V.S. Mullis, Eugenio J. Gonzalez, Teresa A. Smith, and Dana L. Kelly. 1999. *School Contexts for Learning and Instruction: IEA's Third International Mathematics and Science Study (TIMSS)*. Chestnut Hill, MA: Boston College.

Mathews, Jay. 2000. "The Downside of High-Stakes Tests," *Washington Post*, Aug.1, p. A9.

Mathews, Jay. 2001a. "The Chosen Ones: Students Say Favoritism by Teachers Can Affect the Entire Class; Educators Say It's Hard to Avoid." *Washington Post*, January 2.

Mathews, Jay. 2001b. "Pupils Cheat Expectations: Schools Hope Students Learn From Mistakes Without Harsh Penalties." *Washington Post*, October 28, C1, C9.

Mathews, Jay. 2002. "Don't Panic Over Test Scores." *Washington Post*, February 19.

May, Lucy. 1995. "Test Don't Have All the Answers to How Ky. Kids Rank." *Lexington Herald-Leader*, July 6.

May, Meredith. 2001. "Measuring Minds: Backlash Hits High-Stakes Test." *San Francisco Chronicle*, April 29.

McMillan, James H. 2001. "Secondary Teachers' Classroom Assessment and Grading Practices." *Educational Measurement: Issues and Practice*, Vol. 20, No. 1 (spring).

McMorris, Robert F., and Roger A. Boothroyd. 1992. "Tests that Teachers Build: An Analysis of Classroom Tests in Science and Mathematics." Paper presented at the Annual Meeting of the National Council on Measurement in Education, San Francisco, CA, April.

McNeil, Linda M. 2000. *Contradictions of School Reform: Educational Costs of Standardized Testing*. New York: Routledge.

McNeil, Linda, and Angela Valenzuela. 2000. "The Harmful Impact of the TAAS System of Testing in Texas: Beneath the Accountability Rhetoric," The Civil Rights Project, Harvard University,

Mehrens, William. 1998. "Consequences of Assessment: What is the Evidence?" *Education Policy Analysis Archives*, Vol. 6, No. 13, July 14.

Mehrens, William, and Gregory Cizek. 2001. "Standard Setting and the Public Good: Benefits Accrued and Anticipated," in Gregory J. Cizek ed. *Setting Performance Standards: Concepts, Methods, and Perspectives*. Mahwah, NJ: Lawrence Erlbaum.

Meier, Deborah. 2000. *Will Standards Save Public Education?* (with a foreword by Jonathan Kozol). Boston: Beacon Press.

Merrow, John. 2001. "That Sinking Feeling." *Education Week*, October 17, pp. 32, 35.

Merrow, John. 2002. "Testing Our Schools" (radio interview). *Washington Post Live Online*, March 29, 11a.m. (EST).

Messick, Samuel, and Ann Jungeblut. 1981. "Time and Method in Coaching for the SAT." *Psychological Bulletin* 89: 191-216.

Meyers, Susan Luscetti. 2001. "DETRIMENT TO STUDENTS: Education ReformersTake Aim at Flawed, Incomplete Research." *Atlanta Journal-Constitution*, October 3, A14.

Mintz, John. 2000. "An Education 'Miracle' or Mirage?" *Washington Post*. April 21, A1, 4.

Mitchell, Joyce Slayton. 1998. "A Word to High School Seniors—SATs Don't Get You In." *Education Week*, May 29, p.33.

Mohring, Herbert. 1983. "The Value of Travel Time." Chapter 5 in *Transportation Economics*. Cambridge, MA: Ballinger.

Molpus, David. 1998. "Improving High School Education." *National Public Radio Morning Edition*, September 15.

Moore, K. 2000. *State-Mandated Educational Assessments: Survey of Parents' Perceptions*. Education Research Division, Harris Interactive, April.

Mullis, Ina V. et al. 1993. *1992 NAEP Trial State Assessment Data Compendium*. Washington DC: U.S. Education Department, National Center for Education Statistics.

Mullis, Ina V.S. 1997a. "Benchmarking toward World-class Standards: Some Characteristics of the Highest Performing School Systems in the TIMSS." Paper presented at panel "International Benchmarking: New Findings," at the Annual Meeting of the American Educational Research Association, Chicago, Illinois.

Mullis, Ina V.S. et al. 1997b. *Mathematics Achievement in the Primary School Years: IEA's Third International Mathematics and Science Study*. Chestnut Hill, MA: Boston College.

Mullis, Ina V.S., Michael O. Martin, Albert E. Beaton, Eugenio J. Gonzalez, Dana L. Kelly, and Teresa A. Smith. 1998. *Mathematics and Science Achievement in the Final Year of Secondary School: IEA's Third International Mathematics and Science Study*. Chestnut Hill, MA: Boston College.

Murnane, Richard J., John B. Willet, and Frank Levy. 1995. "The Growing Importance of Cognitive Skills in Wage Determination." *The Review of Economics and Statistics*, Vol. 77, No. 2 (May): 251-266.

Murray, David, Joel Schwartz, and S. Robert Lichter. 2001. *It Ain't Necessarily So: How Media Make and Unmake the Scientific Picture of Reality*. Lanham, MD: Rowman & Littlefield Publishers.

Murray, David W. 1998. "The War Against Testing." *Commentary*, September, 34-37.

National Association for College Admission Counseling. 1996. "Members Assess 1996 Recruitment Cycle in Eighth Annual NACAC Admission Trends Survey." *News from National Association for College Admission Counseling*, October 28, pp. 2, 4.

National Association for College Admission Counseling. 1998. Telephone correspondence, August 14.

National Commission on Excellence in Education. 1983. *A Nation at Risk: The Imperatives for Educational Reform*. Washington, DC: U.S. Government Printing Office.

National Commission on Testing and Public Policy. 1990. *From +Gatekeeper to Gateway: Transforming Testing in America*. Chestnut Hill, MA: Author.

National Education Goals Panel. 2000. *Rising to the Test: Meeting the Challenges of Standards, Assessment and Accountability*. Downlink Site Facilitator's Guide. Author, December 6.

Nathan, Linda. 2000. "Habits of Mind." *Boston Review*, February/March.

NEA Today Online. 2001. "News: Interview: Lorrie Shepard: How to Fight a 'Death Star.'" Washington, DC: Author, January.

Neill, Monty. 1998. *High Stakes Tests Do Not Improve Student Learning*. Cambridge, MA: FairTest, January.

Nolan, Susan Bobbitt, Thomas M. Haladyna, and Nancy Haas. 1992. "Uses and Abuses of Achievement Test Scores." *Educational Measurement: Issues and Practice* (summer): 9-15.

Nolin, Mary Jo, Cassandra Rowand, Elizabeth Farris, and Judi Carpenter. 1994. *Public Elementary Teachers' Views on Teacher Performance Evaluations*. National Center for Education Statistics: Statistical Analysis Report, March.

Oakes, Jeannie. 1985. *Keeping Track*. New Haven, CT: Yale University Press.

Office of Technology Assessment. 1992. *Testing in American Schools: Asking the Right Questions*, OTA-SET-519, Washington, DC: U.S. Government Printing Office, February.

Olson, Lynn. 2000a. "Officials Worry About Pressures Placed on Assessments." *Education Week*, July 12.

Olson, Lynn. 2000b. "Poll Shows Public Concern Over Emphasis on Standardized Tests." *Education Week*, July 12.

Olson, Lynn. 2000c. "Test-Makers' Poll Finds Parents Value Testing." *Education Week*, August 2.

Olson, Lynn. 2000d. "CRESST to Become More Active in Guiding Accountability Systems." *Education Week*, September 27.

Orfield, Gary, and M. Kornhaber, eds. 2000. *Raising Standards or Raising Barriers? Inequality and High Stakes Testing in Public Education*. New York: Century Foundation.

Organisation for Economic Co-operation and Development. 1996. *Education at a Glance: OECD Indicators*. Centre for Education Research and Innovation, Paris.

Patterson, Chris. 2002. *From TAAS to TEKS: A Progress Report on New Assessments for Texas Public Schools*. Texas Public Policy Foundation, January.

Pelavin, Sol, and Michael Kane. 1990. *Changing the Odds*. New York: The College Board.

Perera, Andrea. 2002. "Death Threats Mailed to 6 Taft High School Teachers." *Los Angeles Times*, May 11.

Pertschuck, Michael. 1986. *Giant Killers*. New York: W.W. Norton

Peter, Lawrence J. 1993. *Peter's Quotations: Ideas for Our Times*. New York: Quill.

Phelps, Richard P. 1993a. "The Weak and Strong Arguments Against National Testing." *Education Week*, May 9.

Phelps, Richard P. 1993b. "National Testing: Pro and Con." *The Education Digest*, November.

Phelps, Richard P. 1994a. "Benefit-Cost Analyses of Testing Programs." Paper presented at the annual meeting of the American Education Finance Association, Nashville, TN.

Phelps, Richard P. 1994b. "The Economics of Standardized Testing." Paper presented at the annual meeting of the American Education Finance Association, Nashville, TN.

Phelps, Richard P. 1994c. "The Fractured Marketplace for Standardized Testing," book review. *Economics of Education Review*, Vol. 13, No. 4: 367-370.

Phelps, Richard P. 1996a. "Are U.S. Students the Most Heavily Tested on Earth?" *Educational Measurement: Issues and Practice*, Vol. 15, No. 3 (fall): 19-27.

Phelps, Richard P. 1996b. "Mis-Conceptualizing the Costs of Large-Scale Assessment." *Journal of Education Finance*, Vol. 21, No. 4 (spring).

Phelps, Richard P. 1996c. "Test Basher Benefit-Cost Analysis." *Network News & Views*, Educational Excellence Network, pp. 1-16, March.

Phelps, Richard P. 1997. "The Extent and Character of System-Wide Student Testing in the United States." *Educational Assessment*. Vol. 4, No. 2: 89-122.

Phelps, Richard P. 1998a. "Benefit-Cost Analysis of Systemwide Student Testing." Paper presented at the annual meeting of the American Education Finance Association, Mobile, AL.

Phelps, Richard P. 1998b. "The Demand for Standardized Student Testing." *Educational Measurement: Issues and Practice*, Vol. 17, No. 3 (fall): 5-23.

Phelps, Richard P. 1998c. "How U.S. Students Have it Easy (and Hard)." *Education Week*, September 9.

Phelps, Richard P. 1998d. "Test Basher Arithmetic." *Education Week*, March 11.

Phelps, Richard P. 1999a. "Education Establishment Bias? A Look at the National Research Council's Critique of Test Utility Studies." *The Industrial-Organizational Psychologist*, Vol. 36, No. 4 (April): 37-49.

Phelps, Richard P. 1999b. *Why Testing Experts Hate Testing*. Washington, DC: Thomas Fordham Foundation.

Phelps, Richard P. 2000b. "Cheating on Standardized Test Polls: School Administrators Tell the Public How to Think." *Commentaries and Reports*, EducationNews.org, July 11.

Phelps, Richard P. 2000c. "Estimating the Cost of Systemwide Student Testing in the United States." *Journal of Education Finance* (winter).

Phelps, Richard P. 2000d. "High Stakes: Testing for Tracking, Promotion, and Graduation," book review. *Educational and Psychological Measurement*, Vol. 60, No. 6 (December).

Phelps, Richard P. 2000e. "That 'Backlash' That Testing Opponents So Desperately Crave." *Commentaries and Reports*, EducationNews.org, August 8.

Phelps, Richard P. 2000f. "The Research Sez...Standardized Tests are Horrible and Terrible." *Commentaries and Reports*, EducationNews.org, July 25.

Phelps, Richard P. 2000g. "Trends in Large-Scale, External Testing Outside the United States." *Educational Measurement: Issues and Practice,* Vol. 19, No. 1: 11-21.

Phelps, Richard P. 2000h. "Walt Haney's Texas Mirage: Parts 1-4." *Commentaries and Reports*, EducationNews.org, September12-October 3.

Phelps, Richard P. 2000i. "Your Tax Dollars at Work: Testing Research at CRESST." *Commentaries and Reports*, EducationNews.org, October 17.

Phelps, Richard P. 2001a. "Test Bashing Texas." Opening Remarks: Debate on High-Stakes Testing, Annual Meeting of the American Association of Publishers—School Division, Austin, Texas, January 23.

Phelps, Richard P. 2001b. "More One-Sided Coverage of Testing Coming: CBS Sunday Morning." *Commentaries and Reports*, EducationNews.org, March.

Phelps, Richard P. 2001c. "The Formidable Anti-Student Testing Alliance." *Commentaries and Reports*, EducationNews.org, April.

Phelps, Richard P. 2001d. "An Encounter with the Politburo at the Peoples' Republic of the Web." *Commentaries and Reports*, EducationNews.org, August.

Phelps, Richard P. 2001e. "Benchmarking to the World's Best in Mathematics: Quality Control in Curriculum and Instruction Among the Top Performers in the TIMSS." *Evaluation Review*, Vol. 25, No. 4, (August): 391-439.

Phelps, Richard P. 2001f. "'School' Flunks." *Commentaries and Reports*, EducationNews.org, September.

Phelps, Richard P. 2001g. "SAT Bashing." *Commentaries and Reports*, EducationNews.org, November.

Phelps, Richard P. 2001h. "The Public Broadcasting System and the SAT: Secrets of the Education Press." *Commentaries and Reports*, EducationNews.org, November.

Phelps, Richard P. 2001i. "Three Essays in Public Policy: ...Issue Visibility in Congressional Voting." Ph.D. diss., University of Pennsylvania.

Phelps, Richard P. 2002a. "If 'Mainstream' Educators Trained the U.S. Olympic Team." *Commentaries and Reports*, EducationNews.org, January.

Phelps, Richard P. 2002b. "Estimating the Costs and Benefits of Educational Testing Programs." *Education Consumers ClearingHouse*, February.

Phelps, Richard P. 2002c. "Testing, Testing, Testing, Testing, Testing." *Commentaries and Reports*, EducationNews.org, April 2.

Phelps, Richard P. 2002d. "The *Merrow Report* on Standardized Testing: Can Education Journalism Get Any Worse?" *Commentaries and Reports*, EducationNews.org, April 16.

Phillips, Gary W., and Chester E. Finn, Jr. 1988. "The Lake Wobegon Effect: A Skeleton in the Testing Closet?" *Educational Measurement: Issues and Practice* (summer): 10-12.

Picus, Larry O., and Alisha Tralli. 1998. *Alternative Assessment Programs: What are the True Costs?* CSE Technical Report 441, Los Angeles: CRESST, February, p. 47.

Polivka, Anne E. 1996. "A Profile of Contingent Workers." *Monthly Labor Review*, October, pp.10-11.

Popham, W. James, and W. N. Kirby. 1987. "Recertification Tests for Teachers: A Defensible Safeguard for Society." *Phi Delta Kappan*, September.

Portner, Jessica. 2000. "Pressure to Pass Tests Permeates Va. Classrooms." *Education Week on the Web*, December 6.

Powers, Donald E. 1993. "Coaching for the SAT: A Summary of the Summaries and an Update." *Educational Measurement: Issues and Practice* (summer): 24-30, 39.

Psacharopoulos, George. and Eduardo Velez, World Bank. 1993. "Educational Quality and Labor Market Outcomes: Evidence from Bogota, Columbia." *Sociology of Education*, Vol. 66, No. 2 (April).

Public Agenda. 1997. "Good News, Bad News: What People Really Think About the Education Press." A presentation by Public Agenda for the 50th Anniversary Seminar of the Education Writers Association, Washington, D.C., May 1-3.

Public Agenda.2000. *Survey Finds Little Sign of Backlash against Academic Standards or Standardized Tests*. Author.

Public Agenda. 2001. *Reality Check 2001*. New York: Author.

Public Agenda. 2002. *Reality Check 2002*. New York: Author.

Raimi, Ralph A. 2000. "Judging State Standards for K–12 Mathematics Education," in Sandra Stotsky, ed. *What's at Stake in the K–12 Standards Wars: A Primer for Educational Policy Makers*. New York: Peter Lang.

Rand Corporation. 2000. "What Do Test Scores in Texas Tell Us?" Memo to Reporters and Editors, October 26.

Ravitch, Diane. 2000. *Left Back: A Century of Failed School Reforms*. New York: Simon and Schuster.

Roberts, Michelle A-M. 1996. "An Assessment of the Writing Proficiency Examination at Delta State University." Ed.D diss., Delta State University.

Robinson, John P., and Geoffrey Godbey. 1997. *Time for Life: The Surprising Ways Americans Use their Time*. University Park: Pennsylvania University Press.

Roderick, Melissa, and Mimi Engel. 2001. "The Grasshopper and the Ant: Motivational Responses of Low-Achieving Students to High-Stakes Testing." Consortium on Chicago School Research, University of Chicago, *Educational Evaluation and Policy Analysis* (fall).

Rodgers, Natalie et al. 1991. "High Stakes Minimum Skills Tests: Is Their Use Increasing Achievement?" Paper presented at the Annual Meeting of the American Education Research Association, Chicago, IL, April 3-7.

Roeber, Edward et al. 1994. *State Student Assessment Programs Database, 1993-1994*. Oak Brook, IL: CCSSO and NCREL, October, pp. 213-215.

Rothstein, Richard. 1998. *The Way We Were?* New York: Century Foundation.

Rothstein, Richard. 2000. "Lessons: Polls Only Confuse Education Policy." *New York Times*, November 15, B15.

Rudman, Herbert C. 1992. "Testing for Learning." Book Review, *Educational Measurement: Issues and Practice* (fall): 31-32

Sacks, Peter. 1999a. "Standardized Testing: Meritocracy's Crooked Yardstick." *Change* (March/April): 26.

Sacks, Peter. 1999b. *Standardized Minds: The High Price of America's Testing Culture and What We Can Do to Change It*. Cambridge, MA: Perseus Books.

Sanders, William L., and Sandra P. Horn, University of Tennessee. 1995. "Educational Assessment Reassessed: The Usefulness of Standardized and Alternative Measures of Student Achievement as Indicators for the Assessment of Educational Outcomes." *Education Policy Analysis Archives*, Vol. 3, No. 6, March 3.

Sandham, Jessica L. 1998. "Ending SAT May Hurt Minorities, Study Says." *Education Week*, January 14, p. 5.

Schafer, William D., Francine H. Hultgren, Willis D. Hawley, A. L. Abrams, C. C. Seubert, and S. Mazzoni. 1997. *Study of Higher-Success and Lower-Success Elementary Schools*, School Improvement Program, University of Maryland.

Schleisman, Jane. 1999. "An In-Depth Investigation of One School District's Responses to an Externally-Mandated, High-Stakes Testing Program in Minnesota." Paper presented at the Annual Meeting of the University Council for Educational Administration, Minneapolis, October (ERIC: ED440465).

Schmidt, Frank L., John E. Hunter, R. C. McKenzie, and T. W. Muldrow. 1979. "Impact of Valid Selection Procedures on Work-Force Productivity." *Journal of Applied Psychology*, Vol. 64, No. 6: 609-626.

Schmidt, Frank L., and John E. Hunter. 1998. "The Validity and Utility of Selection Methods in Personnel Psychology: Practical and Theoretical Implication of 85 Years of Research Findings." *Personnel Psychology*, Vol. 51.

Schmitt, Neil, Richard Z. Gooding, Raymond D. Noe, and Michael Kirsch. 1984. "Meta-Analysis of Validity Studies Published Between 1964 and 1982 and the Investigation of Study Characteristics." *Personnel Psychology*, Vol. 37, No. 3.

Schouten, Fredreka. 2001. "Poll: Teachers Expect Less of Poor, Minority Teens." *Gannett News Service*, October 3.

Schrag, Peter. 2000. "High Stakes are for Tomatoes." *Atlantic Monthly*, August.

Shepard, Lorrie A., Amelia E. Kreitzer, and M. Elizabeth Grau. 1987. *A Case Study of the Texas Teacher Test*. CSE Report No. 276, CRESST/UCLA.

Shepard, Lorrie A. 1991a. "Effects of High-Stakes Testing on Instruction." Paper presented at the Annual Meeting of the AERA, Chicago, April.

Shepard, Lorrie A. 1991b. "Will National Tests Improve Student Learning?" *Phi Delta Kappan* (November): 233-234.

Sivalingam-Nethi, Vanaja. 1997. "Examining Claims Made for Performance Assessments Using a High School Science Context." Ph.D. diss., Cornell University.

SmarterKids.com. 2000. "National Survey Reveals Widespread Parental Confusion Over Standardized Tests." Needham, MA., June 20.

Smith, Mary Lee, and Claire Rottenberg. 1991. "Unintended Consequences of External Testing in Elementary Schools." *Educational Measurement: Issues and Practice* (winter): 10-11.

Smith, Mary Lee. 1991a. "The Role of Testing in Elementary Schools." *CSE Technical Report 321*, Los Angeles, UCLA, May.

Smith, Mary Lee. 1991b. "Put to the Test: The Effects of External Testing on Teachers." *Educational Researcher*, Vol. 20, No. 5 (June).

Smith, Mary Lee. 1991c. "Meanings of Test Preparation." *American Educational Research Journal*, Vol. 28, No. 3 (fall).

Solmon, Lewis C., and Cheryl L. Fagnano. 1990. "Speculations on the Benefits of Large-scale Teacher Assessment Programs: How 78 Million Dollars Can be Considered a Mere Pittance." *Journal of Education Finance*, Vol. 16 (summer): 21-36.

Southern Regional Education Board. "High Schools That Work: Case Studies." Atlanta, GA.

Stake, Robert, and Paul Theobald. 1991. "Teachers' Views of Testing's Impact on Classrooms," in Rita G. O'Sullivan and Robert E. Stake, eds. *Advances in Program Evaluation: Effects of Mandated Assessment on Teaching*. Greenwich, CT: JAI Press.

Starch, D., and E. C. Elliot. 1912. "Reliability of the Grading of High School Work in English." *School Review*, 21, 442-457.

Starch, D., and E. C. Elliot. 1913a. Reliability of the Grading of High School Work in History. *School Review,* 21, 676-681.

Starch, D., and E. C. Elliot. 1913b. Reliability of Grading Work in Mathematics. *School Review*, 22, 254-259.

Steinberg, Lawrence. 1993. "The Use of Out-of-School Time." Chapter 6 in Lorin W. Anderson and Herbert J. Walberg, eds. *Timepiece: Extending and Enhancing Learning Time*. Reston, VA, National Association of Secondary School Principals.

Stiggins, Richard J., and Nancy Faires Conklin. 1992. *In Teachers' Hands: Investigating the Practices of Classroom Assessment*. New York: SUNY Press.

Stiggins, Richard J., David A. Frisbee, and P. A. Griswold. 1989. "Inside High School Grading Practices: Building a Research Agenda." *Educational Measurement: Issues and Practice*, Vol. 8, No. 2: 5-14.

Stigler, George W., and J. Hiebert. 1997. "Understanding and Improving Classroom Mathematics Instruction: An Overview of the TIMSS Video Study." *Phi Delta Kappan*. Bloomington: Phi Delta Kappa (September): 14-21.

Stone, John E. 1995. "Inflated Grades, Inflated Enrollment, and Inflated Budgets: An Analysis and Call for Review at the State Level." *Education Policy Analysis Archives*, 3 (11).

Stone, J. E. 1996. "Developmentalism: An Obscure but Pervasive Restriction on Educational Improvement." *Education Policy Analysis Archives*, 4 (8).

Stone, John E. 1999. "Value-Added Assessment: An Accountability Revolution," in *Better Teachers, Better Schools*. Thomas B. Fordham Foundation, Education Leaders Council, July.

Stotsky, Sandra. 2000. "The State of Literary Study in National and State English Language Arts Standards: Why It Matters and What Can Be Done About It," in Sandra Stotsky, ed. *What's at Stake in the K–12 Standards Wars*. New York: Peter Lang.

Stricherz, Mark. 2001. "Many Teachers Ignore Cheating, Survey Finds." *Education Week on the Web*, May 9, 2001.

Teicher, Stacy A. 2001. "Where in the World is that No. 2 Pencil." *The Christian Science Monitor*, September 4.

Texas Education Agency, Division of Assessment. 1994. Telephone conversations, February through May.

Thomas, John W. 1992. "Expectations and Effort: Course Demands, Students' Study Practices, and Academic Achievement," in Tommy M. Tomlinson, ed. *Hard Work and High Expectations: Motivating Students to Learn*. December.

Thomson, James A. 2000. "Statement of Rand President and CEO James A. Thomson." Rand Corporation, October 26.

Toch, Thomas. 1992. "Schools for Scandal." *U.S. News & World Report*, April 27.

Toenjes, Larry A., A. Gary Dworkin, Jon Lorence, and Antwanette N. Hill. 2000. *The Lone Star Gamble: High Stakes Testing, Accountability, and Student Achievement in Texas and Houston.* Department of Sociology, University of Houston, August.

Traub, James. 1999. "Better by Design?: A Consumer's Guide to Schoolwide Reform," Thomas P. Fordham Foundation, December (http://www.edexcellence.net/library/bbd/better_by_design.html).

Traub, Ross E. 1993. "On the Equivalence of the Traits Assessed by Multiple Choice and Constructed-Response Tests," in R. E. Bennett and W. C. Ward (eds.), *Construction Versus choice in Cognitive Measurement.* Hillsdale NJ: Lawrence Erlbaum.

Trotter, Andrew. 2000. "Educators Turn to Anti-Plagiarism Web Programs to Detect Cheating." *Education Week on the Web*, December 13.

Tuckman, Bruce W. 1994. "Comparing Incentive Motivation to Metacognitive Strategy in Its Effect on Achievement." Paper presented at the Annual Meeting of the American Educational Research Association, New Orleans, LA, April 4-8. ERIC: ED368790.

Tuckman, Bruce W., and Susan Trimble. 1997. "Using Tests as a Performance Incentive To Motivate Eighth-Graders To Study." Paper presented at the Annual Meeting of the American Psychological Association, Chicago, August. ERIC: ED418785

Tyler, John H., Richard J. Murnane, and John B. Willet. 1997. "Estimating the Impact of the GED on the Earnings of Young Dropouts Using a Series of Natural Experiments." Mimeo. July.

USA Today. 2001. "High Schools Inflate Grades, and Parents are Fooled." Author, 12A.

U.S. Bureau of Labor Statistics. 1995. Division of Labor Force Statistics, "Household Data: Annual Averages," Tables 2, 31, 35.

U.S. Bureau of Labor Statistics. 1997. Division of Labor Force Statistics, "Employed Persons by Usual Full/Part-Time Status, Annual Averages, 1968-96."

U.S. Department of Education, National Center for Education Statistics. 1996. *Remedial Education at Higher Education Institutions in Fall 1995*, NCES 97-584, by Laurie Lewis and Elizabeth Farris. Project Officer, Bernie Greene, Washington, DC.

U.S. Department of Education, National Center for Education Statistics. 1997. *State Indicators in Education, 1997*, NCES 97-376, by Richard P. Phelps, Andrew Cullen, Jack C. Easton, Clayton M. Best. Project Officer: Claire Geddes. Washington, DC.

U.S. General Accounting Office. 1993a. *Educational Testing: The Canadian Experience with Standards, Examinations, and Assessments.* GAO/PEMD-93-11. Washington, DC: Author, April.

U.S. General Accounting Office. 1993b. *Student Testing: Current Extent and Expenditures, With Cost Estimates for a National Examination.* GAO/PEMD-93-8. Washington, DC. Author, January.

USA Today. 2001. "High Schools Inflate Grades, and Parents are Fooled." Author, August 30, 12A.

U.S. News & World Report. 2001. "Exclusive Poll: Cheaters Win." *U.S. News & World Report Editors' Advisory.*

Viadero, Debra. 1994. "National Tests in Other Countries Not as Prevalent as Thought." *Education Week*, June 8.

Viadero, Debra. 1998. "FairTest Report Questions Reliance on High-Stakes Testing by States." *Education Week*, January 28.

Wadsworth, Deborah. 2000. Comments for panel on "Testing 'Backlash'." National Forum on Education Policy, Education Commission of the States.

Wainer, Howard, and David Thissen. 1993. "Combining Multiple-Choice and Con-structed-Response Test Scores: Toward a Marxist Theory of Test Construction." *Applied Measurement in Education*, Vol. 6, No. 2 (spring): 103-18.

Walstad, William B., and William E. Becker. 1994. "Achievement Differences on Mul-tiple-Choice and Essay Tests in Economics." *Research on Economics Education* (May): 193-96.

Waltman, K. K., and David A. Frisbee. 1994. "Parents' Understanding of their Children's Report Card Grades." *Applied Measurement in Education*. Vol. 7, pp.223–240.

Wedman, Ingemar. 1994. "The Swedish Scholastic Aptitude Test: Development, Use, and Research." *Educational Measurement: Issues and Practice*, Vol. 13, No. 2 (summer).

West, Mary Maxwell, and Katherine A. Viator. 1992. *The Influence of Testing on Teaching Math and Science in Grades 4-12: Appendix D: Testing and Teaching in Six Urban Sites*. Boston: CSTEEP, October.

Weisbrod, Burton A. 1964. *External Benefits of Public Education*. Princeton, NJ: Industrial Relations Section, Princeton University.

Wildavsky, Aaron B. 1991. *The Rise of Radical Egalitarianism*. Lanham, MD: University Press.

Willingham, Warren W., Charles Lewis, Rick Morgan, and Leonard Ramist. 1990. "Implications of Using Freshman GPA as the Criterion for the Predictive Validity of the SAT." *Predicting College Grades: An Analysis of Institutional Trends over Two Decades*. Princeton, NJ: Educational Testing Service.

Woessman, Ludger. 2000. *Schooling Resources, Educational Institutions, and Student Performance: The International Evidence*. Kiel Institute of World Economics. Kiel Working Paper No. 983, December (abridged version in *Education Next*, summer 2001).

Woessman, Ludger. 2001. "Why Students in Some Countries Do Better." *Education Next* (summer).

Wolf, Lisa F. ,and Jeffrey K. Smith. 1995. "The Consequence of Consequence: Motiva-tion, Anxiety, and Test Performance." *Applied Measurement in Education*, Vol. 8, No. 3: 227-42.

Wolff, Daniel. 2002. "Edu-Speak: A Glossary for Parents." *Education Week*, May 1.

Wolk, Ronald A. 2000. "Crash Test." *Teacher Magazine*, October.

Wolk, Ronald A. 2002a. "Multiple Measures." *Teacher Magazine*, April.

Wolk, Ronald A. 2002b. "Sacred Cow." *Teacher Magazine*, March.

Wooldridge, Adrian. 1998. "A True Test: In Defense of the SAT." *The New Republic*, June 15, pp.18–21.

Wyatt, Edward. 2001. "Schools Found Uneven in Promotion of Students." *New York Times*, August 23.

Zehr, Mary Ann. 2001. "Study: Test-Preparation Courses Raise Scores Only Slightly." *Education Week*, April 4.

Index

Academic credibility strategy, 63-64
Advanced Placement (AP) tests, 62, 94
Alternative comparing strategy, 65-66
Allocative efficiency, defined, 244
Alternative ignoring strategy, 66
American Association of School Admin-
    istrators (AASA), 170, 189-190
American Association for Supervision
    and Curriculum Development
    (ASCD), 171, 191-194
American College Test (ACT), 69-70
    multiple choice questions, 60-61
    as non-curriculum based, 65
    vs Texas SAT scores, 142-143
American Federation of Teachers (AFT),
    183
Annie B. Casey Foundation, 135
Anxiety, testing and, 275
Arizona teacher testing
    CRESST and, 116-117
    expert participants for, 117
    political culture of, 117-118
Association of American Publishers, 6,
    170
Association of American School Admin-
    istrators (AASA), 189
Association for Supervision and Cur-
    riculum Development (ASCD), 191
Atkinson, Richard, 152, 154-155, 160,
    168
Atlantic Monthly, 167
"Attack dog" strategy, 68
Attack strategies
    academic credibility, 63-64
    alternative comparing, 65-66
    alternative ignoring, 66
    "attack dog" using, 68
    data creating, 71-72
    data doctoring, 69-71
    evidence selectivity, 69
    guilt by association, 64

messenger killing, 64
name calling, 72-77
obfuscation, 69
one-side limiting, 67
opposition demonizing, 64
research contrary as non-existent, 66-
    67
self-interest concealing, 63
shame inducing, 64
"validity" proliferating, 64-65
words in their mouths, 67-68
Attack tactics
    test unfairness, 54-63
    testing not natural, 38-46
    testing not working, 46-54
Authentic instruction
    assessment concerns with, 283
    knowledge accumulation as, 282
    portfolios as, 283-284
    skilled trades as, 282
    as time-consuming, 282-283
    vs standardized tests, 284
Authentic instruction, types of, 282

Baker, Eva, 152, 154-155
Ballou, Dale, 152, 154
Bay Area Resisters, 167
Becker, William, 266
Bishop, John, 152, 154, 216, 256
    Canada's student performance, 241
    curriculum vs aptitude basis, 240
    GABT and, 249
    New York's student performance,
        240
    redoublement research, 51
    testing incentive effects, 238-239
Blow, Steve, 206
Bosher, Bill, 165
Boston Arts Academy, 168
Bottoms, Gene, 153-154
Bracey, Gerald, 152-154, 188

Burkett, Elinor, 205
Bush, President George W., 122, 160-162, 165
Business Roundtable, 6

California Coalition for Authentic Reform in Education, 167
California Resisters, 167
Camara, Wayne, 96-98
Canada
    curriculum based exit exams, 241
    IAEP student performance, 241
    school administrator's effects, 241
    teacher effects and, 241
Cannell, John J., 10, 41
Catalyst for Chicago Education Reform, 188
Censorship
    "mainstream" education research and, 3-4
    media's self censoring, 147
    standardized tests and, 1, 5-6
    Yahoo use of, 176
Center for Advanced Research in Human Resources (CAHRS), 184
Center for Research on Evaluation, Standards and Student Testing (CRESST), 2, 4, 199, 216, 218
    Arizona's teacher testing and, 116-119
    basic skill vs "neat stuff" instruction, 43
    citizens input rejecting, 115
    Education Week editorials, 180-181
    political belief study, 68
    primary source non-alienating, 197
    as Rand Corporation client, 123
    status quo maintaining, 115
    TECAT and, 105-107
    unintended consequences study, 47
Center for the Study of Testing, Evaluation and Educational Policy (CSTEEP), 44, 52-53, 60
    Education Week and, 181, 184
Chaddock, Gail, 205
Chase, Bob, 151-154, 168
Chauncey, Henry, 97
Chavez, Tim, 205
Cheating tactic, 48-49
    student cheating tactic, 49
    teacher cheating tactic, 49-50
Chrysler Corporation Foundation, 259

Cizek, Gregory, 11, 153-154, 278
Cliff Notes, 61
Clinton, President Bill, 186
Cole, Nancy, 152, 154
College admissions
    criteria for, 94
    factors influencing, 94
    SAT reasons in, 94-95
College Entrance Examination Board (College Board), 58, 69-70
Costrell, Robert, 153-154
Crossen, Cynthia, 149, 206
Cunningham, George, 153-154
Curriculum standards, high stakes state tests from, 270
Curriculum-based External Exit Examination Systems (CBEEES), 240

Darling-Hammond, Linda, 152, 154-155, 168, 181-182, 205
Data creating strategy, 71-72
Data doctoring strategy, 69-71
Davis, Gray, 165
Debra P. v Turlington (1984), 11
Digest of Education Statistics, 140
Driscoll, David, 165
Dropouts
    defining, 159
    rates of, 159
    TAAS research, 132-137
    vs redoublement, 51
Dropouts increasing tactic
    denying diplomas costs, 50
    reasons for, 50
    testing and, 50-51
    vs redoublement, 51
Duke, Daniel, 156

Earning effects
    incentive effects and, 243
    median value of, 243-244
    student outcomes and, 243
Eckstein, Max, 14
Economic Policy Institute, 19
Education Assessment Insider, 187
Education Commission of the States (ECS), 188
Education consumers
    characteristics of, 3-4
    standardized testing and, 3
    types of, 3
Education Daily

editorial board members, 187
vested interest of, 187
Education providers
types of, 3
vs external testing, 3
Education testing debates
educational consumers fiscal resources, 202
media market access, 201-202
medial reporting unknowledgeable, 202
testing opponent fiscal resources, 201
university education and, 202-203
Education Week, 66, 176, 216
CSTEEP and, 181, 184
FairTest and, 184
homework elimination editorial, 180
testing issue sources, 180-181
testing opposition editorial, 179-180
Education Writer's Association
anti-testing focus, 188
criticisms of, 188-189
"hot topics" sources, 187-188
"new research" sources, 188
Educational efficiency
external examinations hypothesis, 242-243
factors for, 242
Educational Measurement, 200
Educational press
anti-test advocates, 182-183
editorial critiques, 180
editorial false facts, 179-180
high stakes testing accusations, 177-179
information sources for, 180-182
pro-testing advocates, 182-183
research expertise preferences, 183-186
testing editorials, 179
testing research needs for, 177
trade papers for, 176
vs parent wishes, 179
Educational Testing Service (ETS), 6, 170, 186
Education's trade press
expertise sources, 180-187
high stakes testing and, 176-180
testing cop-outs, 187-189
Education's vested interest
journalist bias, 205-206

public interest siding, 203-205
Educators
defining of, 24
mistrust of, 284
stress tactic of, 48
Elected officials, testing political position, 28
Employee testing
economic benefit of, 253
hiring decision from, 247-248
job performance predictive validity, 246-247
reliability of, 248
test measures, 245-247
European testing systems
as elitist, 268
student differentiation in, 269
Evidence selectively using strategy, 69
Exit examinations, Canada's use of, 241
External testing, groups opposed to, 3

Finn, Chester, 152, 154, 168, 185-186
Foreign countries comparison tactics, 53
Foreign country testing
case studies on, 14-15
countries with, 12-14
examination burden by country, 15
examination difficulty by country, 15
exit and entrance uses of, 12-13
increasing use of, 12
popularity of, 15
U.S. reactions to, 12
See also European testing systems
Frontline SAT series
biased background interviews in, 97-98
biased reporting in, 96
media reactions to, 101
minority students and, 100-101
narrator's statements, 96
report contradictions, 102
student subjects in, 98-99
test preparation use, 99-100

Gandal, Matt, 152, 154, 160-161
Gardner, Howard, 152-154, 168, 181
General Accounting Office, 53
General aptitude testing
Board of Assessment report, 249-250
federal government and, 248-249
predictive benefits of, 248
present value calculating, 249

utility estimating, 249
General Aptitude Test Battery (GATB),
  248-249
Gerstner, Lou, 165
Glover, Danny, 205
Godbey, Geoffrey, 258
Goodman, Walter, 101
Government test controlling, test-score
  inflation from, 10, 42
Grayer, Jonathan, 97
Grissmer, David, 123
Guilt by association strategy, 64

Hambleton, Ronald, 152, 154, 185
Haney, Walter, 151-154, 156, 160
Haney, Walter TAAS research
  dropouts, 132-133
  dropouts and, 134-137
  fourth grade retentions, 128-129
  high school completions, 137-141
  IEP and LEP students, 129-130
  LEP excluding guidelines, 131
  NAEP score exaggerating, 129-131
  NAEP score manipulating, 127-128
  NAEP scores levels, 131-132
  TEA lying, 133-134
Harris Interactive, 191
Hart, Peter D., 259
Hauser, Robert, 152, 154-155
Haycock, Katy, 153-154
Heubert, Jay, 152, 154-155
High stakes decision tactics, 55
High stakes external testing
  benefit comparing, 255
  cost benefit reconciling, 253
  state mandated test costs, 254-255
High stakes standardized tests
  educational press and, 176-180
  examination system varieties, 269
  high achieving students and, 266-
    267
  performance targets, 275-266
  "single target" solutions, 267-268
  target quantity, 266
  testing program building, 268-269
  vs middle achieving students, 267
High stakes testing
  anxiety over, 275
  benefit studies of, 231-239
  characteristics of, 226
  court cases over, 11
  downside of, 159

dropouts and, 159
education group's characteristics, 20
education professor's dislike, 20-21
information availability and, 19-20
Lake Wobegon Effect and, 11
non-use of, 12
opposition polls against, 17-18
polling value, 19
public opinion for, 15
quality control measures, 221
school administrators and, 18-19
standardized quality improving, 11-
  12
state administrators vs school officials, 274
state testing directors vs, 27-28
support reasons, 15-17
test quality compromises, 274-275
TIMSS study and, 221
unwillingness to remove, 224
U.S. vs foreign countries, 221-222
vs instructional means ownership, 21
See also Testing benefits
High stakes testing implementing
  sequencing, 271-272
  structuring, 272-274
  supportive technologies for, 270-271
"Higher order" thinking tactic, 59-60
Hirsch, E. D., 4, 76, 152, 154, 168
Holland, Robert, 206, 222
Houston, Paul, 152-154
Human rejection tactic, 56-57
  type one errors, 57
  type two errors, 57
Hunter, John E., 249

Incentive effects
  allocative efficiency, 244
  Bishop's research on, 239
  Canada example, 241
  counties using TIMSS, 241-243
  countries using IAEP, 241
  curriculum vs aptitude, 240
  external exams earning effects, 243-
    244
  information benefits, 244
  information benefits from, 239-240
  New York State example, 240
  student's harder working as, 238
Indiana Youth Poll, 50
Instruction distortion tactic
  creative teaching and, 38

examples of, 39-40
vs standards, 38
Instruction means ownership
anti-testing advocating, 22-23
anti-testing conclusions, 21-22
media reports and, 22
research implication of, 21
standardized testing threat to, 21
International Assessment of Educational
Progress (IAEP), 239
countries with, 241

Jacobs, Joanne, 180, 205
Jacobson, Jonathan E., 143, 266
Jencks, Christopher, 97
Journalist
balanced coverage reporters, 205-
206
as education graduates, 201
education's visibility, 201
established group credibility with,
199
journals non-reading by, 200
memory loss of, 199-200
observations of, 200-201
peer trusting by, 198-199
primary sources alienating, 197
problems as news, 197
reader alienating by, 198
space limitations, 198
spin by, 189-194
time constraints of, 198
See also Media bias; Standardized
testing media sources
Journalist manipulating
AASA poll, 189-190
ASCD and, 191-194
Journalist preferences
AMA vs FTC example, 203-205
teacher independence, 205
Journalist reporting balance
efforts at, 30
fact checking, 149-150
as liberals, 196
non-testing bias, 30
questions about, 30-31
small difference significance in, 149
vs biased outcomes, 31, 96-98, 205-
206

Kaplan, Stanley, 59, 89-92
Katzman, John, 96-97

Kean, Michael, 152, 154
Keegan, Lisa Graham, 117
Kilpatrick, Jimmy, 205
Kirst, Michael, 165
Klein, Stephen, 152-154, 162
Kohn, Alfie, 151-155, 168, 202
Koretz, Daniel, 152, 154, 217
Kozol, Jonathan, 152, 154, 168
Kurtis, Bill, 205

Laccetti Meyers, Susan, 205-206
Lake Wobegon Effect
description of, 10
government control from, 10, 42
high stakes test and, 11
no-stakes tests and, 11
school administrator use, 11
school administrator's return to, 18
test-score inflation as, 10, 41-42
Langland, Connie, 101
Learning incentives tactic, 46
Lemann, Nicholas, 96, 98, 100, 151-
154, 188
Lerner, Barbara, 153-154
Levin, Henry, 216-217
Linn, Robert, 152, 154
Long, Diane, 205
"Lower order" thinking tactic, 60-61

McNeil, Linda, 132, 152, 154-155, 261
Madaus, George, 152, 154, 165
Media
anti-testing research accepting, 22
See also Standardized testing media
sources
Media bias
education consumers and, 206
media's responsibility, 206-207
political policy influencing, 206
public education impact, 206
See also Journalist
Media testing coverage
bias on, 206-207
educator's trade press, 176-189
journalist coverage and, 196-201
journalist manipulating, 189-194
print media, 150-159
self-censoring, 147
standardized testing sources, 147-
150
state education commission biases,
194-196

television coverage, 160-168
worldwide web, 168-176
Mehrens, William, 152, 154, 217
Meier, Deborah, 152, 153-154
Merrow, John, 44, 164, 167
Merrow Report (television program), 71
  bias reporting of, 165
  contradictions in, 166
  false facts in, 166-167
  one-sided purpose, 167-168
  perfection vs alternative comparing, 167
  story format, 164
Messenger killing strategy, 64
Minority unfairness tactic, 55-56
Monthly Labor Review, 251
Multiple-choice artificiality tactic, 61-63
Murray, David W., 56, 153-154
Musick, Mark, 152, 154-155, 185

Name calling as methodology strategy, 72
  culturally biased tests, 75
  educator learning claims, 73
  journalist naturalistic information, 72-73
  school day shortening, 74-75
  student intellectual capacities, 75-76
  Texas testing and, 73-74, 76-77
Narrow the curriculum tactic
  instructional method for, 43-44
  student requirements reassessing, 43
  as tautological, 44
  vs instructional time, 42
  vs learning, 43
  vs non-academic subjects, 42-43
National Assessment Governing Board (NAGB), 131, 155, 274
National Assessment of Educational Progress (NAEP), 54, 76, 123-132, 158, 239, 274
National Association for College Admission Counseling (NACAC), 89, 94
National Association of Secondary School Principals (NASSP), 170-171
National Association of Testing Directors (NATD), 6, 30, 170
National Board on Educational Testing Policy (NBETP), 199
National Center for Education Statistics, 140

National Center for Fair and Open Testing (FairTest), 4, 60, 181
  college admission test waiving, 89
  Education Week and, 184
  Frontline interview, 98
  SAT attacking, 88-89
National Council on Education Standards and Testing (NCEST), 186
National Council of Measurement in Education (NCME), 6, 181
National Education Association (NEA), 171
National Education Longitudinal Study (NELS), 143, 266
National Educational Goals Panel, 123
National Research Council (NRC), 53, 181, 184, 197, 217, 249-251
National School Boards Association (NSBA), 171
Neill, Monte, 151-154
Nellhaus, Jeff, 165
New York State
  curriculum based graduation exams, 240
  student performance, 240
New York Times, 19
No-stakes testing, Lake Wobegon Effect and, 11
Noah, Harold, 14

Obfuscation strategy, 69
Office of Technology Assessment (OTA), 71-72
Ohanian, Susan, 153-154
One-side limiting strategy, 67
Open Directory Project
  control battles in, 172-176
  volunteer editors in, 172
Opposition demonizing strategy, 64
Organization for Economic Co-operation and Development (OECD), 12, 53

Page, Clarence, 101
Paige, Rod, 161-162, 165
Parker, Larry, 206
Perot, H. Ross, 105, 115, 122, 165
Peter, Lawrence J., 18
Phelps, Richard, 153-154
Phillips, Susan, 152, 154
"Placing out," defined, 252-253
Podgursky, Michael, 152, 154

Polivka, Anne E., 251
Popham, James, 156, 165
Portfolios
    as tests, 283-284
    vs standardized tests, 284
Powers, Donald, 91
Predictive validity
    defined, 244
    employee hiring and, 244
    test types for, 244
Presidential elections
    anti-TAAS news articles during, 121-122
    anti-testing books during, 122
    NAEP findings, 124-126
    Rand study challenges, 123-124
    study release timing, 122-127
    TAAS vs NAEP gains, 126-127
    Texas miracle and, 127-144
Princeton Review, 57
    coaching efforts of, 91-92
    Frontline interview, 98
    test preparation by, 89-90
    test preparation value, 98
Print media
    high stakes testing downside, 159
    newspaper articles published, 151-155
    testing expert identifying, 150-151
    testing opponents and defenders, 151-155
    Time magazine articles, 155-157
    Washington Post articles, 157-158
Public Agenda, 19-20, 45, 47, 55, 196-198
Public Broadcasting System. *See Frontline* SAT series
Public support
    reasons for, 215
    vs education aristocracy, 215-216

Qualls, Audrey, 165

Rabinowitz, Nancy, 101
Rand Corporation study
    anti-testing clients of, 123
    claims of, 124-126
    funding threats to, 122
    study challenges, 123
    TAAS vs NAEP gains, 126-127
    Texas study reasons, 122-123
Ravitch, Diane, 152, 154, 168, 185

Redoublement
    defined, 51
    dropouts and, 51
Research nonexistence strategy, 66-67
Robinson, John P., 258
Rock, Donald, 91
Rosen, Sherwin, 266
Rosenberg, Bella, 153-154
Rothstein, Richard, 19

Sacks, Peter, 151-154
Sacramento Bee, 167
San Francisco Chronicle, 167
Sanders, William, 152, 154-155, 183
Schaeffer, Robert, 96-97, 151-154
Schmidt, Bill, 165
Schmidt, Frank L., 249
Scholastic Assessment Test (SAT), 58, 69-70, 141-144
    admission test criticisms, 89
    allocative efficiency of, 95
    attacks on, 87
    college admission decisions, 87-88, 94-95
    FairTest attacks on, 88-89
    Frontline series on, 96-102
    high school curriculum and, 88
    impact of, 89
    journalist trade secrets of, 96-102
    minority unfairness of, 56
    as non-curriculum based, 65
    operation of, 87
    predictive invalidity and, 92-93
    Sunday Morning topic, 160
    tricks for, 89-92
    waiving of, 89
    See also Texas SAT scores
Scholastic Assessment Test (SAT) allocative efficiency
    benefits from, 95
    college application pools, 95
    defined, 95
Scholastic Assessment Test (SAT) predictive invalidity
    benefit-cost ratio for, 93
    college performance and, 93
    defining of, 92, 95
    vs high school grades, 92-93
Scholastic Assessment Test (SAT) tricks
    format review as, 90-92
    limits of, 89-90
    supporters of, 89

test preparation as, 90
School administrators
    Lake Wobegon Effect use, 11
    poll results of, 19
    testing and accountability, 18
Schrag, Peter, 152-154
Schwartz, Robert, 152, 154
Scholastic Aptitude Test (SAT), GPA
    predicting, 63
Scholastic Aptitude Test (SAT), multiple
    choice questions, 60-61
Second chance testing, "placing out"
    principle, 252-253
Self-interest strategy, 63
Sequencing
    defined, 271
    examination adopting, 271
    examination difficulty, 272
    minimum-competency examina-
        tions, 271-272
    political durability, 272
    student failure solutions, 272
Shame inducing strategy, 64
Shepard, Lorrie, 152, 154-155
Signaling. See Incentive effects
Single purpose validity tactic, 54-55
Sizer, Ted, 165
Standardizing instruction tactic, vs in-
    novation, 45
Standardized instruction tactic, curricula
    and, 45-46
Standardized testing
    "cause" oriented educators, 5
    censorship and, 1, 5-6
    debate issues over, 1
    education policy actors, 3-4
    "mainstream" research bias, 4-5
    research conformity, 5
    study censorship about, 1-2
    U.S. educational approaches, 3
Standardized testing alternatives
    authentic instruction, 282-284
    children outcomes, 284
    college remedial programs, 277
    pitfalls of, 281-284
    social promotion system, 277
    standardized curriculum absence,
        279
    student performance non-available,
        277-278
    teacher grading problems, 278-279
    vs standardized testing, 279-281

vs unattainable utopian perfection,
    277
Standardized testing benefits
    benefit types, 224-245
    evidence for, 216-219
    information uses, 245-255
    public support for, 215-216
    student business, 255
    test dropping and reintroduction,
        219-224
Standardized testing media sources
    advocacy group reports, 148
    journalist balance and, 149
    vs fact checking, 149-150
Standardizing minds tactic, 44
State education commissions
    anti-testing group alliances, 195
    bias of, 194-196
    purpose of, 194
    testing resource links, 195-196
    vested interest information, 194
State testing directors, vs high-stakes
    testing, 27-28
Stecher, Brian, 152, 154-155
Steele, Claude, 96-97
Steinberg, Lawrence, 256
Sternberg, Robert, 97
Stix, Nicholas, 205
Structuring
    curriculum branching, 272-273
    defined, 272
    test incentives, 273-274
Student achievement lower tactic, 53-54
Student business vs testing
    education importance signals, 256
    high stakes testing incentives, 255
    homework time value, 255-256
    out-of-school effects, 256-257
    student age and, 256
    student employment, 256
Student coaching tactic, 57-59
Student individuality ignoring tactic, 44-
    45
Student schedule slack capacity
    diary study evidences, 258-259
    international comparisons, 258
    student attention, 260
    time choices, 259-260
Student stress tactic, 47-48
Sunday Morning (television program)
    bias examples of, 160-163
    standardized testing stories, 160

Teacher Magazine, 176
Teaching to the test tactic
    effectiveness of, 40
    testing opponents argument for, 40-
        41
    vs "teaching to" something, 41
Television testing coverage
    CBS's *Sunday Morning*, 160-163
    PBS's *Merrow Report*, 164-168
Test benefits
    accountability from, 225
    categories of, 224-225
    credentialing from, 225
    external measures, 227
    goodwill from, 227
    information from, 225
    motivation, 226
    organizational clarity, 226
    subject-matter mastery, 225
    teacher's role in, 226-227
Test benefits measuring
    challenges of, 228
    measuring methods, 229
    non-jurisdictional comparisons, 230
    studies identifying, 230-238
    teaching to the test, 229-230
Test benefits process
    higher quality work in, 228
    individual benefits, 228
    knowledge student identifying, 228
    student learning in, 227
Test cost tactic
    cost calculations, 52-53
    gap estimates, 53
    standardized test costs, 52
Test dropping
    as common theme, 219
    countries reintroducing process, 220
    era of, 219
    high stakes testing use, 220-222
    need for, 222-224
    as social experiment, 220
    test reintroducing, 219-220
Test publishers
    off-the-shelf sales, 9-10
    Self-interest of, 28
Test score inflation
    government control from, 42
    origin of, 41-42
    solutions to, 10
Test score misusing tactic, 52
Test unfairness tactic

"high order thinking" missing, 59-
    60
high stakes decisions from, 55
"lower order thinking" from, 60-61
minority unfairness, 55-56
multiple-choice artificiality, 61-63
rejecting student as wrong, 56-57
single purpose tests, 54-55
student coaching, 57-59
women unfairness, 55-56
Testing advocates
    educational press and, 182-183
    groups supporting, 24
    organizations supporting, 27
    research characteristics, 26
Testing attack strategies
    anti-testing strategy examples, 35-36
    attack strategies, 63-77
    attack tactics, 38-63
    classification system for, 36-38
    justifying of, 77-79
    opponent fallacy verifying, 77
    overview of, 36-38
    as spin, 35
    testing opponents defenses, 79-82
Testing battlefield
    educators and, 24
    opposition characteristics, 23-24
    radical constructivists and, 25
    "right wing" vs "liberals", 24-25
    testing experts and, 24
Testing benefit evidence
    anti-testing research persistence, 218
    educator's happiness focus, 218
    methods for, 216-217
    opponents' discussion of, 217-218
    research timing and, 218
    vs current advocate, 219
    vs student learning improvement,
        218-219
Testing concerns
    curriculum standards importance,
        269-270
    implementation issues, 270-274
    oversight of, 274-275
    single target performance, 265-269
    test anxiety, 275
Testing with consequences
    instructional ownership and, 21-23
    research on, 19-21
Testing experts
    expert defenders and, 26-27

expert opponents and, 28-30
journalistic balance issues, 26, 30-
    31
pro-testing experts, 26
state testing directors and, 27-28
testing opposition of, 24
Testing importance
    information's function, 31-32
    vs information suppressing, 31
Testing no working tactic
    cheating, 48-50
    dropout increasing, 50-51
    educator stress, 48
    student achievement lowering, 53-54
    student stress, 47-48
    test costs, 52-53
    test score misunderstanding, 52
    unintended consequences, 46-47
Testing opponents
    biased research justifying, 77
    contradiction of, 80-82
    defense of, 79-80
    educational press and, 182-183
    enemy demonizing, 77-78
    established experts groups, 29
    fallacies of, 77-79
    instructional means ownership, 22-
        23
    organizations supporting, 24, 28-29
    vested interest of, 78-79
Testing reasons
    importance of, 224
    as indispensable, 222-223
    non-education test relying, 224
    vs local measures, 223
Testing systems
    battlefields on, 23-25
    external high-stakes standardized test
        and, 9
    foreign country approaches, 12-15
    purposes of, 31-32
    testing with consequences, 15-23
    testing experts, 26-31
    U.S. style of, 9-12
Testing types
    incentive effects, 238-244
    information benefits, 244-245
Testing as un-natural tactic
    curriculum narrowing, 42-43
    instruction distorting, 38-40
    learning incentives, 46
    standardization instruction, 45-46

standardizing minds, 44
student individualization ignoring,
    44-45
teaching to the test, 40-41
test preparation, 43-44
test score inflation, 41-42
Texas Assessment of Academic Skills
    (TAAS), 143
    anti-articles on, 121-122
    Rand Corporation study, 122-127
    school day shortening, 74-75
Texas Education Consumers Associa-
    tion, 77
Texas Examination of Current Admin-
    istrator and Teachers (TECAT)
    Arizona testing policy, 116-119
    cost and benefit analysis, 107-114
    CRESST and, 105-107, 115-116
    as high-stakes test, 105
    purpose of, 105-106
    as teacher's test, 105-115
    testing costs, 115-116
Texas SAT scores
    longitudinal studies, 143-144
    test influences, 141-142
    vs ACT scores, 142
    vs TAAS scores, 143
Texas testing gains
    dropouts and, 132-137
    NAEP score and, 127-128
    NAEP score exaggerating, 129-132
    ninth grade vs high school comple-
        tion, 137-141
    retention rates, 128-129
    SAT scores, 141-144
Third International Mathematics and
    Science Study (TIMSS), 221, 239,
    241-243
Thomas P. Fordham Foundation, 184
Thompson, James A., 122, 162
Time magazine, standardized testing ar-
    ticles, 155-157

Unintended consequences tactic
    types of, 46-47
    vs happiness concept, 47
United States testing
    commercial test publishers and, 9-10
    educational approaches, 3
    government control over, 10
    high stakes testing, 11-12
    "no-stakes" tests, 11

school official preferences, 9
statistical anomaly factors, 10
See also Foreign country testing

Validities proliferating strategy, 64-65
Veciana-Suarez, Ana, 206
Vocational-technical schools, 268
Voluntary National Tests (VNT), 186

Wadsworth, Deborah, 19
Walberg, Herbert, 153-154
Washington Monthly, 205
Washington Post articles
    high stakes tests downside, 159
    lawsuit paid witnesses in, 158
    unbiased reporting and, 158
Wellstone, Paul, 160
Wilkins, Amy, 152, 154
Wilson, Pete, 165
Woessman, Ludger, educational efficiency study, 242-243
Women unfairness tactic, 55-56

Wooldridge, Adrian, 31
Words in their mouth strategy, 67-68
Worldwide web
    directory development for, 171-176
    expert hits on, 169
    links frequency, 169-170
    one-sided reasons, 170
    status quo distorting, 168
    testing expert attention, 168
    websites on, 170-171
    Yahoo link censorship, 176
Worldwide web testing links
    link-censoring, 176
    as politburo, 171-176

Yahoo, link censorship at, 176

Zemal, Jane Elizabeth, 101
Zero-sum labor markets
    arguments for, 252
    as erroneous argument, 251-252
    NRC and, 250-251